# PRINCIPLES AND PRACTICES OF STUDENT HEALTH

## VOLUME THREE

# COLLEGE HEALTH

# PRINCIPLES AND PRACTICES OF STUDENT HEALTH

## THREE VOLUMES

Volume One: **FOUNDATIONS**
Editor: HELEN M. WALLACE, MD, MPH

Volume Two: **SCHOOL HEALTH**
Editors: GUY S. PARCEL, PhD
JUDITH B. IGOE, MS, RN, FAAN

Volume Three: **COLLEGE HEALTH**
Editor: KEVIN PATRICK, MD, MS

PRINCIPLES AND PRACTICES OF STUDENT HEALTH

VOLUME THREE

# COLLEGE HEALTH

EDITORS

HELEN M. WALLACE, MD, MPH • FOUNDATIONS
PROFESSOR, MATERNAL AND CHILD HEALTH
GRADUATE SCHOOL OF PUBLIC HEALTH
SAN DIEGO STATE UNIVERSITY
SAN DIEGO, CALIFORNIA

KEVIN PATRICK, MD, MS • COLLEGE HEALTH
DIRECTOR, UNIVERSITY OF CALIFORNIA, SAN DIEGO, AND
SAN DIEGO STATE UNIVERSITY GENERAL PREVENTIVE MEDICINE RESIDENCY
DIRECTOR, STUDENT HEALTH SERVICES
SAN DIEGO STATE UNIVERSITY
SAN DIEGO, CALIFORNIA

GUY S. PARCEL, PhD • SCHOOL HEALTH
PROFESSOR AND DIRECTOR
CENTER FOR HEALTH PROMOTION
RESEARCH AND DEVELOPMENT
THE UNIVERSITY OF TEXAS HEALTH SCIENCE CENTER AT HOUSTON
HOUSTON, TEXAS

JUDITH B. IGOE, MS, RN, FAAN • SCHOOL HEALTH
ASSOCIATE PROFESSOR AND DIRECTOR
SCHOOL HEALTH PROGRAMS
UNIVERSITY OF COLORADO HEALTH SCIENCES CENTER
SCHOOLS OF NURSING AND MEDICINE
DENVER, COLORADO

with forewords by

ERNEST L. BOYER, PhD
JULIUS B. RICHMOND, MD
VINCE L. HUTCHINS, MD, MPH

THIRD PARTY PUBLISHING COMPANY
OAKLAND, CALIFORNIA, U.S.A.

## ACKNOWLEDGMENTS

The Editors want to express their gratitude to the many experts who have been willing to share their knowledge and expertise, and who have taken the time to write the individual chapters for these three volumes. We also want to acknowledge the significant contribution of Charlotte Shindledecker Seidman, RN, FNP, MHS, MPH, who did the text editing and indexing of all three volumes. Paul Mico, our publisher, gave us important ideas about content in planning the book, especially from his discipline of health education. Chris Morris assisted with many of the graphics used in the book, as did Patrick Kammermeyer. Finally, we would like to thank Dan Nowak, Vice President of Student Affairs, San Diego State University, and the staff of the SDSU Student Health Center for providing some of the support necessary for the production of this book. The publisher joins in the acknowledgment of Charlotte Seidman's contribution. In addition to the able assistance she provided to the Editors and chapter authors on the technical preparation of their manuscripts, she was especially helpful with her advice regarding in-house style and on the overall presentation of this Work.

PRINCIPLES AND PRACTICES OF STUDENT HEALTH
Three Volumes:

        One:    Foundations
        Two:    School Health
        Three:  College Health

Copyright © 1992 by Third Party Publishing Company

Library of Congress Catalog Card Number: 91-67600

International Standard Book Numbers:
For the complete work: 0-89914-034-3
For Volume One: 0-89914-035-1
For Volume Two: 0-89914-036-X
For Volume Three: 0-89914-037-8

Manufactured in the United States of America
Third Party Publishing Company
A division of Third Party Associates, Inc.
P.O. Box 13306, Montclair Station
Oakland, California 94661-0306, U.S.A.
Telephone: 510/339-2323
Fax: 510/339-6729

Publisher, and Design: Paul R. Mico
Electronic Composition: Patrick Kammermeyer

# CONTENTS

VOLUME THREE: **COLLEGE HEALTH**

**Section I:** History, Rationale, and Organizational Issues

# PREFACE

The history of health care for students, from preschool through college, has been wrought with too few resources, insufficient infrastructure to support service delivery, ambiguous roles for health personnel, and confusion surrounding the relationship of the student health program to the school system or university and to other community health systems. Nevertheless, the deteriorating health status of children and youth coupled with the need to take advantage of the school and college settings as ideal environments for developing health life-styles warrants the development of new, and the support and improvement of existing, student health systems. Given the complexity and urgency of the needs that must be met, it is today's challenge to overcome the fragmented approach and institutional inertia that have characterized the past, and design a comprehensive, integrated student health care system guided by an overall philosophy of disease prevention and health promotion.

Health care was first widely provided in schools and colleges in the early 1900s. It was almost always associated with the simple goal of screening for communicable disease. Since then, school health programs have evolved from the provision of basic preventive health care and health education to an expanded focus on the provision of primary health care services and health promotion to students with special health needs. The latter is aimed at the "new morbidities," i.e., early adolescent pregnancy, emotional disorders, sexually transmitted diseases, and other life-style-associated phenomena that require psychosocial and behavioral interventions and new types of services.

It must be emphasized that an increasing number of primary, secondary, and post-secondary students today need basic primary health care due largely to their un- or under-insured status. The 1984 National Health Interview Survey found that at least 4.5 million (14%) students ages 10 to 18 are in these categories, and that those from poor and/or minority households are least likely to have health insurance. Current estimates are that as many as 30 percent of college students lack any form of health insurance and that another

15 percent may be seriously under-insured. For a variety of reasons, this problem has become worse in the early 1990s.

Growing numbers of acute and chronically ill and impaired children and youth are in school and college today as a result of the Education for All Handicapped Children's Act of 1975 (PL 94-142), and the more recent PL 99-457. These individuals require complex nursing and health care and the best place to do so is often at school or in college. Among the common treatments these students require are bladder catheterization; endotracheal suctioning, ileostomy, and ureterostomy care; nasogastric tube feedings; and physical, occupational, and communication therapy.

The traditional primary and secondary school health program that has grown out of this history consists of the three core components of health services, health education, and health protection (measures intended to promote a physically, socially, and psychologically healthy environment). Yet, in spite of this evolution to a varied and sophisticated level of care, these school health programs are commonly a series of unrelated activities and projects for which there exist no unifying mission, goals, or objectives. School nurses orchestrate case management services for medically fragile students independent of health teachers who plan health education curricula, while environmental inspection for health hazards is arranged and implemented by someone else in the school organizational structure. The bottom line is that these school health efforts are fragmented at a time when a consolidated and effective system of health care is needed more than ever to ensure the well-being of students, faculty, and staff.

A similar circumstance has occurred with the evolution of college and university health services. What began as simple dispensaries on a few campuses to deal with the communicable disease problems of students attending college away from home has evolved into a panoply of models of delivery of services ranging from simple triage and referral performed by nurses to full-scale primary and secondary health care centers staffed with a range of health professionals. However, as with primary and secondary education, little in the way of unifying mission, goals, or objectives for these services has developed in the higher education arena. A reactive, "medical model" approach is common, even in the face of overwhelming evidence that the key causes of morbidity and mortality among college students are associated with behavior and life-style and are either partially or completely preventable. It is the rare institution of higher education that explicitly integrates a high level of commitment for the health and well-being of their students, and their graduates, into all levels of institutional policies and procedures.

The logical resolution of these issues is for health planners and providers to redesign student health care systems to meet today's needs. However, planners and providers of student health services have held what sociologists refer to as a "boundary dweller" position: they are members of two organizations – the school or college and the community health care system. Usually, boundary dwellers succumb to a natural inclination to assume the role most frequently in use in, or most acceptable to, their organization. The school nurse may be more comfortable playing the role of teacher than of health care provider and thus may avoid important clinical activities. The college health physician may be best suited to simply "be a doctor" and avoid questioning the impact of institutional alcohol-use policies on patient management. Yet neither of these approaches is satisfactory given what we know about the integrated nature of the causes – and the solutions – of the challenges facing our children and youth.

With this series of volumes, we have chosen to address student health issues for students at all levels of education – primary, secondary, and post-secondary. To our knowledge, this has not been attempted before. It is our conviction, however, that there is much more in common between the "worlds" of school health and college health than has heretofore been acknowledged. Each field responds to health needs in educational contexts. Each has as its central beneficiary a developing human being confronted with the many challenges of growth and identity formation. Each field addresses that most complex period of life known as adolescence. And, in the interest of both a higher order of integration of our activities and a stronger, more unified approach to making our case to others, each field can benefit from a greater level of understanding of the other.

Much remains to be done to design the student health care systems that we need. Key to achieving this is acceptance of the concept that student health care involves many different disciplines commonly associated with multiple institutional and community resources, agencies, and programs. Once accepted, this notion then begs the issue of the need for enhanced communication between and among these resources. This communication is essential if we are to attain the economies of scale, both human and financial, that are paramount to the attainment of the level and complexity of services needed. Of equal importance is a unifying mission of student health care. We posit that the overriding mission of such activities is to promote health, prevent disease, and to provide for environments capable of developing the full potential of each student. It is only in this way that we can insure that the student health care needs of today and tomorrow will be met.

Helen M. Wallace, MD, MPH
Kevin Patrick, MD, MS
Guy S. Parcel, PhD
Judith B. Igoe, MS, RN, FAAN

# FOREWORD
### Ernest L. Boyer, PhD

School and college health professionals have always dispensed more than aspirin, bandaids, and the proverbial "tender loving care." Student health offices have provided not only first aid, but also the first line in health care for many of America's children and young people. It is often the school nurse who discovers that a child has faulty vision or impaired hearing, or who brings a child's need for dental treatment to the notice of the family. In college, the health center is often the first place to which students turn when stricken with disease, addiction, or serious depression and self-doubt.

The publication of *Principles and Practices of Student Health* could not be more timely, because today, more than ever, the primary health care needs of many students will be diagnosed at school, or not at all. The numbers of poor children are rising, thrusting upon school nurses special responsibilities for attending to basic health needs. And adding to the burden is the ever larger role that schools and colleges have assumed in trying to head off or cope with alcohol and drug abuse, sexually transmitted diseases, AIDS, unplanned pregnancies, and the many other perils young Americans face today.

The situation is critical, especially in schools. In a 1990 Carnegie Foundation survey, over two-thirds of the nation's primary and secondary teachers reported that poor health was a problem among students in their school. Teen pregnancy and parenting were cited as a serious or somewhat serious problem by nearly 80 percent of secondary school teachers; while 24 percent said alcohol was a serious problem, and 60 percent said it was a somewhat serious problem for young people in their school.

Wherever one looks, the numbers are numbing, especially given the typically poor resources allocated for student health. For many school professionals, the job is not unlike the approach taken by overworked doctors and nurses on the front lines during times of war. Often, they are so overextended that they must make their own triage decisions and allocate their precious time in ways that leave unattended some student health needs that sorely need to be addressed. Clearly, school health professionals need the best training and guidance they can get in making these decisions, and in organizing their efforts, so as to be efficient while remaining reassuring and humane.

This large territory is well-mapped in these three volumes on Student Health. Here is where nurses, doctors, and others responsible for student health can go for the latest information on how to recognize and evaluate the signs and symptoms of abuse, disease, addiction, and distress. Here is where student health professionals can go for information on the developmental transitions that affect children's health and well-being; on the many subtle connections between health and learning; and for models for organizing school health services, which are informed by a broader vision of what constitutes student health. In this vision, diagnosis, referral, and treatment are essential, but they are only the first steps.

As the authors of *Principles and Practices of Student Health* make clear, wellness is a goal that must be pursued in many ways. If we are to adequately serve the health needs of our children and young people, school and college health professionals must seek – and receive – better support for their task. This means that adequate financial support must be provided for student health services, of course. But it also means that a healthy environment must be created throughout the school or campus, and, indeed, in their surrounding neighborhoods, as well.

Today, there is a growing acceptance of the idea that something constructive about school health can and should be done. In schools and campuses around the country, urgent discussions are taking place on how to mobilize everyone – students, teachers, parents, and staff – for the task. School health professionals are playing a vital role in these discussions, and understanding that the whole community is implicated in the wellness of children and young people is an essential fact that health professionals can help people from varied walks of life to see. Good nutrition, physical fitness, social confidence, emotional stability, and general knowledge about health are essential conditions for wellness. They are conditions that all adults working or living with children have the responsibility to strengthen, foster, or create.

Making schools and colleges and their neighborhoods safer and healthier environments should be a top priority both for health and for education policy today. Throughout the country, innovative ways are being found to fund school health offices, to upgrade the professional status of school health professionals, to extend school health services, and to link them more closely to local community needs. The challenge is to build on these new and promising models that see the connections between health and learning, schools and neighborhoods, and students' academic and non-academic life. School and college health professionals are uniquely situated to help the larger community to understand student health problems, and to envision the breadth of appropriate response.

# FOREWORD

Julius B. Richmond, MD

These volumes on student health are a welcome addition to the library of those interested in improving the health of children and adolescents. It is surprising, since we require all children to attend school, that so little attention has been directed specifically to the health of students. Now, at last, we have a comprehensive sourcebook for those in the various health professions who work with children in their student years.

These volumes go beyond the usual considerations of the practice of health professionals, for they present the context in which students are growing and developing. Today's problems are in part the consequence of historical progress in improving the health of children. The revolution in biology of the past several decades has resulted in a dramatic decline in morbidity and mortality from the acute infectious and gastrointestinal diseases of childhood. Declines in infant mortality rates, although not as great as we would like to see, have resulted in the saving of the lives of many low birthweight infants who are vulnerable to developmental disabilities. These changes have transformed pediatric practices and services in recent years.

A consequence of these changes has been a considerable shift from the acute disorders to developmental disabilities and long-term illnesses, which have major implications for the health of students. The student's primary task is learning, and these are health issues with profound implications for education. Society has recognized this linkage of health and education through the passage of the Education for All Handicapped Children's Act (PL 94-142), to which has been added PL 99-457 to include children in preschool years. Thus all health professionals caring for children and adolescents must be prepared to deal with learning disorders and the impacts of chronic illnesses on learning processes. While the implementation of this legislation is somewhat uneven in communities across the country, there is no question but that it has stimulated improved programs for students and better training and research, which ultimately leads to higher quality programs.

The transformation of student health services has also resulted from other changes in the context of practice. We have witnessed much greater ethnic diversity among the children in our schools. The number of children living in poverty and its intensity has increased; immunization rates in low-income populations have decreased; drug abuse has become a pervasive concern; teenage pregnancy rates are difficult to reduce; and acquired immunodeficiency syndrome (AIDS) has become a major risk, as have other sexually transmitted diseases. These ethnic, social, and economic issues and their political implications are important for every health worker. These volumes provide a state-of-the-art book to help in dealing with these difficult issues; they are also of help in comprehending the health problems for those young people who drop out of school.

The new complexity is resulting in efforts to reorganize services for students. Thus, while the establishment of school-based clinics is not a novel concept, there is considerable movement to expand such programs, probably due in part to the considerable fragmentation of services that has developed over the past several decades. The expansion of Medicaid and other services to low-income populations is a welcome effort that can help those involved in student health to finance the improvement and expansion of their efforts. As we move toward expanded state – and perhaps, ultimately, national – universal health insurance programs, we should make every effort to incorporate adequate provision for better student health programs.

It is interesting to observe the recent improvements in high school and college-age health programs. There is a growing sophistication concerning the opportunities in these programs to foster improved personal health practices that will carry over into adult life. It is also appropriate to note that in the preschool years, programs such as Head Start have comprehensive health services and it is important that students in the school years be assured of continuity of these services.

Student health programs provide unique opportunities to teach health promotion and disease prevention. Since the 1979 Surgeon General's Report, *Healthy People*, and its recent update, *Health Goals for the Year 2000*, our knowledge base for fostering health-enhancing behaviors has improved. In the many settings in which health professionals work with students they can serve as educators as well as service providers.

Thus, it is clear that those who provide student health services face many complex challenges and opportunities. Their activities should result in improved services, training, and research that will lead to better health for children and adolescents. These volumes should go a long way toward establishing an interdisciplinary profession of student health services as it clarifies these issues.

# FOREWORD

Vince L. Hutchins, MD, MPH

With the publication of *Principles and Practices of Student Health,* a longitudinal view is presented of health and health delivery issues concerning school-age children, adolescents, and young people from the perspective of school health.

Health services, health education, and a healthful school environment are generally accepted as the three principal components of comprehensive school health. Despite rather common agreement on these three components of a comprehensive school health program, wide differences exist among the 16,000 school districts in the U.S. Some provide innovative programs of health services and education, including provision of primary care in the school setting, while others make little or no provision for even basic health services for enrolled children. Budget constraints frequently mean a reduction or elimination of some or all health services to school-age children.

Concern is increasing about the health of the millions of school-age children and youth in our society. The focus of this concern has broadened from physical health to other conditions – behavioral disturbances, learning disabilities, substance abuse, mental health disorders, injuries (both intentional and non-intentional), sexually transmitted diseases, child abuse, adolescent adjustment, suicides, and homicides – as well as the age-old health problems such as infectious disease, malnutrition, and vision and hearing defects.

At any one time, approximately 99 percent of 6-to-15-year olds and about 90 percent of 16 and 17 year olds are enrolled in school. Once children are in school, many of their health and developmental problems are identified because a considerable number of these problems relate to their school performance. Many of these children are also seen by health care providers in the private or public sector.

As a result, health information on these children exists in a variety of settings – private sector, public agencies, and the schools. These data could be used more effectively to develop a rational base for delineating policy, planning, allocating resources, and evaluation if there were common recognition and communication.

It is important to understand that school health programs function within a system of health care, including the physician in private practice as well as the community health agencies. School health practice must be integrally related to this network for resolution of the school population's health-related problems.

With their newly evolving role in systems building, the State Title V Maternal and Child Health (MCH) program should be in the vanguard of promoting this network and communication within it. The State MCH program should be identifying the health needs of this population and taking action to plan, promote, and coordinate health services responsive to their needs. All of this should be accomplished through a public process.

The family, however defined, must continue to have a central role in all aspects of child health. The health services and programs should be implemented in ways that work with and for the family, involving and capitalizing on their strengths and supplementing and supporting their roles as necessary.

The health of school-age children should become a community-wide concern and not be viewed as the sole domain of any single part of the system. Services appropriate to a child and a family's needs, as noted, may need to come from the health care delivery system, the educational system, or the community and social services system. Thus, each must be considered in planning for services. Informed leadership, mutually identified goals and objectives, and coordinated action become critical for a successful community-based program, the end result of which will be healthy school-age children and youth.

# Contributing Authors, All Three Volumes

Diana Abramo, Doctoral Candidate, New York University; P. O. Box 1801 Old Chelsea Station, New York NY 10011

Martha Adams, BSN, FNP, MSN, Assistant Professor, University of North Dakota College of Nursing; Co-ordinator, Child Health Program, Grand Forks ND 58202-8195

Richard M. Adams, MD, Director, School Health Services, Dallas Independent School District, Dallas TX 75204

Zili Amsel, ScD, Acting Director, Division of Epidemiology and Prevention Research, National Institute on Drug Abuse, Rockville MD 20857

Elizabeth Bacon, MS, Director, Disabled Student Services, San Diego State University, San Diego CA 92182

Suzanne M. Bianchi, PhD, U.S. Bureau of the Census, Housing and Household Economic Statistics Division, Washington DC 20233

Anne Bourgeois, MS, RD, Obesity Specialist, NHLBI Information Center, P.O. Box 30105, Bethesda MD 20824-0105

Pamela A. Cooper Bowen, MD, MPH, Director, Princeton University Health Services, Princeton NJ 08544-1004

W. David Burns, Director, Student Health Services; Assistant Vice President for Student Life Policy and Services, Rutgers University, New Brunswick NJ 08903

Ernest L. Boyer, PhD, President, The Carnegie Foundation for the Advancement of Teaching, 5 Ivy Lane, Princeton NJ 08540

Willard Cates, Jr, MD, MPH, Director, Division of Training, CDC Epidemiology Program Office, CDC, Atlanta GA 30333

Donald F. B. Char, MD, Director, Student Health Services; Professor of Pediatrics, University of Hawaii at Manoa, East West Road, Honolulu HI 96822

**William A. Christmas, MD, FACP,** Director, Student Health Center; Clinical Associate Professor of Medicine, College of Medicine, University of Vermont, Burlington VT 05401

**Dominic Cittadino, DDS,** Director and Staff Dentist, Student Emergency Dental Service, Southern Illinois University at Carbondale, Carbondale IL 62901

**MarJeanne Collins, MD,** Director, Student Health Service; Associate Professor of Medicine, Associate Professor of Pediatrics, Hospital of the University of Pennsylvania, Philadelphia PA 19104-4283

**James P. Comer, MD, MPH,** Professor, Child Psychiatry; Director, Yale Child Study Center, Yale University School of Medicine, New Haven CT 06510

**Carol N. D'Onofrio, DrPH,** Associate Professor of Public Health, University of California at Berkeley, Berkeley CA 94720

**Murray M. DeArmond, MD,** Director, Student Health Services, University of Arizona, Tucson AZ 85721

**Connie A. Diggs, RN, NP, MPA,** Director, Student Health Center, California State University, Los Angeles, Los Angeles CA 90032-8411

**John M. Dorman, MD,** Director of Public Relations and Outreach, Cowell Student Health Center; Clinical Associate Professor of Pediatrics, Stanford University, Stanford CA 94305

**Johanna Dwyer, DSc,** Professor of Medicine in Community Health, Tufts University School of Medicine, Boston MA 02111

**Linda H. Edwards, MSN, DrPH,** School Health Co-ordinator, Illinois Department of Public Health, Springfield IL 62761

**James H. Evans, MS,** Assistant Professor of Behavioral Sciences; Director, Chemical Dependency Counselor Training Program, San Diego City College, San Diego CA 92101-4787

**Nell Faucette, EdD,** Associate Professor of Physical Education, University of South Florida, Tampa FL 33620

**Gail C. Frank, DrPH, MPH, RD,** Nutritional Epidemiologist, Professor of Nutrition, California State University, Long Beach, Long Beach CA 90840-0501

**Karen A. Gordon, MPH, EdD,** Director, Health Education, Princeton University Health Services, Princeton NJ 08540

**Ted W. Grace, MD, MPH,** Director, University Health Services, The Ohio State University, Columbus, OH 43210-1240

**Joel Grinolds, MD, MPH,** Staff Physician, Liaison to Disabled Student Services, San Diego State University Student Health Services, San Diego CA 92182

**Debra W. Haffner, MPH,** Executive Director, Sex Information and Education Council of the U.S. (SIECUS), West 42nd Street, New York City NY 10036

**Steven L. Harris, MD, MS,** Clinical Assistant Professor of Family and Emergency Medicine, USC; Chief of Medical Staff, California State University, Los Angeles, Los Angeles CA 90032-8411

**Nils Hasselmo, PhD,** President, University of Minnesota, Minneapolis MN 55455

**Karen Hein, MD,** Professor of Pediatrics, Associate Professor of Epidemiology and Social Work, Albert Einstein College of Medicine, New York NY 10467

**Wylie C. Hembree, MD,** Director, Student Health Services, Health Sciences Campus; Associate Professor of Clinical Medicine and OB/GYN, Columbia University, New York NY 10032

**Alan R. Hinman, MD, MPH,** Director, National Center for Prevention Services, CDC, Atlanta GA 30333

**Vince L. Hutchins, MD, MPH,** Consultant, Carnegie Corporation, New York City

**Judith B. Igoe, MS, RN, FAAN,** Associate Professor and Director, School Health Programs, University of Colorado Health Sciences Center, Denver CO 80262

**Elaine M. Johnson, PhD,** Director, Office for Substance Abuse Prevention; Associate Administrator for Prevention, Alcohol, Drug Abuse, and Mental Health Administration (ADAMHA) of the USDHHS, Rockville MD 20857

**Diane H. Jones, MSW, PhD,** Medical Sociologist, Center for Chronic Disease Prevention and Health Promotion, Centers for Disease Control, Atlanta GA 30333

**Richard P. Keeling, MD,** Director, Department of Student Health; Associate Professor of Internal Medicine, University of Virginia, Charlottesville VA 22902

**Steven H. Kelder, BS, MPH,** Doctoral Student, Division of Epidemiology, School of Public Health, University of Minnesota, Minneapolis MN 55455

**Douglas Kirby, PhD,** ETR Associates, P.O. Box 1830, Santa Cruz CA 95061-1830

**Joel C. Kleinman, PhD,** (deceased), former Director of Analysis, National Center for Health Statistics, Hyattsville MD 20782

**David P. Kraft, MD,** Executive Director, University Health Services, University of Massachusetts at Amherst, Amherst MA 01003

**Richard D. Krugman, MD,** Director, C. Henry Kempe National Center for the Prevention and Treatment of Child Abuse and Neglect; Professor of Pediatrics and Acting Dean of the University of Colorado School of Medicine, Denver CO 80262

**Felice D. Kurtzman, MPH, RD,** Assistant Professor, Department of Biological Chemistry, School of Medicine, UCLA, Los Angeles CA 90024-1703

**Myra Lappin, MD, MPH,** Director, Student Health Service, San Francisco State University, San Francisco CA 94132-4200

**Carl G. Leukefeld, DSW,** Director, Drug and Alcohol Abuse Research Center, University of Kentucky, Lexington KY 40506

**Frances Marcus Lewis, RN, PhD,** Evaluator, Cancer Information System, Fred Hutchinson Cancer Research Center, Seattle; Professor, Department of Community Health Care Systems, University of Washington, Seattle WA 98195

**Chris Y. Lovato, PhD,** Assistant Professor, Graduate School of Public Health, San Diego State University, San Diego CA 92182

**Ralph Manchester, MD, FACP,** Chief, Medical Care Section, University Health Service; Associate Professor, Department of Medicine, University of Rochester, Rochester NY 14642

**Mary L. Michal, MD,** Associate Professor, Department of Pediatrics; Director, Developmental/ Behavioral Pediatrics, East Tennessee State University, Johnson City TN 37614-0002

**Brenda S. Mitchell, PhD,** Director, Behavioral Science and Health Promotion, Institute for Aerobics Research, Preston Road, Dallas TX 75230

**Patricia A. Motz, EdD, RNC,** Director, Health Services, Denver Public Schools, Denver CO 80203

**Philip R. Nader, MD,** Professor of Pediatrics; Chief, Division of General Pediatrics; and Director, Community Pediatrics, University of California at San Diego, San Diego CA 92103

**National Health/Education Consortium, c/o Rae Grad,** National Commission to Prevent Infant Mortality, Switzer Building, Washington DC 20201

**Anne Marie Novinger, RN, MA,** Specialist, Health Services, Glendale Community College, Glendale CA 91208

**Patrick W. O'Carroll, MD, MPH,** Chief, Intentional Injuries Section, Epidemiology Branch, Division of Injury Control, National Center for Environmental Health and Injury Control, CDC, Atlanta GA 30333

**Janice Ozias, RN, PhD,** Supervisor of Nursing Services, Austin Independent School District, Austin TX 78757-2147

**Guy S. Parcel, PhD,** Professor and Director, Center for Health Promotion Research and Development, The University of Texas Health Science Center, Houston TX 77225

**Carole Passarelli, RN, PNP, MS,** Editor, Journal of School Nursing; Associate Professor, Pediatric Nursing Program, Child Division, Yale University School of Nursing, New Haven CT 06536-0740

**Kevin Patrick, MD, MS,** Director, UCSD-SDSU General Preventive Medicine Residency Program, University of California at San Diego; Director, Student Health Services, San Diego State University, San Diego CA 92182-0567

**Mary Ann Pentz, PhD,** Associate Professor, Department of Preventive Medicine, University of Southern California; Institute for Health Promotion and Disease Prevention Research, North Lake Avenue, Pasadena CA 91101

**Cheryl L. Perry, PhD,** Associate Professor of Epidemiology; Chair, Community Health Education, Division of Epidemiology, University of Minnesota School of Public Health, Minneapolis MN 55455

**R. Morgan Pigg Jr., HSD, MPH, FASHA,** Editor, Journal of School Health; Professor and Chair, Department of Health Science Education, University of Florida, Gainesville FL 32611-2034

**Deborah Prothrow-Stith, MD,** Assistant Dean for Government and Community Programs, Harvard University School of Public Health; Lecturer, Health Policy and Management Department, Harvard University, Boston MA 02115

**Julius B. Richmond, MD,** John D. and Catherine T. MacArthur Professor of Health Policy, Emeritus, Harvard University School of Public Health, Boston MA 02115

**Frederick P. Rivara, MD, MPH,** Director, Harborview Injury Prevention and Research Center, Seattle; Professor of Pediatrics, University of Washington, Seattle WA 98104

**George M. Robb,** Associate Vice President for External Relations, University of Minnesota, Minneapolis MN 55455

**Carolyn C. Rogers, MA,** Demographer, Economic Research Service (USDA), Washington DC 20005

**James F. Sallis, PhD,** Associate Professor of Psychology, San Diego State University, San Diego CA 92182

**Linda E. Saltzman, PhD,** Behavioral Scientist, Intentional Injuries Section, Epidemiology Branch, Division of Injury Control, National Center for Environmental Health and Injury Control, CDC, Atlanta GA 30333

**Allan J. Schwartz, MA, MS, PhD,** Associate Professor of Psychiatry and of Psychology; Chief, Mental Health Section, University Health Service, University of Rochester, Rochester NY 14642

**John R. Seffrin, PhD,** Professor, Health Education; Chair, Department of Applied Health Science, Indiana University, Bloomington IN 47405

**Toby Simon, MEd,** Associate Dean, Student Life, Brown University, Providence RI 02912

**Bruce G. Simons-Morton, EdD, MPH,** Research Scientist, The Prevention Research Branch, Division of Epidemiology, Statistics, and Prevention Research, National Institute of Child Health and Human Development, Rockville, MD 20892

**Beverlie Conant Sloane, MPH, PhD,** Director, Health Education, Dartmouth College; Assistant Professor, Department of Community and Family Medicine, Dartmouth Medical School, Hanover NH 03755

**Jack C. Smith, MS,** Chief, Statistics and Computer Resources Branch, Division of Reproductive Health, Center for Chronic Disease Prevention and Health Promotion, CDC, Atlanta GA 30333

**Howard R. Spivak, MD,** Associate in Pediatrics, New England Medical Center Hospital, Boston; Associate Professor of Pediatrics, Tufts University School of Medicine, Boston MA 02111

**Richard Strauss, MD,** Associate Professor of Preventive Medicine and Internal Medicine; Team Physician, Athletic Department; Director, Sports Medicine Clinic, Student Health Services, The Ohio State University, Columbus OH 43210-1240

Paula Swinford, MS, CHES, Director of Health Education, Student Health and Counseling Services, University of Southern California, Los Angeles CA 90089-0311

Alex Thomas, PhD, Associate Professor, Educational Psychology Department, Miami University, Oxford OH 45056

Kenneth C. Troutman, DDS, MPH, Professor of Clinical Dentistry; Director, Pediatric Dentistry Post-doctoral Program, Columbia University School of Dental and Oral Surgery, New York NY 10032

Deborah Klein Walker, EdD, Assistant Commissioner for the Bureau of Parent, Child, and Adolescent Health, Massachusetts Department of Health, Boston MA 02111

Helen M. Wallace, MD, MPH, Professor of Maternal Child Health, Graduate School of Public Health, San Diego State University, San Diego CA 92182

Leighton C. Whitaker, PhD, Director, Psychological Services for Swarthmore College; Swarthmore PA 19081

J. Robert Wirag, HSD, Director, Student Health Center, University of Texas at Austin, Austin TX 78713

Joel Yager, MD, Professor, Department of Psychiatry and Biobehavioral Science, School of Medicine, UCLA; Director of Residency Education; Senior Consultant, Adult Eating Disorders Program, UCLA, Los Angeles CA 90024-1703

Laurie S. Zabin, MD, Associate Professor, Department of Population Dynamics, The Johns Hopkins University School of Hygiene and Public Health; Associate Professor, Department of Obstetrics and Gynecology, JHU School of Medicine, Baltimore MD 21205

Christine Heustis Zimmer, BSN, MA, Administrator, University Wellness Programs, Sindecuse Health Center, Western Michigan University, Kalamazoo MI 49008

Joseph E. Zins, PhD, Professor, Department of Early Childhood and Special Education, University of Cincinnati, Cincinnati OH 45221

# Section I

# History, Rationale, and Organizational Issues

# The History and
# Current Status of College Health

KEVIN PATRICK, MD, MS

## INTRODUCTION

College Health theory and practice, from their earliest origins, have been predicated upon the uneasy marriage of two basic concepts – keeping the healthy healthy and restoring the sick to a healthy state. The contemporary embodiment of these concepts may be found in the fields of Public Health and Clinical Medicine. Of course, it has never been as simple as merely getting two camps to agree on something. The historical development of the field is traceable to a number of different ideologic movements, each of which struggled, and in some cases still struggle, with its own identity formation. It has not made matters easier that these struggles have occurred in full view of the academic community. In fact, that they have done so has probably maximized the potential for full fractionation, academics relishing as they do a good turf battle.

This fractional nature explains much of the difficulty that we have in the field of college health today. It is difficult for us to explain ourselves to others, both in and out of the field, because for each of us our primary discipline serves as the basis of our individual perspective. We are physicians or nurses or health educators or psychologists or dentists or public health workers. We even represent subsets within these disciplines. There are great differences between the frames of reference of internists and family physicians, between counseling psychologists and behavioral medicine psychologists. When we are comprised of so many disciplines, miscommunication is a natural by-product. In the midst of this cacophony, it is not surprising that those on the outside with apparently clear messages, such as "cost savings" or "specialization," might ring more true to our non-student health overseers.

The multidisciplinary nature of college health is, however, also the basis of much of its strength. That we are an uneasy amalgam of several disciplines almost certainly serves to keep us in balance with one another. It enables us to be exposed to and absorb new ideas more readily. And it allows us to cast off old modes of doing things more readily than if we were dependent solely upon them. Throughout this process of transformation and rebuilding it behooves all of us to understand something of our history and to comprehend the major forces that shape our present. Table 1 summarizes some important historical markers for college health.

---

### Table 1
#### Selected Historical Events in College Health

1818 - Harvard College establishes a series of lectures on hygiene required of all seniors.

1825-1860 - Harvard, Yale, Williams, and Dartmouth develop physical activity and gymnastics as a means of improving the health of students.

1851 - The College of the City of New York establishes a course on anatomy, physiology and hygiene.

1860 - Amherst College establishes a Department of Physical Education and Hygiene to "secure healthful daily exercise and recreation to all students. . . and to teach them, both theoretically and practically, the laws of health." Dr. John Hooker was the first Professor in this department but, due to ill health, was replaced in the first year by Dr. Edward Hitchcock.

1861 - Mount Holyoke College appointed a physician-in-residence to the staff to look after the health of its students.

1865 - Vassar College appointed a physician-in-residence on its founding staff. The physician was a professor of physiology and hygiene, practiced in a medical unit that included an infirmary, a nurse, and a consultation office, and developed "a positive program for the promotion of health and well-being" of students. Thus, Vassar may qualify as having the first "comprehensive" student health service by modern day standards.

1885 - The American Association for the Advancement of Physical Education (AAAPE) was founded. This was an organization of health-related staff at schools, colleges and universities, and was a precursor organization to the American Student Health Association (ASHA).

1897 - The Society of College Directors of Physical Education (SCDPE) was founded. Initially dominated by "men and women of medical or scientific training" it became, over time, progressively dominated by athletic personnel. It was also a precursor to the ASHA.

1901 - The University of California (Berkeley) developed the first large-scale, comprehensive university health services.

1910 - Princeton University, with the guidance of Dr. Stewart Paton, inaugurated a special section in the health service to deal with "personality problems" among college students, arguably the first such special unit addressing mental health issues.

(Table 1, continued)

Table 1, continued

1918 - The Interdepartmental Social Hygiene Board was created by the U.S. Congress to address the high incidence of venereal disease in the nation. Dr. Thomas Storey, Professor and Director of Hygiene at the City College of New York was appointed the Executive Secretary of this Board. Of its $1.4 million annual budget, $300,000 went to colleges to "develop effective educational measures in the prevention of venereal diseases." In 1922 this Board went out of existence.

1920 - The American Student Health Association (ASHA) was formed by members of AAAPE and SCDPE. These individuals felt that such an organization would more appropriately address the full range of student health issues. This organization became the American College Health Association (ACHA) in 1948.

1922 - The President's Committee of Fifty on College Hygiene was formed " to stimulate the development and extension of instruction and training in hygiene in normal schools, colleges and universities." Dr. Charles Eliot, President Emeritus of Harvard, was Chair, and Dr. Thomas Storey was its Executive Secretary.

1927 - The President's Committee published the landmark report "The Status of Hygiene Programs in Institutions of Higher Education in the United States" through Stanford University Press. Its author was Thomas Storey. This survey of 396 institutions assessed the types of health services offered in colleges and addressed the strengths and weaknesses of these services.

1931 - The First National Conference on College Hygiene was held in Syracuse, New York. Its sponsors were the National Tuberculosis Association (the initial conference organizer), The National Health Council, The President's Committee of Fifty, and the American Student Health Association. For the first time minimum standards for college health services were outlined, in part as a result of the 1927 Storey report. Other such National Conferences followed in 1937, 1947, 1954, and 1970.

1953 - "Health Services in American Colleges and Universities" by Dr. Norman Moore and Dr. John Summerskill was published by Cornell University Press. This was a landmark survey of student health activity nationwide.

1964 - First set of comprehensive standards for college health published by ACHA. Revisions followed in 1969, 1977, 1984, and 1991.

1974 - Macy Conference on Student Health convened in Princeton, New Jersey and was chaired by Willard Dalrymple, MD, then Director of Student Health at Princeton. The aim of the conference was to discuss the "nature and function" of campus health programs.

1986 - Standards for College Health Nursing Practice published by the American Nurses Association. This led to the creation of a special College Health Nurses Certification Exam.

1990 - Healthy People 2000, Objectives for the Nation for Health Promotion, included specific objectives for health promotion activities on college and university campuses.

1990 - U.S. Public Health Service, Centers for Disease Control, Division of Adolescent and School Health specifically identifies College Youth as one of three overall target groups for surveillance and public health intervention.

## The 1800s

College health in this country began in the early 1800s with activities both in and out of the classroom. There was an effort to import the *mens sana in corpore sano* model of fitness from European higher education with instruction in physical activity and gymnastics. This was coupled with curricula in what was popularly called "hygiene," almost always presented with a strong element of religiosity. For example, Harvard taught courses in hygiene and anatomy "for the purpose of illustrating and bolstering the course in natural theology" and "to furnish knowledge wherewith to construct an argument for the existence and attributes of God."[1] This approach endured for several decades and included activities at a number of institutions including Yale, Dartmouth, and Amherst. At Williams College in 1851 the first item of instruction for first year students was Combe on Health and Mental Education, a text that served as the basis for advice on healthful living habits.[2] In this same year, a course in hygiene was offered at the City College of New York to educate students on "the active duties of operative life, rather than those more particularly regarded as necessary for the pulpit, bar, or medical profession."[3]

During the latter half of the 1800s it was becoming clear to at least a few college presidents, and at least one college trustee, that the health status of college students was important enough to address through the provision of special, dedicated services. In 1856 President Stearns of Amherst noted that "the breaking down of health of students, especially in the spring of the year, which is exceedingly common, involving the necessity of leaving college in many instances, and crippling the energies and destroying the prospects of not a few who remain, is in my opinion wholly unnecessary if proper measures could be taken to prevent it." This quote is taken from a publication entitled Physical Culture in Amherst College written by Nathan Allen.[2] In 1859 Allen, a medical doctor and trustee of Amherst, garnered support from the other trustees to establish a new Department of Physical Education and Hygiene at the College with a physician as its head. In 1860 Edward Hitchcock was appointed to this position and, as such, is generally regarded as the first college health practitioner.

Activities at other colleges happened as well, notably at women's colleges. In 1861 Mount Holyoke appointed a physician-in-residence to its staff. Vassar followed suit in 1865 providing for student health care from the founding year of the institution.[1] At each institution, the physician had both clinical and teaching duties. The pioneering role of these women's college health centers is undervalued in virtually all historical accounts of student health. It can be argued that the first "comprehensive" student health care services were offered at these two institutions. With the combination of physician services, physical space for medical exam rooms and infirmary care, nursing services to nurture the ill back to health, and health promotion activities, these centers combined almost all aspects of current-day student health services. Raycroft's suggested reason for the advanced status of women's college health services is interesting: "(F)or many years college girls enjoyed the benefits of a much more general and better coordinated program of health and physical education than was provided for their brothers. The absence of intercollegiate contests with their peculiar problems and limited objectives, which distracted attention from the importance of every day service for the non-athletic student, was no small factor in providing freedom for the development of a high standard" for health services.[3]

Athletic medical care played a seminal role in the definition of college health practice. In the 1880s and 1890s intercollegiate athletics began to flourish and, with it, a greater level of emphasis upon physical conditioning, strength testing and exercise. Athletic enterprise also lead to a separation of philosophical approaches to health care for students. On the one hand, it is apparent that athletics prompted an increased investment in gymnasiums and exercise equipment, both areas initially under the "cost-centers" of health service leaders. On the other hand, however, decision-making about the uses to which these resources were put made more apparent the frequent differences of opinion that had developed about the goals and objectives of student health.[3] Organizations developed that served to represent these various interests, including the American Association for the Advancement of Physical Education (1885), the Society of College Directors of Physical Education (1897), The National Collegiate Athletic Association (1905) and, ultimately, the American Student Health Association (1920). It is safe to state that it was during such "turf battles" that physical activity and physical fitness took distinctly subordinate roles to that of medicine as the focus of efforts in the majority of student health centers.

## THE EARLY 1900S

The period from around the turn of the century through the early 1920s was an extremely important one with respect to medical issues in general and the health of college students in particular. Four significant things happened. First, the Flexner Report on medical education[4] signaled the end of medical practice as an unsystematic, sketchy enterprise and the beginnings of hegemonic biotechnologic, reductionistic medicine. Through the adoption of Flexner's recommendations, and with the infusion of substantial resources from private foundations, medicine gained a new-found credibility in a rapidly industrializing society.[5] This was a genuine watershed era for medical practitioners as it provided the essential underpinnings of a guild approach to medical practice unequaled in history and maintained to the present day.

The second occurrence was the rise of Public Health with its emphasis upon the control of communicable diseases. A new class of scientists and practitioners emerged, more interested in approaching health problems in the aggregate, through sanitation, legislation, health education, and prevention. The third event was World War I with its need for healthy soldiers, which focused the nation's attention on the health status, or lack thereof, of its youth. The fourth historical process that profoundly impacted health care considerations on college campuses was the evolution of mental health care as a separate, distinct, and respectable field of endeavor.

The second and third factors, the public health movement and the war, were intimately related in their impact upon student health. With the war approaching, great concern was expressed about the problems associated with venereal disease. In 1918 the 65th Congress established and funded the Interdepartmental Social Hygiene Board, comprised of representatives of the U.S. Public Health Service, the Navy, the Army, and other selected agencies. The Board was to address the increasingly vexing problem of venereal disease in America's youth and appointed as its Executive Secretary Dr. Thomas Storey, Professor and Director of Hygiene at the City College of New York. Dr. Ruth Boynton, an early chronicler of the history of college health, has pointed out that Dr. Storey was very influential in insuring that some of the resources expended by the Board, initially allocated for the sole purpose of dealing with venereal disease, were spent to "improve or establish complete college health programs" on several college campuses across the country.[6] Thus, we have what in all probability is the first instance of federal subsidy for college health activities.

Dr. Storey's influence on the practice of student health didn't end with the Social Hygiene Board. After World War I, while the Board was being phased out, Dr. Storey engineered the creation of the "President's Committee of Fifty on College Hygiene." Composed of highly influential individuals, many of whom were college presidents, the Committee was chaired by then-President Emeritus of Harvard, Charles Eliot. One of its tasks was to survey the status of college health at the time, the result of which was a publication, in 1927, entitled "The Status of Hygiene Programs in Institutions of Higher Education in the United States."[7] Authored by Thomas Storey, this report, among other things, served as the stimulus for the consideration and adoption of basic standards for college health at the First National Conference on College Hygiene in 1931.[8] These standards represent the first set of recommended practices for college health centers.

The recognition of the social and emotional problems of students has its earliest manifestations in the early 1900s. The first college mental health service, at Princeton, dates to 1910; it was under the direction of Dr. Stewart Paton.[3] Over the ensuing few decades campus approaches to the mental health problems of students expanded with the continuing development of the disciplines of psychology and psychiatry, although the literature of student mental health did not become extensive until the 1950s. One important survey was undertaken by Dana Farnsworth of Harvard and reported in 1957.[9] Farnsworth has pointed out that the 1950s were also the time in which "the role of the college campus as a social setting worthy of examination in its own right" occurred.[10] Thus, "student life" became legitimate as a research topic for scholars of psychology, sociology, social work, and education. These studies contributed to the creation of a new type of educational administrator important to the recent development of the field of student health, the student affairs professional.

## THE RECENT PAST

The close of the first half of the 1900s witnessed the dawn of a new era of higher education. Optimism about the future of the nation was coupled with the early post-war growth in college campuses and study of the student experience. Moore and Summerskill reported in an extraordinarily comprehensive survey of the status of college health services[11] that the range and extent of these programs was vast, with almost 85 percent of institutions offering some sort of student health care.

Several developments in the early 1960s had a great impact on these providers of student health. First, as noted above, the explosive growth in the numbers of college students from the post-World War II baby boom created unprecedented demand for space in higher education. With the development of new campuses came the need for student services of all types. This involved expansion of existing services on established but growing campuses, and the development of services on new campuses in growth states like California, Texas, and Florida. To oversee these developments, college presidents frequently recruited administrators from the ranks of student affairs professionals weaned on the new "science" of student life. It is not surprising that these individuals often opted for full-service, comprehensive student health facilities, emulating those of the more established institutions that had, perhaps, been the subject of their study.

Second, the development of medical science, expanding almost geometrically as a result of the infusion of massive amounts of federal research support into what Arnold Relman, the Editor of the New England Journal of Medicine, later called the "medical-industrial complex," began to flourish in the 1960s. There was widespread enchantment with this phenomenon. It was imagined by many that there was really very little that could go wrong with the human body that couldn't be "fixed" in one way or another. The health care industry was growth-oriented and paid handsome returns on investments in an era of unquestioned cost reimbursement. The result was a sophisticated and costly role for medical practice and a subordinate one for concepts related to the prevention of disease. If anything, this phenomenon solidified the "medical model" approach to disease within many student health centers, as it did in virtually every other sector of medical practice.

This period of the "engineering approach" to disease, occurring as it did at a time of great reductionism in the university community in general, probably represented the nadir of influence of non-physician student health personnel on college health practice. Health became too important to trust to anyone but the physicians.

Third, despite the clear hope by many that it would not happen,[10] it is in the 1960s that athletic medical services, especially on campuses with substantial intercollegiate athletic programs, experienced a marked drift away from the sphere of influence of mainstream student health concerns. The need for a balance between medical care for the athletic student and services for the student-athlete, a common desire throughout the entire history of college health and higher education, was overwhelmed by the impact of television – and the revenues it produced – upon collegiate athletic endeavors. Although certainly not universal, this phenomenon was common enough to further alienate most remaining individuals whose sentiment might have wedded college health, physical education, and physical fitness.

Fourth, profound social changes occurring in society with respect to such things as sexual activity, alcohol and drug use, campus safety and sexual assault, unplanned pregnancy and abortion all greatly impacted the health – and health care needs – of college students. Campus administrators who had disavowed the precepts of *in loco parentis* could not escape the needs of addressing health issues created by these phenomena. Pressures to do so were strong and came from many constituencies, including parents, community health resources (who felt that colleges should tend to "their own" problems so that community agencies could deal with community indigent and minority groups), and the students themselves.

A final set of historical conditions brings us to where we are today and lays the groundwork for the future. First has been our progressive disillusionment with the yield of high-technology, reductionistic medicine. It is becoming increasingly clear to many that we cannot afford to have our every medical technologic wish come true. To attempt to do so begs unavoidably the economic argument of necessary choice articulated so well by Fuchs.[12] We in student health are drawn into this argument whether we like it or not. Most of the benefits of high technology medicine are realized by the very sick and the very old. This is also where most of the resources go. If these expenditure are not checked, unless we believe that there are limitless supplies of both human and fiscal resources, someone is going to come up short. With an aging population, time will only exacerbate this problem.

A directly related problem is the current crisis in health insurance and access to medical care. College students are among the most poorly insured group in America with from 20 to 30 percent without any medical coverage.[13,14] The escalating cost of medical care is not making this problem better. This creates an unconscionable circumstance in which many of our nation's youth are effectively denied access to even simple health care. Also, student health centers, while not traditionally heavily dependent upon insurance reimbursement for support, may be more-so in the future as college administrators attempt to hold the line on costs. Lack of health insurance will then create even more disenfranchisement.

As a result of the extraordinary cost escalation in the health care industry in general, major changes have occurred in the structure of medical care practice in the United States. Managed health care systems utilizing cost-controlling measures such as pre-payment, utilization review, ambulatory surgical centers, selected physician panels, and a host of other processes are now the rule. While the firestorm of activity has been centered on hospital cost containment there has been no shortage of innovation in the area of ambulatory care. The last decade witnessed an extraordinary stimulation of the private sector in medicine and health care and it is likely that the only thing that has restrained this process from impacting student health centers more directly is that greater financial returns exist in caring for individuals more sick than students usually get. When the industry that has grown as a result of this stimulation begins to "shake out," its impact on student health may increase.

Partly as a reaction to the excesses of technologic medicine, and partly because they were there all along, promising developments have occurred in the areas of health education, health promotion, and preventive medicine. We have gradually come to recognize that it makes more sense to reduce the modifiable risk factors for chronic disease, and thereby the incidence and severity of those diseases, than it does to treat the disease once it occurs. The two disciplines of medical behavioral psychology and health promotion, both beginning in earnest as recently as the 1970s, have begun to produce results. This impacts college health environments in two ways. First, interventions have improved for health problems directly affecting college students while they are in school. Drug and alcohol programs, accident prevention, immunization programs, sexually transmitted disease control – the list goes on and on. As these interventions improve it has become progressively more difficult to justify spending the vast majority of health center resources on medical services for already sick patients.

Second, with the demonstration of the value of **early** interventions on long-range health outcomes, **questions of the contexts** of those interventions are necessarily begged. Smoking cessation, hypertension control, close diabetes management, and the promotion of physical activity to counteract sedentary life-style are all preventive interventions that must be developed early and maintained throughout life to have maximal benefit in late adulthood. At the time of this writing it seems unavoidable that student health practitioners, like others whose principal practice is with the young, will be drawn into discussions of the "when and where" of societal health care dollar investment.

A final important historical development impacting student health is the dramatic shift in the age, health status, and demographic characteristics of the college student population. Much of this occurred during the 1970s and 1980s. Well-addressed in several chapters in the closing section of this volume, suffice it to say that these changes – past and projected – coupled with what is generally acknowledged as an impending and almost universal financial crisis for this nation's colleges and universities, are likely to have deep and lasting effects upon contemporary models of student health care.

## CURRENT STATUS AND PROMISING DEVELOPMENTS

Student health currently enjoys a strong position in many colleges and universities.[15] As outlined in this text, models of student health services range from small nurse-directed health centers at community colleges to comprehensive, full-service health care facilities with medical, psychological, psychiatric and dental care, specialty services of various types, inpatient care, and a full range of health education and health promotion activities. Substantial connections exist on many campuses between student health centers and medical, nursing, allied health education schools, and schools of public health. At these institutions joint appointments for staff are common as are research projects aimed at exploring new ways to prevent, diagnose, and treat ailments common to young adults.

Growth in some existing student health programs is occurring, even to the extent of "bricks and mortar" activity at major institutions. This is not universal, however, and at least one campus, Drexel University, recently closed its student health center citing "drastically rising costs" as the reason.[16] Spokesmen at Drexel maintained that moving to contract its services to a local health maintenance organization would save the university $500,000 in its first full year of transition. The spokesperson was not quoted about whether, or how much, students would save in the move. In an era in which it is popular to cost-shift to potential users of services, irrespective of their ability to afford them, such actions may well occur on other campuses.

Recent developments hold promise for the field of student health. The Fund for the Improvement of Post-Secondary Education (FIPSE) of the U.S. Department of Education has recently financed innovative programs on college campuses to combat alcohol and drug abuse. These FIPSE projects, developed on dozens of campuses, hold substantial promise in our ability to combat these most pernicious problems.

Healthy People 2000, National Health Promotion and Disease Prevention Objectives, was released in the Spring of 1991.[17] This is a follow-up document to the landmark 1979 publication Healthy People,[18] and is comprised of dozens of specific and measurable objectives for the nation to attain by the year 2000. Notably, many of these pertain directly to activities now common to comprehensive student health centers. Several student health professionals played key roles in the development of this report. Healthy People 2000 will serve as an invaluable reference point for all those interested in improving the health of young people.

The Division of Adolescent and School Health of the U.S. Public Health Service, Centers for Disease Control, Center for Chronic Diseases has recently developed a major nationwide initiative focusing on the development of risk factor surveillance and health promotion activities for college students. Supported in large part from resources aimed at the prevention of HIV infection, the overall goal of this initiative is to strengthen the capacities of colleges and universities to address the major preventable health problems of college students including accidents and injuries, tobacco consumption, alcohol and drug abuse, nutritional problems, unintended pregnancy, and sexually transmitted diseases. So history repeats itself. As Dr. Storey did in 1919, we see that federal officials are taking an opportunity to use a compelling concern about a particular "venereal disease" and amplifying it to the betterment of health promotion and disease prevention of all kinds among college students.

## CONCLUSION

The origins of college health in America can be traced back almost 175 years. The field has enjoyed the influence of an extraordinary group of professionals from a wide array of disciplines. Substantial transformation has occurred as the field has reacted and responded to countervailing social, economic, educational, political, and scientific forces. The most constant influence has likely been the college students themselves. There to partake of what society characterizes as the "intergenerational transference of knowledge and values" they come to the campus with idealism, enthusiasm, and an almost uniform sense of invulnerability. They come to change, and often find the process more painful, and more enlightening, than they could ever have imagined.

A resurgence of interest in the quality of the college experience is occurring.[19] The Carnegie Foundation for the Advancement of Teaching has recently published Campus Life: In Search of Community,[20] which outlines precepts for higher education communities to attain. Leading universities such as Stanford and Harvard are re-examining core curricula. Issues of campus racial harmony and tolerance, once thought settled, are gaining new prominence as campus homogeneity is replaced with heterogeneity and as complex, divisive, and unsolved social and economic problems continue unabated.

Student health professionals have a critically important role to play in these deliberations.[21] Unfortunately, and too often it seems, campus quality of life issues are discussed with only passing – if any – reference to emotional or physical health; to designing in at the outset health-enhancing and promoting environmental components; or to services renderable to students to address these issues. The notion still prevails that health is something that occurs separate from cognition, that poor health can be restored as one would fix an automobile, and that a hierarchy exists on campus with, naturally, "academic" considerations at the top.

DeArmond has outlined some considerations for the future of college health.[22] A central theme of his thoughtful treatise is the inseparability of mind, body, and spirit. Society has entrusted academe with the task of exploring and developing knowledge in each of these domains. During the time that student health has evolved from the simple study of "hygiene" to the complex set of tasks embodied in health promotion and clinical medical and psychological services, scholarly activity has burgeoned in psychiatry, psychology, molecular biology, chemistry, physiology, medicine, philosophy, theology, and dozens of other disciplines. This knowledge, reintegrated, allows us to comprehend the interrelationships among mind, body, and spirit. As student health practitioners we do this reintegration in the midst of the academic enterprise and for its primary beneficiaries. Thus, we have the opportunity to interject what we (and only we, because of our unique position) know of the student "mind, body, and spirit" into academic discourse. This will be essential if the highest quality of college and university campus life is to be attained.

**Acknowledgment**

I am indebted to William A. Christmas, MD, who so willingly shared with me his files on the history of college health.

## REFERENCES

1. Quoted by RK Means in Slack CB: Historical Perspectives on School Health. Thorofare, New Jersey, 1975, pp 175, 177; from Rogers JF: Instruction in Hygiene in Institutions of Higher Education. U.S. Department of the Interior, Office of Education, 1936, p 2

2. Ginsburg EL: The College and Student Health, National Tuberculosis Association, New York, 1955, p 2; from Allen N: Physical Culture in Amherst College. Lowell MA, Stone and Huse, 1869, p 3

3. Raycroft JE: History and Development of Student Health Programs in Colleges and Universities, Proceedings of the 21st Annual Meeting, American Student Health Association, 1940, pp 39, 41

4. Flexner A: Medical Education in the United States and Canada, Bulletin no. 4. New York, Carnegie Foundation for the Advancement of Teaching, 1910

5. Brown RE: Rockefeller Medicine Men: Medicine and Capitalism in America. Berkeley, University of California Press, 1979

6. Boynton RE: Historical development of college health services. Student Med 10(3), 1962, p 298

7. Storey TE: The Status of Hygiene Programs in Institutions of Higher Education in the United States. Stanford, Stanford University Press, 1927

8. Boynton RE: The first fifty years: A history of the American College Health Association. J Am Coll Health Assoc 19:273, 1971

9. Farnsworth DL: Mental Health in the College and University. Cambridge, Harvard Press, 1957

10. Farnsworth DL, Prout C, Munter PK: Health in colleges and universities. N Engl J Med 267:1290-1295, 1962

11. Moore NS, Summerskill J: Health Services in American Colleges and Universities 1953: Findings of the American College Health Association Survey. Ithaca, NY, Cornell Univ Press, 1954

12. Fuchs V: Who Shall Live. New York, Basic Books, 1974

13. Brown RE, Valdez RB, Morgenstern H et al: Californians Without Health Insurance: A Report to the California Legislature. Berkeley, University of California/California Policy Seminar, 1987

14. McManus MS, Greaney AM, Newacheck PW: Health insurance status of young adults in the United States. Pediatrics 84(4):709-716

15. Patrick K: Student health: Medical care within institutions of higher education. JAMA 260(22): 3301-3305, 1988

16. Nicklin J: Citing high costs, Drexel will close its health center. The Chronicle of Higher Education, May 16, 1990, p 32

17. U.S. DHHS, Public Health Service: Healthy People 2000: National Health Promotion and Disease Prevention Objectives. Washington, DC, U.S. Government Printing Office, 1990

18. U.S. DHEW, Public Health Service: Healthy People, The Surgeon General's Report on Health Promotion and Disease Prevention, 1979

19. Boyer EL: College: The Undergraduate Experience in America. New York, Harper Row, 1987

20. The Carnegie Foundation for the Advancement of Teaching: Campus Life: In Search of Community. Princeton, NJ, The Carnegie Foundation, 1990

21. Patrick K, Grace TW, Lovato CY: Health Issues for College Students. Ann Rev Public Health, 13:253-68, 1992

22. DeArmond MM: Designing the future of college health. NASPA Journal 27(4):275-280, Summer, 1990

# 2

# A University President's Perspective on College Health

NILS HASSELMO, PhD WITH GEORGE M. ROBB

I have been given the opportunity to address, from the perspective of a University President, the value of personal and community health to an academic community and the students, staff, and faculty it serves. While the editors were too circumspect to add admonishments that I should offer more than the commonplace tributes to the importance of health and wellness – and more than a recitation of "how it's done at Minnesota"– I will impose those on myself.

Personal and community health is an imperative in any organization, large or small. Many American organizations, possibly even most, recognize this already. Certainly most now recognize the complexities inherent in delivering health services. Knowing what we want – and why – doesn't impart much insight into how to get it done. We are left with a bewildering array of alternatives – in-house direct services, health insurance, health maintenance organizations, and all manner of wellness and employee/constituent assistance programs – many of which seem exemplary and well-grounded in individual and institutional self-interest. Then we have to decide how to design, redesign, maintain, and, finally, pay for it.

Colleges and universities face virtually all the issues, represent virtually all the circumstances of need and delivery alternatives, and provide virtually all – and none – of the answers. Even considering our own situation in the five-campus University of Minnesota system illustrates the breadth of the challenges and the problems in meeting them. Within our system, we have the full range of models, from a comprehensive student health center serving one of America's largest campuses in a metropolitan community to one- or two-person health service offices serving two-year colleges in rural communities. Even respecting, as I surely do, the profession-alism of the University of Minnesota providers in dealing with their widely differing demands in widely differing models, I cannot hold up our programs as exemplars for other institutions to emulate. There are simply too many variations and too many unresolved problems to stake out any general truths for institutional health services in the 1990s, let alone a more extended future.

On our Twin Cities campus, the debates over individual and community responsibilities and individual and community self-interests have gone on for years. Like other major university campuses, we evolved an *in loco parentis* student health service over many years, providing both home-away-from-home health services for students and a "public health" protection for the campus community. We developed an on-campus alternative for faculty and staff members who preferred to use University colleagues rather than private practitioners in the metropolitan community. And, because of the special requirements of the University's international roles (long before most businesses began dealing in the global arenas), we developed the more specialized capabilities to serve students from abroad and University people traveling to areas of the world that require special preventive services – and sometimes treatment of exotic ailments.

But, the debates are still unresolved here. Many students arrive with full insurance coverage, and particularly in Minnesota, that coverage often involves full-service health maintenance organizations. Those students argue that such coverage meets both their personal needs and the legitimate public health needs of the institution. On the other hand, those family insurance policies and HMO memberships are also in a state of significant threat and change as part of the general health care delivery and insurance crisis. The University of Minnesota's circumstances are further complicated by the change in student demographics. Our students are older (60 percent are 22 or older) and increasingly part-time (now 37 percent). Some older students carry personal or group insurance or HMO coverage, yet many are uninsured or underinsured, and many have dependents.

In the past, required student service fees have supported a health service providing both individual care and meeting institutional public health needs. In recent years, we have explored, full circle, the issue of exemptions for those with other coverage, returning more recently to a "no exemption" fee in order to maintain the health service infrastructure needed to assure the community health standards. That many students have double coverage is indisputable; whether we can maintain the infrastructure while allowing exemptions – and evaluating which coverage warrants those exemptions – is equally clear. We cannot.

The issues are further complicated by health insurance and HMO coverage for faculty and staff members falling under a State Health Plan that now governs all state government employees. There, the intricacies may be particular to this state; then again, they may not. The fundamental issues are national, and it's not at all clear how those issues will sort out in state and local programs.

Finally, those special services that developed in colleges and universities to address their international roles are now far more broadly available in the private sector. More Americans are traveling abroad, requiring both preventive and diagnostic/therapeutic services from private practitioners, and in international business enterprises, those services are increasingly common fare in corporate health programs, either in-house or through provider contracts.

In all of these changing circumstances, the clear message is that no university's health service either solves all the issues or serves as a definitive model. We all face an uncertain future that is shaped by larger health care delivery issues well beyond our control as academic communities.

**As academic communities,** however, colleges and universities have not been, and must not be, uninvolved bystanders in the larger social arena of individual and institutional health care delivery.

Some academic communities are obviously and properly long-standing participants in that arena. They provide the teaching, research, and public service expertise that fuels the health care delivery systems – and that fuels the on-going debates over its strengths, shortcomings, and future. Depending on perspectives – and there are plenty to go around – our colleges and universities that have health sciences programs are clearly part of the solution, part of the problem, part of both.

So, too, I would submit, are all the other colleges and universities as academic communities, regardless of whether their programs include the health sciences. As academic communities, they are in the business of finding, testing, and imparting knowledge. That body of knowledge surely includes the topics of individual and community health, but the uncomfortable and uncompromising truth is that educational institutions have failed to impart the knowledge that they have.

At all educational levels, clearly including higher education, we talk about the educational aspects of the AIDS epidemic, of substance abuse, of sexual violence, of all the other health subjects that are, indeed, the other chapters of this book. We recognize, over and over again, that these are public problems that call for public education solutions. Then, by and large, we give them little attention in our own curricula, we create all manner of problem-solving programs to deal with our failures to educate in the first place, and we generally avoid the controversial policy decisions that logically follow the body of knowledge that is, after all, quite clear in its policy implications.

We know, for instance, that condoms and sterile hypodermic needles are important to halting the spread of AIDS. Yet, we're not comfortable even discussing the policy and service options this knowledge presents, lest we, as educational institutions be perceived as condoning high-risk behaviors.

We know that tobacco use is destructive, addictive, and expensive. Yet, we continue to subsidize the industry, we publish warnings that pass for public education, and we are barely beginning to require smoke-free environments. Even in hospitals, surely the most obvious facilities with a *prima facie* case for banning smoking, such bans are only very recent and by no means generally accepted. For academic communities at any level, the body of available knowledge calls simply and clearly for more effective education, campus-wide smoke-free environments, and very tenacious programs to help students and employees break the habit.

The same applies to alcohol and other chemical abuse, where we have clear evidence that educational efforts have generally failed, only modestly successful treatment programs, and, generally, institutional policies that side-step what we know about the fundamental health issues by tacitly accepting some alcohol use, as long as it falls below some level that we can define as abuse.

Taking this a step further, the whole area of nutrition is another example of failing to take seriously what we really know. I will grant that general nutrition is a subject of much debate and many unknowns, but I cannot accept the notion that we know so little that we dare not modify our institutional food services to provide healthier fare. We know far more than we are willing to put into practice, and we are generally willing to accept the "customer's" preferences as guidance, especially when we have to live with the marketplace realities of self-supporting services.

A local newspaper columnist recently referred to Minnesota as "The State Where Absolutely Nothing is Allowed," and I recognize quite self-consciously that my foregoing comments must certainly strengthen just that perception. That's a risk I have to take. The weight of the health evidence is simply preponderant, even in the face of the social behavior evidence that argues so strongly that an institution like a university must somehow accept an imperfect world that limits the steps one can feasibly take toward fundamentally rational behavior. Like it or not, enough of the facts are in to challenge individuals and communities, especially academic communities, to practice what they preach – and to do a better job of both.

The fact of the matter is that my own university – and my own administration of the institution – has not been any more aggressive or effective in dealing with these issues than most, possibly any, of America's colleges and universities. I have suggested or implied program and policy steps that my own institution has not been willing or able to take – at least not yet.

The fact that we haven't found the answers doesn't make the questions – or the facts behind them – go away. They remain until we address them, either with full solutions or, much more likely, with stated goals against which we can measure partial, step-by-step action.

In 1990, in cooperation with the American Council on Education, The Carnegie Foundation for the Advancement of Teaching published Campus Life: In Search of Community. In an effort to address academic community values and standards of behavior, this report proposes six principles and urges their adoption in *campus compacts* to be used as the basis for day-to-day decision-making on campus. The principles deal with a college or university being:

> ...an educationally purposeful community, a place where faculty and students share academic goals and work together to strengthen teaching and learning on the campus.
>
> ...an open community, a place where freedom of expression is uncompromisingly protected and where civility is powerfully affirmed.
>
> ...a just community, a place where the sacredness of the person is honored and where diversity is aggressively pursued.
>
> ...a disciplined community, a place where individuals accept their obligations to the group and where well-defined governance procedures guide behavior for the common good.
>
> ...a caring community, a place where the well-being of each member is sensitively supported and where service to others is encouraged.
>
> ...and a celebrative community, one in which the heritage of the institution is remembered and where rituals affirming both tradition and change are widely shared.[1]

These are compelling principles. They are certainly not the final answers to the circumstances that inspired the study and report, but they do provide what we can hope will be a common framework for the kind of "community building" that seems generally warranted in American higher education. Perhaps these are general enough to encompass the issues of individual and community health, but I believe there is a case for adding a seventh principle:

> A college or university is a healthy community, one in which personal and public health is an accepted institutional commitment, backed by policies and programs that apply the knowledge we have acquired.

We have, I submit, the knowledgeable faculty, staff, and students who can write the goals that reflect the facts, however uncomfortable and challenging those facts may be to our personal and institutional behavior. Then the responsibilities fall to those who manage and govern to develop and begin implementing the practical steps toward using what we know. Without question, those steps will fall somewhat short of the ideal. Our institutions are too complex, too preoccupied with other priorities, and in the final analysis, too human to reach the rational ideal. On the other hand, individual and community health is too important to ignore.

## REFERENCE

1. The Carnegie Foundation for the Advancement of Teaching: Campus Life: In Search of Community. Princeton, NJ, The Carnegie Foundation, 1990

# 3

# Medical Services for College Health

WILLIAM A. CHRISTMAS, MD, FACP

## RATIONALE AND GOALS

Medical services provided by college and university health centers are the foundation upon which a comprehensive student health program is built. The lay public has an oversimplified concept of a health center and thinks of it only as a place to go to have an illness diagnosed and treated by a physician. There is not a good understanding of the sophistication and complexity of the modern university health center. In general, the larger the enrollment at an institution of higher education, the better potential there is to establish a comprehensive health center.

Depending upon a traditional, local, medical practice, or a hospital emergency department as the sole provider of health services to college students is generally unsatisfactory. For traditional-aged students, going to college is usually their first sustained attempt at independent living away from the family unit. They are unprepared to handle the complexities of our health care system and require much guidance and compassionate understanding. Many of their visits are for so-called trivial problems, which may be seen as a nuisance to busy practitioners, but are apt to be appreciated by college health professionals as an opportunity for a meaningful interaction and for some pertinent health education. Knowledge of the developmental goals of college students is also an important factor in caring for this population.[1] The campus environment, and specifically the student affairs division, acts as a powerful nurturer in the achievement of these developmental goals. Because of this the student affairs area is the natural organizational home for the health center.

The basic goal of the medical service area is to provide students easy access to health care services. The services available often depend on the size of the institution. For example, at a small college, access may be provided by a registered nurse who can make assessments, give advice, and triage selected patients to the appropriate providers in the community. At a medium-sized institution both the initial evaluation and the referral may take place internally, depending on the range of services provided. Large institutions often have a wide spectrum of in-house medical services, and several of them have evolved into self-contained health maintenance organizations (HMOs). Accessibility to care can be enhanced by provision of 24-hour, on-site services or an on-call system via answering service and beeper. Acceptability, and therefore utilization, by student-patients will be improved by the professionalism of the staff and by conducting medical services in modern facilities. A survey of patient satisfaction with health care services at Kent State University[2] found that the most satisfying factors were perceived technical competence of the practitioner, perceived adequacy of the interpersonal aspects of the practitioner-patient relationship, adequate health education related to the problem for which care was sought, and short waiting time.

Another goal of the medical service area is to provide as comprehensive a scope of services as resources permit at a reasonable cost to the student. With large increases in medical care costs over the past decade, this goal has become increasingly important to students already hard pressed by the escalating costs of a college education. Making available low-cost group health insurance to cover medical services not available at the health center is also a part of this goal.

The importance of preserving confidentiality of medical information both within and without the institution cannot be overemphasized. This includes not only medical records, but the results of laboratory tests, telephone communications, and conversations among staff. Every health center should have a written policy on confidentiality of medical information, and all staff should review it annually.

To summarize, a well organized and adequately funded college health center should strive to meet the following goals through its medical services activities:

1. accessible medical services;
2. reasonable cost to the student for these services;
3. emphasis on preventive and health education services, especially within the context of the provider-patient relationship;
4. integration with (other) student affairs departments, i.e., residential life, counseling center, and international educational services; and
5. confidentiality of medical information preserved.

## TYPES OF SERVICES OFFERED

Over the past three decades the national trend in health care has been for greater specialization. This trend has been reflected in the college health field by the increased variety of medical services provided. Many of these services are offered in health centers at smaller institutions by integrating them into their primary care activities. As the number of visits for medical services increases at larger schools, it becomes possible to establish specific medical services by "clinic." The following discussion recognizes the more common examples of these services and is not meant to identify all the components of a comprehensive health service.

## PRIMARY/EMERGENCY/URGENT CARE

These services merge imperceptibly into one another and for practical purposes constitute the activities of the primary care area of the health center. Tables 1 and 2 (next page) list the most common diagnoses seen and health maintenance procedures performed in the clinical areas of the University of Vermont Student Health Center; they are probably representative of all health centers regardless of size.

Primary care services are the backbone of the health center and should be supervised by a physician. Nurse practitioners and physician's assistants can play an important role. At present the registered nurse is limited in this setting by the scope of nursing practice, but can make important contributions in such areas as nursing assessment and triage. The use of nursing diagnosis in a nurse-managed college health center was studied reviewing 100 randomly selected patient records; it was

---

Table 1

**Rank Order of Most Common Medical Conditions
Seen at the University of Vermont Student Health Center**

July 1, 1988 - June 30, 1989

1. Upper Respiratory Infections, including pharyngitis, bronchitis and sinusitis
2. Viral Syndrome
3. Urinary Tract Infection
4. Conjunctivitis
5. Vaginitis
6. Otitis media
7. Genital Warts (HPV)
8. Dermatitis/Rash
9. Common Warts
10. Ankle sprain
11. Chlamydia suspect
12. Abdominal pain
13. Molluscum contagiosum
14. Gastroenteritis
15. Abscess/boil
16. Skin laceration
17. Low Back Syndrome
19. Fatigue
20. Infectious Mononucleosis

found that 66 percent of patients were treated by nursing interventions alone.[3] The efficiency of all health professionals in the primary care area can be improved by utilizing non-professional support staff or medical office assistants, who with appropriate training can act as receptionists, medical records clerks, appointment secretaries, and clinical assistants. Many health centers also provide limited medical services to faculty and staff (occupational health). Provision of emergency and urgent care services suggests 24-hour operation or an alternative site, e.g., hospital emergency room, nearby for use when the health center is closed. College students tend to overuse emergency medical services for reasons of convenience and lack of knowledge about economical and appropriate use of the health care system. This behavior was recently studied and strategies developed to encourage more appropriate use of emergency services.[4] Many health centers sponsor student-run ambulance services to improve access and response to students with serious health problems. A student-run ambulance service was developed at the University of Delaware ten years ago.[5] A similar emergency medical service utilizes student Emergency Medical Technicians (EMTs) at Brandeis University.[6] Many centers require annual CPR recertification for all professional staff as on-going preparation for clinical emergencies.

---

### Table 2

**Rank Order of Most Common Health Maintenance Procedures Performed at the University of Vermont Student Health Center**

July 1, 1988 - June 30, 1989

1. Allergy shot
2. Oral contraceptive prescription
3. Health assessment for athletics, study abroad, etc.
4. Annual Gyn exam including Pap smear
5. Immunization
6. Suture removal
7. Administrative visit for medical withdrawal from courses, remedial physical education, re-enrollment after absence
8. Initiation of contraceptive measures, not oral contraceptive
9. Abnormal Pap smear
10. Pregnancy examination or test

## SPECIALTY CARE INCLUDING ATHLETIC MEDICINE

Depending on the local situation, it may be possible to contract with local specialists, often at a financial advantage to the student-patient, for such services as orthopedics, dermatology, gynecology, and allergy. Services may be rendered on- or off-site, but convenience to the student is better served on-site if equipment and space permit. In large health centers, specialists may actually be full-time staff members. The medical specialty referrals from the Duke University Student Health Service were studied in 1981: Specialties receiving the most frequent referrals were orthopedics (31%), ophthalmology (16%), general surgery (10%), and gynecology (10%).[7] It was concluded that in this clinic, referrals occurred somewhat infrequently and therefore did not justify provision of in-house specialty consultation at their institution.

Care of athletes may be supervised by a physician trained in primary care who has a special interest in athletic medicine, an orthopedic consultant, or it may be shared. Non-physician professionals can also make important contributions in this area. The author believes that the best interests of the athlete are served if medical care of the athlete is the responsibility of the health center. The professional staff at the Student Health Center is often called upon to furnish medical care at campus events such as concerts and athletic contests. A model has been proposed for providing medical care in large stadiums based on the findings that 85 percent or greater of cardiac arrests were successfully resuscitated even though true medical emergencies are very uncommon at these events.[8]

## SPECIAL CLINICS

Many health centers establish gynecology or family planning clinics that may be in space distinct from the primary care area. This permits a better sense of privacy and allows for a less hectic atmosphere. Nurse practitioners and physician's assistants function very well in this area and often need minimal physician supervision, since the problems encountered are generally well defined in number and complexity. Similar clinics have been established for men to deal with sexually transmitted diseases and sexuality issues. A number of special areas are particularly suited for staffing by registered nurses. For example, allergy shot and immunization clinics, screening and health advice, travel clinics, and special sessions to orient international students are all important areas where registered nurses can contribute.

## INFIRMARY CARE

Because of the high cost of overnight bedcare, a number of institutions have phased out their infirmaries in recent years. Low utilization, high cost of staffing, increased premiums for liability insurance, and lack of reimbursement by insurance companies for these services have all contributed to this trend. At the University of Vermont the decision was made to close the infirmary in 1981 and dedicate the resources to establishing a health promotion program.

Nevertheless, many institutions have retained an infirmary for reasons of location, convenience, and scope of services. Staffing requires 24-hour nursing staff, 24 hour availability of a physician, and appropriate support staff, e.g., housekeeping and food service.

## SUPPORT SERVICES

### LABORATORY

Ready access to a clinical laboratory is essential to a modern medical practice. Ideally the laboratory should be on-site and staffed by a licensed medical technologist. Recent directives from the federal health regulators suggest that regulation of outpatient laboratories may become a reality in the near future. The scope of procedures offered should be determined by demand and feasibility; those procedures not offered can be sent out to commercial laboratories.

### RADIOLOGY

These services usually require a certified radiology technician, and a major investment in equipment and facilities including lead shielding, a storage area for films, and availability of a radiologist for official interpretation. Compliance with state radiation standards is also required. Most health centers are limited to the provision of basic procedures and must refer outside the health center for contrast studies, ultrasound, scans, and other complex procedures.

### PHYSICAL THERAPY

With the increase in recreational and intercollegiate sports participation in the past decade, the demand for rehabilitative therapy on campus has intensified. For continuity of care the author prefers licensed physical therapists who are also certified athletic trainers to staff the Sports Therapy department at the University of Vermont. In this way the student athlete can be evaluated on the field and also rehabilitated in the sports therapy facility by the same staff member. The team athletic trainer function insures excellent communication with the coaching staff. The author advocates that all such services should be provided by the health center and not duplicated by the athletic department.

## Pharmacy

Provision of prescription medications by the health center enhances both convenience and medication compliance for the student-patient. It was found in a 1985 survey of ACHA member institutions that 34 percent had an in-house pharmacy with a pharmacist in control.[9] In general the larger the institution, the more likely it was to have an in-house pharmacy. Although drug dispensing can be done by a physician, it is to everyone's advantage to have this done by a licensed pharmacist with the help of as many pharmacy assistants as necessary. Medical staff should agree on a limited formulary to keep inventory and costs down.

## Medical Records

The importance of this area is often overlooked in the delivery of medical services. Medical records require careful organization and frequent review to select out inactive charts, a common situation in a health center where there is high patient turnover. A medical records librarian can best organize and oversee the support staff who work in this area. If this is not possible, then a consultant should be engaged to make periodic reviews of policies and procedures.

A decision will have to be made on the format of the clinic record. Hopefully this will be an informed decision made democratically among the professional staff who use the records. The author prefers the problem-oriented medical record as advocated by Weed.[10] Many health centers have adopted this system in the past 25 years for reasons of clarity and ease of review and performing quality assurance functions.

This discussion of services has assumed that the professional staff performing the services described are properly credentialed according to the regulations of the state in which they occur. Also, certification of some service area (e.g., clinical laboratory, radiology, and infirmary) may be required.

# Dental Services

Factors to be considered in developing a dental program within a student health center have been described: Emergency and preventive care should be the foundation of the dental service, with provision of prepaid preventive care resulting in higher student participation and acceptance.[11] Priorities for other traditional services like restorative and endodontic procedures must be established and offered as time and resources permit. Staffing should include dentists, hygienists, assistants, aids, and secretaries. (See also this volume, Chapter 17, for further discussion of dental services in student health.)

## ORGANIZATION OF MEDICAL SERVICES

Primary care is the hub of student health center medical activities. Distinct medical service components can be readily identified in larger health centers, and these form the spokes of the Wheel of Medical Services (Figure 1).

The most basic configuration of a primary care clinic consists of a room, desk and two chairs, telephone, examination table, file cabinet, instrument and supply table, and basic equipment like a sphygmomanometer, oto-ophthalmoscope, stethoscope, and thermometer. Such an arrangement could accommodate only one health care professional and one patient and would have no waiting area for other patients.

A basic ambulatory clinic consists of a waiting room, reception and medical records area, exam rooms, offices for clinical and administrative staff, restrooms, basic laboratory

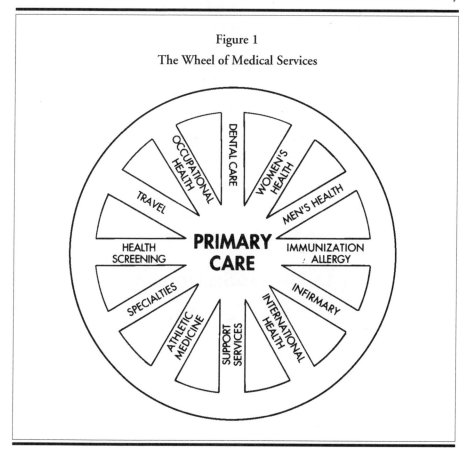

Figure 1

The Wheel of Medical Services

area, utility room, storage area, and staff lounge. Some medical service components require dedicated space, e.g., infirmary and women's health, while others can take place in common space, e.g., primary care and occupational health.

A ratio of 2:1 between support staff and care providers is ideal and usually results in maximum efficiency for the health care professionals. However, most student health centers have a ratio closer to 1:1. This often results in professional staff performing many of the functions of support staff and is inefficient. Also, care providers should have two exam rooms to use when seeing patients. This permits preparation of the next patient by an assistant while the provider is busy with the first patient, thus increasing productivity. Examination rooms should be no smaller than 8 feet by 10 feet. For basic guidelines on how to design and construct medical facilities, consult the guide produced by the American Medical Association.[12]

Traditional primary care practices strive to achieve three or more patients per provider hour. Because of the nature of college health practice described at the beginning of this chapter, a more realistic goal in college health is probably 2.5 patients per hour in the primary care area and closer to 2.0 in the gynecology area. Provider productivity is a complex issue and is very dependent on the physical layout of the clinic and the availability of well-trained support staff.

Campus ambulatory care clinics demonstrate the whole spectrum between walk-in and appointment systems. The author favors a full-appointment system because it dramatically decreases patient waiting time and is "more professional" – that is, it emulates traditional practice settings. Such a system requires that provision be made for emergencies and urgent problems by such mechanisms as an urgent care team with a same-day appointment schedule, nurse triage of patients to blocks of provider time held open for urgent problems, or in very large centers an emergency department. A full-appointment system increases the administrative duties of the nursing and appointment desk staff. Because of an inadequate level of support staffing, many health centers cannot implement an appointment system; and if they do, it is often limited in scope. One approach to the development of an appointment system at a college health center that had offered previously only walk-in care is described in reference no. 13.

In larger health centers the medical services area should have a medical director, who is usually a physician, as well as a person responsible for the daily operation of the clinical area, e.g., clinic coordinator or nursing coordinator. The medical director usually reports directly to the director of the health center, if these positions are separate. Special areas such as women's health, athletic medicine, and dental care may have an individual designated as coordinator of that activity. Each health center seems to evolve an organizational structure that best suits its needs; the possibilities are almost endless.

As the staff size increases, the need for better communication, ownership, and problem solving among staff members increases. Also, the more potential there is for community interaction about health related issues. Finally, increasing size means a larger health center budget, which requires community support and justification. The best way to realize these disparate goals is through committees and task forces in which membership may be comprised exclusively of health center staff, other campus constituencies, or a combination of these. Occasionally, individuals from outside the college community may be invited to join. It is important that any committee or task force have clearly defined goals and objectives, and that it be appointed by the appropriate person on campus (e.g., health center director, Vice President of Student Affairs, or President) to assure the broadest institutional support and maximum visibility. The following are examples of committees and task forces at the University of Vermont in recent years:

### In-House:

**Standing Committees:** Executive Committee, Medical Clinic Operations Committee, Computer Committee, Quality Assurance Committee, Continuing Medical Education Committee, Medical Records Committee.

**Ad-Hoc Committees:** Wellness Program Advisory Committee, Task Force on Satellite Clinic, Task Force on Pharmacy.

### Campus Committees:

**Task Forces:** on AIDS; on Sexual Violence; on Student Trainer Program; on Student Health Insurance.

**Advisory Committees:** to Alcohol and Drug Education Program; Student Health Advisory Committee.

To establish a high-quality college health center requires meeting defined standards of excellence. The American College Health Association (ACHA) has developed standards for college health centers based on AAAHC and JCAHO standards. Persuasive arguments have been made in favor of health centers seeking accreditation.[14]

Since college students never seem to have enough time, a major effort should be made to offer high-quality medical services in an efficient and professional manner while preserving a supportive and educative approach to the patient.[15] This is one of the major challenges to be met in the field of college health.

The medical services area can make important contributions to the overall mission of the health center. The basic philosophy of the medical services area should extend beyond attending to sickness; it should address campus wellness and make a sincere commitment to health promotion activities. The full integration of these concepts has been addressed recently.[16]

## CONCLUSIONS

It is not possible to describe the intricate details of a medical services area of a college health center in depth here. There are a myriad of topics such as immunization programs and policies, medical excuses, withdrawal from courses for medical reasons, quality assurance programs, peer review activities, and supervision of non-MD providers, which are beyond the scope of this discussion.

The author believes that the greatest resource for obtaining knowledge about college health is from other health centers. Planned visits to institutions of similar size and philosophy will often be most rewarding. Also, meeting health professionals from other institutions and disciplines at national and regional college health meetings is another effective method of information diffusion. And finally, a number of national associations, such as the American College Health Association, National Athletic Trainers Association, American Nurses Association, and the American Medical Association are important resources for obtaining specific information.

## REFERENCES

1. Margolis G: Developmental Opportunities, College Psychotherapy. Edited by PA Grayson, K Cauley. New York, The Guilford Press, 1989, pp 71-91

2. Gillette JL, Byrne TJ, Cranston JW: Variables affecting patient satisfaction with health care services in the college health setting. J Am Coll Health 30:167, 1982

3. Bugle LB, Frisch N, Woods T: The use of nursing diagnosis in a nurse-managed college health service. J Am Coll Health 38:191, 1990

4. McKillip J, Courtney CL, Locasso R et al: College students' use of emergency medical services. J Am Coll Health 38:289, 1990

5. Body RB: The development of a student-run ambulance. J Am Coll Health 31:164, 1983

6. Meisel JL: Student-run voluntary emergency medical services: A case study at Brandeis University. J Am Coll Health 35:227, 1987

7. Hansen JP, Brown SE, Sullivan RJ Jr et al: Medical specialty referrals from a student health service. J Am Coll Health 31:200, 1983

8. Spaite DW, Criss EA, Valenzuela TD et al: A new model for providing pre-hospital medical care in large stadiums. Ann Emerg Med 17:825, 1988

9. Hak SH, Reid G: National survey of student health pharmaceutical services, 1985. J Am Coll Health 37:65, 1988

10. Weed LL: Medical records that guide and teach. New Eng J Med 278:593-652, 1968

11. Lubin H: A dental program in the health service. J Am Coll Health 26:154, 1977

12. American Medical Association: Planning guide for physician's medical facilities. AMA, 535 N Dearborn, Chicago IL, 60610

13. Marshburn DM, Elesha-Adams M: From a 24-hour facility to time-limited ambulatory care. J Am Coll Health 38:293, 1990

14. Averill B: Accreditation of college and university health programs - Why have it and who should do it? J Am Coll Health 30:221, 1982

15. Christmas WA: College health service and the fast-food value system. J Am Coll Health 39:51, 1990

16. DeArmond MM: The future of college health. NASPA J 27:275, 1990

## RECOMMENDED READING

American College Health Association Publications
P.O. Box 28937
Baltimore, MD 21240
Telephone: 410/859-1500

1. Recommendations for an institutional pre-matriculation immunization requirement
2. Optimizing health care for foreign students in the United States
3. Student Health Committee Handbook

Hurst JW, Walker HK (ed): The Problem-Oriented System. New York, MedCom, 1972

# 4

# Mental Health Services for College Health

## Leighton C. Whitaker, PhD

Several recent developments underscore the need for campus mental health services. First, the practice of *in loco parentis* began fading in the 1960s and is seldom practiced now, so students no longer have the institutionally imposed strict guidelines and security precautions of earlier eras. Second, Section 504 of the 1973 National Rehabilitation Act, which prohibits discrimination against the handicapped, allows mentally handicapped or disturbed persons easier enrollment and more protection against dismissal.[1] Third, the mental hospital deinstitutionalization movement has had a major impact on college enrollment beginning in the 1970s. Fourth, there have been sharp increases in certain forms of mental disturbances in youth since the 1950s, notably suicide,[2,3] acts of violence toward others, eating disorders,[4] and alcohol and other drug use.[5,6] Fifth, the stigma against using mental health services has lessened. No college or university can be wholly free of the enormous impact of these sweeping societal changes.

Students are often outspoken in their demands for professional help with both mental disturbances and developmental challenges. They may pressure administrators to provide mental health professionals who are not only knowledgeable about college student issues but also practice on the campus; this makes them both highly accessible to the students and familiar with the particular college or university.

Administrators and faculty tend to have different (although overlapping) concerns compared to students. As every dean knows, student behaviors often raise issues about the safety and well-being of both individuals and portions or even all of the campus community. Most modern deans probably could not see themselves carrying out their own disciplinary and guidance functions without being able to call readily upon mental health professionals for referral or consultation.

Campus mental health service goals reflect attempts at comprehensiveness within resource limitations. At small colleges the mental health services offered on campus rarely include inpatient facilities, whereas large universities with medical schools have available to them emergency room and other crisis services as well as hospital treatment. On the other hand, the small college may have more generous provisions for outpatient and outreach services, which probably helps to lessen demand for hospital-based services. All campus mental health services should provide directly, or have ready geographic and logistical access to, a full spectrum of mental health services. Failure to design and implement adequate mental health services will result not only in frustration for students and administrators but may also result in otherwise avoidable tragedies, such as preventable suicides and psychotic breakdowns.

While the goal of comprehensiveness means an extensive range of services that are readily available, it seldom includes much emphasis on long-term services. For example, a small college may have mandatory student insurance that will cover the first three or four days of a hospitalization, time enough to make further management decisions, but not time enough to provide complete treatment. Similarly, outpatient counseling and psychotherapy may be readily available to all students but not be prepaid or "free" at many institutions except for the first ten or fifteen sessions.

There are many situations that may call for more prolonged service, which may be met in part by referral to private practitioners. Many students will resist referral for reasons of distance from campus, transportation time and expense, inability to pay private fees, reluctance to inform parents who are needed for insurance or other financial coverage, and resistance to seeing therapists in unfamiliar places. In some cases, a student's great need and motivation and/or lack of financial resources may persuade therapists to provide relatively long-term treatment[7] though institutions of higher education have little interest in providing psychotherapy per se.[8] Communicating the value of psychotherapy to college students[9,10] is an important approach to obtaining funding for campus mental health programs.

When starting a new mental health service or attempting to operate one within a very limited budget, it may be necessary to think primarily in terms of brief consultation and referral to off-campus resources. At the very least, one should plan to have an astute clinician do the interviewing since sizing up the student's needs in only one session can be a difficult challenge and the success of an outside referral will depend greatly upon the rapport and follow-through engendered by the clinician. Furthermore, since referral can be such a difficult art, the clinician may need more than one session to do the job even if referral is planned. The clinician should have available, at least for consultation, a psychiatrist who has access to a local hospital and crisis service as well as expert knowledge of psychopharmacology. While it is almost always inadvisable to prescribe psychiatric drugs for someone after a single visit, some students will have need to renew medications that they are already receiving.

Where a more adequate but nonetheless limited budget is available, the mental health service should include, at the least, clinicians capable of short-term counseling and psychotherapy. These staff should also make themselves available for consultation to health personnel and other college staff to assist with the evaluation of crisis situations. Such staff can come from the ranks of clinical psychologists and clinical social workers as well as psychiatrists. Except for the specific psychiatric functions noted above, the most important selection criteria should be the skill of the professionals to develop rapport with college students and to carry out effective psychotherapy.

The expected outcomes of mental health services vary with the types of problems encountered, the student's motivation, and available resources. In the final analysis mental health services should be capable of helping students through the college or university and should provide a favorable and enlightening learning experience with the mental health system. They should also be able to discern which students should be advised to take time out from college to prepare themselves better emotionally for what may be for them a very difficult developmental challenge.

## TYPES OF SERVICES AND PATTERNS OF USE

The full range of campus mental health services includes emergency on-call accessibility and service, hospitalization, individual and group counseling and psychotherapy, consultation, and "outreach" programs designed to promote awareness of the other services and of important mental health issues. Colleges lacking some of the necessary staff or personnel on campus can form contractual relationships that ensure accessibility to off-campus facilities for emergency service and hospitalization.

By far the largest component of service is outpatient counseling and psychotherapy. In any year, a typical college mental health service can expect that from 5 to 25 percent of the student population will use mental health services for such counseling. At most institutions the average number of sessions per user per academic year ranges from four to twelve. Substantial college-to-college variation in utilization of mental health services occurs. This is due to a number of factors including the level of student sophistication or experience with mental health care, the accessibility and quality of services, and the presence of mental health care in the surrounding community. Utilization tends to be higher at small, selective colleges, some of which have utilization rates of 15 percent of the student population per year. Swarthmore College yearly rates are between 13 and 20 percent and, by the time they graduate, approximately one-third of the student body will have used Psychological Services.

Graduate students use mental health services more than undergraduates and female students tend to use counseling and psychotherapy at twice the male utilization rate. Males tend to develop more serious emotional problems overall, particularly in terms of suicide risk and drug use, including alcohol, although females are much more likely to have eating disorders. The "macho" orientation may explain the overall male pattern of lower usage rates in combination with a greater tendency to severe emotional breakdown.[11] Males tend to have equal or greater rates of hospitalization, while schizophrenic breakdowns are more likely to occur in college men than their female counterparts, and suicide occurs twice as often in college men than it does in college women.[12]

Most mental health services have outreach programs consisting of education and consultation that address both individuals and groups. Group counseling can occur for students with alcohol and other drug problems, for adult children of alcoholics, post sexual assault students, and students in need of assertiveness or social skills training. While these group formats can serve important needs, small colleges often find them difficult to maintain because of the special confidentiality problems of the small campus.

Large universities often have a counseling facility in addition to a mental health service, the former usually staffed by counseling and/or clinical psychologists, the latter by psychiatrists, psychologists and clinical social workers. Many counseling centers also offer academic assistance, career and vocational testing and advising, and provide links to potential employers. Thus counseling may have a very generic meaning and be more developmentally focused than mental health services, which often relate more to a medical model and to medical facilities. Students may choose between the two types of service centers or may be referred from one to the other. In recent years there has been a trend toward consolidating counseling and mental health centers, due often to the desire to reduce costs.

## CONFIDENTIALITY AND
## RELATIONSHIPS WITH MEDICAL CARE

While no campus mental health service can succeed without guaranteeing and maintaining a high level of confidentiality, there are situations in which it is crucial to share information in order to prevent harm and to ensure good care.

Threat-to-life situations pose the need to share information with those in a position to minimize the threat. Potential suicides, homicides, and psychotic breakdowns all require some sharing for both clinical and legal reasons. So-called "failure to warn" a potential victim of homicide resulted in the 1976 precedent-setting case of Tarasoff vs Regents of the University of California[13] in which the court declared that mental health professionals have a duty to warn. For suicide threats, although the need to warn – much less the duty – is not always clear, state laws generally permit involuntary hospitalization on the basis of such threat when it can be shown to be imminent.

A mental health service occupies an especially sensitive position among health services. The need for high standards of confidentiality is nowhere more evident than in the provision of counseling and psychotherapy. Students will not readily use a service to meet very personal emotional needs if it fails either to be quite confidential or if it even **appears** to lack strict confidentiality safeguards. Slippage in confidentiality can result in ruined reputations and even legal suits.

Information about student drug use, both prescribed and illicit, should be shared within a campus health service lest there be "cross-medication" and polypharmacy as well as stockpiling. Otherwise, students may deliberately or unwittingly mix drugs that should not be taken in combination as well as accumulate drugs to use in suicide attempts. One precautionary system requires any prescriber to note for both mental health and medical records all prescribed drugs complete with dates, dosages and supplies. One may argue, when such information comes from the mental health service, that the system violates the usual extremely tight protection of confidentiality that characterizes a good mental health service. This confidentiality issue is but one of many emblematic of the inherent dilemma of trying to provide both optimum health care and maximum mental health confidentiality.

The confidentiality-care dilemma is never wholly resolved[14] but it can be accommodated providing there is good will between students and caregivers who can be trusted to practice respect and to make carefully considered judgments of the "need to know" in any given case. Often the dilemma can be handled well by consulting the student in particular situations and explaining the need to share information. Medical and mental health caregivers should take into account student wishes as well as clinical considerations.

Certain student populations are especially important to reach in order to prevent tragedies such as suicide, homicide, psychotic breakdowns, and "accidental" deaths through dangerous forms of behavior such as alcohol and other drug overdoses. However, as every referring dean, residence hall advisor, physician or nurse soon learns, referral for mental health care itself needs to be developed into a fine art[15] since the students who are most in need are often the most resistant to accepting help. On the other hand, many students, seeking to enhance their personal growth and knowing of the positive experiences of others with psychotherapy, are highly motivated to learn about themselves and their interpersonal relationships. Thus, it is common to see an admixture of students using mental health services, representing both the most disturbed and some of the "strongest" and most insightful students.

## FINAL CONSIDERATIONS

College psychotherapists find themselves well utilized overall but never to the complete satisfaction of college administrators who may wish them to help solve campus disciplinary problems. While mental health staff may have to share information, albeit in strictly limited ways, with other college personnel, confidentiality dilemmas that are difficult even within a college or university health center are more difficult outside of the health center. Deans and campus security personnel, faculty, residence hall advisors (RAs), and, more rarely, other students may need to be apprised of certain dangerous or harmful situations. Security may be called upon most readily when there are blatant and apparently imminent threats to life and/or when a student is having a psychotic breakdown and it is decided to hospitalize the student involuntarily. Alternatively, security might be asked simply to help monitor a situation, for example, to be in the area of a threatening confrontation.

Confidentiality is less problematic when deans, security staff, or any member of the campus community are just informing the mental health service of their concerns and asking for interventions. In these cases, mental health staff may elect to receive the information without breaking the strictest confidentiality restrictions adopted by the mental health service: the "we-can-always-listen" policy. Nevertheless, there may be complaints even when this policy appears appropriate to the mental health service. For example, an RA who refers a suicidal student may want to be reassured by the therapist that the referred student is making and keeping appointments. In reply, the therapist can advise the RA to ask the student who will probably answer the question straightforwardly and feel more secure about confidentiality.

Psychotherapists profess, correctly in most instances, that they can help to change only those patients who want to change. Frequently, everyone, with the exception of the student, wants that student to change. Successful counseling is a painstaking fine art in itself and, although therapists cannot solve all the behavior problems referred to them, in most instances college mental health centers can produce gratifying results for all concerned.

## REFERENCES

1. Pavela G: The Dismissal of Students with Mental Disorders: Legal Issues; Policy Considerations; and Alternative Responses. Asheville, NC, College Administration Publications, Inc, 1985

2. Whitaker LC: Suicide and other crises, College Psychotherapy. Edited by P Grayson, K Cauley. New York, 1989, pp 48-70

3. Whitaker LC, Slimak RE (eds): Special issue on college student suicide. J College Student Psychotherapy 4: 3/4, 1990

4. Whitaker LC, Davis WN (eds): The bulimic college student: Evaluation, treatment and prevention. J College Student Psychotherapy (Spec Iss) 3: 2/3/4, 1988/1989

5. Burns WD, Sloane DC (guest eds): Students, alcohol, and college health: A special issue. J Am Coll Health 36:2, 1987

6. Rivinus TM (guest ed): Alcoholism, chemical dependency and the college student. J College Student Psychotherapy 2:3/4, 1988

7. Webb R, Widseth J: Students we don't refer: "Holding" the unheld. J College Student Psychotherapy 5:2, 1991

8. May R: Definitions of psychotherapy in an academic setting, or: Life in the fun house. J College Student Psychotherapy 5:2, 1991

9. Whitaker LC: Communicating the value of psychotherapy with college students. J Am Coll Health 33, 159-162, 1985

10. Whitaker LC: What parents need to know about counseling and psychotherapy. J College Student Psychotherapy 2, 1/2, 187-204, 1988

11. Whitaker LC: Macho and morbidity. J College Student Psychotherapy 1:4, 1987

12. Schwartz AJ, Whitaker LC: Suicide among college students: Assessment, treatment, and intervention, Suicide Over the Life Cycle. Edited by SJ Blumenthal, DJ Kupfer. Washington, DC, American Psychiatric Press, 1990, pp 303-340

13. Tarasoff vs Regents of the University of California, 551 P. 2nd 334 (Cal., 1976)

14. Whitaker LC (ed): Voices and boundaries in college mental health. J College Student Psychotherapy, 1:2, 1986

15. Boswinkel JP: The college resident assistant (RA) and the fine art of referral for psychotherapy. J College Student Psychotherapy 1:1, 1986

# 5

# Health Education and Health Promotion on Campus

BEVERLIE CONANT SLOANE, MPH, PhD, CHRISTINE HEUSTIS ZIMMER, MA

Health education and health promotion are interactive disciplines that stem from a need to assist both individuals and society with the prevention of disease and functional impairment and with the promotion of quality of life. This need gained intensity through the large-scale epidemiologic studies of the early 1970s establishing smoking as the primary source of most lung cancers, and certain risk factors such as elevated cholesterol, smoking, and hypertension as associated with the development of coronary heart disease. The shift of emphasis to life-style causes of premature death and disability has occurred. Finally, the need for assisting individuals and communities with the development of healthful living skills and environments has been established as a primary national goal.

Healthy living strategies are extremely significant to the youth of our nation, whose health potential is greatest when influenced prior to the onset of risk behaviors and chronic disease and whose abilities to make healthful decisions may help reduce unnecessary injury. Healthful choices at an early age can lead to a life free of chronic disabling diseases and conditions, and can help young adults carry future responsibility for building healthy families, worksites, social norms, and political structures essential to a process that will contribute to improved health for all.

Institutions of higher education have an opportunity and an obligation to make colleges and universities healthful places in which to live and learn, where faculty, staff, and students share common goals and work to support one another in the development of positive health behaviors, healthy environments, and social arenas that promote health and prevent disease. Higher education institutions have a wealth of resources not available to others to accomplish this task.

## THE HISTORY OF HEALTH EDUCATION AND HEALTH PROMOTION IN HIGHER EDUCATION

Many pioneering visionaries have led the way for public health and personal approaches to health behavior change within institutions of higher education. Leaders in both student health services and academia have contributed to this process. In the early 1800s, health care and health education on college campuses were the responsibility of a local physician who cared for students' health needs and offered short courses on hygiene and anatomy.[1,2] Gradually, these physicians were replaced by health services, which only slowly recognized the need for separate health education programs.

Principles of health education were first introduced to college students by physical education instructors in the nineteenth century. Dr. Edward Hitchcock, director of physical education at Amherst College from 1861 to 1911, was the most prominent pioneer of health and physical education in higher education. Hitchcock's program attempted to improve what he considered the failing health of nineteenth-century students. Hitchcock even collected anthropomorphic measurements and studied student health records, thus becoming a pioneer evaluator of the link between health education and improved health status.[2,3,4]

American women's colleges were also early promoters of physical and health education. From its opening in 1836, Mt. Holyoke offered a course on hygiene and physiology. Women's colleges quickly offered physical education, more often than men's colleges, accrediting both the courses and their instructors.[5] In the mid-nineteenth century, Catherine Beecher and other women promoted the popularization of exercise programs, helping to expand opportunities for physical activities for both men and women.[3]

Hitchcock, Beecher, Dudley Sargent at Harvard, and other pioneers in physical education throughout the country focused primarily on developing the body. Lifestyle practices such as alcohol/drug use, nutrition, injury prevention, or reproductive concerns were only sporadically integrated into programs, usually as part of a lecture series on health, hygiene, and physiology. College health officials rarely had the mandate for open discussions of personal health issues.

The bacteriologic revolution of the late nineteenth century and the expansion of public health activities in the early twentieth century lead parents to demand more effective health programs at colleges and universities.[6] During the first decade of the twentieth century, a growing number of institutions, including state universities in Michigan and California, established college health services.[7] During World War I, the great number of ineligible draftees spurred construction of college health centers.[6] By 1934, most major institutions of higher education had a separate health service.[8] These new health centers, however, emphasized only medical care rather than health counseling or health education/health promotion services. Health education remained suspended between physical education programs, academic health and hygiene departments, and the medical clinics of the new health services. (See also Chapter 1, this volume, for further discussion of the history of college health.)

Reconsideration of the role and definition of public health activities spurred physical education theorist Thomas Dennison Wood to clarify the role of health education. Wood defined health education as "the sum of experiences, in school and elsewhere, which favorably influence habits, attitudes, and knowledge relating to individual, community and racial health."[9,10] With this new definition Wood for the first time separated health and physical education, with physical education becoming only one aspect of a more comprehensive health education field. Wood became the first professor of Health Education at Columbia's Teachers College, which awarded its first degree in health education in 1922. Significantly, the first degree was awarded to a woman.

The University of Minnesota Health Service, headed by Dr. Ruth Boynton, hired the nation's first college health educator in 1954. Preventive health concepts previously taught to college students in various forms now began to evolve into comprehensive health education and health promotion programs. Campus health education and health promotion programs have become increasingly sophisticated and now include healthy life-styles and behavior change programs, self-care decision-making, and education about the appropriate use of the health care delivery system.[5,11] A recent survey conducted by the American College Health Association suggests that at least 20 percent of institutions now offer health promotion programs for students.[12] Priority areas for programming include nutrition, reproductive health, substance abuse, sexual assault, self-care, injury prevention, fitness, and gender-related and sexual preference health education.[13] A growing number of college health services now consider health education and health promotion an integral component of their mission within their clinical services and the campus community.

## CURRENT PERSPECTIVES

National health strategies for health promotion and disease prevention were initiated in 1979 with the publication of Healthy People: The Surgeon General's Report on Health Promotion. Healthy People was the first federal document to reflect a national commitment to improvement of health through the prevention of disease and the promotion of positive health behaviors. Healthy People described specific life-style behaviors that affect the health of Americans and targeted specific risk reduction goals for the nation. In 1980, a second report entitled Promoting Health/Preventing Disease: Objectives for the Nation was published, which defined a national health promotion plan for the decade. It listed 226 measurable objectives within 15 priority areas established to achieve the goals identified in Healthy People.

The process for the 1980s was considered by public health professionals to be so successful that, towards the end of the decade, consideration of objectives for the next decade began. In September, 1990, Healthy People 2000: National Health Promotion and Disease Prevention Objectives was published. With contributions from thousands of professionals from many disciplines this document defines prevention as the "single most important factor in maintaining good health." Healthy People 2000 encourages state and local health departments, communities, school systems, businesses, and the practice of medicine to improve the health of all Americans. It is a strategic planning tool that will guide education for all medical and allied health professionals. Healthy People 2000 encourages health education and health promotion providers to combine scientific knowledge, professional skills, individual commitment, community support, and political power to enable Americans to live full and active lives. It outlines: 1) health promotion priorities related to individual life-style, 2) health protection strategies that confer environmental or regulatory protection to university communities, and 3) preventive health services that define patient education priorities and preventive health screening needs by gender, age, and risk factors. There are 298 measurable objectives organized into 22 priority areas ranging from fitness, nutrition, and tobacco to HIV infection, alcohol and other drugs, mental health, and clinical preventive services.[14]

Healthy People 2000 can serve as a planning instrument for college health services to define priority services and to measure health status and health behavior change over the next ten years. Institutions of higher education are specifically addressed in the following ways:

1. Increase to at least 50 percent the proportion of post-secondary institutions with institution-wide health promotion programs for students, faculty and staff.

2. Reduce the proportion of college students engaging in recent occasions of heavy drinking of alcoholic beverages to no more that 32 percent of college students.

3. Provide HIV education for students and staff in at least 90 percent of colleges and universities.

4. Increase immunization levels of basic immunizations among children through post-secondary education institutions to at least 95 percent.

The challenge for campus health education and health promotion has become increasingly complex as the demographics of students enrolled in higher education change. As noted elsewhere in this book, student populations are no longer limited to 18- to-21-year olds. Colleges and universities contain increasingly older, more culturally and ethnically diverse, and more female students than ever before. Limited resources coupled with competition for the attention of students will force institutions of higher education to address quality of life issues on campus more creatively and to be accountable for the health protection of students in their charge.

Health education for all ages and cultures involves competition with manipulative media and a "do it now" culture, complicated by serious gaps in health information, and a reliance on uninformed peers for assistance with many painful concerns and dysfunctions students bring with them to college. The key lies in the provision of learning experiences and opportunities for changing knowledge, attitudes, and behaviors. For health educators dealing primarily with 18- to 21-year-old students, the developmental issues of profound denial, risk-taking behavior, an "it can't happen to me" belief system, and feelings of immortality, make education for changing behavior a priority that will demand peer support as well as campus-wide strategies.

# DEFINITIONS, MODELS, AND THEORIES USEFUL FOR HEALTH PROMOTION AND HEALTH EDUCATION

## DEFINITIONS

The definitions of **health education** reflect many perspectives, but all emphasize behavior change.

1. "Health education attempts to close the gap between what is known about optimum health practice and that which is already practiced."[15]
2. Health education is "bringing about behavior changes in individuals, groups, and larger populations from behaviors that are assumed to be detrimental to health to behaviors that are conducive to present and future health."[16]
3. Health education is "any combination of learning experiences designed to facilitate voluntary adaptations of behavior conducive to health."[17]
4. Health education is "the process of assisting individuals, acting separately or collectively, to make informed decisions about matters affecting their personal health and that of others."[18]
5. "Health education covers the continuum from disease prevention and promotion of optimal health; to the detection of illness; to treatment, rehabilitation, and long-term care."[19]

How is **health promotion** different from **health education**?

1. "Health promotion [is] intended to underscore the broader social structural context of health behavior more clearly than health education."[19]
2. Green proposes that "health promotion is a broader term than health education because health promotion methods do not always include an educational component."[20]
3. Green defines health promotion as "health education and related organizational, economic, and environmental supports conducive to health."[20]
4. The World Health Organization Working Group defines health promotion as "a process of enabling people to improve their health by synthesizing personal choice and social responsibility."[21]
5. The Ottawa Charter adds that "health promotion includes creating healthy policies and supportive environments, and reorienting health services beyond clinical and curative care."[22]
6. "Health promotion is a combination of health education and health advocacy."[23]

Each of these definitions underscores that the ultimate goal of health education and health promotion is to improve health through behavior change, social support systems, and healthy environments.

## MODELS AND THEORIES

Health education and health promotion practitioners use a wide variety of theories, models, and conceptual frameworks for understanding human behavior and designing effective programs based on that understanding. Pioneering research includes Lewin's seminal Field Theory (1935), initiating the exploration of how individuals make decisions concerning health, and Rosenstock and Hochbaum's work in the 1940s and 1950s. More contemporary health behavior and learning theories are utilized in creating health education and health promotion interventions. Understanding these theories enables practitioners to appreciate the complexity of human behavior relating to health. Applying these theories to the design of health education and health promotion programs creates strategies that can effectively influence health-related behaviors.

**The Health Belief Model** – why people accept preventive health care and why they do or do not comply with a variety of health care practices.[24]

**PRECEDE Model** (Predisposing, Reinforcing, and Enabling Causes in Educational Diagnosis and Evaluation) – this planning model is designed to help apply the Health Belief Model to the real world by developing interventions based on "diagnosing the multiple layers and dimensions of a health problem."[17,25]

**Value Expectancy Theories** – describe ways to identify and assess aspects of making health decisions.[17]

**Theory of Reasoned Action** – behaviors and behavioral intentions result from a rational process.[26]

**Multi-attribute Utility Theory** – predicts behavior from a person's assessment of the consequences associated with being involved or not involved in a specific behavior.[17]

**Attribution Theory** – the processes that individuals use to explain events in their lives as they attempt to understand the world around them and the process of developing "personal cognitive explanations about factors affecting their levels of health or illness...these cognitions [then influence their] health-related behaviors."[27,28]

**Consumer Information Processing Theory** – how people process information and how consumer choices affect consumer health behavior.[29]

**Stages of Change Model** – There are many versions of this model, but the basic concept includes the precontemplation of change (when a person has no knowledge or reason to consider a behavior change), contemplating change (the interval during which a person moves toward change), action (initiating specific behavior changes), and maintenance (retaining the gains achieved).[30]

Numerous disciplines offer additional philosophies, theories, and models that contribute to understanding of behavior. Over 100 years of extensive research and practice in the field of psychology have contributed immensely to knowledge about "individual differences, motivation, learning, persuasion, and attitude as they relate to behavior change."[17] Likewise, research and professional practice in the art and science of medicine, nursing, social work, and other human services provide essential understandings of how to integrate health education strategies within a clinical setting. Finally, organizational communication, social marketing, and management theories contribute to the development of leadership skills, team building, positive visibility, and the process of planning and evaluating all facets of the "process" of health promotion.

# THE PRACTICE OF
# HEALTH PROMOTION AND HEALTH EDUCATION

## THE ROLE OF THE HEALTH EDUCATOR

Many individuals on college campuses can chart the course for health education and health promotion. Nurses, nurse practitioners, counselors, physicians, faculty, staff, and administrators all have opportunities to address the health of students and the roles that a health service and an institution play in promoting positive life-style choices for students.

With the emergence of the health education professional in the 1950s, a unique partner in health was created. Health educators can assess individual and community needs for health education and can plan, develop, implement, and evaluate those educational interventions most likely to maximize resources and sustain behavior change. Professional health educators possess community organization skills necessary to create supportive social environments. They have become key members of teams that plan, develop, and integrate health education and health promotion into the clinical setting as well as the campus community. Most colleges and universities committed to health promotion have hired a professional health educator to guide this process.

In recent years, credentialing has become an issue for determining appropriate qualifications and skills for individuals responsible for the development and oversight of health education and health promotion activities. In 1988 the National Commission for Health Education Credentialing, Inc. (NCHEC) established a voluntary credentialing system to certify health education specialists, to promote professional development, and to strengthen professional preparation.[31] There is currently no estimate on the number of health education specialists in college health that have applied for and received this certification.

## PROGRAM DEVELOPMENT AND IMPLEMENTATION

Ideally, the concept of health promotion planning, implementation, and evaluation within institutions of higher education needs to involve a "systems" approach, integrating health promotion strategies into community norms and campus-wide services as well as programs and counseling designed to reduce specific risk behaviors. Institutions of higher education are rich with resources that can be tapped to create a community-based network of support and intervention.

Regardless of whether the person responsible for health promotion is a certified health education specialist or another key player in a health service, student service, academic or human resource division, activities need organization and continuity to maximize resources and effectiveness of outcome.

Every health professional has some responsibility for health education. Whether this individual is responsible for broad-based, multidimensional community programs or simply the development of one-on-one health counseling and screening protocols, a series of steps for program planning is required to enhance the likelihood that an intervention will result in education for behavior change rather than simply the giving of information. Planning models for health education are varied, but generally deal with both administrative and educational components.

The following steps are reflected in most models and were used to create the Model Alcohol Education Program described in Appendix A at the end of this chapter.

1. **Assess need and identify priority problems.** This is usually accomplished through the use of literature review, surveys, focus groups, or data collected at the health service, student affairs, or institutional level. Utilizing faculty colleagues with expertise in psychology, marketing, or other human services, as well as members of an intended audience to help define health promotion needs and to develop multidimensional approaches also increases the potential effectiveness of any intervention.

2. **Identify an intended target market and its current knowledge, attitudes, values, and perceptions.** Target markets for health promotion on a college campus include administrators and policy-makers, faculty, clinical health service personnel, or students. Variations in age, ethnicity, genetic risk, behavioral risks, and disabling conditions can be taken into account.

3. **Develop clearly stated goals and learning objectives to define needed changes in knowledge, attitudes, or behavior that can be observed or measured.** Behavioral goals and learning objectives help to define skills and tasks that must be mastered in order to achieve a desired behavior change.

4. **Analyze alternative teaching/learning approaches and select the most appropriate combination of activities designed to achieve the educational goals defined.** No single method of learning can be expected to be effective for all persons or all disease-prevention issues. Behavior change requires the use of a variety of methods, combined into a systematic approach that focuses on interactive learning and decision-making. Methods can include one-on-one counseling, small group discussion, workshops, academic classes, peer educator-led strategies, computer-assisted instruction, interactive video programs, and other print or electronic media.[28]

5. **Develop specific content, scripts, and protocols to be followed to achieve designated learning objectives.** Scripts and protocols help to ensure consistent quality and ultimately lead to clear expectations for the educator and a higher quality experience for the learner.

6. **Evaluate human, financial and technical resources available or needed to implement designated learning activities.** Everyone in college health is faced with constraints imposed by limited resources. Acknowledging the realities of budgetary and staffing limitations helps any health promotion planner prioritize learning activities. It also encourages creativity for blending resources with others. (See Appendix B)

7. **Decide what role the educator will play** (i.e., instructor, facilitator, initiator of a self-help intervention) **and who the educator(s) will be** (i.e., nurse, physician, peer educator, health educator). Campus health promotion can be implemented through recruitment of interested and caring faculty and the training of peer counselors and educators who can bring a dimension of reality to others like themselves. Outside community agencies can be integrated into campus and community networking to enhance the health of both a college and the community it influences.

8.  **Provide training and feedback for those designated to teach, coordinate, or facilitate the educational interventions,** and monitor their performance to maximize continuous quality improvement. Health professionals and peer educators need training and supervision to facilitate mastery of prevention information as well as methods of education most likely to impact a learner's behavior.

9.  **Evaluate the process of the learning experience as well as knowledge, attitude, and behavior outcomes defined on learning objectives.** Evaluation should be part of the entire framework of any health education intervention. Evaluation is critical because it helps document program participation and satisfaction. Evaluation can also be used to measure intended and reported behavior change. Tracking health status change through health service statistics (such as using ICDA-9 codes), local health care facilities used by students (such as emergency rooms, family planning clinics) can help assess trends in health status that programs may be affecting. Using one evaluation measure alone, such as how many students attended a program, can help justify how many people are being reached. Using several measures can help track behavior change.

    For example, if 90 percent of entering students are exposed in their first week on campus to an innovative alcohol education intervention, then report on a survey that they intend to decrease or abstain from drinking based on the program, and again report in a survey mid-term that they have indeed not been drinking or drink less, and emergency room alcohol admissions are significantly fewer for this group than "untreated" sophomores, your educational intervention may be having an impact. Doing a randomly selected "treatment" versus "delayed treatment" evaluation would be the next step in attempting to "prove" that an educational intervention is working to help reduce abusive drinking among those students who are exposed to the intervention. Demonstrating that health education programs are making behavior changes on campus can be very satisfying and a powerful political tool for maintaining or expanding your efforts. Behavior change is also what fund-raisers look for in model programs.

10. **Strategic Planning.** Create a five-year plan that takes into account where you are in your overall program goals and objectives now and where you want to be in five years. Using the Year 2000 health objectives will give you some nationally recognized health goals that will help you justify your strategic plan. Your strategic plan needs to take into account the strengths, weaknesses, opportunities, and threats of your health education/health promotion program from a political, financial, educational, and epidemiologic perspective. A strategic plan will help you map your needs for the future and plan accordingly as your strengths develop, weaknesses change, and your opportunities and threats shift.

Institutionalizing health promotion involves understanding and working with key decision-makers who are a part of the political process of the college community and who can facilitate integration of health promotion into the broader network of the institution. Utilizing networks already in place for faculty, staff, and students can create community-building teams that help health promotion become a more visible integrated component of university life.

To achieve a "Healthy Campus 2000," institutions of higher education will need to own the promotion of health as an organizational goal. Strategic planning for institutionalizing health promotion will involve implementation of the national health objectives from four perspectives: those of a community, a worksite, a school, and a medical delivery system. It will require the development of university-wide groups representing a variety of constituencies. It will necessitate the development of health promotion activities that encourage faculty to model and support physical and emotional health. It will include health promotion course requirements for graduation that integrate knowledge of health promotion and protection with the development of skills in values clarification, decision-making, communication, and management of stress. It will also facilitate the development of health promotion course modules at all levels of study.

Health promotion will involve the development of environments conducive to healthful living that will enhance the quality of university life. University policies will be needed to support healthy social norms and services will evolve to provide healthful choices, including an emphasis on low-fat food and a focus on activities that provide healthy outlets for stress, relaxation, and socialization.

Within the clinical setting of the health service, health promotion and patient education will be viewed as equal in value to diagnosis and treatment. This will involve a collaborative, integrated, and coordinated approach, utilizing a variety of allied health professionals to identify students at risk and provide education and support for risk reduction. Prevention will be facilitated by the development of specific health education objectives for each clinical encounter, with standard sets of questions and counseling protocols. It will also require continuing education for all health professionals for both the content and process recommended for effective preventive health education.

## CONCLUSION

Healthy People 2000 cites institutions of higher education as one of the few environments outside of military services where large numbers of 18 to 24 year olds can easily be reached. Currently more than 12 million students (5 percent of the population of the United States) are enrolled in our country's colleges and universities. If our nation is to be successful in addressing chronic disease prevention, violence, and risk behaviors associated with substance and sexual health, young adults in higher education will be a crucial group to influence.

The future of college health promotion must be data-driven, with ongoing participation in interdisciplinary research that will help us better understand health behavior change. In addition, comprehensive and consistent evaluation strategies must be developed that will identify and track institutional health status, risk behaviors, protective policies, preventive health services, and health behavior change. Longitudinal data collection will be necessary to demonstrate our ability to influence risk reduction and health outcomes over the next decade.

Higher education has been recognized as a key constituency and partner in achieving the national health objectives. This challenge will require all of us to embrace health promotion on both a personal and professional level. No matter how limited our resources, each one of us can contribute to the collective process of achieving priorities for the Year 2000 on campuses throughout our nation.

## REFERENCES

1. Means RK: A history of health education in the U.S. Philadelphia, PA, Lea-Febiger, 1962

2  Boynton RE: Historical development of health services. Student Medicine 10:294-305, 1962

3. Lockhart AF, Spears B: Chronicle of American Physical Education: Selective Readings, 1885-1930. Dubuque, IA, WC Brown, Co, 1972, p 66

4. Hitchcock E: An Anthropometric Manual Giving the Average and Mean Physical Measurements and Tests of Male College Students, and Methods of Securing Them. Amherst, MA, JE Williams, 1889

5. Rogers JF: Instruction in Hygiene in Institutions of Higher Education. Washington, DC, United States Department of the Interior, Bulletin no. 7, 1936, pp 2-10

6. Sloane D, Conant Sloane B: Changing opportunities: An overview of the history of college health education. J Am Coll Health 271-273, 1986

7. Forsythe WE: Health services in American colleges and universities. JAMA 1926-30, Nov. 28, 1914

8. Mitchell OWH: Health services in colleges and universities of New York state. N.Y.S.J. of Medicine 1:30(20): 1283-1286, Nov 1930

9. Davenport J: Thomas Denison Wood: Physical educator and father of health education. JOPERD 63-65, 68, Oct. 1984

10. Physical Education, reprinted in Weston, Arthur, The Making of American Physical Education. New York, Appleton-Century Crofts, 1962, pp 154-158

11. Boynton RE: The development of student health services. Student Medicine 4-8, Oct. 1952

12. U.S. DHHS, Public Health Service: Healthy People 2000: National Health Promotion and Disease Prevention Objectives. Washington, DC, U.S. Government Printing Office, 1990 p 15

13. Keeling R, Downy P, Gould J: Health Promotion on Campus: Resources and Referral Directory. Baltimore MD, American College Health Association, Maryland, 1991

14. U.S. DHHS, Public Health Service: Healthy People 2000: National Health Promotion and Disease Prevention Objectives. Washington, DC, U.S. Government Printing Office, 1990

15. Griffith W: Health education: Definitions, problems, and philosophies. Health Educ Monogr, 12-14, 1972

16. Simonds FK: Health education in the mid-1970s: State of the art. New York, Preventive Medicine USA, 1976

17. Green LW et al: Health Education Planning: A Diagnostic Approach. Mountain View, CA, Mayfield Press, 1980

18. National Task Force on the Preparation and Practice of Health Educators, Inc.: A Framework for the Development of Competency-based Curricula for Entry Level Health Educators. New York, National Task Force on the Preparation and Practice of Health Educators, 1983

19. Glanz K, Lewis FM, Rimer BK: Health Behavior and Health Education: Theory, Research and Practice. San Francisco, CA, Jossey-Bass Publishers, 1990, p 8

20. Green LW: Health education model, Behavioral Health: A Handbook of Health Enhancement and Disease Prevention. Edited by JD Matarazzo et al. New York, Wiley Press, 1984

21. World Health Organization Working Group: Report of the Working Group on Concepts and Principles of Health Promotion. Copenhagen, World Health Organization, 1984

22. Ept L: Achieving Health for All: A Framework for Health Promotion in Canada. Toronto, Health and Welfare, Canada, 1986

23. Minkler M: Health education, health promotion in the open society: A historical prospective. Health Educ Q, pp 17-30, 1989

24. Janz NK, Becker MH: The health belief model: A decade later. Health Educ Q, p 1-47, 1984

25. Green LW, Kreuter MW, Deeds FG et al: Health Education Planning: A Diagnostic Approach. Mountain View, CA, Mayfield Publishers, 1980

26. Fishbein M, Ajzen I: Belief, Attitude, Intention and Behavior: An Introduction to Theory and Research. Reading, MA, Addison-Wesley, 1975

27. Weiner B: A theory of motivation for some classroom experiences. J Educ Psychol, 3-25, 1979

28. Abramson LY, Seligman MEP, Teasdale JD: Learned helplessness in humans: Critique and reformulation. J Abn Psychol, 49-74, 1978

29. Bettman JR: An Information Processing Theory of Consumer Choice. Reading MA, Addison-Wesley, 1979

30. Prochaska JO et al: Self-change processes, self-efficacy and self-concept in relapse and maintenance cessation of smoking. Psychol Rep, p 983-990, 1982

31. National Commission for Health Education Credentialing, Inc.: Self-assessment for Health Educators. New York, NCHEC, Professional Examination Service, 1990

# KEY RESOURCES

## Books

Frederiksen L, Solomon L, Bahoney K (eds): Marketing Health Behavior. New York, Plenum Press, 1984

Gochman DS: Health Behavior: Emerging Research Perspectives. New York, Plenum, 1988

Green L, Kreuter M: Health Promotion Planning: An Educational and Environmental Approach. Mountain View, CA, Mayfield Publishers, 1991

Health Education in College Health Services, AHA/CDC Health Education Projects, Balitmore MD, American College Health Association, 1981

Hill L, Smith N: Self-Care Nursing: Promotion of Health. Norwalk , CT, Appleton & Lange, 1985

Kanfer F, Goldstein A: Helping People Change. New York, Pergamon Press,  1991

Meichenbaum D, Tura D: Facilitating Treatment Adherence: A Practitioners Handbook. New York, Plenum Press, 1987

Ross H, Mico P: Theory and Practice in Health Education. Palo Alto, CA, Mayfield Publishing Co., 1980, pp 230

Rubinson L, Alles W: Health Education: Foundations for the Future. St. Louis, Mosby College Publishing, 1984

Squyres W: Patient Education and Health Promotion in Medical Care. Palo Alto, Mayfield Publishing Company 1985

Ward WB et al: Advances in Health Education and Health Promotion. Greenwich, CT,  Jai Press, 1986

## Journals

Advance Data, From Vital Statistics of the National Center for Health Statistics, U.S. Department of Health and Human Services, Public Health Service, Centers for Disease Control, National Center for Health Statistics, Hyattsville MD

American Journal of Public Health, American Public Health Association, Washington, DC

FDA Consumer, U.S. Dept Health and Human Services, Public Health Service, FDA, Rockville, MD 20857

Health Education Quarterly, John Wiley & Sons, New York, NY

Health Education, Association for the Advancement of Health Education, New York

Health Psychology, American Psychological Association, Hillsdale, NJ

Higher Education Quarterly, Basil Blackwell, Oxford and Cambridge, MA

Higher Education, The International Journal of Higher Education and Educational Planning, Kluwer Academic Publishers, The Netherlands

Journal of Health and Social Behavior, American Sociological Association, Washington, DC

Journal of Health Education, American Alliance for health education, recreation and dance, Reston, VA

Journal of Healthcare Education and Training, The Journal of the American society for healthcare education and training of the American hospital association, Chicago, IL

Journal of Youth and Adolescence, A Multidisciplinary Research Publication, Plenum Press, New York & London

Patient Education and Counseling, Elsevier Scientific Publishers, Ireland

The Journal of American College Health, Heldref Publishers, Washington DC

## APPENDIX A
### Model Alcohol Education Program

- Establish the position of an Alcohol Educator/Counselor full time with clerical support
- Assess campus educational needs
- Assess campus alcohol problems
- Special speakers such as nationally known athletes
- Student Panels
  —"Alcohol and Athletes: Choices in Crisis"
- Alcohol peer education outreach program
- Alcohol information in existing campus health education training efforts such as:
  —health aides
  —student residential life staff
  —fraternity and sorority leadership
- Special Alcohol Awareness programing for incoming students (freshmen and women) and their parents
- Alcohol lectures in academic courses
  —literature
  —sociology
  —history of medicine
  —psychology
  —education
  —biology (consider effects of alcohol on cells, tissues, organs)
  —statistics (use data from campus alcohol surveys)
- Alcohol information displays
  —campus libraries
  —student union
  —health service
  —dean's office
- Radio, television, newspaper: Alcohol-related
  —public service announcements
  —articles
  —editorials
  —radio and television documentaries devoted to Alcohol Education
- Alcohol topic files with articles, clippings, journals, and books
  —in health service
  —campus libraries
- Consequences of alcohol use integrated within reproductive health clinics and peer outreach programs
- Special programs for fraternities, sororities, athletes, and other special interest groups
- Unique marketing techniques for each campus such as high-profile Alcohol Awareness Week activities
- Alcohol information available in as many campus locations as possible:
  —health service
  —student union

——campus residences
——in student health aide kits
——library
——bookstore
——student food store
- Alcohol information at:
——health fairs
——registration
——student services and activities fairs
- Compile comprehensive list of community alcohol resources and providers
- Fund the training of faculty/administrators/clinicians and support staff to recognize signs of alcohol problems
- Invite alumni to actively participate in alcohol programming
- Alcohol video and audio tapes available for individuals and groups
- Evaluation of the impact of education programs on attitudes, knowledge, and behavior of students
- Evaluation of dorm damage, injuries, health status, disciplinary actions, academic performance related to alcohol
- Counseling and treatment programs accessible to campus community
- Legal and policy issues made clear to campus community
- Provide housing options for students who want the option to live in an entirely alcohol-free environment
- Incentives for social organizations to offer alcohol-free social events
- Empower students to choose healthy lifestyles and be role models for entire community

## Appendix B
## Funding Health Education Programs

With shrinking budgets and increasing competition for the student services dollar, health education practitioners need to be aware of other resources to supplement their shrinking budgets. While federal, state, local and foundation and corporate monies are highly competitive, they are usually earmarked for very specific objectives. Half of the battle in fundraising is knowing where the potential funds are and the other half is finding the time to write grants, letters of intent and respond to Requests for Proposals (RFPs). Other sources of money or in-kind services are often on campus or in your community. A third source of budget relief can be goods and services. Giving presentations for an honorarium, selling T-shirts with your most popular peer education logo, or consulting with a local school about how to start an alcohol education program can help raise dollars to run programs.

### Grants

Many people shy away from grant-writing because of fear of the grant-writing process. It can be time consuming, but grant writing does not have to be difficult or overwhelming. Usually a campus development officer is willing to suggest funding sources and offer tips on writing successful letters of intent or full-fledged grants.

1.   Consider writing letters of intent first or calling the grant administrator to be sure that your ideas match theirs.
2.   Follow the directions of the grant form to the letter. Often federal grants are set aside and never read because they exceed the required length or some other detail important to them.
3.   Know what you want to do and state your request clearly and briefly.
4.   Know what they want and be sure your goals match.
5.   Ask for help in creating a draft and editing the final copy.
6.   Allocate time for grant writing into your schedule. Be sure your supervisor knows what you are doing and agrees. Fund raising is very time consuming and there is no guarantee of success, so it is a calculated risk of time spent (which costs money) versus results.
7.   Many resources exist on how to write grants. For example, The National AIDS Clearinghouse provides free grant-writing materials, called "Writing a Successful Grant Application," by Liane Reif-Lehrer.
8.   Writing one grant helps you write the next. Once you have your idea down in writing, you can tailor it to the next RFP or letter of intent.

### Honorariums and "Merchandise"

The AIDS Memorial Quilt funds its massive operation primarily by selling T-shirts, buttons, books and charging a reasonable honorarium for quilt displays. As often as possible, health education practitioners do professional courtesy consulting and community service lectures and other activities.

However, many schools do have grants, in K-12 and in higher education, and would appreciate your expertise, a peer education demonstration or a workshop and are willing to pay a fee. The key is not to overcharge or undercharge. Determine what your time is worth and offer a fair price for your consultation. Consider taking less if what they offer is all that they have. Often, they will have to go back and raise the money from their own community resources. Suggest that several similar schools or organizations combine resources to attend your presentation and share the fee. Getting a good reputation for providing excellent services at reasonable fees will increase your opportunities for this kind of fund raising. A key objective is to plan this work as part of your schedule rather than adding it to an already overwhelming list of responsibilities.

### "Friends" of Health Education and Health Promotion

Parents, alumni, and students can give to your program or a special part of your program. While many institutions of higher education find this a new concept for health services, usually athletic groups on campus have this tradition (i.e. "Friends of Rowing"). Alumni often prefer to give to a program they enjoyed, participated in, or benefited from rather than to the general college gift fund.

### On-Campus Resources

Often the student assembly, Greek houses, residence hall councils, student activities office, athletic associations, academic departments, residential life, dining services or student clubs and organizations are willing and anxious to co-sponsor events. Although it is time consuming to develop connections with these organizations initially, create a list of resources, update it annually and create a relationship of collaboration in funding events, pamphlets, health fairs, fundraisers, speakers, awareness weeks, etc. Sharing the costs also increases the input and commitment that these contributors have to the event. Higher turnouts may be a result and a distinct advantage to this strategy.

### Community Resources

Local businesses are usually swamped with requests for free goods or services for events and raffles. Develop a professional relationship with local merchants. Explain your goals, assess their interest, willingness to participate, the types of activities they would be willing to be involved in and the level and type of financial help they can supply. In return, they have advertising budgets that support contributions and will expect credit or co-sponsorship for their participation. Developing ongoing relationships, perhaps one business per event, can help eliminate work in the future. Remind them that donating a gift certificate for as little as one pizza or T-shirt a year is peanuts for the advertising it provides them.

The bottom line: Be creative, fearless, innovative, and assertive. Ask for help, allocate time to raise money, and don't be intimidated by rejection.

# 6

# Unique Issues for Nurse-directed College Health Centers

ANNE MARIE NOVINGER, RN, MA

Nurse-directed student health centers exist in private and public colleges, universities, and special institutions across the nation. In these health centers, rather than the traditional chief physician or administrative manager, a nurse-director is responsible for creating, operating, and evaluating the student health program. Such centers may employ physicians, nurse practitioners, mental health professionals, health educators, and other support staff but the individual responsible for the overall operation is typically a career College Health nurse.

Nurse-directed health centers usually are smaller in size and have a more limited scope of service than those in major university settings. They typically serve as ambulatory care and preventive health clinics without over-night facilities. Populations served range from traditional college-age students attending small private colleges to diverse student bodies representing all ages and cultures. Students may live in dormitories, off-campus housing, or commute long distances. Nurse-directed health centers may be located in rural settings, suburban areas or large metropolitan regions. Nurse-directed health centers are as varied in size and services as the institutions, geographic areas and populations they serve. The extent of their health service offerings is significantly affected by budgetary politics, community resources, and institutional traditions.

## PROGRAMMATIC ISSUES

The program philosophy of a nurse-directed health service tends to be less medical and more wellness-oriented with distinct emphasis placed on health promotion, disease prevention, self-care, and consumer advocacy. This emphasis matches the philosophy of the student services component of many institutions. This philosophy holds that college students are at a time of growth and transition in their lives and need to develop personal responsibility and independent decision-making skills. An important goal of the nurse-directed health service is to promote lifelong attitudes and behaviors that will result in optimum health and quality of life.

Services provided by most nurse-directed health programs focus upon triage, health education, and primary health care rather than the provision of comprehensive, specialized, and ongoing medical care. The scope of services may include nursing assessment; diagnosis and treatment of minor health problems and injuries; screening and immunization programs; consultation with campus physicians; family planning clinics; referrals to specialists, clinics, and other community health resources; and crisis intervention. Many nurse-directors feel that an environment that concentrates on preventive care, health teaching, and self-care contributes the most to the well-being and ultimate success of students in their college experience. Countless examples exist of creative wellness-oriented programs in nurse-directed health services: nutrition and weight-control groups; fitness awareness programs; periodic health fairs; self-care centers for headaches, colds, and abrasions; substance abuse programs; AIDS prevention programs; and multi-media resource centers.

Physician services are usually limited and may be available only on a consultant basis because of budgetary restrictions. The same is true for most mental health services. Nurse practitioners and physician-approved standardized procedures (standing orders) may be utilized in an effort to provide safe, cost-effective, legally authorized, high quality student health services. Although the scope of services offered is influenced by the amount of institutional support provided, many nurse-directed health services are models of innovative programming accomplished with little budgetary support.

An annual assessment of campus needs and community resources is an important component of a cost-effective health program and should be the first step in maintaining a realistic and justifiable scope of practice in the student health center. In this way appropriate planning, policy development, and personnel deployment can occur. The nurse-director has the "opportunity to use skills and knowledge . . . to create a program which is unique to the institution, not only in direct consumer care, but through teaching, counseling and serving as a campus consultant on health-related matters."[1]

Special cooperative arrangements commonly exist with college academic nursing programs, disabled student programs, and other campus departments. The health service might provide, for example, health resource materials, mental health stress reduction groups, physical examinations, and immunizations for prospective nursing students. The academic nursing program may be valuable as a mutually beneficial support system to the student health service. Faculty members of the nursing program could provide a source of part-time (hourly) service to the facility, making possible participation in college activities and meetings as well as off-campus conferences. Teaching faculty also offer current professional expertise and consultation in specialized areas of nursing and community resources.

## STAFFING AND ORGANIZATIONAL ISSUES

Successful and well-respected nurse-directed student health services represent a wide range of organizational patterns affected by variables such as the student population served, funding limitations, availability of community resources, and the qualifications and experience of the nurse-director. As noted above, such centers include programs ranging in staff from simply the nurse-director and a part-time clerk or student worker, to facilities with a full clinic staff including physicians, nurses, nurse practitioners, mental health providers, and other allied health personnel.

Nurse-directors perform many duties including direct patient care; planning and organizing; developing policy; preparing and negotiating a budget; participating on committees, either in the health center or elsewhere on campus; recruiting, screening, orienting, evaluating, and supervising employees; participating in disaster planning and drills; publishing newsletters and other health-related materials; and serving as a safety specialist for laboratories and other areas on campus. Other duties may necessarily include accounting and clerical work; preparing and maintaining examination rooms; selecting, ordering and maintaining equipment and supplies; and teaching health-related classes. With such a vast array of activity there is a potential for role confusion. Hourly physicians may be puzzled by the nurse-director who recruited and hired them and yet also cleans up the exam room between patients.

It is common for nurse-directors to have faculty status in the institution, especially those who are involved in the education of health professionals. It is not uncommon to find nurse-directors with a broad base of health care experience and knowledge in medical, ambulatory, and rehabilitation settings.

The nurse-director may report to an administrator of student services, student affairs, student activities, business, counseling, or an academic nursing program. Because very few of these administrators have had education or training in health care, the nurse-director has the challenge of educating them about the health-related needs and problems of a student population and, thus, the requirements of a student health program.

When one individual is the administrative head of a student health program as well as a provider of direct service to students, the scope, utilization, and effectiveness of the health service program is likely to be determined primarily by the balance of managerial ability, clinical skills, creativity, motivation, and communication skills of that director. The most successful nurse-directors are characterized as outgoing self-starters who are friendly, flexible, diplomatic, professional, cooperative, energetic, highly motivated, and creative, especially with regard to program innovation. They must demonstrate ingenuity, initiative, and the ability to balance the demands of the health service with the public relations activities so necessary in a health center.

Nurse-directors, as well as other staff in small student health services, need professional development, continuing education, and the opportunity to network with colleagues. Professional isolation can occur because of solitary work environments or because of few colleagues in close geographic proximity. If this is the case, staff of such centers should arrange time for regular meetings with colleagues for mutual peer-review.

Roles and responsibilities of the nurse in college health are unique, and the particular professional needs of nurse-directors may not be addressed adequately by the generic nursing organizations on the state and national levels. The need for managerial/administrative skills is an important one for nurse-directors who must plan and manage budgets, negotiate staff salary increases, and negotiate contracts with staff professionals. Membership and active participation in the American College Health Association, its regional affiliates, and state college health service organizations are essential for nurse-directors, bringing them into the mainstream of national college nursing issues, practices, and procedures. Membership provides numerous opportunities to network, update skills, obtain new ideas and information, and learn about standards of care in college health, current research, new resources, and successful programs.

Many colleges struggle with the selection of an appropriate and descriptive title for the nurse-director position, an important symbol in good health services management. The title should accurately reflect the level of administrative responsibility and be comparable to the titles of other department heads at the institution. Titles used include Director, Coordinator, Campus Nurse, College Nurse, Health Counselor, Health Services Specialist, and Wellness Coordinator. The recent trend toward accurate reflection of responsibility in other health care settings should provide support for needed changes. A comprehensive job description, clearly defining the reporting relationship on the college organizational chart, should be available in the health center and in appropriate administrative files. Other documents necessary to the legal operation of a nurse-directed health service include current manuals of policies, procedures, and protocols. If necessary, of course, these must comply with appropriate federal, state, and local regulations.

Unique to the nurse-director's role are issues surrounding the "management" of physicians. This can include responsibility for planning and coordinating medical clinics and services; defining the package of services needed from the physician; developing recommendations about payment for physician services; and hiring, supervising and firing physician staff. This role reversal requires sensitivity, diplomacy, and well-defined management policies. Basic to the success of this relationship is a clear administrative statement describing the responsibilities of each professional employee. Full administrative support is essential in the delineation of the nurse-director's ultimate responsibility for the operation of the health service. The nurse-director must be assertive enough to perform the supervisory duties implicit in this assignment while respecting the physician's role as manager of medical diagnosis and treatment. Management duties are quite distinct from these medical functions.

If conflicts develop over policy issues, such as the purchase of expensive medical equipment, the supervising administrator or the advisory committee may need to be consulted. The boundary issue is critical in relationship to two basic management tenets: 1) Only one person is in charge, and 2) that person must be knowledgeable about health care management and supervisory skills. The physician must accept and respect the supervisory role of the nurse-director who, in turn, must fully accept the limitations imposed by the nursing license in all contacts with students. Clear, comprehensive job descriptions and open communication among all health service staff are key factors in avoiding role identity and authority problems. Balancing this unique distribution of roles and responsibilities of the nurse and the physician is vital to successful nurse-directed health care management.

## FACILITIES AND FUNDING

The physical plant of a small, nurse-directed health service may vary considerably, ranging from one room, with a restroom down the hall, to an extensive clinic with several offices, examination rooms, laboratory, radiology room, pharmacy, mental health therapy rooms, and a conference room. In some instances, nurse-directed health services exist in very cramped quarters lacking office space, storage space, and consultation or examination rooms, contributing to a loss of privacy for students. In such circumstances it is incumbent upon the nurse-director to develop as strong a case as possible to higher level college administration about the need for adequate space.

Funding for small, nurse-directed student health centers might come from any combination of pre-paid student health fees, general institutional funds, fee-for-service, insurance reimbursement and, if the institution is public, state funds. A 1988 survey of the nation's largest institutions suggested that during the 1986-87 academic year an average of $102 per student per year was spent on student health centers.[2] A 1990 survey of California community colleges demonstrated that an average of $14 per student per year (not including summer session) is collected in student health fees.[3] However, the range of expenditures is broad: Examples of nurse-directed health center expenditures include Glendale Community College in California where health services are provided to 14,000 students for $15 per student per academic year; the College of Lake County in Grayslake, Illinois, where the expenditure per student for an academic year is $17; and the University of Pittsburgh at Bradford, Pennsylvania, where services cost $32 per student per year.

The financial commitment of an institution varies dramatically depending on the educational philosophy of the administration and its governing board, general budgetary constraints, and the availability and accessibility of community resources. Tradition, student expectations, and student health care needs on each individual campus may also influence budgetary decisions.

Health services typically compete with other student services for financial support. To insure stability in funding, and to develop new funding sources, nurse-directors need to develop and maintain positive relationships with all members of the college community, including the governing board. The challenge for adequate funding is often compounded by the preventive care nature of nurse-directed student health centers mentioned above. Because typical medical care reimbursement pays poorly for preventive care, support for prevention generally occurs through the combined efforts of a far-sighted college administration and a convincing nurse-director.

In addition to regular reports and written communications, the most effective way to market health services is for the nurse-director to be visible by serving on committees, accepting special assignments, consulting on health-related issues, and working cooperatively with key administrators and campus leaders.

## OTHER CONSIDERATIONS

Nurses (and, the author would add, women) are traditionally socialized to be "all things to all people" and to focus on meeting the needs of others before self. Due to this, and because of numerous clinical and administrative responsibilities, the nurse-director is highly vulnerable to stress. Although academic breaks, holidays and summer vacations may provide a measure of relief, it is imperative that the nurse-director develop strong skills in time-management, assertiveness, delegation, negotiation, and self-care.

In order to develop appropriate health services standards, all nurse-directors should be well acquainted with Recommended Standards for a College Health Program and The Development of Health Programs in Junior/Community Colleges and Universities with Nurse-Directed Health Services, both issued by the American College Health Association. These important publications provide the framework for a quality health service program.

Accreditation is an important mechanism to evaluate and improve quality, enabling comparison of performance with established national or state standards. While many college health services have been accredited by the Joint Commission on Accreditation of Healthcare Organizations or the Accreditation Association for Ambulatory Health Care, few nurse-directed health services have done so. In part this is because of the time and expense involved in the accreditation process. It also may be due to the fact that accreditation instruments developed so far seem to be more appropriate for larger, more sophisticated health centers.

## FUTURE CONSIDERATIONS

Issues of importance to College Health nursing in the coming years will include the expanding role of nurses in the health care arena, the availability of – and salaries for – health care practitioners of all types, the increasing scope of medical services potentially available due to new technologies, and advances in preventive health care. Important goals for long-range planning should include creation of an appropriate accreditation instrument for nurse-directed health services, active participation in the accreditation process, and improved means of communication among and between nurse-directors.

In an effort to enrich the quality and enhance the image of college health nursing, the American College Health Association has worked with the American Nurses Association (ANA) to develop a college health certification offering at the generalist level. In the fall of 1991, more than 900 nurses took the first ANA College Health Nurse certifying examination, setting an ANA record for the largest number of first-time test takers. For information about the certification examination, call 1-800/274-4262. This is an exciting development for College Health nursing and promises to usher in a new era of nursing's involvement in the provision of health care to college and university students nationwide.

### Acknowledgments

Acknowledgment and appreciation are extended to the following people who were responsible for contributions to this chapter: Janet DeVoe, RN, CSE, University of Pittsburgh, Pittsburgh PA; Jacquelyn A. Hassett, RN, MS, College of Lake County, Grayslake, IL; Paula Liska, BSN, MPH, PhD, San Diego City College, San Diego, CA; Linda McDermott, RN, MSN, FNP, University of Southern California, Los Angeles, CA; and Carol Mulvihill, RN, BSN, University of Pittsburgh at Bradford, Bradford, PA.

# REFERENCES

1. American College Health Association: The Development of Health Programs in Junior/ Community Colleges and Universities with Nurse-Directed Health Services. Rockville, MD, The American College Health Association, 1986

2. Patrick K: Student health: Medical care within institutions of higher education. JAMA 260:3301-3305, 1988

3. Novinger AM: Survey of health fees in California community colleges. Unpub. data. June 1990

# RESOURCES AND HELPFUL MATERIALS

Council of Community Health Nurses: Standards of College Health Nursing Practice. ANA Publishing, 1986, Ch 15, pp 1-20

Dirschel KM: Changing a student health service to primary nursing. Nursing and Health Care 4(5): 252-256, 1983

Douglas K: College health nursing. Kansas Nurse 63(10):1, 1988

Heffern M: College health nursing: State of the art. J Am Coll Health 34(3)148-149, 1985

Kalma S: Guidelines for directing college health services. Nursing Outlook 53(1):45-49, 1983

McEvoy MD, Vezine M: The development of a nursing center on a college campus. J Advanced Nursing 11(3):295-301, 1986

White DH: Justifying the existence of the nurse-directed health service. J Am Coll Health 30(4): 191-192, 1982

**Author's Note:** Many helpful and important articles written about the college/university health setting and nursing administrators may be found in professional journals such as the Journal of American College Health, American Association of Occupational Health Nursing Journal, American Journal of Public Health, Family and Community Health, Health Education, Journal of Advanced Nursing, Journal of School Health, Nurse Educator, Nursing and Health Care, Nursing Management, Patient Education and Counseling, and Public Health Reports. Other interesting and helpful periodicals include FDA Consumer, Health Affairs, Health Values, Healthline, Lovett's Letters, Stethoscope, and University of California Berkeley Wellness Letter. Lovett's Letters, a national newsletter for Nurse-Directed Health Services, is published ten times per year; article submission is requested and encouraged (Editor, Joy Corcoran, Health Center Director, S.B.1.03.02, University of Texas at San Antonio, San Antonio, Texas 78285). The Morbidity and Mortality Weekly Report, published by the Centers for Disease Control in Atlanta, Georgia, is another relevant and important publication for following infectious disease and public health issues. A current copy of the state Nurse Practice Act is also an essential document for nurse-directors.

# 7

# Administrative and Financial Issues for College Health

## J. Robert Wirag, HSD

The nature, scope, size, configuration, location, and financial support for campus health service programs differ widely from campus to campus. Some programs are free-standing, offering a wide range of ambulatory care and health education services with an array of professional and support staff. Other programs have been relegated to a single room in a facility that serves other student needs and are limited to education, care for common illnesses, minor injuries, or assessment and referral services managed by one person, usually a nurse. Many variables come into play when analyzing campus health service programs: philosophy of campus administration, availability of services proximal to campus, value to the students for whom the services are directed, means of financing the program, and the ability to recruit and retain quality staff, to name a few. Although a model that has universal application for all colleges and universities (including junior and community colleges) does not exist, there are some common elements to be considered.

This chapter recognizes that if a commitment is made to institute a health service program on campus or to enhance an existing program, some attention must be devoted to the following fundamentals, regardless of the size of the institution: a **program** that is tailored to fit the health needs that most of the students have most of the time; **human resources** to manage and deliver the program's services; a **facility** to house the program and the staff; and some means of **financing** the program. Each fundamental will be addressed, followed by a discussion of associated administrative issues for consideration.

## THE PROGRAM

Ideally, form should follow function. The campus health center that reaches beyond the year 2000 should be designed to meet the medical, health education, and the counseling and mental health needs of the population to be served. A number of questions must be addressed to establish this design: What is the mission of the program? Will the health center program be limited to students or will its services be extended to include students' dependents and employees? Who determines eligibility for services? Is it a Student Health Center or a University Health Center?

In the perfect world, the first order of business would be to identify the health needs of the population to be served as a basis for designing a facility and program to serve those needs. What do they want? What do they need? Surveys would help determine what they want. A combination of survey research and experience based on utilization reports would help determine what they need. Rarely, however, is a blank check issued to design and offer a program of services tailored to fit the needs of a given population. From a planning perspective, it is more realistic to consider change for the future in evolutionary terms. From the present, identify strengths and weaknesses of the current program. Take advantage of existing opportunities or create new opportunities to enhance or expand services.

**Planning** a program for the future is an ongoing process. It means having a clear understanding of the status of the current program, knowing its strengths and weaknesses, recognizing its unmet needs, forecasting the needs of a changing population, having an awareness of the forces that impede progress, and committing oneself to finding the means necessary to assure success. Planning involves dreaming alone and aloud with others. It means looking at things the way they can be, not necessarily the way they are. It means developing a plan, a strategic plan, to make things happen.

Set the foundation. Start with a broad-based view. Know what the overall mission of the institution is as well as the mission of the unit (e.g., Student Affairs) of which the campus health service program is a part. Prepare a mission statement for the campus health service program that supports the broader mission of the larger administrative unit and the institution. For example:

> The mission of the student health center is to provide ambulatory health-care services and offer health education programs that promote healthy life-styles to help students achieve satisfying and successful college experiences.

Goal statements flow from the mission statement according to "expected outcomes." That is, ask the following question: "At the end of the coming year, what do I expect (hope) to have accomplished?" Follow each goal statement with "SMART" (Specific, Measurable, Attainable, Realistic, Time-framed) objectives. For example:

> **Goal:** Delivery of health education messages for Health Education services is enhanced through the use of peer instructors and student volunteers.

**Objective:** Recruit, train and use three full-time peer instructors for Health Education programs during the 1991-92 year.

**Goal:** Increase the use of volunteers, student interns and practicum students in health education programming and evaluation efforts.

**Objective:** Increase the number of hours per week of volunteer and student intern time to at least 200 by the end of the 1992 academic year.

With clear direction in terms of where the program is and what the intentions are for enhancing its value, attention must be paid to the administrative tools that are necessary to manage the program. One such tool is the handbook of policies and procedures specific to the health service program. A policy is a statement that guides or directs decisions. A procedure refers to the step(s) to be taken to support a policy. Policies and procedures are dynamic, subject to change as circumstances affecting the program change. Policies and procedures are established or changed by official action.

Policy-making is a process that should include individuals representing parts of the organization who will be affected by the policy or who will be involved in the procedures that will be instituted to support it. Policies are operational at various levels. Schools that are part of a larger system of campuses will have a book of policies and operating procedures. Each component institution may have its own subset of policies and operating procedures, according to the unique features of that campus. Likewise, the various units of operation (colleges, divisions, or departments) will, or should, have their own set of policies and procedures to govern the activities of their respective programs but which also support the policies and procedures set by a higher administrative authority.

The campus health service's policies and procedures should be reviewed periodically but not less often than once each year. This process should not be merely an administrative exercise. When changes are instituted, every effort must be made to inform those affected by the change – staff and consumers alike – either through group discussion, by formal memoranda to campus officials and student leaders, or by using campus media.

## HUMAN RESOURCES

With a clear picture of the type of program that is desired to address the needs of the population to be served, decisions about staffing, lines of authority, duties and responsibilities must be made. Who will direct the program? To whom will this person be responsible? How will the staff be organized? How will staff be recruited, evaluated, or terminated? How will staff development needs be managed?

Director, CEO, Executive Director, Administrator, Manager, Nurse-Director are all titles used to designate leadership responsibilities for the campus health service program. Professional training of directors varies from MDs to RNs to Nurse Practitioners to individuals with doctoral or masters degrees in health planning, health education, psychology, or business. Because of the size and complexity of student health programs, professionally trained individuals and/or those with proven administrative skills are essential for these positions.

Directors must have a fundamental knowledge of higher education to help the campus health service staff understand their unique fit in, and their relative contributions to, the academic community. On the other hand, the chief campus health official must be sensitive to the changing landscape of the larger health care system, must assess the impact of such changes on the campus program, and must be skillful in addressing those changes. To be an effective leader in this rapidly changing world of higher education and health care requires deliberate attention to the essential elements of administration: planning, organizing, coordinating, directing and evaluating. Strategic planning is essential and must include setting goals, managing information, marketing and promotion. Leaders must determine what the program is, what it does best, what needs are being met, what needs are not met, how it fits into the larger academic community, what its mission is, where it is going and what the plan is to get it there.

Individuals serving in the principal leadership capacity for the campus health program generally have a reporting relationship with a higher administrative official. The typical, direct reporting lines point to a Dean of Students, a Vice President for Student Affairs or, in rare instances, to the President. The title of the up-line administrator is not as important as the individual's understanding of the need for and value of the campus health service program and a willingness to support the program.

Managing the human resources for the organization means organizing the staff for the purpose of accomplishing predetermined goals and objectives. The formal organizational structure varies with the size of the program and the community to be served and with the breadth of services provided. The structure may be organized along lines of functional units according to the menu of services provided with a member of the professional staff delegated administrative authority and responsibility for areas such as medical care (with overall supervision provided by a physician or other clinically trained professional for lab, x-ray, physical therapy, or pharmacy services), health education, mental health, nursing, and business services (including personnel, accounting, housekeeping, and data management).

Regardless of its size, however, clear lines of authority must be established that consider: responsibility relationships, division of work, job design descriptions, work flow, and information feedback systems. Larger programs will be organized along departmental lines with supervisors or department heads providing the leadership for their individual administrative unit. Smaller programs tend to be less formal in their organizational structure with fewer people having broader responsibility. Again, regardless of the size, the purpose of an organization's structure is to provide quality health services efficiently.

There is no definitive, universally accepted theory about the way a campus health service should be designed. Administrators are free to choose from, adapt, and combine many concepts of organization design. In doing so, it is important to recognize that each program has both a "formal" and an "informal" organization. The informal organization consists of those relationships that occur spontaneously from the activities and interactions of various staff, but are not set forth in the formal structure. It is an administrative challenge to utilize fully the positive benefits of the informal organization and at the same time minimize its negative impact. The informal organization is a fact of organizational life and there is value in integrating the interests of the informal organization with those of the formal organization.

Human resource management decisions are necessary to assure that the organization has the right culture and that personnel fit the needs of the program. Positions need to be constantly re-evaluated and redesigned. Laws that govern recruiting, hiring, and dismissal practices must be understood and followed. Hiring, firing, performance appraisals and other personnel tasks are commonly performed in conjunction with campus departments of human resources or personnel services that serve employee needs institution-wide. The often unique nature of health center employees to these personnel units must be anticipated and addressed.

## FACILITIES

With the program defined and the staff in place, what about the facility to support the delivery of services? The unprecedented changes taking place in the U.S. health care system are having a substantial impact on college health service programs and the buildings that house them. Student health centers built in the 1950s and 60s are being rebuilt, either by major renovation or new construction. The shift from hospital care to ambulatory care services and the emphasis on prevention and health education render obsolete those facilities that provided around-the-clock hospital care for students in the 1950s, 60s, and 70s. Attempts to retrofit old buildings constructed for very different purposes have resulted in inefficient and costly operations; they little resemble the modern health service facilities to which students were accustomed before arriving on campus. Consequently, student health center personnel constantly battle the poor image students have about the program. Students tend to make decisions about quality with their eyes. They are greatly influenced by the environment, including furnishings, traffic flow, lighting, and air conditioning. If it doesn't look or feel like they are receiving quality services, they quickly become convinced they are not.

Fortunately, a number of campuses have been reconfiguring their health centers to focus their services on ambulatory care and incorporate wellness as the pervasive theme; to provide disease prevention and health promotion activities through a well-planned and coordinated campus health service program. Substantial investments in "bricks and mortar" have been made, or are being planned, by many colleges and universities including "the Universities of" Virginia, Arizona, Michigan, Florida, Illinois, Texas, and UC Berkeley. This is testimony to the commitment these institutions have made to the provision of health services for their campuses. These changes are not reserved, however, for the larger schools. As the spotlight gets turned up on the health issues facing students today and as health care costs continue to escalate, higher education officials at all types of institutions are recognizing the value of supporting a campus health service program through a facility that is adequate in size to support the program tailored to fit the needs of its students, appropriately staffed, properly financed, and well-managed.

Health centers of the future will build flexibility into their programs and services in order to adapt to the changing environment. They will be designed to move away from the "fixed wall" architecture, will cater to the users, and will be more cost effective and efficient to operate. The function of the facility should be the first consideration. Start with the services currently offered, decide what new services are to be added, and develop a plan to do it. Space guidelines should relate to the functions, activities, and productivity of the area. Consider: scope of services in various areas, hours of operation, automated vs manual equipment, full time and part time staff, patient/consumer mix, and procedures to be performed. Additional considerations include: interdepartmental relationships; flow of patients, visitors, staff, and supplies; confidential nature of medical and mental health services; health screenings and assessments; interactive and didactic health promotion activities; site development, including parking needs and traffic patterns; and future expansion of services and programs.

In addition to matters of appearance, infrastructure that promotes efficiency in all aspects of the operation is essential. The information age requires the application of available technology to facilitate the collection and expression of data as a means of expediting and improving the appropriateness of administrative decisions. Computer hardware and software are readily available and affordable. The successful campus health service of the future, regardless of size, will be computer-connected, both internally among its functional units and externally to programs and departments in the academic community. Information generated can be used for a variety of purposes. Computers will be used extensively to order and perform tests, record notes in the electronic medical record, order prescriptions, access medical information for diagnostic purposes and pay for services.

# FINANCING

Now that the program has been determined, the staff is in place, and a facility has been built or renovated to support the program, how much will it cost? Ideally, the needs of the program should drive or determine the budget. Rarely is this the case. Typically, someone sets the budget either through negotiation or a unilateral decision is made by an up-line administrator and the program is retooled to fit the budget. How will the program be financed? There is no uniform means of financing campus health service programs. The trend, however, is toward a separate, identifiable health fee to cover the delivery of specified services. The discussion that follows identifies the various financing schemes and the pros and cons of each.

## HEALTH FEE

The decision to establish a student health fee recognizes the distinctiveness of the campus health service program and the fact that costs of providing such services are separate from all other tuition-related benefits of the institution. On some campuses the health fee is set by a "fee committee" composed of students, faculty and staff. The health service administrator is competing for a funding level along with other groups who depend on separate student fees to support their programs. Two health fee approaches can be applied:

1.  Set the fee to cover the fixed costs of the program. The fixed costs will include primarily salaries, wages, and benefits. This method of financing establishes a funding base to guarantee coverage of the people-costs of providing the services. The balance of the budget to cover costs of operations would have to be made up by charging for services available, such as lab tests, x-rays, screenings, or physical therapy.

    **Advantages:** Places a value on health services; provides security for staff; eliminates competition for institutional funds; as the student population increases, each student pays less.

    **Disadvantages:** The Student Services Fee Committee may not value the health services program and either maintain the fee at a level that will not provide adequate support, reduce the fee, or eliminate it entirely in favor of some other form of financing; students may refuse to pay the fee if they lack confidence in the quality of the services available; requires a business operation to collect charges for services; if student population decreases, each student pays more.

2.  Set the fee to cover all the costs of the program. This method of financing is designed to cover all fixed and operations costs. The fee is set according to the total budget divided among the student body. It is a form of self-insurance that provides specified services to students regardless of how often they need them.

    **Advantages:** Eliminates the need for a business operation since all services are covered; encourages early contact with health services staff, eliminating the "I can't afford to go there" excuse; does not compete with tax or tuition monies needed to operate other areas of the campus.

**Disadvantages:** Budget may be exceeded due to unexpected increase in consumers needing services; student Services Fee Committee may arbitrarily reduce or eliminate the fee.

## FEE FOR SERVICE

Fees are set according to a predetermined level for a specified period of time and levied for services received.

**Advantages:** Non-users do not underwrite the costs of providing the services for those who use them; no institutional funds are required to support the services (except, perhaps, the costs of maintaining the facility).

**Disadvantages:** Users are penalized in the sense that they have to pay more for the services they receive than they would if all students shared in the costs of underwriting the services available; uncertainty in meeting budget is increased; non-revenue-generating services, such as health education, either do not exist or are severely limited; the competitive advantage over similar community-based services may be lost; business costs associated with collections would have to be accounted for in the fees.

## GENERAL FUND ALLOCATION

Monies needed to support the campus health service program can be taken from the general fund consisting of allocated funds such as from the state in public institutions, tuition or other resources such as gifts, grants and fund-raising.

**Advantage:** Demonstrates the institution's commitment to make health services available on campus.

**Disadvantages:** The allocation to the campus health service may be reduced if funds need to be redirected because of a shortfall in tax monies available to support higher education, fewer tuition dollars available because of a decline in enrollment, or because the campus health service is not as highly prized as other parts of the campus community; fosters adversarial relationships with other administrative units competing for the same pool of money; the nature and scope of the program is driven more by the availability of institutional finances than by the services required to meet students' basic, primary health service needs. (Restricts the administrator's ability to set the funding according to the community's need for specific student health services.)

## MANAGED CARE

Campus health service programs are potential candidates for not-for-profit or for-profit organizations to manage their care services on a contract basis. Financing for such a program can take several forms, such as a health maintenance organization that includes subscribers on a per capita basis with, perhaps, deductible or co-pay provisions in the membership arrangement. The captive student population with relatively predictable health problems makes it an attractive target group for off-campus health care organizations.

> **Advantages**: Expertise in organization and administration skills; eliminates need for institutional funds; may be connected with a larger network of health care services available to students.

> **Disadvantages**: Campus can lose control over the nature and scope of services provided; primarily medical care-related revenue generating services provided to the exclusion of non-revenue producing but necessary services involving prevention and organized, planned health education; profit motive may increase costs of services; health service personnel unavailable to advise community on matters of health or to serve on academic community committees such as campus health and safety or the Institutional Review Board; developmental needs of students may be unrecognized or ignored; commitment to the higher education community is suspect.

## COMBINATIONS OF THE ABOVE

Another option to finance the costs of providing on-campus health services is to pool the financial support from several sources. For example, the institution may regard the health service program as a facilitating resource that helps keep students attending classes and in school because it is readily accessible and encourages early intervention as a hedge against complications and higher costs of cures. The institution may, therefore, accept some of the financial responsibility to support the program by making a contribution from institutional funds up to a certain percentage of the total health service budget. The balance of the budget can then be covered by spreading the financial risk among the student body with a per capita charge or by charging fees for services to users. Part of the funding formula may also include reimbursement from health insurance claims for services provided at the campus health service.

## STUDENT HEALTH INSURANCE

Reimbursement from claims to insurance companies for services rendered students at the campus health center constitutes another means of partially funding the program. Some schools participate in the claims-filing process and accept assignment of claim checks directly from commercial insurance companies. Other schools do not provide assistance in filing claims and do not accept assignment. Rather, the schools expect to be reimbursed directly from the student for whom the services were provided and leave it to the student to file the claim for direct reimbursement from the insurance company.

Schools that participate in the selection or sponsorship of a student health insurance (SHI) program for their campus usually can arrange a simplified claims-filing procedure involving ledger billing. Students enrolled in the SHI plan who receive services covered by the plan at the student health center do not have to file a separate claim. Rather, the claim is made for them, either by the health center staff or by a health center-based SHI representative of the health insurance company, on a form specifying the services, the associated charges, and the amount to be reimbursed. These ledger billings can be done at various intervals. The company will review the claims and mail a check to the school's health center for the total amount of eligible claims in the period specified. The students involved would be notified of any uncovered charges.

SHI plans vary in their benefits and premium costs. An emerging trend is to require students to participate in a school-sponsored mandatory SHI program or provide proof of comparable coverage. Schools are concerned about protecting their investment in students on their campuses. The risk of injury or serious illness with excessive medical costs is real, and without adequate insurance protection or other means to pay for medical expenses, a student's college career could be cut short. In addition to protecting its investment, the associated benefit of using the SHI program as a vehicle to help finance the campus health service program is worth considering. There are numerous formulas that can be applied to combine a health fee with the anticipated claims associated with either a mandatory or voluntary SHI program. For example, the SHI premium and the health fee could be combined into one fee that covers specified services or the SHI premium could be separated from the health fee. Furthermore, a formula could be developed in setting the health fee based on the anticipated utilization of the services provided and the associated reimbursement from the SHI plan. The extent of service provided, size of the staff, charges for services, size of the population to be served, and the experience of students' utilization patterns are other variables that would have to be considered in setting the fees to avoid any budgetary shortfall.

Campus officials, in increasing numbers, recognize the excessive costs of medical care, the extent of risk to which students are exposed, and the need to be forthright in either recommending or requiring health insurance as a pre-matriculation requirement. Caution is advised in either approach, voluntary or mandatory. There is a lack of uniformity in the student health insurance marketplace in terms of experience ratings from one campus to another, the scope of benefits that are available, the premiums that are set, and the manner in which claims are administered and satisfied. The American College Health Association has established standards for student health insurance as recommended guidelines for colleges and universities that want to improve their prospects for a successful student health insurance program. There is no easy way to proceed through the request for proposal (RFP) and bid-letting process to select an affordable plan tailored to fit the health care needs most students have most of the time. As the health insurance industry continues to change and corporate America changes with it by curtailing dependent coverage as an employee benefit, student health insurance plans may be used more frequently as primary coverage plans.

## SUMMARY AND CONCLUSIONS

College health is an integral part of the more encompassing system of health services. In its difference lies its greatest potential as a model for the future for the nation. The unique blending of medical care, health promotion, health counseling and mental health services distinguishes college health from any other organized system of care serving the needs of our communities. Since its principal motive is not profit, college health service programs can be streamlined to provide excellent services at reasonable costs. College health is strategic. It is entry level services in terms of medical care. It has major roles to play in terms of early recognition, early intervention, primary prevention, secondary prevention, and, if necessary, referral to higher level (more costly) services that students as patients or health service consumers may require. The college health model is attracting increasing interest, especially from business and industry where corporate health service programs are being instituted to contain costs. They are hiring their own physicians, nurses and allied health staff including health educators to help their employees manage their acute care and wellness needs. Cost savings may be the motive but in the process they are experiencing more productive employees, which enhances the corporate bottom line. Likewise, the college health service program serves as a special resource to the higher education community. It serves as a magnet in recruitment efforts to attract students to a school that respects the need for quality health services at reasonable costs when they are needed. Parents, in particular, are concerned about their sons' and daughters' access to medical care and want to know how the school is addressing the health problems endemic to the college-age population, namely substance abuse (alcohol and other drugs), sex (STDs including AIDS, contraception), and nutrition (obesity, over/underweight, eating disorders). Just as business and industry are concerned about reducing medical care costs and enhancing their profit margin, colleges and universities are concerned about retaining their students and helping them fulfil their academic and life goals. To do so requires a well-conceived program that has the full support and appreciation of campus officials.

# 8

# Standards, Quality Assurance, and Quality of Care in College Health

DAVID P. KRAFT, MD

The first U.S. college health program was established at Amherst College in the 1860s.[1] By 1988, an estimated 1,500 of the 3,400 U.S. institutions of higher education provided some form of direct health care for students.[2] As more colleges assumed responsibility for student health care, mechanisms were needed to assure that such health care was of high quality.

Prior to 1960, many colleges organized "visiting committees" to review periodically and help improve college health services.[3] In 1964, the American College Health Association (ACHA) published Recommended Standards and Practices for a College Health Program,[4] which became the basis for more formal evaluation and certification efforts. Finally by 1979, two different accreditation associations had been established that would evaluate college health services using the same standards of care applied to other ambulatory health care organizations, including peer review and quality assurance activities.

University health programs and services present unique challenges to the evaluation of quality of care efforts. College health services strongly emphasize education and prevention as well as treatment services. Certain college health programs also help maintain a safe and healthy campus environment. Finally, the delivery of confidential, high-quality health care for students through college health programs must take precedence over the primary educational or research goals of the institution.

## ACHA STANDARDS DEFINE HIGH-QUALITY CARE

The 1964 Recommended Standards and Practices for a College Health Program described various aspects of a comprehensive college health service. The Standards, as revised in 1969, outline an "ideal" health service comprised of 20 programs, services, and support functions, including medical, nursing, mental health, athletic medicine, dental, health education, and environmental health and safety services.[4] Further revisions in 1977 and 1984 strengthened certain sections judged important to the delivery of college health services.[5] During 1991, the ACHA published a completely revised set of Recommended Standards...(5th edition) that conforms more closely to the format of existing accreditation manuals (see Appendix A).[6] The ACHA documents include the following areas:

1.  **Clinical Care Services.** Primary clinical care services usually include the use of nurse practitioners and physicians' assistants, in addition to primary care physicians (chiefly family practitioners and internists). A basic primary care program provides acute care services during week-day hours, with limited or no on-campus evening and weekend availability.

    After-hours' services are often referred to neighboring health care facilities, such as hospital emergency rooms. Medical specialty services are referred to physicians in the community by most college health services, although larger college health programs may provide some specialty medical care on-campus.

    In-patient or "infirmary" care is still provided by some larger institutions, or smaller institutions in rural settings. However, most clinical problems presented by students can be treated on an ambulatory basis so that few schools continue to offer on-campus in-patient care.

2.  **Mental Health Services.** Sound emotional health is as important to the college student and his/her success as medical care services. Up to 10 to 15 percent of students seek professional mental health assistance each year because of emotional difficulties, either through the college's mental health or counseling services or from mental health providers in the surrounding community. Emergency mental health services are increasingly important to most campuses, especially for students who become acutely disturbed or suicidal.

3.  **Support Services.** College health programs may have a variety of services supporting clinical efforts. Health records are maintained in a manner that safeguards the confidentiality of personal health information. Laboratory services range from minor in-office tests only to fully accredited on-campus laboratory facilities, using established standards of quality control. Radiology services range from referrals to off-campus facilities to comprehensive, certified on-campus services. Pharmacy services range from practitioner-distributed "starter supplies" of antibiotics or pain medication, to licensed, comprehensive on-campus pharmacies.

4.  **Special Services.** Most colleges provide some additional specialized services or programs. Sports Medicine Programs medically supervise physical education and sports activities, helping to prevent and treat acute injuries. Dental programs on some campuses include emergency care as well as prevention and education services. Health Promotion and Community Health Education programs offer expanded prevention and education services outside of, as well as within, health service facilities, often with assistance from student "peer educators."

Preventive Medicine programs emphasize immunization requirements and public health surveillance, including periodic screening. Occupational Health services minimize distress and disruption of faculty and staff due to illness and adverse environmental factors. Environmental Health and Safety Services combine on-campus and community services in such areas as water, food and facility sanitation; fire protection; physical, chemical, biological and radiation safety protection; and hazardous waste disposal.

5.  **Ethical and Professional Relationships**. A number of ethical and professional issues arise when providing care to college students. Confidentiality practices maintain the privacy of student health care information from college faculty and staff, except in extreme "need to know" situations. Admissions health information is required in order to determine health status and to maintain adequate immunization levels with all students. The college health service protects student-patients from use as research subjects unless participation is voluntary and with informed consent. Health excuse policies at most colleges require students to be responsible for meeting academic performance standards, except in extreme circumstance, when prolonged hospitalization or unexpected illness will be verified by the college health service after informed consent.

The ACHA Recommended Standards defines the characteristics of an ideal campus program for large and small colleges alike. The Recommended Standards defines what services the college or university needs to provide as an institution, without specifying how to provide each service. For example, a small college that employs a nurse practitioner to provide limited on-campus evaluation and treatment of acute problems would need to arrange adequate referral and emergency mechanisms off-campus to protect its students adequately. Appendix A presents the outline of chapter headings from the 1991 version of The Recommended Standards for a College Health Program,[6] to give some idea of the scope of topics covered.

# JCAHO AND AAAHC ACCREDITATION STANDARDS

Although accreditation standards for hospital services were established in 1951 by the Joint Commission on Accreditation of Hospitals (JCAH), standards for the accreditation of ambulatory health care services were not published until about two years later. In 1978, the Accreditation Council for Ambulatory Health Care (ACAHC) of JCAH published the first Accreditation Manual for Ambulatory Health Care (renamed The Ambulatory Health Care Standards Manual shortly thereafter).[7] In 1979, the Accreditation Association for Ambulatory Health Care (AAAHC) was formed by seven organizations, including the ACHA, and published the Accreditation Handbook for Ambulatory Health Care.[8] Both the JCAH and AAAHC manuals describe standards for organizations that provide ambulatory health care services, and are used as the basis of peer evaluation of services. Standards are written in general terms, so that they can be applied in a variety of ambulatory care settings, including health maintenance organizations, medical group practices, and ambulatory surgery centers, as well as college health services.

Accreditation standards define areas of practice that apply to outpatient settings. Many of the chapters are similar to the ACHA Recommended Standards but are more generally applicable to all types of health care settings (see Appendices B and C). Initial chapters focus on the rights of patients, governance, and administration. Quality of care issues include: accurate definition of services offered, regular credentialing of staff, and provision of timely and accurate clinical records. A separate chapter focuses on the quality assurance process, including regular monitoring and special studies with follow-up.

Separate chapters define surgical and anesthesia services, pharmaceutical, laboratory, and radiology services, which may apply only to some college health programs. General chapters give attention to professional education, research, teaching and publication services. Finally, a detailed section on facilities helps to evaluate the adequacy of the health service physical environment.

An accreditation survey generally involves a team of two or three surveyors who review materials describing the health service and then visit the site for one to three days. Organizations meeting published standards are accredited for up to three years, although organizations that only partially comply in major areas are given a six-month deferral or a one-year accreditation. Non-compliant areas must be improved by the time of the next survey. Standards failed by many college health services include clinical records and quality assurance.

The strength of the accreditation process is the review of activities of the organization by "peer" professionals, which can apply even to a nurse-directed health service on a small college campus. The chief weakness of accreditation is the limited emphasis on non-clinical activities, especially areas of health promotion, health education, environmental health, occupational health, and college institutional relationships.[9]

## QUALITY ASSURANCE ACTIVITIES

One mechanism to improve health care involves quality assurance (QA) activities. QA relies heavily on peer review mechanisms to identify clinical problems, assess the magnitude and type of problems, develop standards of care in such areas, institute corrective actions, and reassess the success of changes. Chart audits have been a typical mechanism to study clinical problems. For example, chart audits have been used to study: legible and complete chart entries; follow-up of abnormal

Pap tests; routine charting of vital signs; diagnosis and treatment of common problems, such as pharyngitis, urinary tract infections, sexually transmitted diseases, and alcohol/drug abuse problems; receipt of consultation reports following off-campus referrals; and follow-up of referrals to emergency facilities. Summary statistical data on patient visits may also be used to identify problems, design QA activities and evaluate the results of changes instituted. High-cost services have also been analyzed by QA programs to determine their clinical benefits or necessity.

Recent advances in quality assurance programs have included on-going monitoring activities to spot potential problems and develop interventions before formal studies are needed. For example, patient complaints, adverse medication reactions, or emergency referrals off-campus are reviewed concurrently to help identify potential or actual problems that need to be evaluated by the QA committee.

Quality Assurance programs have generally been dominated by physicians and other independent health care professionals, with the assumption that "bad clinical practices" or "poor practitioners" produce poor quality care. Recent reviews of these issues[10-15] have emphasized models borrowed from industrial settings, and have been influenced by concepts developed by W. Edwards Deming and Joseph M. Juran. Studies suggest that only 15 percent of poor quality comes from the performance of people while 85 percent comes from poor systems or management of those systems. The evaluation of health care quality is moving away from quality assurance as an activity of health professionals using fixed standards of care to identify "poor performers," toward Quality Improvement as an activity of the health care team, seeking to improve health care practices by continuously using data to eliminate waste, rework and complexity. The focus of quality improvement is on the average producer, not the "outlier," and on learning, not blaming.

Many college health services have used an integrated health team approach to student health care for years, chiefly because they have had to rely upon the limited funding of essentially prepaid ("free") services, with limited staff time from physicians. As a result, current trends in health care in the United States toward quality improvement and managed care approaches will be adapted and assimilated readily by many college health services.

# UNIQUE CHALLENGES FOR UNIVERSITY HEALTH PROGRAMS

The college health service must maintain confidential practitioner-patient relationships, to avoid the reputation of being the "last place to go" if a student needs help but does not want college officials to know of sensitive problems (i.e., unwanted pregnancies, suicidal ideation, and problems with drinking or drugs).

A college health service located on a medical school campus needs to provide confidential, personal health care services for all students, including medical and nursing students, even if it means limiting use of the health service as a training ground for medical and nursing students. As a result, better services separate the reporting relationship of the college health service from the clinical departments of the medical and/or nursing schools.

The college health service provides an excellent opportunity to increase prevention and early intervention efforts with students. College health service staff can augment a student's education by explaining what health care is indicated and by giving the student opportunities to learn more about his/her health care. Health education efforts can also involve students before they seek clinical care, especially in residence halls and other locations outside the health services, using residence assistants and student peer educators. The challenge for college health is not only to maintain high quality standards of care, consistent with general medical community standards, but also to enhance the general educational enterprise of the institution.

# REFERENCES

1. Dalrymple W, Purcell EF (eds): Campus Health Programs. New York, Josiah Macy, Jr. Foundation, 1976

2. Patrick K: Student health: Medical care within institutions of higher education. JAMA 260:3301, 1988

3. Farnsworth DL (ed): College Health Administration. New York, Meredith Publishing Co, 1964

4. American College Health Association: Recommended Standards and Practices for a College Health Program (including a statement on ethical and professional relationships). Evanston, IL, American College Health Association, 1964

5. Recommended Standards and Practices for a College Health Program (4th ed). J Am Coll Health 32:135, 1984

6. American College Health Association: Recommended Standards for a College Health Program (5th ed). Rockville, MD, ACHA, 1991

7. JCAHO: Ambulatory Health Care Standards Manual, 1988. Chicago, Joint Commission on Accreditation of Health Care Organizations, 1987

8. Accreditation Handbook for Ambulatory Health Care, 1989-90 Edition. Skokie, IL, Accreditation Association for Ambulatory Health Care, 1989

9.  Kraft DP: Quality of care and the accreditation of health services: What is the relationship? J Am Coll Health 37:109, 1989

10. Berwick DM: Continuous improvement as an ideal in health care. N Engl J Med 320: 53, 1989

11. Berwick DM: Peer review and quality management: Are they compatible? Qual Rev Bull 16: 246, 1990

12. Bliersbach CM: Quality assurance in health care: Current challenges and future directions. Qual Rev Bull 14: 315,1988

13. Gottlieb LK, Margolis CZ, Schoenbaum SC: Clinical practice guidelines at an HMO: Development and implementation in a quality improvement model. Qual Rev Bull 16: 80, 1990

14. Laffel G, Blumenthal D: The case for using industrial quality management science in health care organizations. JAMA 262:2869-2873, 1989

15. Merry MD: Total quality management for physicians: Translating the new paradigm. Qual Rev Bull  16: 101, 1990

## RECOMMENDED READING

Batalden PB, O'Connor JP: Quality Assurance in Ambulatory Care. Germantown, MD, Aspen Systems Corp, 1980

Berwick DM: Continuous improvement as an ideal in health care. N Engl J Med 320: 53, 1989

Donabedian A: Explorations in Quality Assessment and Monitoring, Volume I: The Definition of Quality and Approaches to Its Assessment. Ann Arbor, MI, Health Administration Press, 1980

Donabedian A: Explorations in Quality Assessment and Monitoring, Volume II: The Criteria and Standards of Quality. Ann Arbor, MI, Health Administration Press, 1982

Gottlieb LK, Margolis CZ, Schoenbaum SC: Clinical practice guidelines at an HMO: Development and implementation in a quality improvement model. Qual Rev Bull 16: 80, 1990

Kraft DP: Quality of care and the accreditation of health services: What is the relationship? J Am Coll Health 37:109, 1988

Laffel G, Blumenthal D: The case for using industrial quality management science in health care organizations. JAMA 262: 2869, 1989

McBride TC: Making quality assessment work for you - not against you. J Am Coll Health 30:230, 1982

## APPENDIX A

### Table of Contents of *ACHA Recommended Standards for a College Health Program*, 1991 (ACHA 1991)

Introduction

Table of Contents

Section A. General Characteristics
Introduction
Windows of Opportunity
1. Community Responsibility—Health Service Roles
2. Issues in Ethics
3. Patient and Provider—Shared Responsibilities
4. Student Participation/Relations
5. Sexuality Education, Counseling, and Health
6. Mental Health, Counseling, and Psychotherapy Services
7. College Health Clinicians
8. Support Staff
9. Dental Health
10. Athletic, Sports, and Recreational Medicine
11. Physically Challenged Patients
Conclusion

Section B. Generic Standards
Introduction
12. Rights and Responsibilities of Patients
13. Governance
14. Administration
15. Institutional Relationships
16. Health Promotion, Health Protection, and Disease Prevention Services
17. Quality of Care Provided
18. Quality Assurance Program
19. Health Records
20. Health Education
21. Professional Development
22. Facilities and Environment
23. Immediate/Urgent Care Services
24. Other Professional and Technical Services

Section C. Specific Standards
Introduction
25. Pharmaceutical Services
26. Laboratory Services
27. Diagnostic & Therapeutic Imaging Services
28. Emergency Services
29. Surgical and Anesthesia Services
30. Inpatient/Infirmary Services

31.   Environmental Health and Safety
32.   Occupational Health Services
33.   Teaching and Publication Activities
34.   Research Activities

Glossary of Selected Terms
Appendix A – References to AAAHC and JCAHO Standards

## APPENDIX B

### Table of Contents of *Accreditation Handbook for Ambulatory Health Care*, 1989-90 EDITION (AAAHC, 1989)

**Accreditation Policies and Procedures**

Consultation Services
Eligibility for Survey
Purpose and Application of the Standards
Survey Process
Transfer of Accreditation
Public Recognition
Confidentiality

**Core Standards**

1.   Rights of Patients
2.   Governance
3.   Administration
4.   Quality of Care Provided
5.   Quality Assurance Program
6.   Clinical Records
7.   Professional Improvement
8.   Facilities and Environment

**Adjunct Standards**

9.   Anesthesia Services
10.   Surgical Services
11.   Overnight Care and Services
12.   Dental Services
13.   Emergency Services
14.   Immediate/Urgent Care Services
15.   Pharmaceutical Services
16.   Pathology and Medical Laboratory Services
17.   Diagnostic and Therapeutic Imaging Services
18.   Occupational Health Services
19.   Other Professional and Technical Services
20.   Teaching and Publication Activities
21.   Research Activities

Appendices

    A. Revisions to Standards Since the 1987-88 Edition
    B. Appeal of Accreditation Decision
    C. Supplemental Checklist for Ambulatory Surgery
    D. Risk Management
    E. Quality Assurance Program Analysis
    F. Clinical Record Worksheet
    G. History of the Accreditation Association for Ambulatory Health Care, Inc.

## APPENDIX C

### Table of Contents of *Ambulatory Health Care Standards Manual,* 1988 (JCAHO, 1987)

Using the Manual
General Administrative Policies and Procedures

Standards

    1. Quality Assurance (QA)
    2. Quality of Care (QC)
    3. Medical Records (MR)
    4. Rights and Responsibilities of Patients (RP)
    5. Governing Body (GB)
    6. Administration (AD)
    7. Plant, Technology and Safety Management (PT)
    8. Educational Activities (EA)
    9. Surgical and Anesthesia Services (SA)
  10. Pharmaceutical Services (PS)
  11. Laboratory Services and Pathology (LP)
  12. Radiology Services (RS)
  13. Emergency Services (ES)
  14. Infirmary (IN)
  15. Teaching and Publication Activities (TP)
  16. Research Activities (RA)

Appendices

    A. Revisions since the 1986 Edition
    B. Accreditation and Appeal Procedures
    C. Surveyor Materials

Glossary
Index

# Section II

# Problems of Unique Importance in College Health

# 9

# Alcohol on the College Campus

## W. DAVID BURNS

A white male physician working in college health described the following encounter with a patient:

> A 20-year-old, Christian, American-born white male came to the clinic one Friday morning with two injured hands—both were badly bruised and swollen. In response to the questions "What happened?" and "How did your hands get this way?" the student somewhat sheepishly reported that he had gotten "mad and punched a wall during a card game." The clinician asked if he had punched it with both hands. The student replied "no," he had hit the wall first with one fist and then later, when he was angry about something else, he had punched it with his other fist. The clinician then inquired, "Were you drinking?" The student responded, again somewhat sheepishly, "Yes." Then the physician reported telling/asking the patient, "That wasn't very smart, was it?!" Again, the student nodded in agreement.

The clinician then described the advice he gave to his patient for getting some relief from the pain in his hands.

The clinician did not follow up on the drinking part of this incident by taking a more detailed history, inquiring about prior injuries or incidents, or eliciting a sense from the patient as to how he felt or thought about the incident. The clinician reported feeling pressed for time – there were other patients waiting. More significant, however, is how the clinician appraised the seriousness of the incident. He reported that he did not really think that patient needed any further investigation or intervention. After all, he said that what the patient reported "wasn't **that** unusual." The clinician described having seen a lot of injuries of this same general etiology, which is exactly why he thought to ask the patient, "Were you drinking?"

## SKILLS AND NORMS

This story illustrates, for those practicing in college health, what we now are coming to know about prevention, in general. We used to think that, in order to

589

prevent disease or achieve a desired health outcome, we needed to concentrate on education about the disease, its causes and what prevents it from happening or lessens its subsequent effect on the patient. Yet, we all know examples of students who know that drinking alcohol, even in quantities that they would consider moderate, impairs judgment. Nevertheless, these students drink to the point of impairment and claim that they will still know "when to say when." Knowledge does not necessarily, or even often, translate into some direct action: In the words of Richard Keeling, "We often do not do what we know."

In the place of knowledge, by itself, we are coming to believe that what will affect alcohol use – and, by extension, what will improve the capacity of those in student health who are charged with dealing with it – boils down to two things: improving skills and having a clear idea about social norms.

To illustrate this point, let's return to the story that begins this essay. At first glance, the report reveals less than optimal history-taking – one of the most important skills a clinician needs. While it was good that the clinician thought to ask about alcohol, the value of the inquiry was diminished when the clinician essentially told his patient that what he did "wasn't very smart." In doing so, he was, of course, judging the behavior, and he was expressing his sense of a norm. But, by not really finding out what happened or why, the clinician missed a chance to engage with the patient and pursue a question about how "normal" it was for the patient to injure both hands in a drinking episode. (There is also present in this exchange another "norm": that someone is capable of being a "smart drunk." This is opposed to something resembling a fact: that given certain quantities of alcohol consumed, no matter how smart you are, you can wind up getting hurt.) By this time in the encounter, the student was already on the defensive and, now, to escape from the accusation that he had not been very smart, the student would have had to embrace the embarrassing position of arguing that punching the wall was evidence of his own good judgment. To another observer, it seems entirely possible that punching a wall, as opposed to punching a person, was the smart (or at least, preferable) thing to do, if you had to punch something. That judgment, though, is also beside the point.

In this example, the presence of alcohol serves to explain, and ironically also to explain away, the behavior (after all, you wouldn't hit a wall if you were sober). In a twisted way, it becomes "normal" for a drunk person to do something that is not "very smart." The clinician described this drinking (and his estimation that the student was drunk) as certainly not unusual but somehow "normal" – stupid, but normal. Given his sense of how normal the behavior was and the press of other business, the encounter ended and the contributing behavior and perhaps, even, the underlying problem that led to the behavior and the injury – excessive drinking –

went unexamined and untreated. The student got help for his hands, but no attention was paid to his drinking. What was left of this encounter in the records of the clinic would probably have been a "contusion," or "hand trauma," or "accidental injury." Alcohol, the not-so-silent partner in this event, most likely did not show up on the record of that clinician's day's work. A chance to make a difference in the student's life was lost. The best practice should lead in a different direction: The presence of alcohol should serve as a point of departure for further investigation.

## ALCOHOL ON CAMPUS

Alcohol, as the common expression has it, is a drug. Indeed, on college campuses, it is the drug of choice. Alcohol is marketed to college students as a "specific" remedy for a range of conditions college students commonly report having: loneliness, fear of rejection, desire to be popular, stress, impostor anxiety, worries about the future, concern about appearance, sexiness, depression, over-work, and being under-appreciated. The manufacturers' claims about alcohol's magical properties – and indeed, the testimony from some of its most ardent users – tells us that alcohol helps you make friends, it increases your chances of having sex, it makes you more attractive, it loosens you up, it rewards you for the hard work that you do that no one seems to care about, it gives you a sense of security, it makes you feel no pain, it tastes great, and it gives you an excuse for doing something that you might not have had the courage to do if you did not have the help that the drug provides. As a drug, it is relatively pure, is commonly available (without a prescription), can be purchased cheaply, has relatively predictable and short-term effects, and, since it is self-administered (at least some of the time) it can be dose-adjusted to fit a particular need (or, when it is administered to others, to achieve a desired result). Even though it is illegal for underage students to purchase it, alcohol is commonly available and most parents would rather that it be used than any other drug around.

From a health perspective, alcohol use to the point of impairing judgment or producing intoxication is probably the single most important factor in the undoing of several critical health practices that lead to significant risks of morbidity and mortality. You will find alcohol at the intersection of virtually every collision between prevention and risk-taking behavior from seat belt use to condom use. Alcohol use, because of its prevalence on college campuses, demands the attention of anyone who seeks to have an impact on reducing a whole range of common conditions that lead us to practice college health. Failure to pay attention to alcohol use on college campuses will undermine most of the outcomes desired from the practice of college health.

## INCIDENCE AND PREVALENCE

Alcohol use and abuse on college campuses has been described in many studies. It is estimated that some 90 percent of college students drink at one time or another, and that a very substantial proportion – probably much more than half of white male college students – drink to the point of potential intoxication at least once every other week. (Heavy drinking in most studies is defined as five or more drinks on any one occasion. For many college students, this "standard" of heavy drinking would not even qualify as their notion of moderate drinking, which is just one more illustration of the problem with "norms.") A good deal of drinking in college is heavy drinking in party settings, with drinking to intoxication as an expected norm of behavior. While a significant proportion of college students essentially abstain from drinking, about four times as many college students would qualify as heavy drinkers, as compared to the population at large and its drinking patterns. Even though the weekend drinking, which now seems to begin on Thursday nights, describes "campus culture," a good deal of the drinking by college students resembles the binge drinking of adult alcoholics.

## THE NATURE OF THE RISKS

From an epidemiologic perspective, the amount and pattern of consumption of alcohol is sufficient to suggest that there are two major risks to college students, their friends and those with whom they come into contact:

1. Acute risks - these embrace a set of immediate consequences that come with or result from alcohol consumption to the point of impairment or intoxication, including alcohol poisoning, accidents, injuries, unwanted pregnancies, sexually transmitted diseases, regretted sex, acquaintance rape, embarrassment, missed obligations, damaged reputation, disciplinary or legal consequences, and a range of injuries to others; and,

2. Chronic risks - these embrace a set of long-term consequences that come from persistent and continuing use of alcohol at quantities that result in damage to the vital organs of the body and produce patterns of behavior that damage the drinker's capacity to sustain relationships, obligations to work and community, and lead to premature mortality. These risks are commonly described in connection with addiction.

This distinction, between acute risks and chronic risks, is helpful to a point, but it can interfere with the effective practice of college health if the clinician remains stuck in thinking that alcoholism is the chief risk of drinking. Alcoholic drinking and heavy drinking carry the same short-term, acute risks. It probably matters very little to the victim that she was sexually assaulted by someone who was drunk for the first time or by someone who had been drinking alcoholically for a long time. This will matter, however, in the treatment and disposition of individual cases, once a good history is taken.

## PRINCIPLES AND PRACTICES: WHAT SHOULD WE BE DOING?

The first principle applying to college health and alcohol is the same principle that would seem to be applicable to all that we do: We need to be engaged with our patients and help them with their lives. How can this be done?

Following a public health model, the Task Force on Alcohol and Other Drugs of the American College Health Association has suggested a series of practices that apply to acute and chronic risks at primary, secondary, and tertiary levels of prevention.[1] These standards emphasize, among other things, learning about the incidence and prevalence of alcohol use among your students, developing good skills at history taking and referral, intervening to adjust the environment that influences drinking, and making inquiries about alcohol use a relatively routine dimension of general care.

The clinical management of students with alcohol problems or problems related to alcohol is an area too large to cover in this brief essay. Fortunately, Jean Kinney and Phillip Meilman have given a very good, comprehensive introduction to alcohol issues within the college health clinical setting in their article, Alcohol Use and Alcohol Problems: Clinical Approaches for the College Health Service.[2] The article contains an excellent series of references for further reading that will help clinicians who want to increase their skills and capacity. Among other things, Kinney and Meilman describe a variety of screening methods to use in history taking (including CAGE, Brief MAST, and the Trauma Scale; the latter, if used in conjunction with additional questions, would have helped the clinical encounter described in the opening story.) In brief, trauma secondary to drinking is a significant indicator of an alcohol problem that should have merited additional inquiry.

Given the widespread use of alcohol at levels that impair judgment or have toxic effects, it seems fair to recommend that virtually all clinical encounters in a college health service should include some questions about alcohol use, not just use by the patient but of those whose lives touch the patient in significant ways (e.g., sexual partners, parents, siblings, roommates, and so forth). Once this information is known, it is important to have a plan to evaluate what it means. This evaluation will require several things.

To be effective, the clinician will need to:

1.  **Develop a clear sense of what is "normal" and what needs further attention and intervention.** What may have kept the clinician in our story from going any further in his encounter with our patient was the clinician's sense that nothing was really out of the ordinary in the picture presented by the patient. In fact, the clinician might have engaged in similar behavior when he was a college student (hence the point of noting the gender and race of the clinician, along with the other obvious similarity: both had college experience). The sense of what is "within normal range" will vary from clinician to clinician. If you concentrate on the outcomes you desire from your encounter with the patient, then heavy drinking that impairs judgment will merit your increased attention because it interferes with so many of the other goals you may have for your patient. For example, if you want your patient to do well academically, blackouts and binge drinking won't help achieve that goal. If you want to help your patient practice safer sex, then you need to know that drinking interferes with condom use.

    You can begin to understand norms for your campus by asking students what they think heavy drinking or dangerous drinking is. You can also look at the vast literature on college drinking that will give you a sense of what is happening on the campuses where drinking has been studied. How different do you think your campus is, and why? You will also need to pay attention to differences in gender and culture, and to those at some special risk: members of organizations that have exaggerated drinking norms (like many fraternities and some athletic teams); children of alcoholics; and gay, lesbian, and bisexual students.

2.  **Listen carefully to the patient, ask questions and do not hesitate to give your patient your evaluation of his/her drinking behavior.** Our clinician was not exhibiting good listening skills. He didn't ask many questions, and he didn't hesitate to give his judgment, but he failed to give an evaluation of what was happening. It would have helped if he had followed this advice. In spite of what we know and will later say about denial, students do seem willing to talk about their behavior. They may be wondering just as you are, if their behavior is "normal." This interest in some external measure, "Am I all right?," is what is contained in the CAGE question: "Have you ever been concerned about your drinking?"

    Such discussion may make a positive difference in the patient's life. There is at least one study that reports that 29 percent of students said "they changed their drinking behavior" as a result of having a physician discuss the consequences of that behavior with them. The unfortunate part of the study's results is that only 15 percent of students were ever asked about their drinking to begin with.[3]

People seem to want to believe that what they are doing is pretty much what everybody else is doing. When they learn that their behavior is out of the ordinary – or not what they think everybody else is doing – it can change what they do. Promising work suggests that students overestimate the amount of heavy drinking others do.[4,5] When they get the facts, they can be expected to bring their own behavior back away from the misperceived norm. The clinician's evaluation can help with that process.

3.   Get beyond a social/moral construction of drinking to something that accounts for its risks and its potential toxicity. Excessive drinking seen as some necessary dimension of adolescent development is a particularly dangerous myth. And, despite what some would say, drinking is not a sign of some moral defect or shortcoming. It may not be smart, but lots of smart people do it.

What if our clinician had developed a little better picture of his patient? If he had, he would have been better able to predict future problems, and trace any issues from past episodes, if there had been any (and there is a great likelihood that there were). He would have been able to help the patient.

The degree to which we have such confused and ambivalent attitudes about alcohol is remarkable. If a student came to the health center and reported drinking something poisonous at what could be toxic levels, it is highly unlikely that the appropriate treatment would be to advise "sleeping it off." Yet, we do not often think of alcohol intoxication as "poisoning." We use a more value-laden name when we say someone is "drunk" – or "wrecked" or "trashed" as the students say. The social construction of inebriation prevents us from engaging in optimal treatment.

4.   Understand denial and learn how to deal with it. We do not know enough about the encounter to tell just who may be in denial in our story: the patient, the clinician, or both. Denial is a tough subject, but to understand it we need to see how what we hope might be the case (that our patient is really all right) might be part of the patient's agenda as well (that he or she hopes we think everything is fine). Accomplished drinkers have accomplished skills at arranging their lives to keep drinking from interfering with what they have to do (recall the weekend drinker, or the student who manages to schedule classes to avoid certain morning obligations). Sometimes there will even be convincing external signs of success (good grades, athletic prowess, apparently successful relationships). In other cases, highly elaborated defenses will resist penetration. The patient might genuinely believe that everything is all right.

Clinicians, too, may be part of the denial – preferring to believe that all is well or that what they are seeing is just a transient episode. Those responsible for colleges and universities as institutions may also be disinclined to face the consequences attending to a conclusion that their campus has an "alcohol problem." The thoughts of parents and friends will often trace similar patterns.

To overcome denial, good history taking is essential and there are several techniques that can work, including making an arrangement with the student to get back to you if something that the student believes is an isolated event re-occurs. Again, confronting the student with your findings and evaluations in a helpful way may assist in the student's coming to terms with a problem. If you can arrange it, getting a patient into a group can be helpful: Not only will the student come to see the possibility that there is help but that others are in similar circumstances.

A health service can assist in dealing with institutional denial by providing anonymous information gleaned from clinical encounters to campus officials along with other surveillance data obtained from systematic survey research or generalizable anecdotal information. Vern Johnson's classic book, I'll Quit Tomorrow, should help any clinician come to understand denial in a way that will help clinically.[6]

5. **Coordinate what you do with health education and health promotion efforts and help the patient make the connection between drinking and other outcomes desired by the student.** Alcohol use on the college campus is a cultural phenomenon; that is, much energy has been expended connecting drinking with being a college student. Successful interventions will require a cultural/environmental dimension as well.

The clinician in our story was able to disconnect drinking from his treatment of the patient. He never reached for an educational opportunity, nor did he explore the context of the drinking.

A student health program should have a health promotion dimension that emphasizes, in addition to knowledge about alcohol, skills needed to reduce risks and harm. These include skills to avoid peer pressure (to increase resistance and resiliency), skills in negotiation and conflict resolution, and skills at improving one's sense of self. Linking to these programs offers clinicians the opportunity to magnify the effects of their encounter with patients and connect patients to some of the larger issues in life. Of course, for the alcoholic student, a course in assertiveness training may just make for a less angry but more assertive drunk. Such students will require referral to more specialized treatment.

6. **Know what resources (services, specialists, clinics, self-help groups) are available to your patient and know how to make effective referrals.** Good principles and practices entail knowing what services are available on campus, in the community, and beyond, and having sufficient familiarity and confidence in those resources to make an effective referral.

The most obvious source of free help is Alcoholics Anonymous. Ironically, outside its membership AA seems shrouded in mystery; however, it is easy to clear up that mystery. Every clinician in college health should attend an open

AA meeting, just to get a sense of it. Colleges should invite AA to meet on campus and clinicians should make arrangements for students in AA to sponsor other students in the program. Bruce Donovan has written a wonderful essay that de-codes AA for physicians.[7]

On-campus resources need to be identified, but care should be taken to insure that these services are capable of seeing the alcohol use as a primary problem, if it is. It does little good to get an alcoholic enrolled in a time-management program, where referral to someone for a more appropriate therapy is indicated. In the event that a patient needs intensive, in-patient treatment, the optimal service will include a referral to a program of high quality with effective arrangements for aftercare.

Making successful referrals is an art in itself. Part of what makes a referral work is the relationship between the clinician and the patient and the match between the patient and provider to which he or she is referred.  It is helpful to be able to let a patient know that you know the quality of the person or place that you think will help them, and your authority – and chances for success – will be enhanced if you can vouch for the quality of your suggestion.

It is important to know that to have a program of high quality does not require that all services be offered by your health service. To have quality, you need to know how to identify problems, gain the confidence of your patient, and make a successful referral.

7.  **Feel confident that you can help the student to make a difference in his/her life.** Your work matters. Again, this last piece of advice has a general applicability. If you know what is happening with patients and have the ability to enter the patient's world, you can and will make a difference in the life of your patient. Your confidence – and the ease with which you handle complicated problems and topics – will help your patient get better. Effective work with alcohol, as with other topics, can start with a searching self-examination ("How do I feel and what do I think about drinking?").  It can then be enhanced by reading and research. It will be informed by the clinical experience you gain in trying to make a difference. Lastly, there are people to whom you can turn for help.

# WHAT IS KEEPING THINGS FROM GETTING BETTER?

To sum up this brief discussion of alcohol as an issue in college health, it is worth considering why more is not being done, and to identify some of the impediments to success and what can be done about them.  Here are a few things to think about.

## TIME, TALENT, AND THE TERROR OF THE "YES" ANSWER

Pressed for time and lacking the confidence and capacity to handle the possible range of answers that a question might elicit, clinicians might exhibit what can be called "the terror of the 'yes' answer." It makes one's job harder to go beyond the obvious – the bruised hands, in our example – to a line of questions that will take time and to answers to them that will require engagement with the patient. If you have just asked a patient about incest, and you learn that her father did try to have sex with her once, your next question can not be, "How do you think the weather will be tomorrow?" or "Who's going to win the Super Bowl this year?" Your natural inclination might be to avoid the subject altogether. This may seem like an efficiency consideration. After all, there are patients waiting to see you.

The answer is not simple, but it is obvious. If you are committed to making a difference in the lives of your patients – and in the quality of life on the campus and beyond – you will have to develop the skills to ask the question and deal with the answer. And you will need to schedule another appointment with the patient, or juggle your next patient, to make the time to do it right.

This "terror" is real, however, and may be related to other factors that will be discussed here. What we find is that such a terror is present, especially in those who know how to ask the questions, because they are the ones who are most likely and most inclined to get themselves into a situation where once receiving the "yes" answer, they then feel and take on an obligation to do something about what that answer means.

## ALCOHOL ABUSE IS JUST A TRANSIENT PROBLEM THAT STUDENTS NEED TO LIVE THROUGH

Another major impediment is the belief that alcohol use and abuse is essentially a transient problem, with a cure that consists of living long enough to get through the risky period of adolescence. This belief comes from some relatively well-supported evidence, which suggests that the abusive drinking going on in college does not lead, in most cases, to chronic alcoholism. But, of course, the defect in this thinking is that it connects drinking to only one kind of problem, namely the chronic problem of alcohol abuse or addiction. It is a mistake to use a statistical determinant, such as the low probability of someone's drinking becoming alcoholic or non-alcoholic, as a reason to refrain from intervention. After all, it is an individual who is being treated. But the larger mistake in this thinking is that somehow the task of the clinician is to simply help the student live through this period of *Sturm und Drang* to emerge later as some adult who will not have the stress, or situational, or age-determined excessive drinking that seems to be the case in college. The most significant threats of acute injury, or infliction of injury to one's self or others, are the reason why one cannot reasonably take the position that the unlikelihood of alcoholism is a reason for refraining from intervention today. There are too many risks to take that chance.

## THE PROBLEM IS INTRACTABLE

A third impediment to better care is the belief that alcohol use among college students is so entrenched that it is essentially an intractable issue. No matter how fiercely one is devoted to solving the problem, it will make no difference. This is essentially an argument that sees abuse as inevitable and not amenable to any special intervention or change. There is a certain power to this argument because, among other things, it allows one to preserve the status quo. And in so doing, it reduces the call on any one of us to be actively engaged.

The problem with this argument is that it is false – and dangerous. We know that treatment for students can work and that early intervention makes a difference. We also know that our missions cause us to take an interest in preventable disease and avoidable problems that lead to loss of academic productivity. Most important, we would never say the same thing about something that we considered more "medical." Here we return to the problem of an exaggerated norm as a cover for a lack of confidence in our skills. That the problem is large and seems, therefore, intractable suggests the priority and vigor with which it should be pursued.

## I DON'T WANT TO LABEL SOMEONE "ALCOHOLIC," AND NO ONE CARES ABOUT WHAT I DO, ANYWAY

It is true that we tend to value what we measure and we do not measure much about alcohol, clinically speaking. We see effects, not causes or contributing factors, and our accountability reports force us into choices that might hurt the patient.

Clinicians are reluctant to apply labels that have potentially long-term and serious consequences, if they are unsure about the correctness of the diagnosis. But, to pursue a student's alcohol problem does not require determining that he or she is alcoholic, no more than getting a mammogram on a breast lump means that a woman has cancer. We need to be careful about tossing labels around, but we can pursue a clinical inquiry without making these mistakes and we can protect the patient from harm.

All this can be accomplished in a clinical context that is supportive of serious work and interested in broad definable outcomes related to patient care. Such a service would be one most likely to provide support for the staff development required to assure a maximal level of staff capacity and an accountability system that took cognizance of the importance of dealing with subtle, difficult problems. It would be a practice that measured the right things.

# CONCLUSION

The clinician who saw the patient with the bruised hands was a very good doctor. He had the courage to talk about his practice and a willingness to learn. He worked in a department that was interested in results and committed to developing his talents. He worked at a university that wanted to do something about its alcohol problem. This doctor cared deeply about what happened to his patients and wanted to make a difference in their lives. He knew all the reasons why he couldn't do better, but his commitment to his practice and his patients told him what was wrong with his excuses. He knew that he, at his election, took time for things that interested him, even though others were waiting. He knew he had made a difference in the lives of patients who had "impossible" problems. (He had prevented suicide, for example.) Now, he turns his attention to another issue – one that received scant coverage in his medical training – and armed with new knowledge, equipped with new skills, and animated by his commitment to his patients, he is doing better and students are getting better. He and others like him are working to avoid the collision between risk-taking and prevention.

## REFERENCES

1. American College Health Association: Recommended Standards: Alcohol and Other Drug Use, Misuse, and Dependency. ACHA, Task Force on Alcohol and Other Drugs, January 1988

2. Kinney J, Meilman P: Alcohol use and alcohol problems: Clinical approaches for the college health service. J Am Coll Health 36:73-82, 1987

3. Hickenbottom JP, Bissonette RP, O'Shea RM: Preventive medicine and college alcohol abuse. J Am Coll Health 36:67-72, 1987

4. Perkins HW, Berkowitz AD: Perceiving the community norms of alcohol use among students: Some research implications for campus alcohol education programming. Int J Addict 21:961-976, 1986

5. Haines M: Drinking on campus: Not as much as you'd think. Psychol Today, Aug 1989

6. Johnson VE: I'll Quit Tomorrow. New York, Harper & Row, 1980

7. Donovan B: What the practicing physician needs to know about self-help for chemical dependents. Rhode Island Med J 72:443-449, 1989

## Recommended Reading

Johnston LD et al: Drug Use, Drinking, and Smoking: National Survey Results from High School, College, and Young Adults Populations. National Institute on Drug Abuse, 1989

Kinney J: Clinical Manual of Substance Abuse. St. Louis, Mosby-Yearbook Inc., 1991

# 10

# Tobacco Use Among College Students

### Chris Y. Lovato, PhD

Tobacco use is responsible for more than one of every six deaths in the United States and is the single most preventable cause of death and disease in our society.[1] The use of tobacco has been identified as a major risk factor for heart disease; chronic bronchitis and emphysema; cancers of the lung, larynx, pharynx, oral cavity, esophagus, pancreas, and bladder; and other health problems such as respiratory infections and stomach ulcers. Exposure to second-hand smoke has also been identified as a health concern for adult nonsmokers.[2,3]

## CIGARETTE SMOKING

The most recent statistics available from the National Health Interview Survey show a steady decline in tobacco use from 1974 to 1985 among the general population.[4] The prevalence for men decreased .91 percentage points per year to 33.5 percent in 1985 and the prevalence for women decreased .33 points per year to 27.6 percent in 1985.[5] The decline in smoking rates has occurred among both men and women; however, the rate of decrease has been greater for men. There is evidence that these differences are due to higher initiation rates among women. Although there appear to be differences in rates related to gender and ethnicity, there is mounting evidence that educational status is becoming the primary predictor of smoking status.[6]

Substance abuse, including abuse of alcohol, drugs, tobacco, and food, has been identified by experts in the field of college health as second only to sexual health concerns in terms of level of concern for college students.[7] Indeed, the American College Health Association adopted a strong no-smoking policy in 1988 that encourages colleges and universities to establish tobacco/smoke-free environments for students, faculty, and staff.[8] Although the number of campuses initiating no-smoking policies is unknown, it has been estimated that approximately 50 percent of all private-sector companies have adopted such a policy.[1] The evidence for the effects of no-smoking policies on cessation has been mixed; however, there is evidence to support the reduction of consumption among smokers.[9,10] Clearly, the college campus can play a key role in the control of smoking and the prevention of exposure to secondary smoke.

According to data from a national survey on smoking, the 30-day prevalence of cigarette smoking among college students declined from 26 percent to 22 percent between 1980 and 1985.[11] The daily smoking prevalence fell from 18.3 percent in 1980 to 12.7 percent in 1986. As shown in Figure 1, although there has been a downward trend, smoking rates among this population have not gone down by more than two percentage points since 1985. Current estimates indicate that approximately 12.4 percent of college students smoke cigarettes on a daily basis.[11]

One of the most striking observations in smoking rates among college students relates to differences between genders. Since 1980 smoking has been higher among female than male college students, despite the fact that there have been large decreases for both groups. Daily smoking rates currently are estimated at 9 percent for males and 15 percent for females.[11] As shown in Table 1, next page, 1988 estimates comparing males and females indicate that females have higher annual, 30-day, and daily prevalence rates. These data clearly suggest that tobacco use interventions that target female college students should be a priority. The preva-

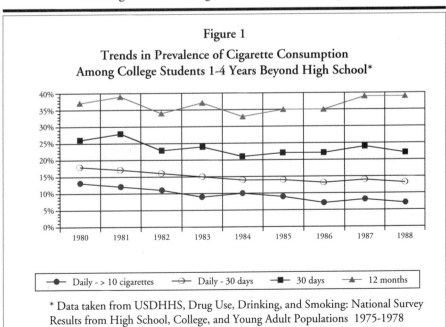

**Figure 1**

**Trends in Prevalence of Cigarette Consumption Among College Students 1-4 Years Beyond High School***

Daily - > 10 cigarettes    Daily - 30 days    30 days    12 months

* Data taken from USDHHS, Drug Use, Drinking, and Smoking: National Survey Results from High School, College, and Young Adult Populations 1975-1978

lence rate of tobacco use and the high rate of birth control pill use among women in this age group place them at high risk of heart disease, in addition to the other negative health consequences of tobacco consumption.

As shown in Tables 1 and 2, the 30-day and annual prevalence rates of cigarette use are very high. According to these data, nearly one in every four college students (23 percent) had smoked at least one cigarette within the previous 30 days. These data, together with evidence that 37 percent of those surveyed had smoked within the previous year, suggest that college students are experimenting with the substance and are potentially at risk of addiction. This high rate of experimentation supports the need for prevention activities, no-smoking policies, and cessation programs as important components of a comprehensive campus program.

Table 1

Prevalence of Cigarette Use, 1988: Full-time College Students

|  | Total | Males | Females |
|---|---|---|---|
| Annual Prevalence | 36.6 | 31.2 | 40.7 |
| 30-day Prevalence | 22.6 | 18.7 | 25.6 |
| Daily Use (any) | 12.4 | 9.0 | 15.0 |
| Daily Use >10 cigarettes | 7.3 | 5.3 | 8.7 |

Table 2

30 Day and Annual Prevalence Rates of Cigarette Use

|  | 1980 | 1981 | 1982 | 1983 | 1984 | 1985 | 1986 | 1987 | 1988 |
|---|---|---|---|---|---|---|---|---|---|
| Daily - > 10 cigs | 13% | 12% | 11% | 9% | 10% | 9% | 7% | 8% | 7% |
| Daily - 30 days | 18% | 17% | 16% | 15% | 14% | 14% | 13% | 14% | 13% |
| 30 days | 26% | 28% | 23% | 24% | 21% | 22% | 22% | 24% | 22% |
| 12 months | 37% | 39% | 34% | 37% | 33% | 35% | 35% | 39% | 39% |

"Light smoking" or "social smoking" may account for the high level of irregular cigarette consumption; however, little is known about these patterns among college students. There is evidence that cigarette smoking has a different function or purpose for social smokers than for addicted smokers.[12] There are also significant differences between "chippers" (very light smokers) and smokers who use tobacco on a regular basis.[13] Thus, it would appear that further examination of smoking patterns is warranted and would contribute to our understanding of addiction among this age group.

## SMOKELESS TOBACCO USE

Recently, the use of smokeless tobacco has increased in popularity among adolescents and young adults. There are three types of smokeless tobacco: 1) moist snuff, 2) dry snuff, and 3) chewing tobacco. Moist snuff, which is held between the lower lip and the gum, is the most popular type of smokeless tobacco among youth. The concentration of nicotine in a pinch of snuff is three times the amount found in a cigarette.

Data from the National Health Interview Survey indicated that between 1970 and 1986 snuff use increased fifteenfold and chewing tobacco use more than fourfold among males between the ages of 17 and 19.[1] Based on results from a national survey on adult tobacco use, males who ever used smokeless tobacco began use before age 21, more than one-third began before age 16, with a median initiation age of 19.[14] Among males aged 17 to 19, 8.2 percent were current users, while 5.9 percent of males between 20 and 29 were current users. The prevalence of smokeless tobacco use among women has always remained very low. A national survey of college students revealed that 22 percent of college men and 2 percent of college women were current dippers or chewers.[15] In addition, results of this survey indicated that 18 percent of smokeless tobacco users also smoked cigarettes.

In a stratified, random sample of college students in physical activity classes across the country (n=5,069), it was found that of those who initiated smokeless tobacco use or cigarette use, most began at age 16 or older.[16] In addition, subjects were more likely to switch from smokeless tobacco to cigarettes than from cigarettes to smokeless tobacco.

Among smokeless tobacco users, college athletes have often been cited as a high-risk group. In a survey of varsity and intramural football and baseball players from a large urban university, it was found that 15 percent of those surveyed used some form of smokeless tobacco.[17] Use was associated with the varsity sports, with baseball players using and experimenting with the substance more frequently than football players (52 percent vs 19 percent). Players reported using the substance most frequently when they were actively participating in their sport, but also when they were getting ready or waiting to play.

In a similar study at two major southwestern universities, one-fourth of those athletes surveyed were smokeless tobacco users. Varsity players were about 20 times more likely to use smokeless tobacco than to smoke.[18]

Further research related to determinants of smokeless tobacco use, particularly among college athletes, would contribute to understanding the etiology of use and the development of effective intervention methods.

## INTERVENTION APPROACHES

Experts have concluded that smoking is determined by multiple causes including psychosocial, pharmacologic, and physiologic forces. Social influences, educational and economic disadvantage, alcohol and other drug use, as well as antisocial behavior have been associated with the onset of tobacco use.[19]

A number of barriers contribute to the difficulty in reducing the prevalence of tobacco use in college students, including developmental issues of young adults, advertising by the tobacco industry, and economic support provided by the tobacco industry to college campuses. Special characteristics associated with college-age individuals include a sense of invincibility and immortality.

The high rates of risk-taking behavior and experimentation place this age group at high risk for use of tobacco, as well as alcohol, marijuana, and other drugs. In fact, substance abuse often represents a "rite-of-passage" to adulthood. Because there is evidence that smokers exhibit significantly less-healthy attitudes and behaviors than nonsmokers[19,20,21] and that tobacco may be a "gateway" drug to the use of other dependence-producing substances, multiple risk intervention methods may represent the most promising approach to promoting healthful behaviors.

The sections that follow concentrate on prevention and cessation of tobacco use and describe current intervention approaches.

### PRIMARY PREVENTION OF TOBACCO USE

Since the 1960s, the target groups for tobacco-use prevention have shifted from high school and college students to middle school and junior high school students. The major factor contributing to this trend has been evidence that adolescents in grades six to eight are at highest risk for experimenting with cigarettes.[1]

Early anti-smoking programs were primarily information-oriented media-based campaigns. Contemporary approaches targeting young adolescents have utilized models of social influence and life-skills training that are incorporated into multicomponent school health education programs.[1,22] In general, the prevention of smoking initiation has been less effective than efforts to promote cessation and it has been suggested that an emphasis should be placed on the prevention of smoking among young adolescents, while cessation programs should be directed at older adolescents.[1]

Three major stages have been used to describe the continuum of smoking behavior: 1) development, 2) maintenance of regular smoking, and 3) cessation. The development stage is comprised of the processes of preparation, initiation, experimentation, and transition to regular smoking.[23]

Movement from the early stages of initiation and experimentation with tobacco to regular use and addiction corresponds roughly to the period of transition that occurs between adolescence and adulthood,[1] thus making the young-adult years a critical time for intervening on the development of heavy addiction patterns. Unfortunately, most tobacco-related research has focused on preadolescents, teenagers, and adults, resulting in a lack of tested intervention methods that address smoking issues relevant to college-age individuals.

## SMOKING CESSATION

Recent data suggest a need for additional research that focuses on smoking cessation among college students. Based on data from a national survey that included cessation items, it was found that smokers who were 17 to 24 years of age and had completed 16 or more years of education were more likely to make an attempt to quit smoking than any other age group, regardless of educational level.[24] The overall quit rate (for seven or more days) was 25.5 percent for smokers aged 17 to 24, with 32.5 percent of these succeeding in maintaining cessation for at least three months. These data suggest the need for interventions that: 1) capitalize on the high level of receptivity to cessation that appears to occur during the college years, and 2) concentrate on providing the skills that will reduce relapse among those who attempt to quit smoking.

One study specifically targeting college students reported positive results in reducing the rate of smoking among freshmen using a health risk appraisal and feedback counseling. In this study, 22 percent of nonsmokers in a control group, as compared to 5 percent in a treatment group, had started smoking at a one-year follow-up. Furthermore, 26 percent of the smokers at pretesting had quit smoking at follow-up as compared to 6 percent in the control group. Both sets of results were statistically significant.[25]

College student health centers play an important role in the health care delivery to a majority of students, consequently college health personnel are in an opportune position to motivate and provide counseling related to tobacco-use cessation. Short-term health conditions such as a bronchitis, shortness of breath, pharyngitis, or sinus problems were identified as the primary reason for quitting smoking among a sample of college students who had made successful and unsuccessful attempts to quit,[26] thus supporting the importance of the student health center as a setting for intervention.

Among the general population, counseling by physicians and other clinicians has been identified as having a strong positive influence on patient motivation to stop smoking.[27] In fact, simple, brief advice from a physician is a cost-effective method of intervention.[28]

A recent meta-analysis of 39 controlled trials of the attributes of successful smoking cessation intervention activities in medical practice found that the most effective techniques: 1) used more than one modality for motivating behavioral change, 2) involved both physicians and non-physicians in face-to-face sessions, and 3) provided motivational messages on multiple occasions over the longest possible period of time. The authors concluded that firm, consistent, and repeated help and advice to stop smoking is the key element for successful quit attempts.[29]

As discussed earlier in this chapter, the higher rates of smoking among college-age women make women an important target for tobacco-use intervention programs. Research exploring gender differences has identified important differences in college populations that should be taken into consideration in developing intervention approaches.[30,31,32] For example, in a survey of 382 undergraduate smokers and ex-smokers, which focused on smoking outcome expectancies, females had more positive expectations than males related to the effects of cigarette use for control of appetite and weight.[30] Female ex-smokers reported more positive expectancies such as relief from anxiety, anger/irritability reduction, and depression reduction. The authors suggest that smoking may play a more important role in coping with negative affect for females than for males. These results corroborate earlier findings, which showed that, for college women, coping with stress was an important motivation for continuation of cigarette consumption.[31] Health effects ("how bad it was for me," "trouble... breathing") were reported by ex-smokers as the strongest reason for quitting, followed by loss of control of their lives ("being a slave"), and social effects ("breath smell," "affect my children," "boyfriend asking me to quit").

A stages-approach to understanding the modification of smoking behavior has become widely used in interventions designed to change risk behaviors and has been the basis for much of the work in the area of smoking cessation. There is empirical evidence to support five distinct stages in the cessation process: precontemplation, contemplation, action, maintenance, and relapse.[33,34]

An individual in the precontemplation stage is neither considering quitting smoking nor actively processing the information that tobacco use is a health hazard. During the contemplation stage the individual is considering cessation, but has not yet made an attempt to quit. An individual who has not smoked for less than six months is in the action stage. In the maintenance stage, long-term abstinence is established, and relapse refers to resumed tobacco use. When relapse occurs, the individual recycles back into any one of the three earlier stages of change. According to the stages model, an intervention should address the issues relevant to the individuals stage of change. For example, an individual at the precontemplation stage may need personalized information on smoking and health, versus a contemplator who may benefit from encouragement and social support to attempt cessation. The individual in the action phase may benefit most from acquisition of relapse-prevention skills.

While there are a lack of intervention methods tested for use with college populations, there are many programs available through various profit and non-profit agencies that target general adult populations. The American Lung Association's (ALA) "Freedom from Smoking" and the American Cancer Society's "Freshstart" self-help programs are easy to obtain in most communities. In addition, the ALA holds training sessions and certifies facilitators for those interested in conducting group sessions. The ALA program incorporates the stages-of-change model described earlier and places an emphasis on relapse prevention.

## PREVENTION OF SMOKELESS TOBACCO USE

Based on the results of a campus survey, it was concluded that the concentration of smokeless tobacco users among varsity athletes, combined with the high number who initiated use after age 15 or quit use during their college years, highlights the need for educational programs targeting this population.[17]

In a study designed to test an interactive video lesson and a corresponding film version of a lesson on smokeless tobacco among college students, the interactive video demonstrated the most accurate and comprehensive recall of information, regardless of gender or ethnicity.[35] The researchers concluded that an interactive video offers health professionals a useful tool for developing prevention programs.

The development and testing of intervention methods targeting tobacco use have focused primarily on smoking, due to the general magnitude of the problem. While the etiology and maintenance of smokeless tobacco use differ, it can be assumed that the basic findings related to cessation of smoking would also apply. These include the importance of firm, consistent, and repeated advice to quit use, stage-appropriate intervention techniques, and a focus on relapse prevention.

# SUMMARY

While the rate of smoking and smokeless tobacco use among college students is lower than that among the general population, the college campus remains an important setting for tobacco-use control. We know that among college students: 1) smokers attempt to quit more frequently than any other age group of smokers, 2) almost 25 percent smoke on an infrequent basis, 3) smoking rates are higher among females than males, and 4) smokeless tobacco use is a problem, particularly among athletes. There is currently a lack of tested intervention approaches that address the needs of young adults. By and large, programs have been designed to target young adolescents and older adult populations.

The college campus represents an ideal community setting for influencing youth during a critical time in their development. Programs can be integrated into existing structures for providing students prevention and cessation intervention approaches. Campus no-smoking policies and media can also be used to influence individual and community norms that provide the environmental support necessary to influence and maintain healthful behavior.

# REFERENCES

1. U.S. Department of Health and Human Services: Reducing The Health Consequences Of Smoking: 25 Years Of Progress: A Report Of The Surgeon General, 1989

2. Eriksen MP, LeMaistre CA, Newell GR: Health hazards of passive smoking. Annu Rev Public Health 9:47-70, 1988

3. Fielding JE, Phenow KJ: Health effects of involuntary smoking. N Engl J Med 39:1452-1460, 1988

4. Pierce JP, Fiore MC, Novotny TE et al: Trends in smoking in the United States: Projections to the year 2000. JAMA 261:61-65, 1989

5. Fiore MC, Novotny TE, Pierce JP et al: Trends in cigarette smoking in the United States: The changing influence of gender and race. JAMA 261:56-60, 1989

6. Pierce JP, Fiore MC, Novotny TE et al: Trends in cigarette smoking in the United States: Educational differences are increasing. JAMA 261:61-65, 1989

7. Guyton R, Corbin S, Zimmer C et al: College students and national health objectives for the year 2000: A summary report 38:9-14, 1990

8. American College Health Association: Statement on Tobacco Use on College and University Campuses. Rockville MD, ACHA, 1988

9. Gottlieb NH, Eriksen MP, Lovato CY et al: Impact of a restrictive work site smoking policy on smoking behavior, attitudes, norms. J Occup Med 32:16-23, 1990

10. Borland R, Chapman S, Owen N et al: Effects of workplace smoking bans on cigarette consumption. Am J Public Health 10:(2),178-180, 1990

11. U.S. DHHS, Public Health Service, Alcohol, Drug Abuse and Mental Health Administration: Drug use, drinking, and smoking: National survey results from high school, college, and young adult populations 1975-1988 (ADM) DHHS 89-1638

12. Leventhal H, Clear PD: The smoking problem: A review of the research and theory in behavioral risk modification. Psychol Bull 88:270-405, 1980

13. Shiffman S: Tobacco "chippers" - individual differences in tobacco dependence. Psychopharmacology 97:539-547, 1989

14. Novotny TE, Pierce JP, Fiore MC et al: Smokeless tobacco use in the United States: The adult use of tobacco surveys. (NIH Publication No, 89-3055) National Cancer Institute Monogr No. 8. Bethesda, MD, NCI, 1989

15. Glover ED, Laflin M, Edwards SW: Smokeless tobacco use among American college students. J Am Coll Health 31:81-85, 1989

16. Glover ED, Laflin M, Edwards SW: Age of initiation and switching patterns between smokeless tobacco and cigarettes among college students in the United States. Am J Public Health 35:207-208, 1989

17. Levenson-Gingiss P, Morrow JR, Dratt LM: Patterns of smokeless tobacco use among university athletes. Am J Coll Health 38:87-89, 1989

18. Levenson-Gingiss P, Gottlieb N: A comparison of smokeless tobacco and smoking practices of university varsity and intramural baseball players. Addict Beh 16(5): 335-340, 1991

19. Castro FG, Newcomb MD, McCleary C et al: Cigarette smokers do more than just smoke cigarettes. Health Psychology 8:107-129, 1989

20. Dews PB: Maintenance of behavior by "Scheduled": An unfamiliar contributor to the maintenance of the abuse of substances and the like, Substance Abuse, Habitual Behavior, and Self Control. Edited by PK Levison. Boulder, CO, Westview, 1984, pp 49-80

21. Levison PK: An analysis of commonalities in substance abuse and habitual behavior, Behavioral Pharmacology of Human Drug Dependence. Edited by T Thompson, CE Johnson. NIDA Research Monograph No 37. Rockville, MD, National Institute of Drug Abuse, 1981

22. Best JA, Thomson SJ, Santi SM et al: Preventing cigarette smoking among school children. Annu Rev Public Health 9:161-201, 1988

23. Flay BR, D'Avernas JR, Best JA et al: Cigarette smoking: Why young people do it and ways of preventing it. Vol 1. Pediatric and Adolescent Behavioral Medicine. Edited by P McGrath, P Firestone. New York, Springer Publishing, 1983, pp 132-183

24. Hatziandreu EJ, Pierce JP, Lefkopoulou M et al: Quitting smoking in the United States in 1986. J National Cancer Institute 82:1402-1405, 1990

25. Chan CW, Witherspoon JM: Health risk appraisal modifies cigarette smoking behavior among college students. J Gen Int Med 3:555-559, 1988

26. Hellman R, O'Shea RM, Kunz ML et al: University health service physician intervention with cigarette smokers. J Am Coll Health. 37: 91-93, 1988

27. U.S. Preventive Services Task Force: Guide to Clinical Preventive Services. Baltimore, Williams and Wilkins, 1989

28. Cummings S, Rubin S, Oster G: The cost-effectiveness of counseling smokers to quit. JAMA 261:75-79, 1989

29. Kottke T, Battista R, DeFries G et al: Attributes of successful smoking cessation intervention in medical practice: A meta-analysis of 39 controlled trials. JAMA 259:2883-2889, 1988

30. Brandon TH, Baker TB: Smoking outcome expectancies among college students. Paper presented at the annual meeting of the Society of Behavioral Medicine, Chicago, IL, April 1990

31. Gottlieb NH: The effect of health beliefs on the smoking behavior of college women. J Am Coll Health 31:214-221, 1983

32. Page RM, Gold RS: Assessing gender differences in college cigarette smoking intenders and nonintenders. J Sch Health 53: (9) 531-535, 1983

33. DiClemente C, Prochaska J: Process and stages of self-change: Coping and competence in smoking behavior change, Coping and Substance Use. Edited by S Shiffman, TA Willis. Orlando, FL, Academic Press, 1985

34. Prochaska J, DiClemente C: Self-help interventions and the stages of smoking cessation. Paper presented at the annual meeting of the American Public Health Association, Boston, MA, 1988

35. Levenson PM, Morrow JR: Learner characteristics associated with responses to film and interactive video lessons on smokeless tobacco. Prev Med 16:52-62, 1987

# Licit and Illicit Drug Use Among College Students

JAMES H. EVANS, MS

While alcohol drinking by college students dates back centuries, the use and abuse of other drugs, particularly the illicit drugs, are more recent phenomena.[1] Although there has probably always been a sub-set of college students who experimented with mind alteration through the use of psychoactive substances, the 1960s saw a significant rise in the use of substances such as marijuana, stimulants, and the hallucinogens. This increase in use reached near epidemic proportions in the society as a whole and on college campuses in particular.

Annually, the University of Michigan's Institute for Survey Research collects data on the drug-use patterns of young Americans. The Institute's collegiate surveys show annual prevalence patterns on campuses by type of drug and year. The data for 1986 and 1987 (Table 1, next page) provide some insight into the extent to which drug use has penetrated into higher education.

These data point to a slight downward trend in annual prevalence, which anecdotal information shows continuing into 1990, but the extent of use by college students is still disturbing.[2] Young adults in America use more licit and illicit psychoactive substances than in any other nation in the Western world. While drug use cuts across all socioeconomic levels and is a phenomenon of all ethnic groups, collegiate chemical abuse is overwhelmingly a problem of Caucasian, middle-class students.

## PATTERNS OF USE

Four classes of drugs are used most often by college students: marijuana, stimulants, hallucinogens, and depressants.

## MARIJUANA

Other than alcohol, marijuana is the most prevalent drug used on college campuses. Most college students who smoke marijuana began doing so in high school; only an additional 1 to 5 percent start to smoke it in college. (Between 36 percent and 39 percent of high school students smoke "pot," while 37 percent to 41 percent of the collegiate population does.)[3] Researchers find marijuana use correlates with counter-culture attitudes. Many collegiate marijuana smokers support the Jamaican politico-religious philosophy of "Rastafarianism," in which marijuana (called "ganga" in Jamaica) smoking is raised to a sacrament. While few students are, in fact, Rastafarians, many enjoy the music of Jamaica, "reggae," and marijuana is seen as integral to the enjoyment of reggae music. Even in the 1990s, many marijuana smokers feel a strong affinity for the values, sub-culture, and music of the 1960s. Musical groups, such as "The Grateful Dead," continue to be cultural icons and their music and life-style are viewed as supportive of marijuana use.

The problems associated with marijuana use include: an "amotivational syndrome" in which heavy users tend to loose vitality in living and show lower grades and higher absenteeism; increased sexual activity and associated problems such as sexually transmitted disease; and association with those using other, and potentially more dangerous, illicit substances.[4] Also, the marijuana being smoked on campuses today tends to be a much more potent form of the substance than that

---

### Table 1

Trends in Annual Prevalence for Eleven Types of Drugs, 1986 and 1987:
College students, 1-4 years beyond high school

| Drug | 1986 | 1987 |
|------|------|------|
| Alcohol | 92% | 91% |
| Marijuana | 41 | 37 |
| Cocaine | 17 | 14 |
| Stimulants | 10 | 7 |
| LSD | 4 | 4 |
| Heroin | 0.1 | 0.2 |
| Other Opiates | 4 | 4 |
| Sedatives | 3 | 2 |
| Barbituates | 2 | 1 |
| Methaqualone | 1 | 1 |
| Tranquilizers | 4 | 4 |

Source: Reference 2

which was smoked in the 1960s and 1970s and is, therefore, more likely to produce psychological dependence – wherein the user finds it very difficult to refrain from use.

## CNS STIMULANTS

The central nervous system stimulants, cocaine and amphetamine (primarily methamphetamine), are the next most prevalent class of drugs used on college campuses. The pharmacologic actions of these drugs – increased alertness and diminished fatigue, increased feelings of well-being, heightened competence in motor skills and mental acuity, and inhibition of appetite[5] – allow their use to be rationalized as integral to the school experience, i.e., to have the alertness to study for examinations. While both cocaine and methamphetamine are used recreationally to produce a "high" or a feeling of euphoria, they are also used instrumentally, to aid in the educational process. This practice of using stimulants to study, for energy, or for weight control is especially dangerous in that students can quickly come to depend on these drugs to assist them with the work of being a student and therefore, not look at the physical, social and ethical consequences of their use.

Cocaine produces a subjective, mind-oriented experience in which the user feels increased power and competence; it is correlated with an upwardly mobile socioeconomic life-style among some college students. Amphetamines produce more body-oriented feelings of elation or euphoria; these drugs are generally cheaper than cocaine, so they are not as tied to the "jet-set" life-style to which many cocaine users aspire.

Both cocaine and methamphetamine are primarily inhaled nasally, but both drugs can be used by injection or transformed chemically and smoked. The smokeable forms of cocaine (freebase and crack) and methamphetamine ("ice") are extremely dangerous and have very high potential for producing chemical dependence. Larger, urban universities where students live and associate with poverty urban neighborhoods will experience higher percentages of students smoking these drugs. Both cocaine and amphetamines are used in conjunction with heavy drinking to "mellow out" the stimulant experience. Both drugs can produce profound depression, paranoia, high blood pressure, and increased risk of heart attack, among other negative consequences of abuse.

## HALLUCINOGENS

Another group of drugs with significant prevalence of use on college campuses are the hallucinogens. The primary types of drugs seen in this class include LSD, which has made a comeback from the 1960s; mescaline, which is derived from the peyote cactus; psilocybin or its naturally occurring form, the *Psilocybe* mushroom; and a relatively new drug on the street scene, MDMA, the slang name for which is "ecstasy."

These drugs are used for "mind-expansion," as they were in the 1960s, and also because the perceptual distortions they produce are thought to be fun to experience by some college students. Hallucinogens cause colors, shapes, and people to appear altered. All activities and events appear to be more profound. These drugs appeal to many students' need to do things that involve risk-taking. Hallucinogenic drugs can produce panic-reactions, brief reactive psychoses, flashback experiences and "bad trips," which can be disturbing at best and terrifying at worst. Negative reactions to these drugs are much more likely to occur when they are used in conjunction with alcohol, but negative reactions can occur at almost any time since they seem to act on the subconscious or unconscious parts of the mind, over which the user has no conscious control.

As with all illicit chemicals, adulteration, misrepresented potency, and poorly synthesized products increase the likelihood of negative health consequences of use. The illicit drug market is truly a place where the expression "caveat emptor" ("let the buyer beware!") should prevail. "Street" drugs are notoriously contaminated and misrepresented.

## DEPRESSANTS

Other classes of drugs – the narcotics and sedatives such as the barbiturates, methaqualone, and tranquilizers – are also used in college environments. Narcotics are the drugs derived from the opium poppy, including heroin, morphine, demerol, and methadone, among others. Use of both heroin and the prescription narcotics can be found among medical students and nursing students, due to accessibility to these drugs in hospital settings. Some students become dependent on narcotics after receiving  prescriptions for them for the relief of pain. Also, colleges located, and students living, in inner-city neighborhoods are likely to have greater exposure to street narcotics. A small percentage of marijuana smokers decide to try opium smoking as a stronger, but related, high.

Other depressant drugs, such as barbiturates, tranquilizers, and methaqualone (Quaalude), are also used. Pharmacologically, these drugs produce physiological, behavioral and psychological effects almost identical to alcohol. Students, therefore, use them to produce drunken comportment and to potentiate an existing alcohol intoxication. Methaqualone, in particular, gained a reputation as an aphrodisiac because, in the drunken state it produces, users can be very suggestible. Barbiturates, such as Seconal, have been called "alcohol in a pill" by college students. Tranquilizers, such as Valium and Xanax, are among the most prescribed drugs in America and they are often prescribed for college-related problems such as anxiety, insomnia, and phobias. Students can come to depend on these drugs' calming effects but they also find that when used in combination with alcohol, these drugs produce a dysphoric "high" that some find very pleasurable. The depressant drugs are the most likely classes of substances to produce serious health problems and even death – from respiratory arrest due to accidental overdose or intentional overdose, or from convulsions during acute withdrawal. The barbiturates in particular correlate with violent behavior in males.

In the final analysis, poly-drug abuse (the abuse of and dependence on several classes of drugs) is the rule rather than the exception among serious drug abusers on college campuses. Alcohol is used in conjunction with all the licit and illicit drugs mentioned above.

## PREVENTION

Prevention of substance abuse disorders on the college campus involves a myriad of concepts, programs and procedures operating interdependently. There are two distinct philosophies of primary prevention in the alcohol and drug field. The first is called Social Competency-based Prevention and it is aimed at the **individual** college student under the theory that if we produce healthy, whole, self-actualized people, they will be less likely to abuse mood-altering substances.

Alcohol and drug education provides factual, chemically specific information to students to deter them from irresponsible and problematic chemical use. Education is a fundamental method of social competency-based primary prevention, but it is not the only way. Programs, classes and projects that promote growth to full human potential, including values clarification programs, teaching social skills and decision-making skills, encouraging peer interaction, and providing healthy, chemically free alternatives to alcohol and drug abuse are also included in this category of prevention programming. The classroom is an appropriate venue for these activities, although extracurricular clubs and organizations are also important places to build the social competencies of students. To be effective, these programs must target and outreach to students at high risk for substance abuse – those who rarely join clubs and organizations.

The second form of prevention activity is social policy-based primary prevention. This complement of programs, policies and activities is designed to influence the **environment** in which chemical use takes place. Often these approaches are termed "environmental strategies." Social policy-based primary prevention attempts to establish normative behavior in communities. This supports the concept of "chemical health" as opposed to the disease process of "chemical dependency." Federal, state and local laws and the operant societal norms on chemical use form the basis of social policy prevention. In any community, like the college or university community, the response to the following series of questions forms the core of whether an environment promotes health or promotes disease, with regard to chemical use and abuse. The questions that must be answered are:

1. What chemicals are legitimate to use?
2. When is use acceptable?
3. Why should chemicals be used?
4. Where should chemicals be used?
5. What behaviors are acceptable under the influence of the legitimated chemicals?
6. How are the rules established for chemical use communicated to members of the college community?
7. What accountability systems exist for those who break the rules?
8. Are there functional, non-chemical methods available for rites of passage to adulthood?
9. Are there functional, non-chemical methods available to cope with emotional stress?

Where colleges and universities answer the questions listed above with clear, concise, unambiguous, non-hypocritical answers, alcohol and drug misuse can be minimized. Social policy-based prevention is predicated on the belief that abstinence from all illicit chemical use and either abstinence or moderate, socially appropriate use of the legal drugs, alcohol and prescription drugs, are the only responsible and healthy chemical-use patterns.

## TOWARD A MODEL PROGRAM

A model campus alcohol and other drug program involves three levels of prevention services: primary, secondary, and tertiary, organized into a Continuum of Care for Chemical Abuse (CCCA). Primary prevention programming seeks to stop chemical health problems before they start. It focuses on keeping students abstinent from illicit chemical use or responsibly using the licit drugs, only when one is above the legal age and only in low-risk situations. Further, it defines low-risk situations for chemical use.

Secondary prevention is intervention into chemical-use problems, hopefully, early enough to prevent long-term damage. Secondary prevention involves policies and procedures to identify, intervene and refer students with chemical health problems. Tertiary prevention is treatment and aftercare. The object is to prevent an existent chemical health problem from continuing. Further, it involves returning a chemically dependent student to healthy functioning.

A CCCA model program begins with alcohol and drug policies agreed to by all segments of the college community. The issue of "dry" versus "wet" campuses pertaining to alcohol dispensation on campus must be addressed. Campus policies should address the nine social policy-based prevention questions posed above. Social competency-based prevention includes good alcohol and drug education, diversified across the curriculum. Clubs and organizations should offer specific programming to present viable alternatives to chemical abuse.

Intervention services are accomplished through employee-assistance and student-assistance programs that involve training for supervisors and faculty in recognition of the signs and symptoms of abuse and referral procedures. A diversion program involving mandatory education for driving under the influence (DUI) and other criminal behaviors is an important component of a model program.

Treatment services should be available, on-campus and at no cost, offered through a student counseling center or student health center. Both individual and group counseling should be available for students with chemical abuse problems. Additionally, self-help support groups such as Alcoholics Anonymous, Narcotics Anonymous, Adult Children of Alcoholics, and Co-dependents Anonymous should be offered. Psychological counselors and student health providers should make referrals to community-based chemical dependency rehabilitation programs, when warranted. Aftercare services in the form of on-going, open support groups, led or co-led by peer counselors, should be available for students recovering from chemical use problems.

A CCCA model program establishes a comprehensive, logical flow of services and programs spearheaded by an administrative commitment to work on these issues. It is coordinated by a multi-disciplinary, oversight committee of students, faculty and staff charged with the responsibility for program monitoring, research, and evaluation with emphasis on collecting and interpreting data on the behavioral indicators of chemical abuse. A comprehensive program can do much to reduce the incidence and prevalence of alcohol and drug abuse on the college campus.

The very small college health service may not have the person-power to accomplish the comprehensive program outlined above. Small college health services may need additional linkages to community-based services. Most county or state alcohol and drug administrative programs can provide technical assistance in planning and implementing such a program. Local drug and alcohol prevention agencies and rehabilitation centers are also helpful in providing services to college health centers. At the very least, self-help groups like Alcoholics Anonymous and Narcotics Anonymous can be offered. They are free and require no staffing, just meeting space. Using peer counselors is another low cost, low staffing way to accomplish drug and alcohol programming.

## REFERENCES

1. Goodale TG (ed): Alcohol and the College Student, New Directions for Student Services no. 35. Edited by MJ Barr. San Francisco, Jossey-Bass, 1986, p 1

2. Johnson LD, O'Malley PM, Bachman JG: Drug use among American high school students, college students, and other young adults: National trends through 1985. Rockville, MD, National Institute on Drug Abuse, 1986, table 28

3. Johnson LD, O'Malley PM, Bachman JG: Drug use among American high school students, college students, and other young adults: National trends through 1985. Rockville, MD, National Institute on Drug Abuse, 1986, pp 47, 48, 49

4. Goode E: Drugs in American Society, Third Edition. New York, McGraw Hill, 1989, pp 85, 95

5. Weiner N: Norepinephrine, Epinephrine, and the Sympathomimetic Amines, Goodman and Gilman's The Pharmacological Basis of Therapeutics, Seventh Edition. New York, MacMillan, pp 145-160, 1985

## Resources

Several professional journals are recommended for more information on substance abuse issues. They are available in many college libraries and include:

The Journal of The Addiction Research Foundation
The Journal of Drug Education
The Journal of Psychoactive Substances

Also, each state has a central state agency for alcohol and drug problems, usually located in the state health or welfare department. That agency serves as a conduit for drug information from the federal government's alcohol and drug information clearinghouses. All the information available from the federal government – papers, articles, research, books and pamphlets – is easily accessible through a system of cooperative arrangements with local lending libraries in each state. This drug information network is known as RADAR. Check with any state alcohol and drug agency to see which local libraries may be a part of the RADAR network;  if none are, make sure that they join.

Finally, the U.S. Department of Education's Fund for the Improvement of Post-Secondary Education (FIPSE) provides two-year grants and technical assistance for the development of primary prevention programs at two- and four-year colleges and universities. These resources can be of tremendous assistance in initiating prevention programming.

# 12

# Human Immunodeficiency Virus Disease in the College Population

## Richard P. Keeling, MD

## DEFINITION AND SPECTRUM OF DISEASE

The human immunodeficiency virus (HIV) causes a chronic, progressive immune deficiency disorder, the entire spectrum of which comprises HIV disease (HIVD). People with HIVD experience a series of manifestations that define several phases, or stages, of the disease. These phases ordinarily follow one another in predictable sequence. Current data and a number of projective models indicate that the ultimate outcome of HIVD will routinely be severe immune deficiency unless therapy alters the natural history. On the other hand, the rate at which persons with HIVD progress from phase to phase, and eventually to advanced disease, varies extensively.

The usual phases of HIVD include:

1. Acute (primary) disease: a flu-like, or mononucleosis-like, illness associated with initial HIV infection but preceding seroconversion. Generally self-limited, this primary phase typically manifests itself within a few days to three weeks after infection. It is seldom recognized while present and can be firmly diagnosed only retrospectively. It is significant because:

   a. Levels of viremia are high, but the HIV antibody test is negative; thus, primary HIV disease argues strongly for "universal precautions" in health care.

   b. The laboratory pattern of primary HIV disease is that of seronegative infectious mononucleosis: atypical lymphocytosis with a normal differential heterophile and no serologic evidence of acute infection with Epstein Barr virus.

621

    c.  It may serve as a marker of development of HIVD among people known to have had high-risk exposure. A health care worker who develops a consistent clinical syndrome 14 days following a high intensity needle-stick injury might well have been infected with HIV.

    d.  The severity of illness during the primary phase is inversely related to the duration of the subsequent asymptomatic phase: The worse the symptoms of primary HIVD, the shorter the chronic asymptomatic phase.

2.  Chronic asymptomatic disease: a long phase which, while deceptively silent clinically, is characterized by ongoing HIV replication and gradual, insidious immunologic deterioration. The HIV antibody tests become positive during the early part of this phase, generally within four to six months of infection. This phase is neither latent nor permanent; it is not an alternative expression of disease among a group of patients who will never become symptomatic. People with chronic asymptomatic disease are not simply "HIV-positive" – their seropositivity is the laboratory marker of a progressive disease. Nor is this phase an incubation period; it is best considered a pre-symptomatic condition. The chronic asymptomatic phase may last for a few months to more than a decade, depending on a variety of co-factors, including the age at time of infection, means of transmission of HIV, and strain variant of HIV. Most students with HIVD are asymptomatic for 7 to 11 years.

3.  Chronic symptomatic disease: differentiated from the previous phase by the presence of symptoms, and from the subsequent one by the absence of life-threatening manifestations. Over the several months to two or three years of this phase, people with HIVD experience constitutional symptoms (especially fever, night sweats, and weight loss) and often manifest adenopathy. Any of several dermatologic disorders (seborrheic dermatitis, porphyria cutanea tarda, chronic folliculitis) are common, as are aphthous ulcers, dental abscesses, and herpes zoster. The development of hairy leukoplakia (an oral lesion related to reactivation of Epstein Barr virus) and oral thrush ordinarily portend a transition to advanced disease within 12 to 18 months. These clinical features coexist with further immunologic progression as measured by declining white blood cell, lymphocyte, and $CD_4$ (helper lymphocyte) counts, and by rising levels of beta-2 microglobulin, serum neopterin, and HIV antigen.

4.  Advanced (severe) disease: severe, life-threatening illness meeting the criteria of the surveillance definition of the acquired immunodeficiency syndrome (AIDS). Four major categories of complications are recognized:

a. Major opportunistic infections – especially pneumonia caused by *Pneumocystis carinii*, meningitis from *Toxoplasma* or fungi, and systemic infection with mycobacteria.

b. Neoplasms – especially Kaposi's Sarcoma (KS) and both Hodgkins and non-Hodgkins lymphoma. KS now seems to represent a separate sexually transmitted disease that requires immunosuppression (and, perhaps, HIV specifically) for its expression.

c. Psychoneurologic disease – especially HIV-associated dementia. Much of the psychoneurologic disease appears to result from dysfunction, rather than destruction, of neural tissue.

d. Wasting with cachexia.

Major influences on the pace of HIVD through these phases include:

1. Age at the time of infection; among infants, HIVD develops rapidly, but among adolescents and adults, the older the person, the faster the progression of disease.

2. Means of transmission: Ordinarily, HIVD moves more quickly after infection by parenteral exposure, transfusion, or needle-sharing.

3. Co-factors: Cigarette smoking, other infectious diseases, poor general health, and, perhaps alcohol and drug dependency are associated with faster progression, whereas aerobic exercise and good general health promote a slower course.

4. Strain of HIV: More virulent strains (as assessed *in vitro*) are associated with faster disease progression. The virulence of HIV during early phases is typically less than that of strains isolated later in the course of illness.

5. Therapy: Treatment with a combination of medical, psychological, and social strategies may retard the progress of HIVD. Early treatment with zidovudine (ZDV), in particular, delays the onset of severe disease.

## EPIDEMIOLOGY

HIV is transmitted during:

1. Intimate sexual contact. Both insertive and receptive anal and vaginal intercourse can result in transmission of HIV. Although the risk of transmitting HIV from passive to active partner during fellatio seems small (and is decidedly lower than the chance of transmission during anal or vaginal

intercourse), this form of oral sex has been associated with infection with HIV. There is no clear data regarding the likelihood of transmitting HIV during cunnilingus. Kissing has not been implicated in transmitting HIV in epidemiologic, virologic, or clinical studies.

2. Direct contact with infected blood, through sharing needles for any purpose (notably injecting intravenous drugs or anabolic steroids); transfusion of infected blood or blood products; transplantation of organs or tissue from an infected donor; artificial insemination; and accidents in health care involving parenteral exposure or splash on mucous membranes or non-intact skin.

3. Gestation and birth: perinatal transfer from mother to fetus or infant. Breast milk may contain HIV and it is possible that otherwise uninfected infants born to infected mothers might acquire HIV postnatally through breast-feeding.

Both extensive epidemiologic studies and the secure weight of a decade's experience confirm that HIV does not spread through any kind of casual, nonintimate contact. HIV is not transmitted by insects, animals, surfaces, air, water, or fomites.

Among students, the overwhelming preponderance of HIV infections are acquired through sexual exposure. While current data do not allow precise determinations, estimates of the frequency of HIV infection on campuses, obtained through blinded seroprevalence surveys, indicate that approximately one in 500 college and university students has HIVD. The research completed thus far demonstrates substantial geographic variation, with higher rates of HIVD on campuses in areas with a higher incidence of AIDS. Seropositivity is strongly associated with male sex and older age within the student population, but HIV is also found in women and among younger undergraduates.

Because of the long pre-symptomatic period, the likelihood of transmission through sexual (rather than blood-related) means, and the youth of college students, most students with HIVD will have chronic asymptomatic disease. Relatively few students will progress all the way to advanced illness during their stay in the college community. Therefore, the major clinical responsibility of campus health care providers will be prevention and early intervention to promote health and delay the onset of severe, symptomatic disease. Nonetheless, since the age of initial infection with HIV is younger now than in the past, and since some campuses have large numbers of older, graduate, or non-traditional students, some students will require complex and inter-related services as symptoms and complications arise.

The significance of HIVD on campus is great, and pertains to:

1.  Chronic illness: HIVD is a chronic manageable illness requiring identification, diagnosis, and treatment as early as possible. Each phase demands specific, sequenced interventions. Ongoing, careful follow-up is vital.

2.  Risk: Patterns of sexual (and, to a lesser extent, needle-sharing) behavior among students allow transmission of HIV, as is true of other sexually transmissible organisms. Students with HIVD may pose risk to health care providers.

3.  Development: The associations of intimacy, illness, sex, and death with HIV may result in broad changes in the process and outcomes of psychosexual development, especially related to issues of intimacy, trust, sexual orientation, and building relationships.

4.  Education: HIVD emphasizes the need for effective sexual health education and health promotion programs. These needs are neither entirely new nor unique to HIV, but the chronicity and gravity of HIVD demand attention.

5.  Costs: Both financial (health care services, professional training, educational programs, health educators, fringe benefits) and nonfinancial (social change, loss of members of the campus community) costs will follow HIVD at all institutions of higher education.

## PREVENTION

HIVD is a disease of behavior, and changes in behavior can prevent it. Unfortunately, human behavior is complex, and altering it is difficult. The determinants of intimate sexual behavior among students are many, and the absence of simple correlations between knowledge and behavior is exceedingly clear. Repeatedly, studies have demonstrated that college and university students possess high levels of accurate information and awareness about HIV and its transmission, but that their behavior still leaves them at risk.

The challenges in preventing HIVD among students are to:

1.  understand existing behavior and its complex personal, social, and cultural determinants;

2.  build skills among students to promote their **doing** what they know – that is, to train them in ways to protect themselves within the real parameters of campus life;

3.  promote self-esteem and self-determination through programs that help students feel a deep and durable personal commitmet to health; and

4.  build community: foster a sense of community support for healthier behaviors, thereby modifying social norms and challenging the cultural values that, in fact, promote unhealthy intimacy, undermine self-esteem, and glamorize risk.

These goals will require prevention programs that are carefully designed, monitored, and evaluated. Effective efforts will likely be peer-based, skills-oriented, and focused on self-determination. Rather than isolating HIVD as an issue in risk and education, successful programs will recognize and emphasize the connections among behaviors related to other sexually transmitted diseases, unwanted pregnancy, sexual assault, and drug and alcohol abuse. Instead of preaching, moralizing, or demanding compliance with simple-minded behavioral recipes ("just say no"), effective prevention strategies will build on personal values and active decisions about health and the future consequences of current behaviors.

The behavioral basis of preventing HIV disease is complex, because of the multiple determinants of and influences on choices, skills, and risk-taking. On the other hand, the principal scientific prescriptions for reducing the risk of infection with HIV are straightforward. HIV infection can be **prevented** by:

1.  never using a needle that has been used by another person for any reason; and

2.  never having anal, vaginal, or oral sexual intercourse; or having anal, vaginal, or oral intercourse with only one lifetime partner who has never had another sexual partner.

The risk of HIV infection can be substantially reduced by:

1.  cleaning and disinfecting needles used by another person with bleach prior to using these needles on oneself; and

2.  properly using latex condoms for anal or vaginal intercourse. Condoms may also reduce the risk of transmitting HIV during fellatio. It is possible, but unproven, that latex squares (rubber dams) reduce the chance of transmitting HIV during cunnilingus. It is possible, but unproven, that discontinuing fellatio prior to ejaculation will reduce the chance of transmitting HIV.

In prevention programs, it is important to stress relativity both in assessing risk and seeking protection. In the lives of most college and university students, **absolute** prevention may be difficult to achieve – but students are able to succeed in **reducing** risk significantly. Unfortunately, there are certain unresolved questions about the details of transmission of HIV during sexual contact (e.g., Exactly how risky is fellatio? What specific recommendations should educators make about cunnilingus?). Coping with these uncertainties is stressful for both educator and student as long as absolutes are sought. Each person must decide what level of risk he or she can tolerate in life – about many issues – and managing the risk of HIV is an important example. An individual who wants no risk at all, for example, would abstain from all sexual contact. People who can tolerate a little greater risk would use condoms for all intercourse; those who can manage greater risk than that might not use condoms for fellatio, but would stop before ejaculation.

# TESTING/INTERVENTION/TREATMENT

## TESTING

The diagnosis of HIVD is made by confirming the presence of antibodies to HIV, HIV antigens, reverse transcriptase activity, or HIV genome in blood or cells. For all practical purposes, diagnosis currently is accomplished by HIV antibody tests that infer the presence of HIV by detecting highly specific immunoglobulins.

HIV antibody testing requires two steps: a screening test, usually done by enzyme-linked immunosorbent assay (ELISA), and a confirmatory test by immunoblotting techniques (usually a Western blot). ELISA tests are extremely sensitive and highly specific, but the occurrence of occasional false positives demands that all positive ELISA determinations be verified by immunoblotting, which is more specific.

Although technical errors and test kit inaccuracies may produce false negative ELISA tests, the real problem of reliability in negative test results derives from variability in the rate at which individuals develop detectable levels of anti-HIV antibody. Most people develop antibody (and become seropositive) within three to six months of original acquisition of HIV, but a small minority do not seroconvert for a year, and rarely seroconversion is delayed for 18-44 months. Thus, while a confirmed positive test provides **absolute** information, the reliability of negative tests is always **relative**. The longer it has been since the last possible exposure to HIV, the more reliable the test. Generally, tests done six full months after last exposure are reasonably reliable but repeat testing is often necessary to resolve uncertainties.

The social, psychological, legal, and economic aspects of HIVD and society's response to the epidemic have greatly complicated HIV antibody testing. Individuals undergoing HIV antibody testing frequently do so after much hesitation and worry, and the testing process is often surrounded by anxiety, sleeplessness, and depression. Disclosure of test results – and, sometimes, even of the fact that testing was done – has led to discrimination, loss of jobs or housing, termination of insurance coverage, and endangering of relationships. Accordingly, to reduce the psychological and socioeconomic risks associated with HIV antibody testing, every individual seeking testing should have extensive, focused pre-test education and counseling and similarly detailed post-test counseling and support. Clinicians and counselors must advise persons wishing to be tested of the procedures used to protect confidential information and of any statutory or regulatory requirements to report test results **before** the test is done.

The most difficult – and important – component of the process of identifying the presence of HIVD is the earliest: risk assessment. Educational programs ideally prepare audiences not only to alter behavior and build community, but also to take positive steps toward health promotion. In the case of HIVD, a clear and straightforward risk assessment is the first fundamental act in health promotion. Clinicians in all disciplines will have many opportunities to suggest, encourage, and support personal risk assessment by students. Doing so requires comfort with the issues involved, skill in doing a careful and sensitive sexual history, knowledge about HIV testing and referral sources, and an attitude of concern and receptiveness.

## INTERVENTION AND TREATMENT

Given that HIVD is a chronic progressive illness, it is important to offer people who have "tested positive" access to a number of medical, nursing, social, legal, and educational services. Different interventions become appropriate during successive phases of HIVD. Of major importance are:

1. **Education:** about HIVD and its management; reporting requirements; sources of clinical services; available research trials; what symptoms to watch for; preventing transmission of HIV to others.

2. **Self-care Skills:** marshalling an individual's own skills and resources to promote health through proper nutrition, regular aerobic exercise, adequate rest and sleep, stress management, smoking cessation, and moderation in the use of alcohol. For many people with HIVD, self care also encompasses meditation, bodywork, imaging, or self-hypnosis.

3. **Clinical Monitoring and Anti-viral Therapy:** (Note: Changes in recommendations must be anticipated as a result of on-going research. At the time of writing, the following recommendations apply. The reader is encouraged to seek updated advice in these areas from community specialists familiar with the management of HIV infection.) Regular visits to assess clinical and laboratory status. Complete blood count, platelet count, and lymphocyte

subpopulation studies (for $CD_4$ number and percentage, $CD_4$:$CD_8$ ratio, and $CD_8$ number and percentage) should be done with increasing frequency as $CD_4$ number declines. As $CD_4$ number decreases, periodic tests of HIV antigen, serum neopterin, and beta-2 microglobulin also become important.

Once the $CD_4$ count is reliably and reproducibly ≤500/mm³, therapy with zidovudine (ZDV) is indicated. ZDV may be initiated earlier if the $CD_4$ cell percentage has dropped to < 21 percent, the $CD_4$ count is declining quickly, or symptoms clearly referable to HIVD have occurred. Currently, the recommended dose of ZDV is 500 mg/day, given as 100 mg p.o. every 4 hours while awake. Once on ZDV, it is important to watch for toxicity – especially myelosuppression (monitored with blood counts every two to four weeks initially, then monthly for three months, then every second or third month) and myositis (anticipated with periodic creatine kinase levels beginning about four to six months after starting the drug).

4. **Prevention of infectious disease** includes:

   a. immunizations against Pneumococcus, hepatitis B, and measles shortly after HIVD is recognized, and yearly influenza vaccine after symptoms develop;

   b. surveillance for tuberculosis by PPD (if not anergic) or chest x-ray, every six months; and

   c. prophylaxis, especially for Pneumocystis pneumonia, using trimethoprim-sulfamethoxazole (one double strength tablet BID) or aerosalized pentamidine (150-300 mg once a month).

5. **Psychological management** of all individuals with HIVD promotes a healthy adjustment to chronic illness, builds a sense of self confidence and self-determination, works to find strategies to reduce isolation, and deals with symptoms of anxiety, fear, and depression.

6. **Social management** provides referrals to support groups, connection to community agencies, assessment of financial resources and demands, and consideration of work-related issues relevant to HIVD.

This multiplicity of approaches properly emphasizes that "early intervention" for HIVD is far more than prescribing ZDV. Using all of the strategies available promotes health, delays the onset of more severe complications, and leaves individuals with HIVD more prepared to handle serious illness if it occurs. The management of the infectious, neoplastic, and psychoneurologic manifestations of advanced HIVD is well reviewed elsewhere.

# READINGS AND RESOURCES

American Public Health Association: Special initiative on AIDS Report Series; and Preventing AIDS: A Guide to Effective Education for the Prevention of HIV Infection. APHA, 1015 15th Street NW, Washington DC, 20005, 202/789-5600

Benenson AS (ed): Control of Communicable Diseases in Man. 15th ed. Washington DC, American Public Health Association, 1990

CDC: America Responds to AIDS series. Packet of articles for young people from the National AIDS Information and Education Program (NAIEP) at CID/CDC

DiClemente et al: College students' knowledge and attitudes about AIDS and changes in HIV-preventive behaviors. AIDS Educ Prevent 2:201-212, 1990

Keeling R (ed): AIDS on the College Campus (2d ed). Rockville MD, American College Health Association, 1989

Kotloff KL, Tacket CO, Clemens JD, et al: Assessment of the prevalence and risk factors for HIV infection among college students using three survey methods. Am J Epidemiol 133: 2-8, 1991

National AIDS Hotline (CDC): 800/342-2437

National AIDS Information Clearinghouse (CDC): 800/458-5231

Richie ND, Stenroos D, Getty A: Using Peer Educators for a Classroom-based AIDS Program. J Am College Health 39:96-99, 1990

Shapiro SJ, Kotloff KL: Prevention of risk behaviors associated with HIV infection among college students. Nurse Practitioner Forum 2:2, 87-90, 1991

# 13

# Sexually Transmitted Diseases Among College Students

TED W. GRACE, MD, MPH AND KEVIN PATRICK, MD, MS

Infections of the genitourinary system are responsible for a significant proportion of all medical visits to student health centers. As expected, sexually transmitted diseases have higher rates in the most sexually active age groups, older adolescents and young adults between 15 and 34 years (Figure 1, next page).[1-4] Individuals under age 25 actually comprise the majority of STD cases.[5] Changing demographic and sociocultural forces, increasing sexual activity, coitus at younger ages, the likelihood of multiple partners, and the gradual replacement of protective barrier contraceptive methods by oral contraceptives have all contributed to the epidemic increase in sexually transmitted diseases in the college-aged population.

Over the past few decades, the spectrum of microbial agents transmitted by sexual intercourse has expanded to over 50 different organisms and syndromes.[6] Four viral STDs have now assumed distinction as the "modern" sexually transmitted diseases: human papillomavirus (HPV), genital herpes simplex virus (HSV), human immunodeficiency virus (HIV), and hepatitis B virus (HBV). These "four-H" infections can cause significant long-term morbidity, including infertility, ectopic pregnancy, chronic liver disease, neoplasias, and risk of death.

While the traditional STDs fit the medical model of treatment for cure, therapy of chronic viral infections is generally of limited benefit. Treatment guidelines for these STDs in the medical literature tend to emphasize palliative therapies, such as destructive procedures (e.g., laser surgery) and antiviral agents (e.g., AZT and acyclovir). These attempts to prevent the chronic sequelae of acute infections are examples of tertiary prevention. Whereas secondary and tertiary prevention can reduce the prevalence of a sexually transmitted disease, primary prevention may reduce its incidence. The immeasurable physical distress, psychological anguish, and economic burden resulting from STDs can be reduced only by management strategies that emphasize primary prevention techniques.

## PRIMARY PREVENTION

As student health providers strive to obtain the best possible health outcomes for their patients with STDs, the focus of interest must shift toward primary prevention. Health education, individual counseling, and behavioral intervention techniques have effectively reduced high-risk sexual behavior among homosexual men.[7-9] The decline in incidence of many STDs during the AIDS era has not been as dramatic in the heterosexual population.[10] Most studies exploring the knowledge, attitudes, perceptions of risk, and sexual behaviors of college students with regard to HIV infections suggest that they are well informed.[11-17]

While knowledge is necessary and useful, it is not sufficient for behavior change.[18,19] Efforts directed at behavior change have lagged far behind those directed at medical diagnosis and treatment.[20] Value expectancy theories and social learning theory currently represent the state of the art in behavioral intervention.[21] Such approaches, although based on a well-established body of knowledge from the psychological literature, are only recently being used to model students' decisions about high-risk sexual behaviors.

College students in transition from youth to adulthood are more likely to exhibit "magical thinking" characterized by risk-taking behaviors, denial, and

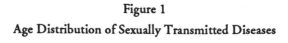

### Figure 1
### Age Distribution of Sexually Transmitted Diseases

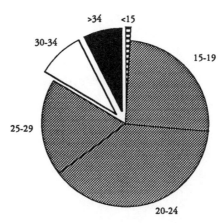

>34    <15

30-34

15-19

25-29

20-24

(typical college-age group included in gray areas.)

feelings of invulnerability. Control programs must stress the reduction of the behaviors that place sexually active students at risk for STDs, including inadequate utilization of barrier-method contraceptives, substance use, and high-risk sexual behavior.

## CONTRACEPTION

Contraceptive behaviors have been linked to both protection from, and to development of, sexually transmitted disease. The use of an intrauterine device (IUD) is a risk factor for pelvic inflammatory disease (PID) and subsequent tubal infertility. Data available on the role of oral contraceptives in acquiring STDs and PID are inconclusive. While oral contraceptives may afford some protection against gonococcal infections and certain forms of PID, oral contraceptive users apparently have more endocervical infections with chlamydia.[22]

The consistent and proper use of latex condoms (not natural skin) is an effective barrier against the most common sexually transmitted infections afflicting the college-age group, including chlamydia, gonorrhea, HSV, HPV, and HIV. Other barrier-method contraceptives, such as the diaphragm used with spermicides containing nonoxonyl-9, have also been found to decrease the risk of some STDs. Women who choose nonbarrier-method contraceptives are potentially at higher risk for sexually transmitted infections and their sequelae. Unfortunately, college students are continuing to decide not to use condoms.[1,23,24] In fact, the use of barrier-method contraceptives may decrease as sexual experience increases.[25]

The National Survey of Family Growth conducted in 1988 shows an increase since 1982 in the use of oral contraceptives for women 15-24 years of age from 24 to 30 percent.[26] Oral contraceptives provide no protection against the viral STDs. As oral contraceptive use increases in college women, clinicians must raise the question of concomitant use of condoms with each patient if the STD epidemic is to be controlled. Teens who carry condoms and who have discussed AIDS with a physician are also more likely to use condoms consistently.[27]

## CO-FACTORS

Substance use is strongly associated with both the acquisition and transmission of STDs. Although sharing of unsterile needles is not the most prevalent method of spreading STDs in the college population, students may be at increased risk by having sexual intercourse with intravenous drug users. The addictive nature of many substances of abuse can result in the exchange of sexual intercourse for drugs.

The use of alcohol, crack cocaine, marijuana, and other non-intravenous drugs is not directly associated with STD transmission, but contributes indirectly to their acquisition. Substance-related sexual disinhibition is commonly associated with failure to use barrier-method contraceptives, multiple sexual partners, or casual sex with a new acquaintance. Alcohol and "recreational drug use" can also contribute to abusive sexual interactions. One survey found that 60 percent of women reported having been targets of other drinkers' sexual aggression at a time when they themselves had been drinking.[28]

## RESPONSIBLE SEXUALITY

Sexual behavior is the most important risk factor for acquisition of STDs, including age at first sexual intercourse; number of sexual partners; and frequency, type, and patterns of sexual activity. Many demographic and social correlates also affect STD rates, including race and socioeconomic status. Sexual intercourse initiated earlier in life is associated with a greater number of lifetime sexual partners and a higher risk for STDs. The average age of first sexual intercourse is 16 years.[29] The proportion of adolescent women 15-19 years of age who reported having had premarital sexual intercourse increased steadily from 28.6 percent in 1970 to 51.5 percent in 1988.[30] Approximately one-third of the increase in premarital sexual experience for the entire period occurred from 1985 through 1988.

The number of sexual partners is also directly associated with the acquisition of STDs, including their long-term sequelae. This relationship is complicated by the sexual behavior of each partner. One study found that 39 percent of males and 17 percent of females ages 18-24 have had three or more sexual partners within a one-year period.[31] A survey of college women comparing the sexual behavior of three cohorts of college women at the same university found little difference in sexual practices over a 14-year period.[32] In all three study years, about 20 percent of women reported having had six or more lifetime male sexual partners, and having had three or more male sexual partners in the year before the study.

High-risk sexual practices are used either as a means of birth control or as a means of sexual experimentation. The above study found no significant differences in the three surveys in the frequency of fellatio, cunnilingus, or anal intercourse.[32] Among 5514 first-year college and university students in Canada, 74.3 percent of the men and 68.9 percent of the women were coitally active. Of those, 14.3 percent of the men and 18.6 percent of the women had participated in anal intercourse, and 5.5 percent reported a previous STD.[1]

## ABSTINENCE

Health care professionals should define what a student means by abstinence. While abstinence from all sexual activity with another person offers protection from sexually transmitted infections, it is usually defined as refraining from penis-in-vagina intercourse. Patients should be well informed that they remain at risk for transmission of STDs through noncoital intimate behaviors, such as anal intercourse, oral sex, and any sex that results in tissue damage or bleeding. Abstainers outnumber those who have had sexual intercourse in the U.S. until age 17.[33] Medical providers should endorse the concept of abstinence by providing the student with encouragement and support.

Besides educating the individual about the advantages of abstinence, it is equally important to provide guidelines on how to abstain, for example, avoiding high-pressure sexual situations, staying sober, setting personal limits in advance, and then sticking to them. Abstainers need to be provided with the knowledge about methods for prevention of infection and pregnancy, should they decide to have intercourse. Include information on both over-the-counter birth control methods, as well as postcoital protection. Students should also be made aware of specific medical indications for abstaining from sexual activity, such as the development of symptoms of an STD.

## EDUCATION

Health education efforts can play an integral part in STD intervention activities by promoting primary preventive behaviors. Educational measures may include one-on-one counseling of patients with sexually transmitted diseases, or may be group-directed efforts. Many health centers provide information about STD preventive behaviors during required family planning classes.

The traditional "scare tactics" approach of teaching about "VD" in didactic health science lectures has clearly been an inadequate method of changing behavior.[34] Sex education courses that increase students' knowledge of AIDS or the full spectrum of STDs are now being woven into the academic fabric of many universities. But the current high levels of knowledge per se are not being translated into safer sexual behavior.[35] The initial results of recently proposed psychological models for promoting protective sexual practices offer more hope for the future.[36-40]

Three components are essential for STD/HIV risk reduction education to be effective:[1]

1. The program has to provide relevant information about STDs/HIV that allows the students both to objectively assess their personal risk and to ascertain the best method of risk reduction within their individual social environment.

2. The program must provide training in the specific behavioral skills that are necessary for actually practicing safer sex, such as how to introduce the topic of safer sex in pre-intercourse discussion, how to negotiate condom use with

a potentially unwilling partner, and how to exit unsafe sexual situations if a partner refuses to comply with safe-sex requests.

3. Individuals must be motivated to act on their knowledge of personal STD/HIV risk by using behavioral risk-reduction skills.

Such multi-method programs have been found to be more effective than interventions designed only to increase knowledge. Other components of a successful program help students process relatively complex information. Peer-led training and skills building allow students to resist peer and social pressure more effectively, negotiate the use of barrier-contraceptives, and anticipate the future consequences of their behavior.[41-44] Sexually transmitted disease prevention programs should incorporate multi-media communication approaches, like role-playing exercises, vignettes or stop-action videos, rehearsal of simulated risky situations, and transmission games.[45-47] Programs with a theoretical framework, such as social learning theory, value expectancy theory and the health belief model, are also more likely to be effective.[21,45,46,48,49] Sexually transmitted infections are no exception to the dictum that diseases are sometimes much easier to understand than the complicated behavioral patterns that cause them.

## VACCINATION

By increasing host resistance, vaccines are by far the most effective available method for primary prevention and control of sexually transmitted diseases. Hepatitis B is the only STD agent for which a vaccine is currently available. Unfortunately, its overall impact on hepatitis B rates has been negligible so far.[50] Some question whether the current strategy of vaccinating selected high-risk groups will ever be effective in lowering the overall incidence of hepatitis B. The populations with high rates of infection are often not aware of their risk, and some 30 percent of patients with hepatitis B have no identifiable source of infection.[50] As the price of the vaccine decreases, universal immunization may become a more practical means of controlling HBV infection. While STD vaccines should probably be targeted toward adolescents and young adults, our most successful approaches to immunization have generally been through efforts to reach children. Vaccines against other STD agents may also become available within the next 5 to 10 years.

## SECONDARY PREVENTION

Secondary prevention refers to activities concerned with the early diagnosis and prompt treatment of health problems before they manifest as more serious problems. The ready availability of diagnostic and treatment services for patients must be an important part of any control strategy for STDs. Most major colleges and universities provide such medical care for their students, and it is now being offered by some high schools. Treatment of STDs is adequately summarized elsewhere,[51-53] so this discussion will concentrate on other components of secondary prevention.

## SURVEILLANCE AND MONITORING

Accurate data collection on STD rates and distribution in the population provides the only sensitive indicator of the effectiveness of intervention control programs. Regular collection, summarization, and analysis of such data also helps to identify trends in disease, and to target resources toward high-risk groups in the population. Unfortunately, many states have not instituted reporting systems for chlamydial or viral STDs, and valid information exists only for the more traditional venereal diseases. Much of the data on chronic viral STDs is collected from the National Disease and Therapeutic Index, which is based on a survey of a stratified random sample of office-based private practitioners in the United States. This includes information about first office visits and total number of visits for the various infections. These cross-sectional surveys estimate the disease prevalence, giving an idea of the burden and age-related trends of the disease in the population. As many patients with chronic viral infections are asymptomatic, seroprevalence analyses are also sometimes performed. These reflect the cumulative STD experience of earlier decades, rather than current experiences. Unfortunately, the true incidence of sexually transmitted diseases in the U.S. can only be crudely estimated from available data presented without denominators.

## SCREENING

Population screening aimed at early detection in presumptively healthy people offers another strategy for controlling STDs. This has traditionally included examining premarital individuals, pregnant women, blood donors, and prostitutes. Screening is sometimes not feasible because of potentially large numbers of sexual partners. Cost is usually the limiting factor, which includes the evaluation of false-positive results. Since the cost-effectiveness is dependent on disease prevalence, screening is often concentrated on high-prevalence groups. Rescreening previously infected individuals is four times as effective in reducing incidence as initial screening.[54] Some STDs are common enough in student populations to warrant universal screening, while others may need screening based only on the presence of identifiable risk factors. Screening programs are most helpful in situations of curable illness. Health-seeking behaviors and the effectiveness of disease control strategies based on early diagnosis and treatment are less important determinants of the incidence of incurable viral STDs.

## CONTACT TRACING

Contact tracing, or partner notification, is a traditional form of medical surveillance whereby the sexual contacts are notified without revealing the identity of the index case. Contact tracing can be thought of as a subset of the general class of screening strategies, based on the risk factor of contact with an infectious individual. Some infections, like gonorrhea, have such a high rate of transmissibility that sexual contact with a carrier is justification for treatment without further testing.[55] Even viral STDs may warrant screening contacts in order to advise those as yet uninfected that they are being exposed, and to allow them to take measures to protect their other partners.

An STD is often the first indication that one of the members of a presumably mutually faithful sexual relationship is having sexual activity outside of the relationship. The best chance of preventing a recurrence of the infection in the patient and its transmission to others is by considering the couple as the unit of disease (Figure 2). However many partners are involved, there is a critical triad of infection: the source, the patient, and the patient's regular partner. Identification and timely referral of sex partners can reduce reinfection rates in all of them, while preventing the spread of infection to future partners. Besides the ethical questions, there are legal requirements. Many STDs must be reported to the public health department, and full disclosure made to the "injured" party.

Students are often willing to assume an active role in locating and referring all of their sexual partners with a high rate of compliance. But student health centers tend to exclude the index patient's sexual partner from care if he or she is not attending the same school. Asking the patient to have his/her partner evaluated and

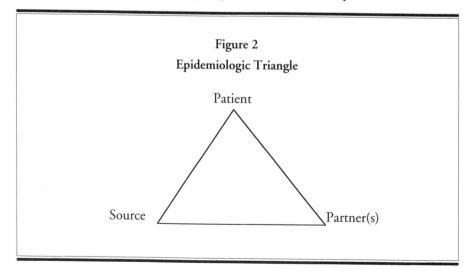

**Figure 2**

**Epidemiologic Triangle**

Patient

Source

Partner(s)

treated elsewhere often results in poor compliance, related to lack of insurance, inconvenience, and fear of parental notification. Sometimes student health providers treat the partner sight unseen, placing themselves in legal jeopardy. Unless institutional barriers are removed that restrict access to individual parts of the whole, STDs may remain uncontrolled on school campuses.

## RISK FACTORS FOR STDS IN COLLEGE-AGE WOMEN

Sexually transmitted diseases are biologically sexist infections![5] Women suffer more serious long-term consequences from the majority of the STDs. These include pelvic inflammatory disease, ectopic pregnancy, chronic pelvic pain, infertility, and cervical cancer. Their infections are more likely to be asymptomatic, and pregnant women can pass many STDs to their newborn infants during delivery. Women are not only infected more often than men, but are also more likely to acquire a sexually transmitted disease from any single sexual event. Several of the STDs, such as human immunodeficiency virus, human T-cell lymphotrophic virus, and hepatitis B virus, are transmitted much more efficiently to the penile-receptive partner. This could be the result of several factors, including the exposure of a larger surface area in women, the retention of the infected ejaculate within the vagina, or the increased possibility of obtaining superficial trauma during intercourse. The latter, along with early lesions, is less likely to be detected by the patient because of its concealed location. Finally, women are more often sexually assaulted, and sexually transmitted diseases are the most common medical problems complicating such assaults.

Others have claimed that both biological and psychosocial characteristics of younger patients make them more vulnerable to genital infections.[56] The average age of menarche has decreased in the U.S. during this century, increasing the sexually mature interval for the female population. In adolescence, the columnar epithelium extends from the endocervical canal into the vagina. This epithelium, not protected by cervical mucus, is the primary site of invasion by both chlamydia and gonococcal pathogens. Until the squamocolumnar junction (transformation zone) has progressed to the endocervical canal, it is also biologically more susceptible to carcinogenic factors. This places younger patients at increased risk for cervical HPV infections, and subsequent cytologic changes.

## SEXUAL-PRACTICES HISTORY

Student health care practitioners typically provide education and counseling for populations at risk of disease. Risk status is based on information derived from a thorough medical history. Primary care providers are also considered an important source of information on sexual matters, but many of them do not take the time or possess the required skills for detecting and preventing potentially high-risk sexual behavior.[57-60] Fewer than one in ten physicians ask new patients questions that are specific enough to identify STD risk.[61] Often with little or no training in sexual history taking, they are uncomfortable asking questions about sexual behavior. In order to provide proper care, college health professionals must be able to obtain a detailed sex, drug, and alcohol history. It takes practice and special skills to overcome specific interpersonal obstacles when asking these questions. The following guidelines for taking a sexual history should assist the provider in gathering the preliminary data necessary for high-risk sexual behavior assessment:[62]

- Do not signal the caregiver's discomfort with the subject by leaving the sexual history until last.
- Establish an appropriate context and rationale for the discussion by introducing the subject in a way that will express your interest in his or her sexual practices, but places that concern within the overall context of an open and honest doctor-patient relationship (e.g., "In order to provide you with optimal health care, I need to ask you some questions about your personal habits and practices.")
- Start with safe questions, such as contraceptive use.
- Be very specific and detailed; not general and euphemistic.
- Unless you are having to probe for specific high-risk behaviors, ask open-ended questions that do not elicit yes and no answers.
- Go slowly, and allow the patient time to mobilize his/her emotional and intellectual resources before changing the subject. Take time to reflect on what a patient says, and how he/she says it (i.e., observe body language).
- Be professional, concerned, sensitive, and self-confident; approach the subject in a nonjudgmental, matter-of-fact way.
- Try to impart a degree of respect and understanding toward the patient's beliefs and values.
- Be aware that different religious and cultural backgrounds may cause communication barriers.
- Use neutral terminology that is comfortable to the patient. If he or she does not understand words for certain sexual parts or activities, teach him/her appropriate terms that have been clearly defined and illustrated.
- Concentrate on the sexual behavior, not on the patient's sexual orientation.
- Practice your technique. Start with simple details, and add more specific questions as level of comfort improves.

Several sources discuss sexual history-taking practices, including specific questions to cover, in more detail. [62-65] Initial inquiries should include broad categories of sexual orientation, i.e., Do you have sex only with men, only with women, or with both?

Follow with questions regarding specific sexual practices that are associated with specific STDs (Table 1, next page). While receptive anal intercourse has a high risk of transmitting HIV infection, genital intercourse has a somewhat lower risk, and oral sex has a still lower risk.

Next, establish the patient's past and present level of sexual activity:

- How old were you when you had sexual intercourse for the first time? Are you having sexual intercourse now?
- Approximately how often?
- When was the last time?
- Do you have a regular partner?
- Have you had other partners? Recently?
- How many partners have you had in the past 6 months? year? lifetime?
- Do you use any preventive measures to protect yourself against STD and HIV infection (e.g., condoms or spermicides)?
- Have you or a sexual partner ever had an STD?
- Have you ever injected drugs, or had sex with someone who might have injected drugs?
- What do you know about your past sexual partners? Did any of them have a history of high-risk behaviors?

This list is not intended to be complete, but only to cover some of the more important aspects of the sexual history questionnaire.

Many students are not aware of the multiplicative effect on risk that can occur with a new partner (Figure 3, page 643). If a person had intercourse with someone new, and that person has had sexual contact with five people in the last year, and each of those have had five sexual contacts, etc., by the fifth expansion of this phenomenon, one sexual encounter could potentially expose someone to 15,625 different people. By having sexual intercourse with five different people who each have that type of exposure, one is exposing him/herself to 78,125 different partners. At some certain level of sexual activity, the risk of acquiring STDs is no longer proportional, but seems to take a quantum leap.[66] This exponential increase in risk demonstrates why serial monogamy is not necessarily "safe sex." Temporary fidelity lasting from months to several years does not provide the same protection as a dual, mutually faithful, long-standing relationship.

Table 1
Infections Associated with Specific Sexual Practices

| Sexual Practice | Possible Infections |
|---|---|
| Oral-genital Sex | Gonorrhea; Herpes Type 1 and 2; Nongonococcal pharyngitis or urethritis (Chlamydia and others); Human papillomavirus; Syphilis; Hepatitis B; Enteric infections; Lymphogranuloma venereum; *Granuloma inguinale*; Chancroid; Influenza viruses; *Neisseria meningitidis*; Human immunodeficiency virus; Candidiasis; Scabies; Cytomegalovirus; Molluscum. |
| Anal Intercourse | Gonorrhea; Herpes Type 1 and 2; Nongonococcal pharyngitis or urethritis (Chlamydia and others); Human papillomavirus; Syphilis; Hepatitis A, B, non-A/non-B; *Lymphogranuloma venereum*; *Granuloma inguinale*; Chancroid; Human immunodeficiency virus; Candidiasis; Fungal infections; Scabies; Cytomegalovirus; Molluscum; Trichomoniasis; Corynebacterium; *E. coli*. |
| Oral-anal Sex (Anilinction) | Gonorrhea; Herpes Type 1 and 2; Human papillomavirus; Syphilis; Hepatitis A, B, non-A/non-B; *Lymphogranuloma venereum*; *Granuloma inguinale*; Chancroid; Human immunodeficiency virus; Candidiasis; *Neisseria meningitidis*; Scabies; Molluscum; *E. coli.*; Shigella; *E. histolytica*; Salmonella; Giardia; Helminthic parasites; *Enterobius vermicularis*; *Strongyloides stercoralis*; Other enteric infections. |
| Fist/Finger Insertion | Human immunodeficiency virus; *E. coli.*; Shigella; Salmonella; Other enteric infections. |

(Adapted from Reference 53)

## SPECIFIC INFECTIONS

The section that follows addresses sexually transmitted *Chlamydia trachomatis,* human papillomavirus, herpes simplex virus, gonorrhea, and syphilis. Two other important sexually transmitted diseases – hepatitis B and human immunodeficiency virus (HIV) infections – are addressed in other chapters of this book. (See Chapters 4, 5, and 6 of Volume One, and Chapters 12 and 15 of this volume.)

### *CHLAMYDIA TRACHOMATIS*

Genital chlamydial infection is the most prevalent bacterial sexually transmitted pathogen in the U.S. today.[67-69] The prevalence rate of genital infections with *C. trachomatis* in female college students ranges from less than 5 percent to nearly 10 percent.[70-76] The infection may result in a wide spectrum of clinical features, although up to one-third of infected men and two-thirds of infected women are asymptomatic.[77] *Chlamydia trachomatis* can be cultured equally as often from the

---

**Figure 3**

**Modern Day Math Problems***

*© Steve Phillips, All Rights Reserved. Reproduced with permission.

urethra as from the cervix in young women, and it is an important cause of the acute urethral syndrome presenting with pyuria in the absence of bacteriuria.[78] Eight to thirty percent of women with untreated cervical chlamydial infection will develop clinically apparent salpingitis.[79] This etiologic agent has been implicated in 20 to 40 percent of salpingitis cases,[80] and one-half to two-thirds of infection-related tubal infertility.[81] The risk of infertility approximately doubles with each new episode of PID (1st=11%, 2nd=23%, and 3rd =54%).[82] Chlamydia apparently causes more severe tubal inflammation and scarring than gonorrhea, although it frequently occurs without symptoms. In fact, two-thirds of women with tubal infertility report no history of past chlamydial infection, in spite of having *C. trachomatis* – specific antibody present.[83]

Consequently, considerable attention has been focused on screening young women at risk for contracting *C. trachomatis*. One study tested a logistic regression model to determine selective screening factors using simple clinical information.[84] Another found universally screening asymptomatic women for chlamydial infection to be cost-effective when the likelihood of infection exceeded 7 percent.[80] Chlamydial infection should be excluded in all sexually active women who have irregular bleeding, whether or not they are on oral contraceptives.[85]

In men, chlamydia causes up to 50 percent of nongonococcal urethritis, and approximately 50 percent of epididymitis.[86] Its role in causing nonbacterial prostatitis remains controversial. Sexually transmitted infections, including chlamydia, rarely produce infertility in men. The paucity of serious complications, and higher proportion of symptomatic infections, give screening for *C. trachomatis* a lower priority in men than in women. Although some recommend screening asymptomatic males[87] this may not become cost-effective until the prevalence rate exceeds 21 percent.[88] The most noninvasive and cost-effective screening method for *C. trachomatis* in males is the identification of pyuria on the first-voided urine sediment. The urine may be screened for pyuria by either the chamber microscopy method or the urinary leukocyte esterase test.[89]

A specific diagnostic test is still necessary to confirm *C. trachomatis* infection in men with first-glass pyuria, and to exclude it in men with minimal or no evidence of urethritis. Isolation in cell culture remains the most sensitive and specific test for detection of *C. trachomatis*, but is expensive and difficult to transport. In a high-risk population for genital chlamydial infections, the antigen detection methods (direct smear test, ELISA test, and DNA probe) are quicker, and provide satisfactory sensitivity and specificity. Antigen detection methods for chlamydia using the urine sediment also show promise as a diagnostic test.

Empirical treatment of sexual partners of patients with *C. trachomatis* infections is recommended even before specific diagnostic test results have returned.[77] The transmission rate has been poorly defined, but studies have found that 45 percent of female partners of men with known chlamydial urethritis were infected, and 28 percent of male partners of women with genital chlamydial infections had positive cultures.[90] Specific testing prior to empiric treatment presents an opportunity to identify still other sexual contacts who should be evaluated and treated.

The Centers for Disease Control STD Treatment Guidelines advises that a test-of-cure evaluation is not necessary after treatment has been completed.[51] However, a test of cure is indicated for therapy noncompliance, circumstances supporting reinfection, pregnancy, complicated infections, requests for psychological reassurance, and evidence of persistent cervicitis. Antigen detection methods are effective starting 10 days after initiation of treatment.[91]

## GENITAL HUMAN PAPILLOMAVIRUS INFECTION

Genital warts are now the most common viral STD,[92] and are three times as common as genital herpes. The peak incidence rate is in the age group of those 20 to 24 years old, with 80 percent of condyloma patients occurring between the ages of 17 and 33 years. Genital HPV infections have an infectivity rate of nearly 66 percent after an average incubation period of two to three months. A 1987 report estimated a 10 percent prevalence of genital human papillomavirus infection in men and women between 15 and 49 years of age in the U.S., although only 1 percent had clinically visible condylomata.[92] The first report on the prevalence of genital HPV infection among women seeking health care at university student health clinics found it to range from 5 to 19 percent.[93] A more recent survey using polymerase chain reaction technology found that 46 percent of the young, sexually active study population of female university students was infected with HPV.[94] It also demonstrated that only 69 percent of the HPV-positive women were infected at both the cervical and vulvar sites.

About one-third of the more than 60 characterized HPV genotypes identified so far primarily infect the anogenital tract. The genital lesions caused by HPV types 6 and 11 (6/11 group) are commonly identified in genital warts or papillary condylomata of the vagina, vulva, cervix, penis, and anus. Lesions from this group of viruses often regress spontaneously. Genital lesions caused by HPV types 16, 18, 31, 33, 35, 39, 51, and 56 (16/18 group) usually occur in flat lesions, and may progress to neoplasia. Unpredictable exceptions also occur, since the 6/11 group lesions have been occasionally associated with neoplastic disease, and the 16/18 group lesions may regress spontaneously. In addition, the clinical value of viral typing is debatable because HPV types from both groups can occur in the same lesion, or at different sites on the same patient.

Molecular and biochemical evidence exists to implicate specific HPV types in the pathogenesis of genital epithelial neoplasia, although the epidemiologic evidence is not totally convincing. Well-controlled prospective clinical studies will be needed to clarify these issues, since carcinogenesis is often a complex, multi-step process. The natural history of cervical neoplasia appears to be changing, with an acceleration in the rate at which cervical neoplastic changes occur.[95,96] The increased frequencies of condyloma and cervical dysplasia in young women suggest that genital HPV infections may be contributing to this change. The exact roles played by HPV infection and changing sexual practices are not yet clear.

Recurrence of genital warts is common. This might result from an incomplete cure of a previous infection, reactivation of a latent infection, new infection with a different HPV type, or reinfection by the same HPV type. Human genital tract papillomaviruses are known to cause persistent, subclinical infections, but how long they persist or how often they become clinically apparent is not known. Like the herpesvirus, a latent human papillomavirus may reactivate. Treatment of this chronic phase of infection has generally not been effective in eradicating HPV or in reducing the risk of transmission to sexual partners.

Some sources advise the partners of women with evidence of genital HPV infections to be examined for warts.[97,98] However, male partners are at low risk of developing penile cancer, and there appears to be an extremely small risk of reinfecting the same sexual partner with the same HPV type after they have been treated.[99] Disappearance of visible condylomata does not mean disappearance of human papillomavirus, as up to two-thirds of patients have evidence of a subclinical infection after the best available therapy.[100] Since the complete elimination of all lesions is unlikely, prevention of the spread of the infection to new partners may be impossible. The Centers for Disease Control STD Treatment Guidelines states, "...the goal of treatment is removal of exophytic warts and the amelioration of signs and symptoms, not the eradication of HPV."[51] Until specific antiviral therapies become available for the management of HPV-related lesions, providers should avoid the misuse of expensive, traumatic, scarring procedures performed primarily for cosmetic reasons.

Many health care providers have been overwhelmed by the recent explosion in knowledge about human papillomavirus as a result of new technological advances. Controversy exists about the appropriate management strategy for atypical Pap smears consistent with HPV infection.[101-103] Replacement of the traditional standard of care practices by more aggressive management strategies should be based on careful evaluation of the soundness of new clinical information, and on consideration of how best to use the limited resources available to most student health centers to combat STD-associated morbidity. Epidemiologists are conducting prospective follow-up studies using sensitive diagnostic techniques on defined populations, and data on the natural history of these infections will be forthcoming. Until then, many practitioners will continue to follow patients with mildly abnormal cervical cytology results with repeat frequent Pap tests.

## GENITAL HERPES

Five different human herpesviruses have been recognized to date, including herpes simplex virus, varicella-zoster virus, Epstein-Barr virus, cytomegalovirus, and the virus recently identified as the etiologic agent of roseola infantum, human herpesvirus 6 (HHV-6). All appear to have the capacity to establish latent infections, and to be subsequently reactivated from the latent state. HSV types 1 and 2 may both infect the genital area, although HSV-1 infection is responsible for only about 25 percent of all first episodes of true primary genital herpes.[104] In addition, genital HSV-2 infections are twice as likely to be reactivated, and recur 8 to 10 times more frequently than genital HSV-1 infections.[105] Approximately 500,000 new cases of symptomatic genital herpes are reported yearly, and student health centers report that genital HSV infections are a major public health problem.[106,107] Genital herpes infections will continue to be of great concern to students based on their morbidity, recurrence rates, and potential for complications, such as neonatal transmission and aseptic meningitis.

Most HSV infections are asymptomatic and unlikely to result in the patient presenting to a physician's office. In the U.S., HSV infection is responsible for 40 to 60 percent of genital ulcers. Transmission of genital herpes can occur by both genital-genital and oral-genital sexual contact with an asymptomatic partner. A primary HSV outbreak may occur 1 to 45 days after sexual contact with an infected partner, although the typical range is 5 to 7 days.

HSV urethritis and/or cystitis may account for the prolonged duration of dysuria in women. A clear, mucoid urethral discharge and dysuria is noted in about one-third of men with primary HSV-2 infection.[104] Most infections present in both sexes with widely spaced bilateral pustular or ulcerative lesions. These patients should be advised not to resume sexual activity until after epithelialization of the lesions, which usually occurs in 17-20 days. The duration of symptoms and frequency of complications are greater in women, perhaps due to the greater surface area involved. Ninety percent of women with primary genital HSV-2 infection, and 70 percent with HSV-1 infection, have concomitant HSV cervicitis. The symptoms of recurrent genital herpes are often milder, the lesions are usually unilateral, and the mean time to complete healing of the lesions is about 10 days. The recurrence rate after primary HSV-2 infection is 90 percent, with a median of five episodes per year over the first two years. Surprisingly, those who develop high titers of HSV-2 complement-independent neutralizing antibody in convalescent sera are more likely to develop recurrences than those who do not.[108]

Since genital HSV lesions exhibit a diverse clinical spectrum, including lesions that resemble traumatic tears, diagnostic laboratory tests can be invaluable. However, they have their limitations. A viral culture is the most sensitive and specific test available if used within the first five days of the outbreak, although the ulcer persists longer than the virus is present in the lesion. The presence of multinucleated giant cells on Tzanck smear may provide a presumptive diagnosis of HSV infection. Differentiation between infections with HSV types 1 and 2 may be desirable, since HSV-2 infections have an increased incidence of recurrence on the genitalia. However, serologic cross-reactions commonly occur between the two HSV types with available assays, making them inadequate for discriminating between HSV-1 and HSV-2 antibodies.[109] While serologic evaluation otherwise has limited utility in the diagnosis of acute herpetic infection, it may be useful to document past infection. Acute and convalescent sera can also be utilized retrospectively to diagnose the primary infection. Serologic assays inadequately predict disease recurrence and transmissibility.

## GONORRHEA

While the annual incidence of gonorrhea appears to have declined in the U.S. in the past three decades, partly because of the behavioral changes related to the AIDS epidemic, these changes have not occurred uniformly within the population. Gonorrhea rates have decreased markedly in homosexual and bisexual men, but have increased slightly in teenagers.[110] Although the highest rates overall occur in the 20- to 24-year-old age group, when adjusted for sexual experience, the reported incidence of gonorrhea is almost twice as high for sexually active adolescents (15- to 19- year olds).[4] Reported cases of gonorrhea are also about tenfold higher in nonwhite than in white populations.

The incubation period for gonococcal infections ranges from 1 to 14 days in men (average of 2 to 5 days), and about 10 days in women. Since co-infection with chlamydia occurs in 15 to 25 percent of heterosexual men, and 30 to 40 percent of women, the use of diagnostic and treatment regimens that cover both organisms is recommended.[77] In men, the initial urethral discharge can be scant and mucoid or nonexistent. For evaluation of urethritis in men, the urethral smear is so sensitive and specific that culture may be considered optional for routine care,[111] although it is useful for determining antibiotic sensitivities. Although more time-consuming, collection and culture of the first 10 to 20 ml. of voided urine is an alternative that avoids the discomfort from use of a urethral swab. Smears from the endocervix or rectum demonstrating typical intracellular gram-negative diplococci are highly specific when performed in settings where the index of suspicion is high.[111] Available serologic techniques are not sufficiently sensitive or specific for routine use.

All partners exposed within 2 weeks prior to the onset of symptoms, or within one  month of an asymptomatic infection, should be treated even prior to the availability of culture results. Test-of-cure cultures are recommended at least 4 to 5 days after finishing treatment, and this should include a follow-up anorectal culture on all women.[112]

## SYPHILIS

The prevalence of primary syphilis is highest in young adults, especially in males and blacks. After a drop in the mid-1980s, the incidence of syphilis in the U.S. has increased significantly among heterosexual populations since 1985.[113] The number of reported cases was over 100,000 in 1988, the highest rate in 40 years.

The delay in reactivity with serologic tests makes dark-field microscopy the diagnostic test of first choice in primary syphilis. The more sensitive FTA-ABS becomes reactive about the time the chancre appears, while the VDRL becomes reactive some 14 days later. If nonreactive initially, these tests should be repeated in three to four weeks in patients with suspicious clinical findings. A rising VDRL titer is suggestive of primary syphilis, while serologic tests are virtually always reactive in secondary syphilis.

All cases should be followed up monthly for the first 3 months, and then 6, 9, 12, and 24 months thereafter, with serial monitoring of VDRL or RPR tests. The VDRL should decline approximately fourfold by three months post-therapy, and eightfold by six months.[114] It should be nonreactive one year after treatment in primary syphilis, and two years after treatment in secondary syphilis. If the titers do not fall as expected, or if clinical signs persist or reappear, retreatment is indicated. The FTA-ABS will remain positive. All sexual partners for the previous three months should be investigated, and at-risk partners for the preceding 6 to 12 months should be examined for secondary syphilis.[115]

## THE "STD CHECK"

After unprotected sex with a new partner, perhaps with the details obscured by alcohol or other drugs, students often present to their college health provider for an "STD check." It is impractical to test or treat for the entire spectrum of infections that could occur, but the typical patient is extremely anxious about STDs and often requests medication. Since most patients do not want to contact a casual acquaintance to inquire about their sexual history, the diagnosis and treatment of infection depends on the development of signs and symptoms, or positive screening tests. Certain infections are associated with specific types of sexual activity (Table 1). Although the relative infectivity of some infectious agents is known, the chance of contracting an STD after a single exposure is difficult to estimate. Most authorities would agree that prophylactic treatment is not routinely indicated in this situation, although the rest of the STD management strategy is the same as for a sexual-assault victim.

Reports on the prevalence rate of STDs in women following sexual assaults have been inconclusive. In one study, vaginal infections (bacterial vaginosis and trichomoniasis) were much more likely to be acquired after rape than were cervical infections (chlamydia and gonorrhea).[116] Genital herpes and human immunodeficiency virus infections have been known to occur, but are rarely transmitted by a single act of vaginal intercourse. The problem with these studies is determining how many of the infections present at the initial examination were present prior to the recent sexual encounter.

The initial visit usually occurs within the first 72 hours, so that postcoital contraception can be discussed. Begin with a vaginal wet mount, cultures or antigen-detection tests for *N. gonorrhoeae* and *C. trachomatis* from all exposed sites, a serologic test for syphilis, and if indicated, baseline HSV, HBV and HIV serologies. This first visit can also be used to educate the patient about the signs and symptoms of the common STDs that would require him/her to return before the next scheduled appointment. The avoidance of future high-risk sexual behavior should be addressed at this time, including the use of barrier contraceptives, especially until the diagnostic evaluation has been completed. Patients should be counseled on the importance of follow-up examinations, as future evaluations would be less likely to miss new infections.

Depending on the prevalence of particular STDs in the local population, and whether or not the contact is considered to be practicing high-risk behavior, follow-up evaluations are repeated at two weeks, two months, and six months (Table 2, next page). At two weeks, cultures and wet mount are repeated, and a pregnancy test can be done. Syphilis serology should be repeated at the two-month visit. If indicated, the viral serologies can be repeated at two months, with the HBV and HIV serologies repeated at six months. Acute and convalescent antibody titers for herpes simplex can be used to determine whether or not this infection was recently acquired, although most reserve this somewhat expensive evaluation for patients who develop characteristic lesions. Some recommend an initial Pap smear for cervical cytology, but a test at two to six months would more likely detect a recently acquired cervical infection with human papillomavirus.

For some students, fears from this affair will focus on the harm that could occur to their "regular" sexual partner, or to their relationship. This guilt contributes to their inability to be reassured that they have not acquired an STD, but the follow-up appointments and diagnostic evaluations will reinforce this. Use of prophylactic antimicrobial therapy can lead to a false sense of security for the patient and failure to return for follow-up evaluations. While these follow-up appointments offer an ideal time to educate the patient on "safer sex" methods, one must also be sensitive to the patient's emotional status. Attempts to scare the patient with frightening statistics during this very vulnerable time might do more harm than good. The astute practitioner will sense the effect of this incident on the patient, and advise formal counseling when indicated.

Table 2
"STD Check"

| | Incubation Period | Diagnostic Tests | Recommendations | Timing |
|---|---|---|---|---|
| Chlamydia | 7-21 Days | Culture or Antigen Detection Methods | Routine | Initial Visit, 2 Weeks |
| Gonorrhea | 1-14 Days Average M=2-5 Days Average F=10 Days | Culture or Gram Stain | Routine | Initial Visit, 2 Weeks |
| Syphilis | 10 Days-10 Weeks Average 3 Weeks | Serology | Routine | Initial Visit, 2 Months |
| Bacterial Vaginosis/ Trichomonas | 7 Days | Wet Mount or Culture | Routine | Initial Visit, 2 Weeks |
| Genital Warts | 2-3 Months | Pap Smear or DNA Probe | PRN | 2-6 Months |
| Genital Herpes | 1-45 Days Average 5-7 Days | Culture or Serology | PRN | Initial Visit, 2 Months |
| Hepatitis B | 45-180 Days Average 60-90 Days | Serology | PRN | Intial Visit, 2 Months, 6 Months |
| HIV | 3-8 Years | Serology | PRN | Initial Visit, 2 Months, 6 Months |

# CONCLUSION

Eleven of the 1990 Objectives for the Nation addressed sexually transmitted diseases.[117] Five priority objectives included syphilis, gonorrhea, gonococcal pelvic inflammatory disease, provider proficiency, and student awareness. In spite of the national attention these focused on sexually transmitted diseases and "safer sex" messages, some of the objectives were not met. While the incidence of some STDs is falling, the incidence of others is rapidly increasing, particularly in adolescent and young adult populations.

Healthy People 2000 contains objectives for reductions of all sexually transmitted diseases.[118] The year 2000 targets include chlamydia, genital herpes, genital warts, sexually transmitted hepatitis B, and special emphasis on HIV infection. The objective aimed at increasing the proportion of sexually active, unmarried people who regularly use condoms to at least 50 percent is particularly pertinent to university-based health care providers. People aged 15 to 29 acquire 86 percent of the 12 million new cases of STDs per year.[6] As college and university officials strive to obtain the best possible outcomes for their students, priorities must shift toward health promotion and disease prevention.

## REFERENCES

1. MacDonald NE, Wells GA, Fisher WA et al: High-risk STD/HIV behavior among college students. JAMA 263:3155-3159, 1990

2. Cates W, Rauh JL: Adolescent sexually transmitted diseases: An expanding problem. J Adolesc Health Care 6:257-261, 1985

3. Bell TA, Holmes K: Age-specific risks of syphilis, gonorrhea and hospitalized pelvic inflammatory disease in sexually experienced US women. Sex Transm Dis. 11:291-295, 1984

4. Centers for Disease Control: Sexually Transmitted Disease Statistics, Calendar Year 1987, No. 136. Atlanta, U.S. Public Health Service, 1988, pp 1-58

5. Hatcher RA, Stewart F, Trussell J et al (eds): Contraceptive Technology. New York, Irvington Publishers, Inc, 1990, p 96

6. U.S. Department of Health and Human Services: Prevention '89/'90: Federal Programs and Progress. Washington, DC, U.S. Government Printing Office, 1990, pp 40-41

7. Handsfield HH: Decreasing incidence of gonorrhea in homosexually active men—Minimal effect on risk of AIDS. West J Med 143:469-470,1985

8. Schultz S et al: Declining rates of rectal and pharyngeal gonorrhea among males—New York City. MMWR 33:295-297,1984

9. Judson FN: Fear of AIDS and gonorrhea rates in homosexual men. Lancet 2:159-160, 1983

10. Becker MH, Joseph JG: AIDS and behavioral change to reduce risk: A review. Am J Public Health. 78:394-410, 1988

11. Dorman SM, Rienzo BA: College students' knowledge of AIDS. Health Values 12:33-38, 1988

12. Edgar T, Freimuth VS, Hammond SL: Communicating the AIDS risk to college students: The problem of motivating change. Health Educ Res 3:59-65, 1988

13. Goodwin MP, Roscoe B: AIDS: Students' knowledge and attitudes at a midwestern university. J Am Coll Health 36:214-222, 1988

14. Gottlieb NH, Vacalis TD, Palmer DR et al: AIDS-related knowledge, attitudes, behaviors and intentions among Texas college students. Health Educ Res 3:67-73, 1988

15. Manning D, Barenberg N, Gallese L et al: College students' knowledge and health beliefs about AIDS: Implications for education and prevention. J Am Coll Health 37:254-259, 1989

16. Price JH, Desmond SM, Hallian C et al: College students' perceived risk and seriousness of AIDS. Health Educ 19:16-20, 1988

17. Thurman QC, Franklin KM: AIDS and college health: Knowledge, threat, and prevention at a northeastern university. J Am Coll Health 38:179-183, 1990

18. Bates IJ, Winder AE: Introduction to Health Education. Palo Alto, Mayfield, 1984

19. Aral SO et al: Genital herpes: Does knowledge lead to action? Am J Public Health 75:69-71, 1985

20. Stone KM et al: Primary prevention of sexually transmitted diseases: A primer for clinicians. JAMA 255:1763-1766, 1986

21. Carter WB, Gayle TC, Baker S: Behavioral intervention and the individual, Sexually Transmitted Diseases. Edited by KK Holmes, P Mardh, PF Sparling et al. New York, McGraw-Hill, 1990

22. Schydlower M, Shafer M (eds): AIDS and other sexually transmitted diseases. Adolescent Medicine. Philadelphia, Hanley & Belfus, Inc, October 1990, p 548

23. Strader MK, Beaman ML: College student's knowledge about AIDS and attitudes toward condom use. Public Health Nursing 6:62- 66, 1989

24. Kegeles SM, Adler NE, Irwin CE: Sexually active adolescents and condoms: Changes over one year in knowledge, attitudes and use. Am J Public Health 78:460-461, 1988

25. Morrison DM: Adolescent contraceptive behavior: A review. Psychol Bull 98:538-568, 1985

26. Mosher WD, Pratt WF: Contraceptive use in the United States, 1973-88. National Center for Health Statistics. Advance Data 182:1-7, 1990

27. Hingson RW, Strunin L, Berlin BM et al: Beliefs about AIDS, use of alcohol and drugs, and unprotected sex among Massachusetts adolescents. Am J Public Health 80:295-299, 1990

28. Klassen AD, Wilsnak S: Sexual experiences and drinking among women in the United States: A national survey. Arch Sex Res 15:363-392, 1986

29. Zelnik M, Shah F: First intercourse among young Americans. Fam Plann Perspect 15:64-70, 1983

30. Centers for Disease Control: Premarital sexual experience among adolescent women - United States, 1970-1988. MMWR 39:929-932, 1991

31. Schydlower M, Shafer M (eds): AIDS and other sexually transmitted diseases, Adolescent Medicine. Philadelphia, Hanley & Belfus, Inc, October 1990, p 600

32. DeBuono BA, Zinner SH, Daamen M et al: Sexual behavior of college women in 1975, 1986, and 1989. N Engl J Med 322:821-825, 1990

33. Jones EF, Forrest J, Goldman N et al: Teenage pregnancy in industrialized countries. Fam Plann Perspect 17:53-63, 1985

34. Brandt AM: No Magic Bullet: A Social History of Venereal Disease in the United States since 1880. New York, Oxford University Press, 1985

35. Shapiro S, Kotloff KL: Prevention of risk behaviors associated with HIV acquisition among college students. Edited by C Seidman. Nurse Practitioner Forum. Philadelphia, London & Toronto, WB Saunders Co, June 1991

36. Fisher WA: Understanding and preventing adolescent pregnancy and STD/AIDS. Edited by J Edwards, RS Tindale, L Health et al. Social Influence Processes and Prevention. New York, Plenum Press, 1990, pp 77-101

37. Kelly JA, St Lawrence JS: The AIDS Health Crises: Psychological and Social Intervention. New York, Plenum Press, 1988

38. Schinke SP: Preventing teenage pregnancy, Progress in Behavior Modification. Edited by M Hersen, RM Eisler, PM Miller. Orlando, Academic Press Inc, 1984

39. Kirscht JP: Preventive health behavior: A review of research and issues. Health Psychol 2:277-301, 1983

40. Fisher WA: Predicting contraceptive behavior among university men: The roles of emotions and behavioral intentions. J Appl Soc Psychol 14:104-123, 1983

41. Shulkin JJ, Mayer JA, Wessel LG et al: Effects of a peer-led AIDS intervention with university students. J Am Coll Health. 40(2) 75-79, Sep 1991

42. Weinstein S, Kezer E, Lew R et al: AIDS risk reduction behaviors of college students related to educational interventions. Int Conf AIDS. 6:270 (abstract no. S.C. 725), 1990

43. Conant Sloane B, Dyer Chamberlain M, Berry K: Innovative AIDS education for adolescents: strategies for behavior change. Int Conf AIDS. 5:831 (abstract no. Th. E. O. 1), 1989

44. Jordheim A: A comparison study of peer teaching and traditional instruction in venereal disease education. J Am Coll Health 24:286-289, 1976

45. Allensworth DD, Symons CW: A theoretical approach to school-based HIV prevention. J School Health 59:59-65, 1989

46. Flora JA, Thoresen CE: Components of a comprehensive strategy for reducing the risk of AIDS in adolescents. Edited by VM Mays, GW Albee, SF Schneider. Primary Prevention of AIDS. Newbury Park, CA, Sage Publications, 1989

47. Brooks-Gunn J, Boyer CB, Hein K: Preventing HIV infection and AIDS in children and adolescents: Behavioral research and intervention strategies. Am Psychol 43:958-964, 1988

48. Flora JA, Thoresen CE: Reducing the risk of AIDS in adolescents. Am Psychol 43:965-970, 1988

49. Kelly JA, St Lawrence JS: Behavioral intervention and AIDS. Behav Therapist 9:121-125, 1988

50. Alter MJ, Hadler SC, Margolis HS et al: The changing epidemiology of hepatitis B in the United States. Need for alternative vaccination strategies. JAMA 263:1218-22, 1990

51. Centers for Disease Control: 1989 Sexually Transmitted Diseases Treatment Guidelines. MMWR 38 (No. S-8):1-43, 1989

52. Abramowicz M (ed): The Medical Letter. Treatment of sexually transmitted diseases. New Rochelle, New York, The Medical Letter, Inc, 32:5-10, 1990

53. Holmes KK, Mardh P, Sparling PF et al (eds): Sexually Transmitted Diseases. New York, McGraw-Hill, 1990

54. Richards EP, Bross DC: Legal aspects of STD control: Public duties and private rights, Sexually Transmitted Diseases. Edited by KK Holmes, P Mardh, PF Sparling et al. New York, McGraw-Hill, 1990

55. Willcox RR: "Epidemiological" treatment in non-venereal and in treponemal diseases. Br J Vener Dis 49:107-115, 1973

56. Cates W: The epidemiology and control of sexually transmitted diseases in adolescents. Adolescent Medicine. Edited by M Schydlower, M Shafer. Philadelphia, Hanley & Belfus, Inc, October 1990, p 418

57. Gerbert B, Maguire BT, Coates TJ: Are patients talking to their physicians about AIDS? Am J Public Health 80:467-469, 1990

58. Merrill JM, Laux LF, Thornby JI: Why doctors have difficulty with sex histories. South Med J 83:613-617, 1990

59. Fredman L, Rabin DL, Bowman M et al: Primary care physicians' assessment and prevention of HIV infection. Am J Prev Med 5:188-195, 1989

60. Lewis CE, Freeman HE, Corey CR: AIDS-related competence of California's primary care physicians. Am J Public Health 77:795-799, 1987

61. Lewis CE, Freeman HE: The sexual history-taking and counseling practices of primary care physicians. West J Med 147:165-167, 1987

62. American Medical Association: Everybody's at risk. Sexually transmitted diseases: Risk assessment, diagnosis and treatment. Symposium monograph, November 7, 1990

63. Johnson MC: Taking sexual histories: Now it's essential. Iowa Med 78:118-120, 1988

64. Ende J, Rockwell S, Glasgow M: The sexual history in general medicine practice. Arch Int Med 144:558-561, 1984

65. Gremminger RA: Taking a sexual history. Wisc Med J 82:20-24, 1983

66. Dan B: Sex and the singles whirl: The quantum dynamics of hepatitis B. JAMA 256:1344, 1986

67. Wiesmeier E et al: Detection of chlamydia cervicitis with Papanicolaou-stained smears and cultures in a university study population. J Reprod Med 32:251-253, 1987

68. Washington AE et al: *Chlamydia trachomatis* infections in the United States. What are they costing us? JAMA 257:2070-2072, 1987

69. Thompson SE, Washington AE: Epidemiology of sexually transmitted *Chlamydia trachomatis* infections. Epidemiol Rev 5:96-123, 1983

70. Malotte CK, Wiesmeier E, Gelineau KJ: Screening for chlamydial cervicitis in a sexually active university population. Am J Public Health 80:469-471, 1990

71. Schachter J: Why we need a program for the control of *Chlamydia trachomatis*. N Engl J Med 320:802-804, 1989

72. Kaplan JE, Meyer M, Navin J: *Chlamydia trachomatis* infection in a female college student population. J Am Coll Health 36:294-296, 1988

73. Pereira CA, Paquette GE, Wood PB et al: Clinical and laboratory screening of *Chlamydia trachomatis* in women at a university health service. J Am Coll Health 36:39-43, 1987

74. Swinker M: *Chlamydia trachomatis* genital infections in college women. J Am Coll Health 34:207-209, 1986

75. Harrison HR, Costin M, Meder JB et al: Cervical *Chlamydia trachomatis* infection in university women: Relationship to history, contraception, ectopy, and cervicitis. Am J Obstet Gynecol 153:244-251, 1985

76. Wiesmeier E, Lovett MA, Forsythe AB: *Chlamydia trachomatis* isolation in a symptomatic university student population. Obstet Gynecol 63:81-84, 1984

77. Stamm WE, Holmes KK: *Chlamydia trachomatis* infections of the adult, Sexually Transmitted Diseases. Edited by KK Holmes, P Mardh, PF Sparling et al. New York, McGraw-Hill, 1990

78. Stamm WE et al: Causes of the acute urethral syndrome in women. N Engl J Med 303:409-415, 1980

79. Stamm WE et al: Effect of treatment regimens for *Neisseria gonorrhoeae* on simultaneous infection with *Chlamydia trachomatis.* N Engl J Med 310:545-549, 1984

80. Phillips RS, Aronson MD, Taylor WC et al: Should tests for *Chlamydia trachomatis* cervical infection be done during routine gynecologic visits? An analysis of the costs of alternative strategies. Ann Intern Med 107:188-194, 1987

81. Lee H: Genital chlamydial infection in female and meal college students. Am J Coll Health 37:288-291, 1989

82. Westrom L: Influence of sexually transmitted diseases on sterility and ectopic pregnancy. Acta Eur Fertil 16:21-24, 1985

83. Moore DE, Cates W Jr: Sexually transmitted diseases and infertility, Sexually Transmitted Diseases. Edited by KK Holmes, P Mardh, PF Sparling et al. New York, McGraw-Hill, 1990, pp 763-769

84. Johnson BA, Poses RM, Fortner CA et al: Derivation and validation of a clinical diagnostic model for chlamydial cervical infection in university women. JAMA 264:3161-3165, 1990

85. Hatcher RA:  Personal communication, 1989

86. Leka TW, Patrick K, Benenson AS: *Chlamydia trachomatis* urethritis in university men: Risk factors and rates. JABFP 3:81-86, 1990

87. Kaplan JE, Meyer M, Navin J: *Chlamydia trachomatis* infection in a male college student population. J Am Coll Health 37:159-161, 1989

88. Randolph AG, Washington AE: Screening for *Chlamydia trachomatis* in adolescent males: A cost-based decision analysis. Am J Public Health 80:545-550, 1990

89. Shafer M, Schachter J, Moscicki AB et al: Urinary leukocyte esterase screening test for asymptomatic chlamydial and gonococcal infections in males. JAMA 62:2562-2566, 1989

90. Lycke E et al: The risk of transmission of genital *Chlamydia trachomatis* infection is less than that of genital *Neisseria gonorrhoeae* infection. Sex Transm Dis 7:6-10, 1980

91. Ferris DG, Lawler FH, Horner RD et al: Test of cure for genital *Chlamydia trachomatis* infection in women. J Fam Pract 31:36-41, 1990

92. Koutsky LA, Galloway DA, Holmes KK: Epidemiology of genital human papillomavirus infection. Epidemiol Rev 10:122-163, 1988

93. Kiviat NB, Koutsky LA, Paavonen JA et al: Prevalence of genital papillomavirus infection among women attending a college student health clinic or a sexually transmitted disease clinic. J Infect Dis 159:293-302, 1989

94. Bauer HM, Ting Y, Greer CE et al: Genital human papillomavirus infection in female university students as determined by a PCR-based method. JAMA 265:472-477, 1991

95. Dunn JE, Crocker DW, Rube IF et al: Cervical cancer occurrence in Memphis and Shelby County, Tennessee, during 25 years of its cervical cytology screening program. Am J Obstet Gynecol 150:861-864, 1984

96. Dunn JE, Schweitzer V: The relationship of cervical cytology to the incidence of invasive cervical cancer and mortality in Alameda County, California, 1960 to 1974. Am J Obstet Gynecol 139:868-876, 1981

97. Ferenczy A: Diagnosis and treatment of anogenital warts in the male patient. Primary Care & Cancer, September:11-23, 1990

98. American College Health Association: Genital Human Papillomavirus Disease: Diagnosis, Management, and Prevention. Rockville, MD, American College Health Association, 1989

99. Richart RM: Causes and management of cervical intraepithelial neoplasia. Cancer 60:1951-1959, 1987

100. Berman A, Berman JE: New concepts in viral wart infection. Compr Ther 14:19-24, 1988

101. Grace TW, Patrick K: An alternate view of the management of cervical human papillomavirus infections. Am J Coll Health 38:241-243, 1990

102. Buck HW: Management of cervical papillomavirus infections: A response. Am J Coll Health 38:298-299, 1990

103. Editorial: The intraepithelial lesion: A spectrum of problems. JAMA 262:944-945, 1989

104. Corey L: Genital herpes, Sexually Transmitted Diseases. Edited by KK Holmes, P Mardh, PF Sparling et al. New York, McGraw-Hill, 1990

105. Corey L, Spear PG: Infections with herpes simplex viruses. N Engl J Med 314:749-757, 1986

106. Sumaya CV et al: Genital infections with herpes simplex virus in a university student population. Sex Transm Dis 7:16-20, 1980

107. Delva MD, McSherry JA: Herpes genitalis in a student population. J Fam Pract 18:397-400, 1984

108. Reeves WC et al: Risk of recurrence after first episode of genital herpes: Relation to HSV type and antibody response. N Engl J Med 305:315-319, 1981

109. Fife KH, Corey L: Herpes simplex virus, Sexually Transmitted Diseases. Edited by KK Holmes, P Mardh, PF Sparling et al. New York, McGraw-Hill, 1990

110. Rice RJ et al: Gonorrhea in the United States 1975-84: Is the giant only sleeping? Sex Transm Dis 14:83-87, 1987

111. Rothenberg RB et al: Efficacy of selected diagnostic tests for sexually transmitted diseases. JAMA 235:49-51, 1976

112. Hook EW III, Handsfield HH: Gonococcal infections in the adult, Sexually Transmitted Diseases. Edited by KK Holmes, P Mardh, PF Sparling et al. New York, McGraw-Hill, 1990

113. Centers for Disease Control: Continuing increase in infectious syphilis - United States. MMWR 37:35-38, 1988

114. Brown ST et al: Serological response to syphilis treatment: A new analysis of old data. JAMA 253:1296-1299, 1985

115. Thin RN: Early syphilis in the adult, Sexually Transmitted Diseases. Edited by KK Holmes, P Mardh, PF Sparling et al. New York, McGraw-Hill, 1990

116. Jenny C, Hooton TM, Bowers A et al: Sexually transmitted diseases in victims of rape. N Engl J Med 322:713-716, 1990

117. Centers for Disease Control: Progress toward achieving the 1990 objectives for the nation for sexually transmitted diseases. MMWR 39: 53-57, 1990

118. U.S. Department of Health and Human Services: Healthy People 2000: National Health Promotion and Disease Prevention Objectives. Washington, DC, U.S. Government Printing Office, 1990 (preliminary edition)

# 14

# Pregnancy, Contraception, and Issues of Sexuality for College Students

PAULA SWINFORD, MS, CHES

> To the young people of this nation
>
> Who must find their way
>
> To sexual health
>
> In a world of contradictions —
>
> Where media scream, "Always say yes,"
>
> Where many adults admonish, "Just say no,"
>
> But the majority
>
> Just say ...
>
> Nothing.[1]
>
> - Peggy Brick, MEd

To the students on a college campus, engaging in sex is much more than an anatomy class. It encompasses a wide range of issues in our society, such as religion, civil liberties, reproductive rights, technology and even politics. College students involved in sexual activity alone or with others may be acting under the influences of a drug (most probably alcohol), simply experimenting, or physically forcing a partner. Students develop a sense of themselves as sexual beings and some choose to express this through abstinence until marriage. Through it all, these young adults are defining themselves, learning their boundaries, and establishing personal values.

This chapter describes some of what is documented about sexual behaviors, unintended pregnancy, and contraception among college students. Some approaches to prevention of sexually related problems are outlined.

## SEXUALITY AND SEXUAL BEHAVIOR

The sexual revolution of the 1960s did not miss the university campus. This has been documented in the 1965 edition of Sex and the College Student and reported by the Committee on the College Student Group for the Advancement of Psychiatry.[2] During the 1950s fear of pregnancy may have postponed sexual intercourse, but the advent of birth control other than barrier methods changed all of that. Suddenly premarital sexual activity was acceptable if there were a "perceived" future in the relationship or sincere affection.

During the 1960s campuses were challenged on many of the *in loco parentis* rules, thus eliminating curfew hours. The birth control pill and the intrauterine device gave women more control and required less thought immediately prior to intercourse. This had the effect of creating a male expectation that it was the responsibility of the female gender to provide the birth control method. Unfortunately, neither of these new methods provided any protection from sexually transmitted disease. The new concept of "living together" entered the campus scene in the 1970s. Even though both partners might maintain a separate mailing address, cohabitation was established as a way of "testing" the relationship. Between 1965 and 1974 only 11 percent of those people who got married had lived together prior to marriage, while between 1980 and 1984, 44 percent of the couples married had lived together.[3]

While some measures of sexual activity among college-age individuals have shown increases, others have not. One study that looked at college women who visited the student health center gynecology clinic in 1975, 1986, and 1989 reported that the percentage of women who were sexually active was virtually the same in all three years – 88 percent in 1975, 87 percent in 1986, and 87 percent in 1989.[4] However, a decrease in the average age of first intercourse was reported from 1970 to 1981 from 18 years for men and 18.8 years for women in 1970, to 17 for men and 17.6 for women in 1981.[5] This same study found that the percent of men who had had intercourse with two to five partners increased from 43.5 percent to 55.6 percent from 1970 to 1981. For women the increase was from 19.4 percent to 48.8 percent. In 1983 only 19 percent of girls under the age of 15 were sexually experienced; today that number is nearly 50 percent higher and some 7 of 10 teenagers have had sexual intercourse by the age 18.[6] The average age for first intercourse of those individuals going on to college is 17.5 years.[6]

In a situation where sexual freedom is assumed if not condoned, many issues are addressed by college health medical[5,7] and counseling[8] professionals. Problems that students identify as associated with sex include too rapid an orgasm, obsession with sex, erection problems, no interest, ejaculation problems, lack of orgasm, painful coitus, and inhibitions about their bodies.[9] Student health professionals may want to adopt a more pluralistic view towards sexuality. Pluralism is the way Americans approach religion and politics and a variety of other issues, but unfortunately with sexuality, often the perception is that there is only one correct way. Sexual Pluralism is based on the moral concept that honesty, equality, and responsibility are essential to a mutual sexual relationship.[10] When working with a student, the health center staff must be sensitive to sexual orientation, beliefs about abortion and birth control methods, and frame sexual activity in an arena of normalcy, one in which sexuality can be gratifying and pleasurable as opposed to one in which disease, unwanted pregnancy, guilt, and irresponsibility are the norm. Another way to look at this would be to think of a society where people valued their sexuality and considered it a gift. This would be a society that is erotophilic vs an erotophobic society where shame, violence, and denial surround sexual imagery and messages. There is more to human sexual behavior than coitus and contraceptive experience. The challenge to college health professionals is to provide services, courses, or workshops on intimacy and sexuality that are erotophilic and deal with these strong human needs.[8,11,12,13]

Expectations surrounding gender play a powerful part in defining adolescent sexual behavior.[14] Men generally hold more positive attitudes toward sex and engage in a greater variety of sexual behaviors more frequently than do women.[15] These expectations revolve around the general focus that women are motivated by sex as an expression of love and men are motivated by sex as a source of pleasure.[16] Other studies support this conclusion showing that women cite emotional reasons for intercourse to a greater extent than do men. Men more often reported pleasure and tension-release.[17] Gender expectations reflect strong socialization pressure on young men to encourage their sexuality and on young women to deny their sexuality, at least until they are married.

There are many gender differences in fantasies. What we know about these fantasies, however, does not reinforce male-dominant female-passive myths.[4] Although men report fantasizing more, they fantasize as much as women do about romantic and tender themes, and as much about being seduced as seducing. Self report of behavior does show college men masturbating and watching erotica and pornography more often than women.

With the continued ethnic and cultural diversification of college campuses, it is important to recognize what we know and don't know about ethnicity and sexual behavior. Very little has been written on this topic specific to the college-age population. One 1985 study showed that between African-American and Caucasian students overall the two racial groups were more similar than dissimilar in their sexual behavior patterns.[18]

## UNINTENDED PREGNANCY AND CONTRACEPTION

No accurate estimates exist of the number of college women who get pregnant, intentionally or unintentionally, each year. In 1981, 15 percent of all women aged 19 became pregnant with 60 percent of these pregnancies ending in birth.[19] With more students outside the traditional 18-24 age range, it is probable that a greater number of college student pregnancies are planned or wanted. Estimates of the number of college women who get pregnant during any year have ranged from 6 to 10 percent.[20] One study noted that college student pregnancies resulted in abortion almost 90 percent of the time, and that 16 percent of all sexually active college women have had at least one abortion.[21]

With respect to contraception, among the teenage females surveyed in 1982, only one of every two reported use of a contraceptive at first intercourse; of these, 47 percent used the condom, 27 percent relied on withdrawal, and only 17 percent used the pill.[20] Once in college, data from over 4,500 female students utilizing a university contraceptive clinic over ten years indicated that the pill was the most popular of three prescription methods.[22] The percentage of women using the pill substantially declined from 1974 (89 percent) to 1983 (73 percent). This percentage slightly increased after 1980 and has remained fairly constant.[22] Oral contraceptives were used by 55 percent of sexually active college women in 1975, 34 percent in 1986, and 42 percent in 1989.

Barrier methods of contraception have become more important in an era of increased recognition of sexually transmitted diseases. Diaphragm use peaked in 1980 (33%) and then declined the following three years.[23] In 1975 only 12 percent reported regular use of condoms during sexual intercourse, in some cases in conjunction with other methods of contraception, as compared with 21 percent in 1986 and 41 percent in 1989.[23]

Contraception behavior is highly complex and influenced by many factors beyond knowledge, attitudes, self concept, and cultural normative expectations. Throughout the literature is the recurrent theme of communication as a means of influencing contraception behavior. Not only family communication about sexuality is important but also the overall pattern of open and honest general communication within the family unit. If the parent-educated teens do engage in sexual activity, they are more likely to use consistent and effective contraception.[24] Conformity to peers' behavior peaks in mid-adolescence and decreases thereafter.[25] Same-age friends and parents are both extremely important influences on the college student.[26] But possibly more important is general and sexual communication with one's partner in predicting regular contraceptive use.[12]

More inclusive than "contraception," the term "birth control" includes abortions. It is estimated that there are now more than 1.5 million abortions performed in the U.S. each year. In recent years a review of literature has shown that students have progressively held more conservative beliefs and values on sexual matters than previously thought.[27] However, attitudes toward abortion may be the exception to the rule. One study[28] reports that college students favor legalized abortion by as high as 82 percent; 78 percent believed that abortion is acceptable if the mother's life is at stake. Fifty-eight percent felt that men should have an "equal voice" in abortion decisions.[29] Of students who had made the decision to terminate pregnancy, 90 percent strongly favored allowing other students to make that same choice, which suggests that the majority of those who choose abortion do not have any serious regrets.[13]

## PREVENTION

Clearly, prevention of unintended pregnancy, education about contraception, and the fostering of a healthy sense of a sexual self begin at home. However, individuals are influenced by many factors including formal education and peers. The challenges lie in both the management of problems and in the promotion of health. These challenges cannot be met effectively on a one-to-one basis, although individual interaction is crucial. The challenge of preventing unplanned pregnancy and fostering individual sexual responsibility and health will be more effectively dealt with on a community level. Communities tend to deny their responsibility in promoting a national norm that approves of using sex, without contraception or conception, to sell everything from toothpaste to handguns. Communities tend to ignore the price that is being paid in deaths, addictions, disease, and pregnancy for the freedom of having alcohol as a substance conveniently available and heavily promoted. Finally, communities promote the endless myth that "nice girls don't." This leads to the need for young women to block conscious consideration of contraception for fear of losing the "nice girl" image. If passion or alcohol use leads to unprotected intercourse, that's "okay." In this case, lack of personal responsibility is forgiven. Over and over again personal rights to privacy and strong beliefs in religious mores clash, leading to confusing messages to young people. This confusion hinders prevention efforts, which, like effective contraception use, requires open thoughtful community communication.

What should the college health center be doing to prevent problems and deal with the problems effectively? The answer to this question depends a great deal on the community in which the health center functions. Community outreach, consensus building, and needs assessment surveys will allow administrators to determine priorities and limits. Focus groups are encouraged as they may answer important questions and challenge commonly held assumptions. On other programmatic decisions, the Health Center may decide to implement a program and see who takes notice.

In the Spring of 1980 when the University of Illinois at Urbana-Champaign McKinley Health Center followed up on a Student Health Advisory Committee resolution that both genders have access to contraception and to make condoms easily available to students (this was before the advent of HIV disease and the epidemic growth in other STDs), the student paper published the minutes of the meeting. Coincidentally, less than a week later both Parade and Hustler magazines printed stories about "Condoms on the College Campus." At the time, the health center director received many calls accusing him of promoting and encouraging sexual intercourse. He stood firm in his decision with data on the need for prevention of STDs as background. In retrospect, his decision to listen to the Student Health Advisory Committee and put condoms in students hands was correct long before the reality of AIDS hit campus five years later.

First and foremost, students need access to reliable contraceptive methods, either through prescription or over the counter. Less than twenty years ago college health physicians were making a radical political statement if they prescribed birth control pills to be filled at the local town pharmacy. Today, Student Health Center pharmacies dispense birth control pills in quantities topped only by cold and possibly acne medication. Now the challenge comes in giving condoms with each birth control pill prescription, explaining the need to prevent STDs as well as pregnancy. If not free through the health center, condoms can be placed in the local convenience, drug, or grocery store check-out lines.

Pregnancy testing should be convenient and inexpensive. Results should be available on a same-day basis if possible. The means by which these results are provided is crucial to a patient's self concept and willingness to use effective contraception in the future. Language is important. Referring to the young woman as a "sweetie," "honey," or "girl" may create a sense of powerlessness and shame. Whoever gives these results – physician, nurse, health educator, or peer counselor – should be formally trained. The local Planned Parenthood can be an excellent community resource for training staff about how to deal with this issue. Student (peer health) counselors can be trained to give confidential quality pregnancy option counseling and are often a cost-effective alternative for health centers with limited budgets. Negative-results counseling is just as important, as it represents a valuable "teachable moment," a critical opportunity for behavior change. It is also a time to explore the possibility of an acquaintance rape or alcohol addiction. Because these opportunities may be lost, pregnancy test results should never be given over the phone.

College health professionals are regularly called upon to provide options counseling. Training will help the professional to be nonjudgmental. Having a packet of prenatal materials available is as important as having a list of adoption agencies or abortion clinics. All referrals need to be part of routine site visits by the

Student Health Center staff. External resources used for referral reflect directly on the Student Health Center. Monitoring and evaluation of quality of medical care and counseling given to these patients should be routine. Coordination with other Student Affairs professionals will allow for the articulation of financial and academic support.

International students, and their spouses, can represent substantial challenges when pregnancy occurs. Pregnancy in the non-student spouse may not be covered by the student's health insurance. Several health centers, for example, those at the University of Oregon and the University of Southern California, will see the spouse for an additional fee. Without health insurance, however, the couple will need special guidance and services. Again, the local Planned Parenthood or other social service agency may be of help. Finally, coordination with the campus International Student Advisor is essential.

Many Student Health Centers provide specialty clinics for women through Reproductive Health Clinics, Family Planning Clinics, Gynecology Departments, or clinic hours for a local gynecologist. Other health centers ensure that each general practice physician is trained in and provides pelvic exams, STD checks, and follow-up after abortion. Prior to receiving oral contraception students need basic information. This is usually covered by a session prior to the clinic visit that focuses on the "hows and whys" of contraception pelvic exams. This session can easily be taught by peer health educators.

Peer Education in the form of Health Advocates, Peer Health Helpers, or sex education paraprofessionals has been documented to be one of the most effective ways of delivering an educational message. With appropriate selection, training, and supervision, peer educators can provide quality outreach programs, one-to-one information, and patient education. Outstanding peer education programs can be found on many campuses. The American College Health Association provides an annual workshop to help start peer education programs.

In 1975, the University of Illinois at Urbana Champaign (UIUC) began to offer a for-credit Human Sexuality course in the residence halls. Now, more than 15 years later there are some twenty sessions of this course offered and still students are turned away. This cooperative effort between the Housing Division and the Academic Department of Health and Safety reaches over 500 students each semester. The course has been evaluated on several occasions showing that knowledge, attitudes, and behaviors change over the progression of the semester. Similar courses could be offered on all campuses. Although not yet common, workshops are beginning to surface on initiating intimacy and sexual negotiation. This type of programming and skills development may be the next generation of preventive sex education.

Studies have shown that most medical school training leaves physicians lacking in both skills and confidence in taking a sexual history. Student Health Center administration must provide extensive in-service training to address issues such as: sexual history taking, removing sexual orientation bias, HIV antibody test referrals, and sensitivity to survivors of rape. Also incorporating CAGE[30] or some other alcohol-use assessment into regular exams is crucial to the prevention of unwanted pregnancies and STDs as well as encouraging treatment for alcoholism.

Small, nurse-directed health centers and those who work in institutions of higher education with a religious affiliation often are faced with unique challenges in provision of sexuality and contraceptive services. Services provided vary substantially from campus to campus. Information and support can be gained by networking through the ACHA nurse-directed Student Health Center section. Nurse educators often have creative and insightful approaches that meet the letter of the law on their campus but also address the needs of individual students. (I will not describe them here in order that they may continue unhindered!)

Creativity, insight, patience, and a willingness to step beyond what is just expected – these are the hallmarks of quality sexuality services provided by college health professionals. College students face many developmental tasks. Separating from home, determining a daily schedule, and making career choices are but a few. This chapter has attempted to provide some guidance to how college health professionals can assist students in developing a healthy sexuality regardless of how it is expressed. Many times professionals are called upon to react by providing treatment for STDs, unplanned pregnancy, or rape, but each clinical interaction with a student is an opportunity to take a sexual history and reinforce healthy choices. "Communication, openness, honesty, and guidance are how we can transform a society that is often angry, jealous, hypocritical, and sexually anxious into a compassionate, safe, erotic, and sex-positive place. In such a society, adolescents can be helped to grow, to flourish, and to become healthy sexual adults."[31] There are many conflicting messages about sex in our society. Given them all, it is a wonder anyone ever learns to feel comfortable and enjoy sex. College Health Services can help to make this happen.

Acknowledgment

I would like to thank M. Ann Hickey, MPH, for using her excellent skills in helping to locate current articles for this chapter.

# REFERENCES

1. Brick P, Charlton C, Kunins H et al: Teaching Safer Sex. Hackensack, NJ: The Center for Family Life Education, Planned Parenthood of Bergen County, Inc, 1989

2. Committee on the College Student Group for the Advancement of Psychiatry: Sex and the College Student. New York, Atheneum, 37: 247-252, May 1989

3. New Haven Register, 1988

4. Person ES, Terestman N, Myers WA et al: Gender differences in sexual behaviors and fantasies in a college population. J Sex Marital Therapy 15:3, 187-197, 1989

5. Earle JR, Perricone P J: Premarital sexuality: A ten-year study of attitudes and behavior on a small university campus. J Sex Research 22(3): 304-310, 1986

6. National Center for Health Surveys: National Survey of Family Growth, Cycle IV, 1970-1988, 1989

7. Yegidis BL: Date rape and other forced sexual encounters among college students. J Sex Education and Therapy 12(2): 51-54, 1986

8. Masters W, Johnson V, Kolodny RC: Sex and Human Loving. Boston, Little, Brown 1986, p 598

9. Wiesmeier E, Forsythe AB, Sundstrom MJ et al: Sexual concerns and counseling needs of normal men attending a university student health service. J Amer Coll Health 35(1): 29-35, 1986

10. Reiss IL: An End to Shame: Shaping Our Next Sexual Revolution. Buffalo, NY, Prometheus Books, 1990

11. Renshaw DC: Sex and the 1980s college student. J Amer Coll Health Vol. 37: 154-157, Jan 1989

12. Byme D: Sex without contraception, Adolescents, Sex, and Contraception. Edited by D Byrne and WA Fisher. Hillsdale, New Jersey, Earlbaum, 1983, pp 3-31

13. Wright LS, Rogers RR: Variables related to pro-choice attitudes among undergraduates. Adolescence XXII: 87: 517-524, Fall 1987

14. Miller PY, Simon W: The development of sexuality in adolescence, Handbook of Adolescent Psychology. Edited by J Adelson. New York, Wiley, 1980

15. Story MD: A comparison of university student experience with various sexual outlets in 1974 and 1980. Adolescence 17: 737-747, 1982

16. Simon W, Gagnon, JL: Sexual scripts: Permanence and change. Arch Sexual Behavior 15:97-1120, 1986

17. Carroll JC, Volk KA, Hyde JS: Differences between males and females in motives for engaging in sexual intercourse. Arch Sexual Behavior 14:131-1139, 1985

18. Belcastro PA: Sexual behavior differences between black and white students. J Sex Research 21:1: 56-67, Feb 1985

19. Hatcher RA, Guest F, Stewart F et al: Adolescent pregnancy, Contraceptive Technology 1988-1989. New York, Irvington, 14: 46-61, 1988

20. Dorman J M: Positive pregnancy tests at Stanford: A follow-up study, 1978-1980. J Amer Coll Health 29: 286-288, 1981

21. Katz J, Cronin D: Sexuality and college life. Change 3, 44-49, 1980

22. Harvey S: Trends in contraceptive use among university women, 1974-1983: A decade of change. J Amer Coll Health 36, Jan 1988

23. DeBuono BA, Zimmer SH, Daamen M et al: Sexual behavior of college women in 1975, 1986, and 1989. N Engl J Med 322: 12, 821-825, 1990

24. Fisher TD: Family communication and the sexual behavior and attitudes of college students. J Youth and Adolescence 16:5: 481-495, 1987

25. Berndt TJ: Developmental changes in conformity to peers and parents. Develop Psychol 15: 608-616, 1979

26. Wilds J: The relative importance of parents and friends in adolescent decision-making. J Youth and Adolescence 15:323-334, 1980

27. Spees EP: College students' sexual attitudes and behaviors, 1974-1985: A review of the literature. J College Student Personnel 28: 135-140, 1987

28. Biasco F, Piotrowski C: College students' attitudes toward abortion. College Student J 23:3, 194-197, 1989

29. Rosenwasser SM, Wright LS, Barber RB: The rights and responsibilities of men in abortion situations. J Sex Research 23:97-105, 1987

30. Heck E: Developing a screening questionnaire for problem drinking in college students. J Amer Coll Health 39:5 227-231, 1991

31. Conant Sloane B: Issues That Arise as a Young Person's Sexuality Unfolds, SIECUS Report  17:5: 5-6 May-July 1989

## Resources

SIECUS Report, the newsletter of the Sex Information and Education Council of the U.S. Janet Jamar, Editor. 130 West 42nd Street Suite 2500, New York, New York 10036. 212/819-9770; fax 212/819-9776

Can We Talk? A description of the videotape and ordering information from: Ms. A. Hill, Student Health Services, The University of Western Ontario, University Community Center, Room 11, London, Ontario, CANADA N6A 3K7

Hatcher RA et al: Contraceptive Technology. Current edition. Irvington Publishers, Inc. 740 Broadway New York, New York 10003

Contraceptive Technology Update: A monthly newsletter for health professionals, Editor, Theresa Waldrom, published by American Health Consultants Inc. 3525 Piedmont Road, Building Six, Suite 400, Atlanta, GA 30305 800/688-2421

Any current sex education text book; e.g., Understanding Human Sexuality by Janet Shibley Hyde, McGraw-Hill Book Company

# 15

# Vaccine-preventable Diseases on the College Campus

MARJEANNE COLLINS, MD

The United States has had great success in the control of vaccine-preventable diseases (VPDs) over the last 25 years. From the pre-vaccine era, the number of measles and rubella cases has declined by more than 99 percent and mumps has decreased by more than 90 percent. For other diseases such as diphtheria, tetanus, pertussis, and polio, even greater reductions have been accomplished. These successes are in large measure due to the school immunization laws that exist in all 50 states, the District of Columbia, Puerto Rico, and the Virgin Islands. These requirements have allowed the U.S. to achieve a greater than 95 percent vaccination level among entering school children. Yet, despite these successes, VPDs continue to create public health problems on college campuses. In recent years outbreaks of measles and mumps have established themselves on campuses and outbreak control has proven costly and disruptive to both the colleges and the students.[1] Rubella has also been reported from colleges and has placed exposed pregnant women at risk for congenital rubella syndrome.[2]

In 1990, ten deaths occurred from measles among people 19-35 years, nine of whom had never been vaccinated. More cases of measles are reported among adults 18 years or older from college settings than any other setting of transmission. From 1985 through 1989, 48 percent of measles cases among adults 18 years or older with a known setting of transmission were reported from colleges.[3] Mumps incidence data for 1985 - 1988 show that the shift in disease occurrence to adolescents and young adults occurred only in states without kindergarten to 12th grade (K-12) school vaccination requirements.[4]

College students are at risk for measles, mumps, and rubella for many reasons, including not being immunized according to current CDC Immunization Practices Advisory Committee (ACIP) recommendations; lack of previous coverage by

K-12 school entry laws or Prematriculation Immunization Requirements (PIRs); decreased opportunity for natural infection; and clustering of susceptibles in residences, classes, laboratories, and during social activities. Excessive mobility and frequent travel to developing countries also enhance the risk for exposure.[5] In an attempt to prevent outbreaks of measles and other vaccine-preventable diseases on the college campus, the American College Health Association (ACHA) recommended in 1984 that all colleges and universities implement a Prematriculation Immunization Requirement (PIR) with review and sanctions imposed for non-compliance. The current recommendation for a Prematriculation Immunization Requirement includes 2 doses of measles, mumps, and rubella (the first at 12 months or later, the second at school entry or later); diphtheria-tetanus primary series and a booster no earlier than 14 years of age; and a record of the dates of polio immunization (Table 1, next page).

What impact has this recommendation had on the institution of PIRs on American campuses? In 1986, ACHA surveyed member schools as well as those belonging to the American Council on Education in order to assess the status of PIRs. Out of 3,210 schools surveyed, 1,085 responded, of which 45 percent had a PIR for measles/rubella.[6] In addition, the Regional Public Health Immunization Program staffs have reassessed the degree of compliance with PIRs on a yearly basis. A comparison of 4-year colleges for 1985 and 1988 reveals an average compliance with a measles requirement of 37 percent in 1985 and 49 percent in 1988 (Figure 1, page 674). Compliance with a PIR for 2-year colleges was 16 percent in 1985, and 24 percent in 1988 (Figure 2, page 674). However, since voluntary vaccination programs are less effective than mandatory programs, it is essential for colleges to move to mandatory PIRs and work out their own system for review of immunization records and the imposition of sanctions for non-compliance. Many college administrators, however, have preferred to wait for the state legislatures to mandate a Prematriculation Immunization Requirement by state law.[7]

At the present time, 22 states and territories have either a law or policy that mandates a PIR (Tables 2 and 3, pages 675 and 676). The coverage of those PIRs varies from state to state but all include measles and rubella. To date two states, New York and Illinois, have already placed the new two-dose measles schedule into their state PIRs. Ongoing surveillance for disease outbreaks and aggressive outbreak control with vaccination of all identified susceptibles are critical adjuncts to mandatory PIRs. The major advantage of maintenance of immunization records of students is that it facilitates the identification of susceptibles in an outbreak, which allows for targeted emergency immunization programs rather than costly mass programs where the majority of students being vaccinated don't need it.

## Table 1
## ACHA PIR Recommendations

| Vaccine | Age Indicated | Major Indications* | Major Precautions* |
|---|---|---|---|
| MMR (if given instead of individual vaccines). | 1st dose at 12 months;** 2nd dose at school entry or later. | All entering college students born after 1956 should have 2 doses of live measles vaccine. Susceptible travelers. | Pregnancy; history of anaphylactic reaction following egg ingestion or receipt of neomycin; immunosuppression. Appropriate for HIV antibody-positive persons. |
| Measles vaccine | Same as for MMR | Same as for MMR | Same as for MMR |
| Rubella vaccine | 12 months** | Both males and females without verification of live vaccine on or after 1st birthday or laboratory evidence of immunity. Susceptible travelers. | Same as for MMR |
| Mumps vaccine | 12 months** | All entering college students born after 1956 should have 1 dose of live mumps vaccine or a history of mumps. | Same as for MMR |
| Tetanus-Diphtheria Toxoid | Primary series in childhood, booster at 14-16, then booster every 10 years. | All persons. | History of a neurologic hypersensitivity reaction following a previous dose. |
| Polio vaccine Killed = E-IPV Live = OPV | Primary series in childhood, booster only if needed for travel after age 18. | Persons traveling to areas where wild poliovirus is endemic or epidemic. OPV not indicated for persons over 18 unless previously immunized with OPV. | OPV should not be given to immunocompromised persons or to HIV antibody-positive persons. |

*Refer to appropriate Immunization Practices Advisory Committee (ACIP) recommendations for more details.
**Public health authorities recommend that a first dose of MMR be given at 15 months of age; however, vaccine administered at 12 months of age is still accepted as a first dose.

Source: ACHA, 1990

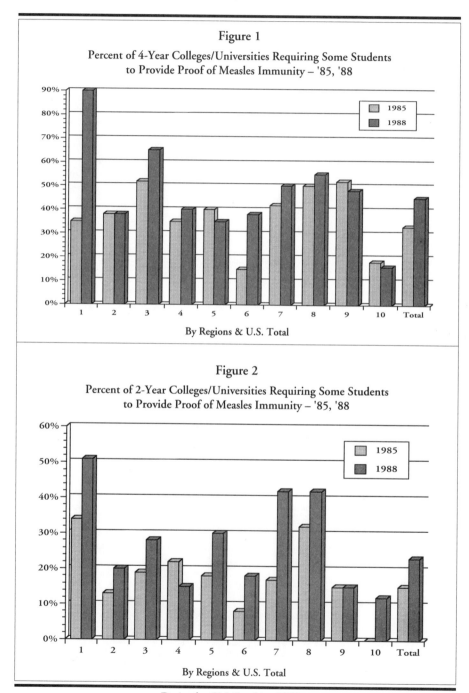

Figure 1

Percent of 4-Year Colleges/Universities Requiring Some Students
to Provide Proof of Measles Immunity – '85, '88

By Regions & U.S. Total

Figure 2

Percent of 2-Year Colleges/Universities Requiring Some Students
to Provide Proof of Measles Immunity – '85, '88

By Regions & U.S. Total

Design by CM Graphics, LTD

## Table 2
## Summary of College Prematriculation Immunization Requirements:
### States with Laws

| State | Date in Effect | Schools Affected | Students Affected | Antigens | Monitor for Compliance |
|---|---|---|---|---|---|
| AK | 1/88 | 2-, 4-year public, private | All | M, R | Yes |
| CT | 7/89 | All | All fulltime born after 1956 | M, R | Yes |
| DC | 1986 | All | All under 26 years | M, R, Mu, T, d, Po | No |
| IL* | 7/89 | 4-year public, private | New enterers | M, R, Mu, T, d | Yes |
| ME | 9/87 | 2-, 4-year public, private | All born after 1956 | M, R, T, d | Yes |
| MA | 9/86 | 2-, 4-year public, private | New enterers | M, R, Mu, T, d | Yes |
| MN | 7/90 | All post-secondary | All born after 1956 | M, R, Mu, T, d | No |
| MT | 7/89 | All post-secondary | All born after 1956 | M, R | Yes |
| NJ | 1/90 | 2-, 4-year public, private | Only out-of-state | M, R, Mu | Yes |
| NY* | 9/90 | All post-secondary | All born after 1956 | M, R, Mu | No |
| NC | 9/86 | 4-yr public, private | New enterers born after 1956 | M, R, T, d, Po | Yes |
| PR | 9/84 | 2-, 4-year public, private | All under 21 years | M, R, Mu, T, d | Yes |
| RI | 1/85 | 2-, 4-year public, private | New enterers | M, R | |
| VA | 1/85 | 4-year public | New enterers | M, R, T, d, Po | |

*New York and Illinois require a two-dose measles PIR.

Immunization is the simplest and most cost-effective intervention in the medical armamentarium. Yet, data show that up to 15 percent of current college students are not appropriately immunized.[8] These students unnecessarily place themselves and their fellow students at risk for morbidity and even death from highly transmissible diseases such as measles, mumps, and rubella. College administrations and Student Health Services cannot afford to wait for passage of a state law in order to institute a mandatory PIR with review and sanctions for noncompliance.

### Table 3

### Summary of College Prematriculation Immunization Requirements: States with Regents' Policies

| State | Date in Effect | Schools Affected | Students Affected | Antigens | State to Monitor for Compliance |
|-------|------|------|------|------|------|
| CA | 9/86 | 4-year public* | New enterers born after 1956 | M, R | No |
| FL | 5/86 | 4-year public | All less than 40 years old | M, R | No |
| MS | 9/84 | 4-year public | New enterers born after 1956 | M, R | No |
| ND | 12/85 | 2-, 4-year public | All | M, R | Yes |
| SD | 3/85 | 4-year public | New enterers | M, R | Yes |
| TN** | 9/90 | 4-year public | All born after 1956 | M | Yes |
| WV | 1/88 | 2-, 4-year public, private | New enterers born after 1957 | M, R | Yes |
| WY | 5/85 | 4-year public | All | M, R*** | No |

\* Does not include UCLA and some other large schools
\** Requires at least one dose of measles received after 1980
\*** R - Health care students only

# UNIQUE ISSUES FOR CERTAIN VACCINES

## RUBELLA VACCINE

Before the licensure of rubella vaccine in 1969, rubella was a common childhood disease with up to 28 cases per 100,000 population. The most important consequences of rubella, which occur in pregnancy, are congenital rubella syndrome (CRS), miscarriage, stillbirth, and fetal anomalies. By 1988 health departments in the U.S. had reported an all-time low of 225 cases of rubella. However, 1989 and 1990 have seen a twofold and an additional threefold increase, respectively, in reported cases. As of January 1991, a provisional total of 1,093 cases, (0.4/100,000) had been reported to the national surveillance reporting system, the highest total since 1982.[2] As of January 1991, ten confirmed cases of CRS had been reported to CDC's National Congenital Rubella Syndrome Registry (NCRSR) and six additional provisional reports have been received.[2] This is the highest number of reported cases since 1980 when 14 cases of CRS were reported to Public Health. The increase in rubella is thought to represent a real increase in incidence rather than just an increase in reporting of rash illnesses.

Twenty-six outbreaks occurred in 1990 that were classified into two categories by CDC. The first occurred in settings where unvaccinated adults were congregated including colleges, workplaces, and prisons. The second occurred in religious communities with low vaccination rates. To date, information from outbreaks in 1990 suggests that failure to vaccinate, rather than vaccine failure, has been responsible for the increase in rubella in contrast to measles, where vaccine failure has been a significant factor.[2] This experience confirms the need to vaccinate women of childbearing age, and to institute aggressive control measures when outbreaks are reported.

Impediments to rubella vaccination of adolescent and adult women have included a fear to vaccinate a woman who might be pregnant and thereby cause a congenital rubella syndrome baby. However, available data indicate that the risk of teratogenicity from live rubella vaccines is small. From January 1971 to April 1989, CDC followed to term 321 known rubella-susceptible pregnant women who had been vaccinated with rubella vaccine within three months before or three months after conception. None of the resultant 324 infants had malformations consistent with congenital rubella infections. This included five infants who had serologic evidence of subclinical infections. On the other hand, there is a more than 20 percent risk of CRS due to maternal infection during the first trimester of pregnancy.[9] Even though the risk of CRS is negligible due to vaccination in pregnancy, vaccination is not recommended in pregnancy because one-third of all pregnancies result in birth defects, one-third of which are serious. This could unjustifiably cause concern that the birth defects were due to rubella. Therefore, it is still recommended that when adolescent and adult women receive rubella vaccine, they be asked if they are pregnant and should be counseled that they must not become pregnant for three months.

Fear of an adverse reaction has constituted a second impediment to vaccination with rubella vaccine. Vaccinees can develop arthralgia and transient arthritis. These reactions occur more commonly in postpubertal females than in males and can begin within one month post-vaccination. Most commonly, they last from one day to three weeks and do not recur. Furthermore, the frequency of chronic joint complaints is higher following natural infection.[9]

In order to be sure that all adolescent and adult women get vaccinated for rubella, it is important to administer MMR when giving the second dose of measles vaccine to entering college students if the student does not have a documented dose of rubella vaccine or serologic evidence of immunity. It is as important to vaccinate men as well as women since unimmunized men may transmit the disease to susceptible women.

Outbreak control should include rapid identification of susceptibles and mandatory vaccination of susceptibles or exclusion from the environment until three weeks after onset of rash of the last reported case in outbreak settings. Voluntary vaccination programs have not been effective in terminating outbreaks. It is critical to confirm a diagnosis of rubella serologically because many other viral illnesses can mimic rubella.

## HEPATITIS B VACCINE

Each year about 300,000 people, mainly young adults, are infected with hepatitis B virus. One quarter of those become ill with jaundice, more than 10,000 require hospitalization and about 250 die of fulminant hepatitis. The U.S. has an estimated pool of 750,000 to 1,000,000 infectious carriers who, unknowingly, transmit hepatitis B to their sexual contacts and children. In addition, 25 percent of this group will develop chronic active hepatitis, and about 20 percent of those will develop cirrhosis, and hepatocellular carcinoma.[10] Recent public health data show that heterosexual as well as homosexual activity with multiple partners (> 1 in 6 months) increases the risk of infection. Intravenous drug users and household or sexual contacts of carriers are also at risk for infection.[11] In addition, immigrants or refugees from areas of high endemicity such as Africa, Eastern Asia, or Pacific Islands have a high risk of infection.[11]

Hepatitis B is the first disease in the history of vaccine development where incidence has continued to increase after introduction of a safe, effective vaccine.

Why? Primarily, because it has been difficult to educate and vaccinate the target high-risk groups. Physician knowledge, attitudes, and behavior have had a serious negative impact on appropriate vaccination of risk groups. Cost of vaccine and inaccessibility of high-risk populations have also been major deterrents. Public health now recognizes that for the vaccine to have a significant impact on the incidence of hepatitis B, a comprehensive strategy must be developed that will provide hepatitis B vaccination to people before they engage in behaviors that will place them at risk of infection. For adolescents, this means universal vaccination in early puberty. The U.S. Department of Health and Human Services now supports the universal vaccination of infants and adolescents as an appropriate strategy to control the transmission of disease.[12]

In 1990, funds were committed to the implementation of universal screening of all pregnant women, with vaccination of infants of carrier mothers, but up to the present time there have not been sufficient funds to implement adolescent vaccination programs.[13] It is important, however, to discuss hepatitis B as another sexually transmitted disease and at least offer the vaccine to all students who present with a sexually transmitted disease or have a history of a multiple sexual partners. Prevention outreach is needed to emphasize the importance of adding hepatitis B vaccine to the routine immunization schedule.

## Hepatitis B Vaccine Dosage Schedule

Primary vaccination is comprised of three (or four) intramuscular doses of vaccine at 0, 1, and 6 months or 0, 1, 2, and 12 months. Hepatitis B vaccine should be given only in the deltoid muscle for adults and children or in the anterolateral thigh muscle for infants and neonates.

For patients undergoing hemodialysis and for other immunosuppressed patients, higher vaccine doses or increased numbers of doses are required. People with HIV infection have an impaired response to hepatitis B vaccine. Since the immunogenicity of high doses of vaccine is unknown for this group, firm recommendations on dosage cannot be made at this time. Table 4 (next page) shows recommended doses and schedules of currently licensed vaccines.

Vaccine doses administered at longer-than-recommended intervals provide satisfactory protection, but optimal protection is not conferred until after the third dose. If the vaccine series is interrupted after the first dose, the second and third doses should be given separated by an interval of 3-5 months. Those who are late for the third dose should be given this dose when convenient. In either situation, post-vaccination testing is not considered necessary.

All hepatitis B vaccines are inactivated (noninfective) products, and there is no evidence of interference with other simultaneously administered vaccines. Data are not available on the safety of hepatitis B vaccines for the developing fetus. However, because the vaccines contain only noninfectious HBsAg particles, there should be no risk to the fetus. In fact, HBV infection of a pregnant woman may result in severe disease for the mother and chronic infection of the newborn. Therefore, pregnancy or lactation should not be considered a contraindication to the use of this vaccine. Hepatitis B vaccine produces neither therapeutic nor adverse effects for HBV carriers. Vaccination of individuals who possess antibodies against HBV from a previous infection is not necessary but will not cause adverse effects. Such individuals will have a post-vaccination increase in their anti-HBs levels. Furthermore, passively acquired antibody, from HBIG or IG transplacental transfer, will not interfere with active immunization.

## Pre- and Post-vaccination Serologic Testing

The decision to test potential vaccine recipients for prior infection is primarily a cost-effectiveness issue and should be based on whether the costs of testing balance

### Table 4
#### Recommended doses and schedules of currently licensed HB vaccines*

| GROUP | Heptavax-B[1,2] Dose (µg) (ml) | | Recombivax HB[1] Dose (µg) (ml) | | Engerix-B[1,3] Dose (µg) (ml) | |
|---|---|---|---|---|---|---|
| Infants of HBV-carrier mothers | 10 | (0.5) | 5 | (0.5) | 10 | (0.5) |
| Other infants and children less than 11 years | 10 | (0.5) | 2.5 | (0.25) | 10 | (0.5) |
| Children and adolescents 11 to 19 years | 20 | (1.0) | 5 | (0.5) | 20 | (1.0) |
| Adults over 19 years | 20 | (1.0) | 10 | (1.0) | 20 | (1.0) |
| Dialysis patients and other immunocompromised persons | 40 | (2.0)[4] | 40 | (1.0)[5] | 40 | (2.0)[4,6] |

* Morbidity and Mortality Weekly Report, Protection against Viral Hepatitis, 39, 1990, p 11
[1] Usual schedule: three doses at 0,1,6 months
[2] Available only for hemodialysis and other immunocompromised patients and for persons with known allergy to yeast.
[3] Alternative schedule: four doses at 0,1,2,12 months
[4] Two 1.0-ml doses given at different sites
[5] Special formulation for dialysis patients
[6] Four-dose schedule recommended at 0,1,2,6 months

the costs of vaccine saved by not vaccinating individuals who have already been infected. Estimation of cost-effectiveness of testing depends on three variables: the cost of vaccination, the cost of testing for susceptibility, and the expected prevalence of immune individuals in the group. For groups with a low expected prevalence of HBV serologic markers, such as health professionals in their training years, pre-vaccination testing is not cost-effective. For routine testing, only one antibody test is necessary, either anti-HBc or anti-HBs. Anti-HBc identifies all previously infected people, both carriers and those who are not carriers, but does not differentiate members of the two groups. Anti-HBs identifies people previously infected, except for carriers. Neither test has a particular advantage for groups expected to have carrier rates of less than 2 percent, such as health-care workers.

Hepatitis B vaccine, when given in the deltoid, produces protective antibody (anti-HBs) in greater than 90 percent of healthy people. Testing for immunity after vaccination is not recommended routinely but is advised for people whose subsequent management depends on knowing their immune status, such as dialysis patients and staff and health care students who are at risk for needle-stick injuries. Post-vaccination testing should be done between three and six months after completion of the vaccine series to provide definitive information on response to the vaccine.

Revaccination of people who do not respond to the primary series (non-responders) produces adequate antibody in 15 to 25 percent after one additional dose and in 30 to 50 percent after three additional doses when the primary vaccination has been given in the deltoid. Therefore, revaccination with at least one additional dose should be considered for health care students who are non-responders to vaccination.

### Indications for Vaccine Booster Doses

Available data show that hepatitis B vaccine-induced antibody levels decline steadily with time and that up to 50 percent of adult vaccinees who respond adequately to vaccine may have low or undetectable antibody levels by seven years after vaccination. Nevertheless, both adults and children with declining antibody levels are still protected against hepatitis B disease. Current data also suggest excellent protection against disease for five years after vaccination among infants born to hepatitis B-carrier mothers. For adults and children with normal immune status, booster doses are not routinely recommended within seven years after vaccination, nor is routine serologic testing to assess antibody levels necessary for vaccine recipients during this period. The possible need for booster doses after longer intervals will be assessed as additional information becomes available. When vaccinated students present with a needle-stick injury, it is important to know their immune status. If a serologic test were performed post-vaccination that showed an immune response, it is not necessary to retest. If immune status were not determined, it is important to perform a titer for anti-HBs. If the titer is undetectable, that student should be given HBIG and a booster dose of hepatitis B vaccine followed by a serologic test for immunity three to six months post vaccination.

## VARICELLA (CHICKENPOX) VACCINE

Varicella (chickenpox) is a common disease of childhood, which in most normal children is a mild, vesicular rash illness with rare serious complications. However, chickenpox does occur in adults and, in particular, on the college campus, which poses major public health problems. Once cases start to appear within a college semester, they tend to continue sporadically throughout the semester. Since it is not possible to effectively isolate students with chickenpox throughout the period of infectivity (which can precede onset of rash by two to four days and continue for seven to ten days), sporadic cases continue to occur among exposed non-immune students with the potential for serious illness, inconvenience, and financial loss.

Normal adults, immunocompromised people, and pregnant women all have a higher risk than normal children of developing complications such as varicella pneumonia and encephalitis. It has been estimated that adults over age 20 are 6 to 12 times more likely to have encephalitis following varicella then are children under 14. In approximately one-third of immunosuppressed patients, disseminated varicella develops involving multiple organ systems. Furthermore, normal adults are ten times more likely than normal children to die from primary varicella, which means a case fatality rate of 6 per 100,000.[14]

A safe, effective vaccine against varicella (Varivax) has been developed, and Merck Sharp Dohme Research Laboratories (MSDRL) submitted an application for licensure to the Food and Drug Administration (FDA) in 1984. This application was favorably reviewed by the vaccine advisory committee for the FDA in January 1990. Licensure is anticipated for the Varivax vaccine in the near future for use in healthy children and adolescents to age 17 years. The Immunization Practices Advisory Committee (ACIP) of the Centers for Disease Control should issue guidelines soon for the use of this vaccine.

The vaccine produced by MSDRL is a live, attenuated vaccine made from the Japanese Oka Strain virus. Studies of normal children show seroconversion rates of 94 percent or greater following a single dose of varicella vaccine. For adults, the efficacy of two doses of vaccine has been estimated to be only 50 percent but no severe illnesses have been reported for adult vaccinees. Possible side effects of vaccination in normal children and adults include a mild generalized rash, usually maculopapular instead of vesicular, in the month following vaccination. Injection site reactions include pain, swelling, and papular or local vesicular lesions, but systemic reactions are rare. Reactivation of varicella (varicella zoster), which is estimated to occur following natural disease in about 8/10,000 person-years, has been only infrequently seen following vaccination of normal people. It has been estimated to occur in such cases in 2/10,000 person-years.[15] Asymptomatic seroconversion has been reported in contacts of vaccinees, but clinical illness secondary to transmission of vaccine virus from healthy vaccinees has not been demonstrated.

If the ACIP and the American Academy of Pediatrics add varicella vaccine to the childhood immunization schedule after it is licensed, the American College Health Association will most likely add it to the Prematriculation Immunization Requirement recommendation.

## IMMUNIZATIONS FOR TRAVEL

In the course of travel for recreation or business reasons, Americans are exposed to many infectious and vector-transmitted diseases that are not a problem in the U.S. This necessitates appropriate counseling and review of routine immunization status as well as administration of other vaccines, depending on the travel itinerary. Many college students do not realize that they encounter special risks as a result of foreign travel and, therefore, do not seek travel consultation. In addition, they are sometimes misinformed by leaders of programs abroad who are not always aware of medical advances with respect to immunization.

Every traveler should have completed routine immunization, including tetanus-diphtheria, measles, mumps, rubella, and polio. Two doses of MMR should have been received or, as an alternative, two doses of measles vaccine one month or more apart with the first dose on or after the first birthday along with one dose each of rubella and mumps vaccines. A primary series of three doses of oral polio vaccine (OPV) should have been completed or, in lieu of OPV, three doses of the new enhanced-potency inactivated vaccine (E-IPV). In addition, all travelers to tropical or developing countries should receive one booster dose of either OPV or E-IPV.[16] OPV has been estimated to cause polio in about one case per 560,000 first doses administered to adults, so previously unimmunized adults should receive E-IPV as a booster for travel.

Additional vaccines may be indicated for areas of poor sanitation, such as developing countries or areas with endemic vector-borne diseases.[17] For areas of poor sanitation, typhoid vaccine, immune globulin, and cholera vaccine should be considered. The new live oral typhoid vaccine is reported to be equally effective and better tolerated than the old parenteral vaccine prepared from killed bacteria. The traveler takes one enteric-coated capsule every other day for a total of four capsules beginning at least two weeks before departure. Cholera vaccine is no longer routinely recommended for tourists because the risk is low and cholera vaccines have limited effectiveness. However, some countries require a single dose within six months of entry for travelers arriving from infected areas. Immune globulin is indicated for susceptible travelers to areas of poor hygiene. It should be given as close to departure as possible in a dose of 2 ml for a stay of less than three months and 5 ml for a longer stay, repeated every five months while in the area of poor sanitation.

Vaccines to be considered for special areas and activities include yellow fever, Japanese encephalitis, hepatitis B, meningococcal, rabies, and plague.[17]

A sample immunization schedule is included (Table 5) that covers most travel needs. It is important to remember that cholera and yellow fever vaccines should be given at least three weeks apart or, if not feasible, given simultaneously. Live virus vaccines should be given at least two weeks prior to immune globulin or, alternatively 6 weeks to three months after immune globulin. In addition, live virus vaccines should be given on the same day or, if not possible, one month apart.

Table 5

Sample Immunization Schedule

| | |
|---|---|
| Visit #1 (DAY 0): | MMR |
| | OPV |
| | Yellow Fever |
| | Typhoid #1 |
| | Rabies #1 |
| Visit #2 (DAY 7): | Rabies #2 |
| Visit #3 (DAY 21): | Rabies #3 (can be given DAY 28) |
| | Cholera #1 (can be given DAY 28, or |
| | DAY zero with Yellow Fever) |
| Visit #4 (DAY 28): | Typhoid #2 (if needed) |
| | Rabies #3 (can be given DAY 21) |
| | Immune Globulin (can be given as |
| | early as DAY 14) |
| GIVE ANY VISIT: | dt |
| | E-IPV |
| | Meningococcus |

## VACCINES FOR SPECIAL RISK GROUPS

Influenza vaccine markedly decreases the incidence of complications from influenza, which in turn decreases the hospitalizations and deaths due to influenza, especially in the elderly. Annual immunization is recommended for patients with chronic pulmonary or cardiovascular diseases, immunosuppressed patients, or people with other chronic diseases.[18] It is also indicated for people who live in group living situations where an outbreak could easily become epidemic. It is not officially recommended for all college students but should be given upon request, since students work, live, and play together in crowded conditions. Because the vaccine changes each year according to early monitoring for influenza, it is important to follow the specific recommendations by CDC for that year.

Like influenza vaccine, pneumococcal vaccine is recommended for patients with chronic cardiac or pulmonary disease. It is also recommended for patients with alcoholism, cirrhosis, diabetes, Hodgkins disease, nephrotic syndrome, renal failure, cerebrospinal fluid leaks, immunosuppression, and other conditions that predispose to pneumococcal infections, such as asplenism and sickle cell anemia.[18] In healthy adults, elevated titers of antibody have persisted for as long as five years after immunizations. High-risk patients who received the earlier 14-valent vaccine should be reimmunized with the 23-valent vaccine.

It is very important to immunize patients who are HIV positive because they are at high risk of becoming quite ill with vaccine-preventable diseases in the event an exposure occurs. All immunizations included in the PIR recommendation except OPV can be given to HIV-positive students; if polio vaccine is still needed, E-IPV vaccine should be given. HIV-positive students should receive pneumococcal vaccine but do not have an increased risk for influenza, so influenza vaccine is not routinely indicated. Live virus vaccines are contraindicated for immunosuppressed people but because people with HIV/AIDS are at high risk of serious illness if exposed to vaccine-preventable illnesses, it is generally appropriate to immunize even though they may not mount an adequate antibody response.

## REFERENCES

1. Sprauer M: Measles, Mumps, Rubella: The Role of Prematriculation Immunity Requirements in Limiting College Outbreaks and an Update on Vaccine Recommendations. Presented Society of Adolescent Medicine annual meeting. Atlanta, GA, March 23, 1990

2. Centers for Disease Control: Increase in Rubella and Congenital Rubella Syndrome - United States, 1988 - 1990. MMWR 40: 93-9, 1991

3. Atkinson W: Measles in Colleges and Universities. Presented National Conference of State Legislators. Nashville, TN, August 7, 1990

4. Centers for Disease Control: Mumps - United States, 1985 1988. MMWR 38: 101-5, 1989

5. Williams W: Immunizations in college health: The remaining tasks. J Am Coll Health 35: 252-60, 1987

6. Collins M: Prematriculation immunization requirements on college campuses: Current status. J Am Coll Health 35: 247-51, 1987

7. Sprauer MA, Williams W, Strikas R: Measles, mumps, and rubella among college-aged adults: Recent epidemiology and new vaccine recommendations. Abstract. Proceedings of the ACHA 68th annual meeting, San Antonio TX, 1990

8. Krause PJ, Cherry JD et al: Epidemic measles in young adults: Clinical, epidemiologic and serologic studies. Ann of Intern Med 90: 873-76, 1979

9. Centers for Disease Control: Rubella Prevention. Recommendations of the Immunization Practices Advisory Committee. MMWR 39:5, 1990

10. Centers for Disease Control: Protection Against Viral Hepatitis: Recommendations of the Immunization Practices Advisory Committee. MMWR 39: 8-14, 1990

11. Alter M, Hodler S et al: The changing epidemiology of hepatitis B in the United States. JAMA 263: 121-22, 1990

12. Margolis HS: The Road Ahead - Future Policy for the Elimination of Hepatitis B Transmission in the United States. 24th National Immunization Conference Proceedings. Atlanta, GA, CDC, 34-35, 1990

13. Collins M: Hepatitis B - The latest sexually transmitted disease. J Am Coll Health 37: 297-8, 1989

14. Fehrs L: Update on Varicella Vaccine. 24th National Immunization Conference Proceedings. Atlanta, GA, CDC, 141-44, 1990

15. Plotkin SA, Starr SE et al: Zoster in normal children after varicella vaccine. J Infect Dis 159: 1000, 1989

16. Centers for Disease Control: Health Information for International Travel 1990. U.S. Government Printing Office, Washington, DC, 81-124, 1990

17. The Medical Letter. Advice for Travelers 32; 33-6, 1990

18. The Medical Letter. Routine Immunization for Adults 32: 54-6, 1990

# General Reading

1. Committee on Infectious Diseases, American Academy of Pediatrics: Report of the Committee on Infectious Diseases Twenty-first Edition. Elk Grove Village, IL, American Academy of Pediatrics, 1988

2. ACIP Task Force on Adult Immunization, Infectious Diseases Society of America: Guide for Adult Immunization Second Edition. Philadelphia, PA, American College of Physicians, 1990

3. Benenson AS (ed): Control of Communicable Diseases in Man. 15th ed. Washington DC, American Public Health Association, 1990

4. Immunization Alert, Computerized information for travel. 93 Timber Drive, Storrs, CT, 06268. 203/487-0611

5. Travel Care from Care Ware, 9559 Poole St, La Jolla, CA 92037. 619/455-1484 or 619/534-2349. Computer program for travel/immunizations, including State Health Department travel advisories.

# 16

# Common Infectious Illness Among College Students

JOHN M. DORMAN, MD

Among the most common problems encountered in college students are those associated with infectious disease. In the first eight months of 1990, almost 30 percent of the visits to Cowell Student Health Center at Stanford University were for some variety of infectious illness. The vast majority of these infections were viral, requiring symptomatic treatment only. The challenges to the college health practitioner are to distinguish which are the infections that need more aggressive antibiotic, antiviral, or antiparasitic treatment, and perhaps more importantly, to assist the students in making these distinctions for themselves in the future.

Particularly in a residential school like Stanford, communications with the rest of the campus community are indispensable. Chickenpox, for example, is not considered by physicians to be a significant medical problem in a healthy young adult, but it can cause much anxiety in a freshman dormitory. Any student health center that has recently suffered through a measles epidemic, or is attempting to implement prematriculation immunization requirements (PIRs), can further attest to the benefit of ongoing communication and cooperation with university officials.

A good health education/promotion program is a great asset in spreading the educational word about infectious disease. The value of racks of pamphlets addressing infectious disease has been contested, but few would dispute the usefulness of a handout or pamphlet on mononucleosis, chlamydia, or herpes being handed to a student who has just received this diagnosis.

## DERMATOLOGIC

Skin infections – bacterial, viral, fungal, and parasitic – are among the most common infections in a college student population. Frequent sports activities and varying levels of hygiene may make these infections more common than in other populations. Though rarely of great medical significance, the infections may have a significant impact on a student's ability to study or on his self image.

Prevention has mainly to do with hygiene, on both an individual and a community basis. Students should be encouraged to wash their clothes – and especially their athletic clothing – on a regular basis. Athletic facilities – gyms, pools, and locker rooms – should also be cleaned on a regular basis.

Most students bring these problems to medical attention because skin problems by their very nature are visible. Practitioners may, however, comment on obvious skin infections when seeing patients for some other reason.

## BACTERIAL SKIN INFECTIONS

**Impetigo** is a bacterial infection, usually streptococcal or staphylococcal, found most often on the face, and manifesting itself as a cluster of macules, vesicles, or pustules. It often has the characteristic golden crust that is most noticeable in the morning. Treatment is most often with a ten-day course of erythromycin, plus an antibacterial soap and an antibiotic ointment. **Folliculitis,** usually involving infected hair follicles, can often be treated with topical approaches only: heat, careful washing, and topical antibiotics.

**Cellulitis** is usually staphylococcal in nature, responding to erythromycin or dicloxacillin. **Abscesses** are notoriously resistant to antibiotics, and often require heat, incision, and drainage as primary treatment. If the problem is recurrent, a course of antibiotics may be indicated as well.

## VIRAL SKIN INFECTIONS

Herpes simplex infections can involve any area of the body. While non-genital infections are usually caused by Herpes simplex type 1, this typing has become of less value as the frequency of oro-genital sexual activity increases. Acyclovir may be of benefit in severe cases, but is not routinely used in non-genital herpes. Wrestlers are a particularly susceptible patient population and may have frequent **herpes gladiatorum**, a herpes infection that prevents them from participating when it is active.[1] **Varicella and herpes zoster** are not uncommon in the student population; varicella may be more severe in this age group than in younger children, but may become less common if the vaccine becomes available and is widely utilized. Acyclovir has been used for herpes zoster, but its high cost and limited effectiveness in mild cases may limit its use for students. Usual treatment is symptomatic and also includes isolation of varicella patients from non-immune individuals until all lesions are crusted over. Aspirin should not be used in these individuals because of the potential risk of Reye Syndrome as a complication; ibuprofen, while it has not previously been implicated, should be avoided as well. Acetaminophen is a preferable substitute for fever and pain.

**Common warts** are a common problem among the student population. In our health service we encourage self-treatment of warts, as many treated warts will return anyway, and many untreated warts will vanish on their own. Often a periodic paring down of plantar warts is sufficient to relieve the pain. More aggressive treatment may include liquid nitrogen or the use of laser.

## FUNGAL SKIN INFECTIONS

The athletic activities of most students often predispose them to **tinea pedis** (athlete's foot), **tinea cruris** (jock rash), and **tinea corporis** (ringworm). Today most of these infections can be easily treated with over-the-counter miconazole. **Tinea unguium**, nail fungal involvement, usually requires treatment either with surgery and/or oral griseofulvin for prolonged periods of time. Students may elect not to treat the problem after understanding the cost. **Tinea versicolor**, causing alterations in skin pigmentation on the trunk and upper arms, may be treated with miconazole, oral ketoconazole, or topical selenium sulfide lotion.

## PARASITIC SKIN INFESTATIONS

Pubic lice are usually sexually transmitted, but may be transmitted by bedding. Scabies can be easily transmitted by any skin contact. Both can be treated with lindane lotion, but environment and contacts must be cleansed as well.

# EYE, EAR, NOSE, AND THROAT INFECTIONS

Upper respiratory infections (URIs) are the most common problem for which students seek medical care. Most of these are viral, and are undoubtedly more common because of the close quarters in which students live and study. Since URIs are self-limited, most medical care is usually indicated only in evaluating and treating complications. Medical efforts are often directed at educating students, helping them to learn in what circumstances they can care for their own URIs, and when they should appropriately seek medical care. A student-run "cold clinic," under the guidance of nurses, has undertaken this task at Stanford.

Indications for medical care include:

1. a fever above 38° C;
2. severe headache or pain over sinuses;
3. ear pain;

4. wheezing or chest pain;
5. severely swollen glands;
6. enlarged and reddened tonsils, exudate; or
7. symptoms for more than 10-14 days.

Otitis media, a middle ear infection, requires antibiotic treatment, usually with amoxicillin or trimethoprim/sulfamethoxazole (TMP/SMX). Otitis externa, infection of the external ear canal ("swimmer's ear"), usually responds to topical ear drops of an antibiotic/steroid combination, as well as keeping the ear dry. Sinusitis normally responds to amoxicillin or TMP/SMX, but occasionally may require surgical intervention.

Streptococcal sore throat is the only unequivocally bacterial cause of pharyngitis, and is treated either with intramuscular benzathine penicillin or by 10 days of oral penicillin or erythromycin. Conjunctivitis may be allergic, viral, or bacterial; however, unless the irritation occurs in a classically allergic setting, a non-ophthalmologist may often choose to treat empirically with topical antibiotic eye drops or ointment. Steroid-containing eye medications should not routinely be utilized by non-ophthalmologists.

## GASTROINTESTINAL INFECTIONS

Most gastrointestinal infections are viral in nature, and respond quickly to supportive and symptomatic treatment. This age group rarely requires intravenous hydration, although occasional parenteral medication is needed. Student travellers may, however, be more likely to be infected by exotic infections than the general population, and recent travel should always be considered. Persistent intestinal symptoms, particularly if present with fever or bloody stools, may raise the question of non-viral etiologies, especially if there is a travel history. Obtaining a stool smear for red and white blood cells will often help in screening for suspected bacterial or parasitic involvement. Students may be infected with Campylobacter, Yersinia, Salmonella, Shigella, or enteropathogenic E. coli (which will not show up on routine culture). Appropriate antibiotic treatment will depend on culture results, but almost all bacterial intestinal infections are susceptible to ciprofloxacin.

Giardia lamblia is the most common cause of parasitic intestinal infestation in students, and may be acquired from stream water or contact with small children, as well as from travel in underdeveloped areas.[2] Hepatitis is not uncommon in the college age group. Hepatitis A most commonly affects those who travel to underdeveloped areas; gamma globulin is recommended prior to departure. Hepatitis B is commonly a disease of international students, particularly from southeast Asia (especially in its carrier state); those with multiple sexual partners, whether homosexual or heterosexual, are also at increased risk. Hepatitis B vaccine is recommended for those at increased risk. At this time, treatment of either disease is supportive only.

## GENITO-URINARY INFECTIONS

Urinary infections in this age group tend to be predominantly in sexually active women. The classic "honeymoon cystitis" category includes any sexually active woman who does not have intercourse on a regular basis, and this description fits most college women.[3] Students who abstain from sexual activity rarely are infected unless they have some anatomical abnormality. Cystitis can often be prevented by emptying the bladder after intercourse and by wiping front to back after voiding.

Most cystitis is caused by E. coli, and simple infections are treated today with the TMP/SMX combination for three days. Single-dose treatment has been utilized, but seems to have a significant failure rate in this population. In complicated infections, a longer course of treatment may be necessary. Over 50 percent of the bacteria causing cystitis at Stanford are now resistant to ampicillin and sulfamethoxazole, the previous mainstays of treatment. Prophylactic doses of TMP/SMX or nitrofurantoin may be used after intercourse for those with frequent recurrent infections. Occasionally women with urinary symptoms may have pyuria but negative cultures; this phenomenon has been named **urethral syndrome**. Some of these patients represent true bacterial cystitis with dilute urine, while others may be infected with chlamydia and would respond better to doxycycline. **Pyelonephritis** is still an occasional complication of urinary infections, but can usually be treated as an outpatient in this population with either TMP/SMX or one of the cephalosporins.

**Gynecologic infections** in this age group are often sexually transmitted (reviewed elsewhere). Most vaginitis, however, is not sexually transmitted. Use of systemic antibiotics, the wearing of nylon tights or underwear, or an undiagnosed case of diabetes may predispose women to **vaginal yeast infections (candidiasis)**. Therefore, cotton underwear is recommended for women who are predisposed to this infection. Indiscriminate use of antibiotics is to be avoided in women for the same reason. Screening is normally done by identification of the budding organisms on a wet preparation of vaginal secretions. Treatment of yeast is with vaginal clotrimazole, miconazole, terconazole, or butaconazole cream or suppositories. Treatment of partners is not necessary. **Gardnerella** is a bacteria that is found in the presence of a watery, malodorous vaginal discharge in so-called bacterial vaginosis. Whether this organism is the actual etiologic agent of the infection is somewhat controversial.[4] Clue cells – epithelial cells covered with gram-negative rods – are seen on the wet preparation. This infection responds to oral metronidazole treatment. Although controversial, it is not currently believed to be sexually transmitted.

*Trichomonas vaginalis* is a parasite that causes a sexually transmitted vaginitis; it is identified on wet preparation and both partners are treated with oral metronidazole.

Most **genito-urinary infections in males** in this age group are likewise sexually transmitted, but there are some exceptions. Uncircumcised males may acquire a **yeast balanitis** if careful hygiene is not practiced; these infections usually respond to hygiene and miconazole cream. **Epididymitis and inflammation of the vas deferens** may occur even in sexually inactive males; these may not be truly bacterial and may respond to anti-inflammatory medication, support, and ice. Others may require antibiotic treatment, particularly if there is evidence of urethritis as well. **Prostatitis** with gram-negative bacteria is an occasional problem that responds well to TMP/SMX.

# RESPIRATORY INFECTIONS

In addition to the previously mentioned upper respiratory infections, students are subject to lower and more serious respiratory infections as well. Living in close quarters, irregular hours, and occasionally irresponsible behavior may predispose students to these infections, although generally good health makes them more resistant. Allergic individuals are more at risk than others, and good monitoring of allergies, especially in those with asthma, will minimize such complications. Smokers are also more at risk than non-smokers, but on most campuses smoking is becoming an uncommon habit. In most locations winter is more the season of risk than other times of year.

**Influenza A** is a viral respiratory infection with a characteristic presentation of high fever, severe sore throat, and a dry hacking cough. If these symptoms are present during the winter influenza season, oral amantadine may be indicated to reduce the severity of the signs and symptoms. High-risk patients (those with underlying chronic conditions involving heart, lung, and kidney) may benefit from annual influenza vaccine in the fall.

**Bronchitis**, with a productive cough and wheezing or rhonchi with or without fever, may be caused by both viral and bacterial agents; over half of presenting cases are probably viral in nature. Most will respond to symptomatic treatment. X-rays are normally not helpful. The white blood count may be elevated in bacterial infections. Treatment of bronchitis is somewhat controversial. Bacterial causes, including mycoplasma and chlamydia, may respond to erythromycin. Antibiotics may be particularly indicated in smokers.

**Pneumonia** is often a further complication in students, and differs little in etiology from the above description of bronchitis. Mycoplasma ("walking pneumonia") and chlamydia are the most common causes in this population, with pneumococcal pneumonia being seen infrequently. Again, the white blood count may be elevated, although this is less common in mycoplasma than with the pneumococcal infections. Blood cultures are less helpful in students, as mycoplasma and chlamydia will not show up. X-rays are usually abnormal, but many physicians will treat on the basis of physical examination alone.

**Tuberculosis** is infrequent in American-born students, but is not uncommon in international populations. The American College Health Association (ACHA) recommends tuberculosis screening with intradermal purified protein derivative (PPD) or chest x-rays of all international students on entry to universities, although students from some developed countries may actually be at the same or less risk as American students. Those students under 35 years of age who have positive skin tests but normal chest x-rays may benefit from isoniazid prophylaxis. Students with pulmonary involvement on x-ray require additional treatment with rifampin and pyrazinamide.

## OTHER SYSTEMIC INFECTIOUS DISEASES

**Infectious mononucleosis** ("mono") is commonly seen in students. Although known as the "kissing disease," it is in fact not particularly contagious, occurring no more often in roommates of those with mono than in the general population. In fact, over half of incoming freshmen in one study had antibodies to the EB virus, the causative agent, upon their arrival at college. Diagnosis is often fairly obvious on clinical examination, with sore throat, pharyngeal exudate, anterior and posterior cervical nodes, and fever. Hepatosplenomegaly may be present, and contact sports are therefore contraindicated. Confirmation of the diagnosis is by the white blood count and differential, with specific mono spot testing as indicated. More specific antibody testing and liver function measurements are rarely needed. Treatment is normally symptomatic only, with prednisone still a somewhat controversial option, ordinarily being utilized mainly in cases with potential pharyngeal obstruction.[5]

**Lyme disease**, a tick-borne spirochete infection, presents initially after a tick bite with erythema migrans, followed if untreated by a disseminated infection with debilitating illness and fatigue and occasional neurologic symptoms, and late involvement of joints.[6-8] The erythema migrans is fairly diagnostic and is treated with 21 days of tetracycline. Some physicians will treat all tick bites, as the screening serology only becomes positive several weeks after the initial infection; this concern is perhaps particularly warranted at this writing in the northeastern United States. In fact, however, Lyme disease is much more feared on campus than it is actually present in most parts of the country.

**Malaria** is occasionally seen in international students, as well as in traveling students upon their return. Normally the symptoms of infection may be prevented using chloroquine or mefloquine prophylaxis,[9] and the disease is relatively straightforward to treat, once it is recognized.

# REFERENCES

1. Selling B, Kibrick S: An outbreak of herpes simplex among wrestlers (herpes gladiatorum). N Engl J Med 270:979-82, 1964

2. Shandera WX: From Leningrad to the day-care center — the ubiquitous *Giardia lamblia.* West J Med 153;154-159, 1990

3. Faigel HC: The relationship between urinary tract infections and the collegiate academic calendar.   J Am Coll Health 39:77-81, 1990

4. Sobel JD: Bacterial vaginosis — an ecologic mystery. Ann Intern Med 111:551-553, 1989

5. Collins M, Fleisher G, Kreisberg J et al: Role of steroids in the treatment of infectious mononucleosis in the ambulatory college student. J Am Coll Health 33:101-105, 1984

6. Steere AC: Lyme Disease. N Engl J Med 321:586-595, 1989

7. Pinger RR, Hahn DB: Is Lyme disease a health threat for your students? J Am Coll Health 37:177-179, 1989

8. Lane R: Lyme disease: A case report. J Am Coll Health 37:180-181, 1989

9. Centers for Disease Control: Recommendations for the prevention of malaria among travelers. MMWR 39 (No. RR-3):1-10, 1990

## Recommended Reading

Abramowicz M (ed): The Choice of Antimicrobial Drugs. The Medical Letter 30:33-40, 1988

Abramowicz M (ed): Drugs for Parasitic Infections. The Medical Letter 28:9-16, 1986

American Public Health Association: Control of Communicable Diseases in Man, fifteenth edition. Edited by AS Benenson. Washington DC, APHA, 1990

Braunwald E, Isselbacher KJ, Petersdorf RG et al.: Harrison's Principles of Internal Medicine, 11th Edition. New York, The Blakiston Co, 1986

Committee on Infectious Diseases, American Academy of Pediatrics: Report of the Committee on Infectious Diseases. 21st Edition. Edited by G Peter. Elk Grove Village, IL, American Academy of Pediatrics, 1988

Goroll AH, May LA, Mulley AG: Primary Care Medicine, 2nd Edition. Philadelphia, JB Lippincott, 1987

Krugman S, Ward R: Infectious Diseases of Children and Adults, 8th Edition. St. Louis, CV Mosby, 1985

Infectious Disease, Scientific American Medicine. Edited by E Rubenstein, DD Federman. New York, Scientific American, section 7, 1990

# 17

# Dental Conditions
# Among College Students

DOMINIC CITTADINO, DDS

Dental conditions and diseases found in the college student population are similar to those found in the general population, with several exceptions. At a typical college dental health service, most of the student patients range in age from 18 to 25 years old. At this age dental health problems are common and expertise in this field is welcome to any student health program.[1] It has been stated that dental patients need more teeth filled between the ages of 15 and 24 years than at any other time of their life.[2] Also, the need for endodontics (root canal therapy) to save restorable teeth and for oral surgery to extract unrestorable teeth and wisdom teeth is high in this age population. Since the student is in an environment that fosters learning, it follows that college students are at an ideal age to develop lifelong attitudes about health behavior, while focusing on improving and maintaining their oral health.[3]

Student health centers should insure the availability of dental health care for all college students. Ideally this should take the form of a dental service within the student health center itself, providing preventive, routine, and emergency dental care. Unfortunately, the number of universities in the United States with student dental services is in the neighborhood of 35 to 40. "High start-up costs and reluctance to embark upon an unknown venture" have been cited as reasons why there is such a paucity of campus-based dental health care provided to college students.[1] There clearly is a need for more college health dental programs. By documenting existing dental needs of the student population, an administrator may begin the groundwork for establishing a dental service at the student health service.

The cornerstone of dental health services at campuses should be a program that focuses upon prevention of dental disease. The dental program at the University of Massachusetts at Amherst is an excellent example of a program that has placed a major emphasis on improving their college population's oral health by making preventive group workshops available for patients that need future comprehensive care and for students who would like to know more about their oral health.[1] Oral hygiene preventive classes are held daily and conducted by a qualified dental hygienist and one or two student health educators. Groups of eight to ten students attend these sessions to learn the correct ways to floss and brush and the preventive significance of these and other oral hygiene measures. These classes are part of the student's prepaid benefit.

## COMMON PROBLEMS

This chapter will focus upon dental problems common to college students. Dental problem statistics have been kept since 1978 at the Student Emergency Dental Service of Southern Illinois University at Carbondale. According to these records, the most common problems encountered in this student population, in descending order, are: 1) dental caries, 2) pericoronitis, 3) abscessed or infected teeth, 4) periodontal disease, 5) trauma, 6) prosthetic problems, 7) oral lesions, 8) TMJ pain dysfunction syndrome, and 9) post-surgical complications.[3]

**Dental caries, or dental decay** as it is called, is seen overtly in the mouth by holes or cavities in the enamel (outside) layer of the teeth. The dental decay process begins when bacteria in the mouth organize in colonies, called plaque. Plaque is a thin, white, sticky film that contains harmful bacteria. These bacteria derive energy by fermentation of carbohydrates. A by-product of this natural process is an acid that can demineralize the crystalline structure of enamel on contact. Several factors affect the speed of cavity formation and its progress. The food one eats, general health, heredity, presence of fluoride during tooth development, and most important, how well one controls the removal of dental plaque are the important modifying influences. Controlling these factors is best for preventing dental decay on an individual level. On the community level, public fluoridation has been found to reduce caries by 30 to 60 percent.[2]

Since dental caries can be detected by x-radiation, one should get a full-mouth set of x-rays every five to seven years. A dental hygienist may be utilized to clean hard plaque deposits (calculus) off the teeth, and to take the x-ray films needed for diagnosis. Students should visit the hygienist every six months.

**Pericoronitis** is inflammation of soft tissue around a developing third molar (wisdom tooth). Third molars are generally the last teeth to emerge in an individual's set of teeth (usually between ages 17 and 22). Frequently, their eruption is blocked by soft tissue, bone, adjacent teeth, or some pathologic process; they are then considered impacted. Pericoronitis may exist around the crown of any erupting tooth, not just a third molar, but because of our student-age population (18-25), erupted and/or impacted wisdom teeth account for almost all episodes. Patients presenting with this disease process may complain of extreme pain (usually in the lower jaw) in the wisdom tooth area and radiating pain sometimes all the way up to the eye (with headache). A foul odor is often noted and swelling of the face and throat can also occur. In many cases antibiotics are necessary if an infection has developed and/or spread.

In addition to good clinical assessment by the dentist, a panelipse x-ray would be the best way to ascertain whether no wisdom teeth, one wisdom tooth, or all four wisdom teeth, should be extracted. If removal of these teeth is necessary one may prevent not only the recurrence of pericoronitis, but also decay of the adjacent teeth, possible infection, jaw pain and crowding of other teeth. Many times the removal of difficult impacted wisdom teeth may require the special skill of an oral surgeon.

**Abscessed or infected teeth** present when an irreversible pulpitis occurs. Most patients with an abscessed tooth will have symptoms such as pain, swelling, pimple on the gums, sensitivity to cold and/or hot, darkened tooth, and pain upon touching down on the tooth. But sometimes there are no symptoms and abscessed teeth are discovered on routine dental x-rays. X-rays are used for the purpose of confirming a diagnosis that the tooth is abscessed and the pulp is irreversibly damaged. Symptomatic and asymptomatic pulpal and periapical (tip of the root) changes are common with a dying tooth and it is the dentist's job to decipher whether the process is reversible or irreversible.[4]

If the pulp is irreversibly damaged the patient is faced with several alternatives. The patient may elect to have nothing done. Untreated, such a condition could lead to a serious infection. Most students want to do something about this dilemma and their other two choices are to have the tooth extracted or root canal therapy to save the tooth. In root canal therapy or endodontics as it is called, the diseased or infected pulp is removed, the root canal is cleansed and made wider, and finally the root canal is permanently filled with an inert material.

Antibiotic therapy should be initiated if signs of infection are present. Hopefully, the student will elect to have the tooth saved by having a dentist initiate a root canal procedure. This can be expensive. Some dental programs such as those at Southern Illinois University at Carbondale[3] and University of Massachusetts at Amherst[1] help the student with this decision by offering a co-payment plan. In this case these dental programs charge the student a partial fee for the root canal, and also subsidize part of that root canal cost by including it in their prepaid package. Many other student dental clinics accomplish the same result by simply charging a reduced fee for this service. In this age of rising medical and dental costs, the students may benefit by not having to pay the full price for a root canal, and still receive the benefits of saving their teeth.

**Periodontal disease**, commonly known as pyorrhea, is generally a slowly developing condition that is the most common cause of lost teeth as a person ages. By age 40, the majority of all tooth loss is from this disease process. Periodontal disease refers to a deterioration of the gums (gingiva) and the bone that support and surround the teeth. Periodontal disease begins when plaque accumulates on the teeth. The saliva will calcify the plaque if it is not removed by proper home care. This calcified plaque is called tartar or calculus, which accumulates at the gum line. An inflammation of the gums (gingivitis) will occur if the calculus is not regularly removed by a dental hygienist or dentist. This initial gingivitis may reveal itself as a mild gum irritation with bleeding during brushing.[2] However, if chronic gingivitis persists, other damage is occurring to the underlying bone, which is being resorbed (melted away). In the advanced stage of periodontal disease (periodontitis), the tooth adjacent to this bone may become infected and have to be removed.

Fortunately, for the college student with a mean age much under 40, simple gingivitis-type conditions are seen more frequently than is periodontitis. Gingivitis problems can be further broken down into two groups called **marginal gingivitis** and **acute necrotizing ulcerative gingivitis**. Marginal gingivitis is simply an inflammation of the gums and a change in the position of the gingival margin, in which there is associated redness and puffiness; the gums bleed easily when brushing or flossing.[5] It occurs in the student population from lack of good oral home care. Proper daily home care and a visit to the dental hygienist every six months for a cleaning are the best ways to prevent marginal gingivitis.[2]

Acute necrotizing ulcerative gingivitis (ANUG), or trench mouth as it is often called, typically presents in young adults.[6] Stress is a main predisposing factor along with poor diet, insufficient sleep, and poor oral hygiene. ANUG is characterized by ulcerated areas on the gums between the teeth that bleed easily, by a foul odor, and by painful and burning sensations on the gums.[6] This disease usually occurs during mid-terms or finals when the students are under more stress. International students tend to contract this disease right after they have left their homeland and family to come to the U.S. Treatment of ANUG involves debridement of the gum tissue with a specialized instrument called a cavitron. Additionally, some medicaments (glyoxide, Ora-5, etc.) may be placed on the gums by the dentist and warm salt water rinses should be advised for several days. A well-balanced diet, water-soluble vitamins B and C, adequate oral home care and sleep will also help. Acute symptoms respond readily to systemic metronidazole or penicillin.[6]

**Dental trauma** accounts for many student dental visits, yet our administrators are just beginning to recognize its significance at the college level. Dental trauma may be as a result of athletic injury (collegiate, intramural, or recreational), horseplay, household mishaps, alcohol or drug related misadventures, automobile accidents, assault, or other traumatic events.[4] A broad spectrum of oral injuries comprises this category, ranging from a simple cut lip, to damage to one or two teeth, to loss of a tooth, to a compound complex fracture of the jaw, to a life-threatening condition in which one's airway may have been compromised. Most dental trauma that a university dental clinic will treat is simple tooth trauma or lacerated soft tissue injuries. In the case of trauma to a tooth there is a protocol that should be followed.

Regardless if a tooth is fractured or intact, but just loose, it should be x-rayed initially for signs of possible root fracture, vertical or horizontal fracture, and injury to the pulp. Clinically, it should be tested for mobility and vitality if the situation warrants. Adjacent teeth should be similarly examined, since it is not unusual for these other teeth to also die because of the force of the trauma to the surrounding periapical tissues.[4] This same type x-ray should be taken and another clinical check for mobility and vitality should be performed two weeks later before any definitive treatment is performed. The reason for delayed treatment is to allow some healing to occur if there were a reversible pulpitis, allow the tooth to get firmer in the socket, or allow the tooth to react adversely, in the case of a dying tooth that would need root canal therapy. Many times a student patient will present with a fractured incisal edge off the front tooth and want it fixed immediately before Mom and Dad find out. The rule of thumb is to wait that specified length of time for these tests to be negative, because if the tooth were restored on the initial visit and then, because of the instrumentation became necrotic, the dentist and dental clinic would be liable.

Sometimes, in an unfortunate situation the tooth is lost (avulsed from the socket). Many times one may still save that tooth by acting quickly and following this protocol established by the American Association of Endodontists excellent brochure entitled, You Can Save That Tooth! Locate the tooth. Handle the tooth by its crown, not by its root. Carefully remove any debris from the tooth. Examine the root for any fracture. There being none, gently replace the tooth in its socket. Another alternative is to keep the tooth moist in a cup of water. If no water is readily available, the tooth may be placed in the patient's mouth next to his cheek. Do not attempt to clean the tooth with vigorous scrubbing or cleaning agents. See a dentist immediately, preferably within thirty minutes of the accident.

It is very difficult to predict when mishaps are going to occur, but there are some safety standards that a university health service could establish. As a service to all athletes, be they collegiate, intramural, or recreational, let them be aware that an athletic protective mouth guard is the best way to prevent needless injury to one's teeth during an athletic event. The dental service may want to get into the business of offering that service for the student population.

**Prosthetic problems** constitute such things as a lost crown or fixed bridge, a broken full or partial denture, problems encountered from a poorly fitting permanent or temporary crown, bridge, partial denture and full denture. Factors such as the number of international students being seen and the socioeconomic status of many of the students have a lot to do with making this prosthetic category sixth on the list of dental problems. Students from these two groups have had little exposure to dental concerns and view the dental clinic as a place to go when an emergency exists. Many of these students have seen the dentist once and only to receive an extraction and a temporary replacement.

An international student, for example, may loose a temporary crown (not even aware that it is a plastic temporary) on a front tooth and wish it to be permanently cemented, even though gingival inflammation may exist and the crown fits poorly. The secret to overcoming this problem lies in educating and becoming empathetic to the patient's concerns. Many times a compromise must be reached between dentist and patient in coming up with a solution that will satisfy the patient's needs and yet be within the realm of dental ethics.

**Oral lesions** constitute a broad area of various lesions. Since the mean age of a university population is in the low 20s, one does not routinely see cancer or lesions associated with the older public.[7] A good rule of thumb for any uncertain lesion that stays in the oral cavity more than two weeks is to biopsy, and that holds true in college dental health as well. The dentist should not delay in the submission of the tissue to the oral pathologist.[8] (See also Volume I, Chapter 14, smokeless tobacco section.)

Recurrent aphthous stomatitis or a canker sore is commonly seen on non-keratinized (movable) oral mucosa. The minor lesions, less than one centimeter, are most frequently seen and they appear as small, shallow, painful ulcerations covered by a gray membrane and surrounded by a narrow erythematous halo.[8] The etiology is unknown but altered immune response, acidic foods, stress, trauma, allergies, and endocrine alterations are predisposing factors. Patients with frequent recurrences should be screened for diabetes mellitus and other systemic debilitating diseases. These lesions heal in seven to ten days on their own. Effective treatment is to place Kenalog (triamcinolone) in Orabase over the lesion after each meal and at bedtime. Students usually respond in one to three days.[8]

Oral tori are hyperostosis (exostosis) of bone occurring most commonly in the midline of the hard palate (torus palatinus) or on the lingual aspect of the mandible in the canine-premolar region (torus mandibularus).[9] Twenty percent of the general population have the palatinus variety, while 8 percent have the mandibularus type. These outgrowths of bone are easily traumatized, tending to grow larger with more irritation and may have to be surgically removed to give the patient true relief.

Many times students present in the dental service because they think the lesion is cancerous and has metastasized because it has grown larger.

A mucocele is usually a spherical swelling of the lower lip due to an abnormal collection of mucin in the underlying tissues.[9] They occur most frequently in the lower lip but may be found wherever there is salivary gland tissue. Trauma is the most likely cause of this lesion, with treatment consisting of excisional biopsy of the entire lesion.[9] Trying to open the lesion and drain the fluid does not help because fluid will fill back into the tissue within the day.

Recurrent (orofacial) herpes simplex is an intraoral lesion appearing in single or small clusters of vesicles that quickly rupture forming painful ulcers.[8] The lesions usually occur on the keratinized tissue of the hard palate and gingiva. Also, the labialis version is clusters of vesicles on the lips that rupture and then crust. Precipitating factors include fever, stress, exposure to sunlight (UV), trauma and hormonal alterations. Lesions may last 14-21 days and treatment such as acyclovir (Zovirax) and PreSun 15 sunscreen lotion work best in the early stage of this disease process.[8]

Primary (acute) herpetic gingivostomatitis is another herpetic viral infection caused by transmission of the herpes simplex virus.[8] Clear vesicles changing to yellow develop both intra- and extra-orally, then rupture, forming shallow, painful ulcers. Patients may have systemic signs and symptoms, including fever and malaise. Treatment includes relieving the symptoms, preventing secondary infection, and supporting the general health of the patient. Palliative oral relief can be obtained by rinses such as Benadryl/Benylin or Benylin/Kaopectate elixirs 50/50 to help the patient eat and drink fluids. Systemic antibiotic therapy may be initiated if signs of secondary bacterial infection are present in susceptible individuals.[8]

Candidiasis is seen less than the other lesions mentioned previously. Its appearance in the oral cavity should act as a beacon for other possible systemic problems in the infected patient, such as xerostomia, diabetes mellitus, pregnancy, poor oral hygiene, prosthodontic appliances and suppression of the immune system with AIDS. Clinically, candidiasis appears as soft, white, slightly elevated plaques that usually can be wiped away leaving an erythematous area. Treatment rationale includes re-establishing a normal balance of oral flora and improving oral hygiene. Medications such as Nystatin oral suspension, ointment, topical powder and troches should be continued for 48 hours after disappearance of clinical signs to prevent its recurrence.

Other common oral lesions seen in the college population – including thermal burns from pizza and nicotine stomatitis from smokeless tobacco – are covered in reference 10.

**Temporo-mandibular joint (TMJ) pain dysfunction syndrome** is a neuro-muscular and/or joint dysfunction that is characterized by some or all of the following symptoms: pain in the lower jaw, TMJ, teeth, neck, or back; pain in the muscles of mastication and muscles that support the head; pain in the temples, vertex, and occipital areas of the head; pain on opening the mouth, yawning, chewing; popping or clicking sounds when opening and/or closing the mouth; trismus or the inability to completely and painlessly open and close the mouth; tinnitus or ringing in ears and reduced hearing acuity; and sensitive teeth. TMJ pain dysfunction syndrome is a multi-causal syndrome being induced by such things as trauma, stress, iatrogenic dentistry, malocclusion, clenching, and occlusal disorders.[11]

The TMJ problem seen almost exclusively with student-patients is myofacial pain dysfunction (MPD), a condition of the muscles of the face and jaw, which are overburdened by excessive clenching or grinding of the teeth, usually uncon-sciously.[12] MPD is usually seen around mid-term and final exam time or whenever a student is under heavy work loads and stress for a long time. Once a diagnosis of MPD is confirmed, the dentist should be supportive of the patient by listening, then offering different types of treatment options. The TMJ on the affected side needs reversible adjunctive therapy, such as heat/cold/heat therapy, soft diet, immobilization of the joint, and avoidance of touching the upper and lower teeth together. Medications (anti-inflammatory drugs, analgesics, and muscle relaxants) can be used. Stress management techniques, cognitive awareness training, biofeed-back, imagery, physiotherapy, myfunctional therapy, hypnosis, occlusal splints, and psychotherapy may be offered to prevent future recurrences.[11]

Finally, **post-surgical complications** are usually associated with the extraction of wisdom teeth. The most common is dry socket (alveolar osteitis) after a wisdom tooth extraction. Dry socket is a condition in which the blood clot disintegrates.[12] At first the clot has a dirty gray appearance, and then it disintegrates, leaving a gray bony socket, bare of granulation tissue. A foul odor is present and severe pain persists for days if untreated. The symptoms usually set in after the second or third day following an extraction. The wound should first be carefully irrigated with warm saline and dried. Usually a dressing containing one of the many analgesic and antiseptic drugs in paste form is placed in the socket area, sometimes followed by a zinc oxide-eugenol compound that is placed over the wound in order to protect it from the oral environment.[12] Even though a dry socket may occur in any type of extraction, it is more common among students who have had their wisdom teeth extracted at home; they usually return to school the night of the extraction and present in the clinic a day or so later with the osteitis problem.

# REFERENCES

1. Lubin H: A dental program in the health service. J Am Coll Health 26:154-157, 1977

2. American College Health Association: Dental Health is Your Choice (brochure), American College Health Association, 1984

3. Cittadino DP, Morgan F: The emergency dental service at Southern Illinois University/Carbondale. J Am Coll Health 29:115-118, 1980

4. Weine FS: Diseases of the pulp and periapex, Endodontic Therapy. Third Edition. St. Louis, CV Mosby Company, 1982, pp 66-171

5. Williams RC: Periodontal disease. N Engl J Med 322:373-379, 1990

6. Strahan JD, Waite IM: Acute periodontal conditions, Color Atlas of Periodontology. Chicago, IL, Yearbook Medical Publishers, Inc, 1978, pp 36-39

7. Wood NK, Goaz PW: History and examination of the patient, Differential Diagnosis of Oral Lesions. Third Edition. St. Louis, CV Mosby Co, 1985, pp 4-30

8. Bottomley WK, Rosenberg SW: Clinicians Guide to Treatment of Common Oral Conditions. New York, The American Academy of Oral Medicine, 1987, pp 2-8

9. Robinson HBG, Miller AS: Developmental disturbances, Diseases of the oral mucosa and the jaws, Color Atlas of Oral Pathology. Fourth Edition. Edited by Colby, Kerr, and Robinson. Philadelphia, JB Lippincott Co, 1983, pp 17-52 and 91-136

10. Bottemley WK, Brown RS, Lavigne GS: A retrospective survey of the oral conditions of 981 patients referred to an oral medicine private practice. JADA 120:529-533, 1990

11. Morgan DH, House LR, Hall WP et al: Initial examination, Diseases of the Temporomandibular Apparatus. Second Edition. St. Louis, CV Mosby Co, 1982, pp 82-116

12. Thoma KH: Extraction of teeth - exodontia, Oral Surgery Volume One. Fifth Edition. St. Louis, CV Mosby Co, 1969, pp 280-318

# 18

# Eating Disorders
# and the College Population

FELICE D. KURTZMAN, MPH, RD AND JOEL YAGER, MD

During the past ten years there has been a remarkable proliferation of research, programs, and services aimed at eating disorders among college students.[1] Stressors inherent in the college environment may precipitate problems in those susceptible to eating disorders or exacerbate symptoms in those with existing problems. These stressors may include separation from family and friends, interpersonal conflicts, group residential living, financial concerns, new food choices, and peer pressures regarding body image, sexuality, and the use of alcohol or drugs.

Media attention and recent research have heightened awareness of the deleterious effects of eating disorders on psychologic and physiologic health. Health professionals providing services to college and university students must be knowledgeable about these disorders and develop effective strategies to deal with their consequences. This chapter will discuss the epidemiology, prevention, assessment, and treatment of eating disorders. The reader should be able to tailor these recommendations to a wide variety of settings, from small, private, rural colleges to large, public, urban universities.

## EPIDEMIOLOGY

Anorexia nervosa, the syndrome of severe self-starvation, and bulimia nervosa, characterized by repetitive episodes of binge eating and purging, have in common extreme preoccupation with weight, marked compulsivity in eating-related behaviors, and many associated medical and psychiatric problems. Diagnostic criteria published by the American Psychiatric Association for anorexia nervosa and bulimia nervosa are listed in Table 1, next page. Although anorexia nervosa and bulimia nervosa may occur independently the two disorders frequently co-exist and may alternate. At the "lower risk" end, they trail off into syndromes of obsessional weight preoccupation without serious starvation or binge/purge behaviors, and various forms of compulsive overeating in normal weight and obese individuals.

The prevalence of anorexia nervosa and bulimia nervosa appears to have increased since the 1960s. Women constitute 90 percent to 95 percent of cases, although male cases are also seen.[2] Diagnosable eating disorders are found in 1 percent to 3 percent of women in select adolescent and young adult populations (e.g., on college campuses) and individual symptoms that do not meet diagnostic criteria may be found in 20 percent to 30 percent of these populations as occasional findings.[3] The disorders are more common among middle- to upper-class women than among those from lower socioeconomic backgrounds. Increasing numbers of poor or culturally disadvantaged patients are being seen, however. Although the etiology of these disorders is uncertain, several contributing factors have been suggested. Over the past few decades society's weight standards for "glamorous" women have shifted downward.[4] Women whose psyches require adherence to these standards but whose bodies are not built to be so, thus attain these unnatural weights

---

**Table 1**

**DSM III-R  Criteria for Anorexia Nervosa and Bulimia Nervosa**

**Anorexia Nevosa:**
  A.  Refusal to maintain body weight over a minimal normal weight for age and height, e.g., weight loss leading to maintenance of body weight 15% below that expected; or a failure to make expected weight gain during period of growth, leading to body weight 15% below that expected.
  B.  Intense fear of gaining weight or becoming fat, even though underweight.
  C.  Disturbance in the way in which one's body weight, size, or shape is experienced, e.g., the person claims to "feel fat" even when obviously underweight.
  D.  In females, absence of at least three consecutive menstrual cycles when otherwise expected to occur (primary or secondary amenorrhea). (A woman is considered to have amenorrhea if her periods occur only following hormone, i.e., estrogen, administration.)

**Bulimia Nervosa:**
  A.  Recurrent episodes of binge eating (rapid consumption of a large amount of food in a discrete period of time).
  B.  A feeling of lack of control over eating behavior during the eating binges.
  C.  The person regularly engages in either self-induced vomiting, use of laxatives or diuretics, strict dieting or fasting, or vigorous exercise in order to prevent weight gain.
  D.  A minimum average of two binge-eating episodes a week for at least three months.
  E.  Persistent overconcern with body shape and weight.

only at the price of severe biological and psychological strain. Binge eating and purging cycles often follow attempts at severe dietary restriction – the diet precipitates the binge. Predisposing psychological traits include poor self-esteem and excessive timidity, anxiety, impulsivity and/or obsessionality. Women with poor self-esteem may gain some sense of control over their lives through altering bodily appearance. Dysfunctional families, particularly those with depression and/ or alcoholism, may also prompt the appearance of these disorders in predisposed children. Familial occurrence is common, with about a 10 percent prevalence rate in first degree female relatives. Finally, some as-yet unclear biological vulnerabilities may exist in the brain or in predisposing metabolic patterns.[5,6,7]

## PREVENTION

Because eating disorders are frequently associated with powerful sociocultural influences and trends, the design of prevention strategies is challenging. In the past few years the "Awareness Week" or "Awareness Day" concept has been a popular and effective tool on campuses to focus attention on a particular issue, including eating disorders. This technique can stimulate a collaborative effort among interested individuals and organizations. Student government, with support from health professionals, can utilize campus media (newspaper, radio stations, television stations), educational materials, and guest speakers from the campus and community to bring notice to eating disorders. Awareness activities can be targeted to student gathering places as well as susceptible groups among whom a high incidence of eating disorders has been documented, such as sororities, dancers, and athletes.

Courses on eating disorders or discussions of eating disorders within course curricula can be targeted for public health, medicine, nursing, nutrition/dietetics, psychology, physical education, dance, and related disciplines. Faculty who discuss eating disorders in the classroom should be prepared to offer support and referrals for students who request such assistance. Health professionals who treat eating-disordered clients should be invited to make presentations in class. Such non-threatening exposures to health care professionals may facilitate help-seeking in students in need of treatment. Additionally, most campuses offer a myriad of opportunities for professional presentations to students outside traditional classroom settings. Programming on timely health topics can occur in sororities, residence halls, women's centers, and recreation facilities.

Food service, athletic and dance departments, health service and counseling staff who may encounter eating-disordered students should be informed about these disorders and should be familiar with local referral resources. Staff in residence hall and sorority settings are ideally situated to educate students concerning eating disorders and to refer for appropriate treatment. Key student leaders such as residence hall assistants and peer health educators also may benefit from knowledge about eating problems as they can play a vital role in disseminating information.

The use of peer educators to provide health information and counseling services has received increased support from traditional health care providers. Peer counseling uses active listening and problem-solving skills by students to help advise or counsel other students. This modality offers several advantages, including the unique empathic qualities of peers who can relate directly to the presenting issues and clients' life-style[8,9] Appropriate training in counseling skills, referral information, and substantive knowledge enables peer educators to present workshops to fellow students on such diverse topics as body image distortion, healthy food choices in the residence halls and the ineffectiveness of "dieting." At UCLA, Peer Health Counselors have designed a series of skits in which women and men are confronted with body image concerns. Students perform the skits and facilitate audience discussion regarding the issues. Competently trained students can be an invaluable resource for information dissemination and co-facilitation of therapy groups with mental health professionals. Students helping students offers an economical, innovative, and practical approach to eating problems.

Primary prevention programs aim at intervention before-the-fact with goals that may include the enhancement of psychological health or the reduction of psychological distress. Programming and services designed to ameliorate stress are essential and feasible, to some degree, at all schools. These can include programs concerned with weight management, stress management, healthy exercise, relationship building, assertiveness training, nutrition, sexuality, alcohol and drug use, and money management. Most of these topics can be addressed by appropriately trained peer educators.

As many prevention programs as feasible should be attempted since the different techniques will variably influence different segments of the campus community. Collectively, these programming suggestions can reduce the prevalence of eating disorders and may favorably impact other issues of concern on campus (e.g., drug and alcohol abuse). Although eating disorders have been ascribed stereotypically to a narrow segment of upper middle class Caucasian students, these disorders are now known to afflict a much wider range of ethnic and socioeconomic groups. Thus, it is also important to target programs to the diverse segments of the campus community.

## ASSESSMENT

Clinicians should maintain a high index of suspicion for eating disorders among young women with marked weight swings; those who are preoccupied with appearance, dieting, nutrition and/or bowel function; whose menses are sparse, irregular or absent; who have swollen salivary glands and poor teeth; who have orthopedic problems related to relentless exercise; or who on routine chemistry panel screening tests have mildly abnormal findings. It is not uncommon for eating disorders to be identified during routine dental or gynecologic examinations.[5,7]

Questions about eating disorders (past and present), eating behavior, and exercise patterns can be asked on routine history questionnaires that students complete in the waiting room before receiving services. It is sometimes easier for students with eating disorders to check the appropriate box on a screening questionnaire than to volunteer verbally their concerns to a clinician. If a student **does** disclose an eating disorder or related concerns on a health history form, it is imperative that the care provider address the issue immediately.

It is best to ask questions about eating patterns and attitudes directly, candidly, and sympathetically. Important information includes a weight history, which collects information on maximum and minimum weight, the weight the patient **desires**, and the reasons for that weight. The severity and chronicity of eating-disorder symptoms should be assessed by inquiring about the following areas:

- weight preoccupation
- body image distortion
- dieting/fasting behaviors
- food avoidances
- binge eating (quantity and frequency)
- purging (vomiting, laxatives, diuretics, emetine)
- regular and compulsive exercise
- use of over-the-counter, prescription and illicit diet pills
- unusual beliefs about nutrition
- a careful menstrual history

While amenorrhea is typically characteristic of anorexia nervosa, approximately 50 percent of patients with bulimia nervosa also experience menstrual irregularity. Eating disorder patients with irregular menses and anovulatory cycles should, nevertheless, be considered fertile unless proven otherwise, and thus, if appropriate, a discussion of contraception should be initiated. Irregular or absent menstrual cycles are a medical consequence of these disorders and patients should be educated about these relationships.

Assessment of psychological features should include attention to early development; temperament and personality traits; self-esteem and self-concept; use of cigarettes, alcohol, and drugs; and concurrent symptoms of depression, anxiety, obsessionality, and compulsivity. Assessment of the family should include a family psychiatric history, attitudes of the family toward eating, weight and appearance, and family communication patterns including the extent of unforgiving, negative criticism and blaming of the patient, often a poor prognostic feature for recovery.

Once an eating disorder is detected, most patients merit a full physical examination and screening laboratory tests including electrolytes, complete blood count, thyroid, calcium, magnesium, and amylase studies. Physical exam should pay special attention to blood pressure (often low with orthostatic changes), heart (small size, bradycardia and other dysrhythmias), skin (excessive soft fuzzy hair called lanugo), teeth (chalky enamel and decay, particularly of incisors), salivary glands (swollen parotid and sublingual glands from overstimulation secondary to vomiting) and the dorsum of the hands (sometimes scarred from abrasions incurred during violent self-induced vomiting). Medical complications related to weight loss and purging are listed in Table 2. For the very thin patient, an electrocardiogram or rhythm strip is also indicated. Usually, the medical work-up of a normal-weight patient with bulimia nervosa is less extensive than that for an anorexia nervosa patient.

---

**Table 2**

**Medical Complications of Eating Disorders**

A. Related to weight loss:
1. Cachexia: Loss of fat, muscle mass, reduced metabolism (low T3 syndrome), cold intolerance, and difficulty maintaining core body temperature
2. Cardiac: Loss of cardiac muscle, small heart, cardiac arrhythmias including atrial and ventricular premature contractions, prolonged His bundle transmission (prolonged Q-T interval), bradycardia, ventricular tachycardia, sudden death
3. Digestive/ Gastrointestinal: Delayed gastric emptying, bloating, constipation, abdominal pain
4. Reproductive: Amenorrhea, low LH, FSH
5. Dermatologic: Lanugo ( fine baby-like hair over body), edema
6. Hematologic: Leukopenia
7. Neuropsychiatric: Abnormal taste sensation (? zinc deficiency), apathetic depression, mild organic mental symptoms
8. Skeletal: Osteoporosis

B. Related to purging (vomiting and laxative abuse):
1. Metabolic: Electrolyte abnormalities, particularly hypokalemia, hypochloremic alkalosis; hypomagnesemia
2. Digestive/ Gastrointestinal: Salivary gland and pancreatic inflammation and enlargement with increase in serum amylase, esophageal and gastric erosion, dysfunctional bowel with haustral dilitation
3. Dental: Erosion of dental enamel (perimyolysis), particularly of front teeth, with corresponding decay
4. Neuropsychiatric: Seizures (related to large fluid shifts and electrolyte disturbances), mild neuropathies, fatigue and weakness,  mild organic mental symptoms

# TREATMENT

Anorexia nervosa and bulimia nervosa are multidetermined eating disorders that require an interdisciplinary team approach for treatment. Ideally the team should include a physician or nurse practitioner; registered dietitian; and psychiatrist, psychologist or psychiatric social worker knowledgeable about eating disorders. The composition of personnel participating on the team depends on the resources of the campus and community. It is imperative that members of the team understand the psychological and physiologic dynamics of the disorder and be willing to work with these challenging patients.

Optimal communication among team members through either formal or informal meetings is essential in providing ongoing care. If resources are available, weekly case management meetings are recommended. The team should also place a high priority on continuing education regarding recent research and therapeutic advances, and consider developing original research endeavors.

Treatment planning for eating disorders must be based on a comprehensive assessment as noted above. Each patient's problem list will have unique aspects, and treatment components should be targeted accordingly. Treatment usually includes attention to weight normalization and symptom reduction through cognitive and behavioral therapy programs, supportive medical care, dietary management, and counseling. Individual and family psychological problems are addressed through individual group and family psychotherapies.[10] Mood disturbances and some eating-disorder symptoms, particularly binge eating and purging, often benefit from psychopharmacologic interventions. The prognosis is better for treated normal-weight bulimia nervosa (75 to 85 percent recovery) than for anorexia nervosa (50 to 70 percent recovery), but considerable residual psychiatric and nutritional illness and even death due to malnutrition or suicide are not uncommon. Prognosis is generally better among younger patients whose disorders have been present for relatively shorter periods of time.[11]

Most student health and counseling services lack the resources to provide long-term or critical care for eating-disordered students. College health services staff should be knowledgeable regarding reliable and affordable community services. Some students may prefer to obtain their care outside the college setting due to concerns about confidentiality. Self-help programs may be useful (see list at end of chapter) and should be considered as adjunctive therapy when appropriate.

Friends or roommates of eating-disordered students are often upset and perplexed by contact with these problems, and their concerns should be addressed. Counseling services should be prepared to provide appropriate services and resources for this group.

Finally, colleges can work together to share resources, design research, and provide support for one another, collaborations that are especially important for smaller schools. As one example, the Western College Eating Disorders Consortium, formed in 1984, is composed of psychologists, physicians, nurses, dietitians, health educators, and peer educators who meet on a regular basis (usually two times per year) to exchange program ideas, problem-solve, discuss research designs, and act as a mutual support system.

## REFERENCES

1. Whitaker LC (ed): The bulimic college student: Evaluation, treatment, and prevention. J College Student Psychotherapy 3(2,3,4) 1988-89

2. Andersen AE (ed): Males with Eating Disorders. New York, Brunner/Mazel, 1990

3. Kurtzman FD, Yager J, Landsverk J et al.: Eating disorders among selected female student populations at UCLA. J Am Diet Assoc 89:45,1989

4. Brumberg JJ: Fasting Girls: The Emergence of Anorexia Nervosa as a Modern Disease. Cambridge, Harvard University Press, 1988

5. Garfinkel PE, Garner DM: Anorexia Nervosa: A Multidimensional Perspective. New York, Brunner/Mazel, 1982

6. Johnson C, Connors ME: The Etiology and Treatment of Bulimia Nervosa: A Biopsychosocial Perspective. New York, Basic Books, 1987

7. Mitchell JE: Bulimia Nervosa. Minneapolis, University of Minnesota Press, 1990

8. D'Andrea VJ, Salovey P: Peer Counseling: Skills and Perspectives. Palo Alto, Science and Behavior Books, 1983

9. Varenhorst BB: Peer Counseling: Past promises, current status, and future directions, Handbook of Counseling Psychology. Edited by SD Brown, RW Lent. New York, John Wiley and Sons, 1984, pp 716-750

10. Garner DM, Garfinkel PE (eds): Handbook of Psychotherapy for Anorexia Nervosa and Bulimia. New York, Guilford, 1985

11. Yager J: The treatment of eating disorders. J Clin Psychiatry 49 (9: supplement): 18-25,1988

## Self-help Group Resources

Anorexia Nervosa and Related Eating Disorders (ANRED), PO Box 5102, Eugene OR 97405

Bulimia, Anorexia Self-Help (BASH), 6125 Clayton Ave., Suite 215, St. Louis MO 63139

National Anorexia Aid Society (NAAS), PO Box 29361, Columbus OH 43229

National Association of Anorexia Nervosa and Related Disorders (ANAD), PO Box 271, Highland Park IL 60035

# 19

## Suicide and Stress Among College Students

ALLAN J. SCHWARTZ, MA, MS, PhD

---

The focus of this chapter is the epidemiology of suicide among students at American colleges and universities. Fifteen sources[1-15] provide the primary data on student suicide. Detailed and critical reviews that consider both methodologic issues and the implications of these studies for assessment, treatment, and prevention have been prepared.[16,17] National suicide data can be found in the annual volumes of Vital Statistics of the United States.[18]

Suicide has been a notable cause of death among persons of traditional college age (18-24) for all of this century. The lowest suicide rates for both men and women of college age occurred in the middle and later 1950s when suicide rates were slightly under 10 (per 100,000 person-years of risk) for men and about 2.5 for women. Over the next 25 years, these rates tripled for both sexes. The suicide rate for men peaked at about 30, in 1977, before settling at about 27.5 over the ten years since that peak. For women the suicide rate peaked at about 7.5, also in 1977, then declined gently but steadily over the next ten years to about 5.0 in 1987, the last year for which national suicide statistics are available. As suggested by these data, men in the 20-24 age group have committed suicide at about four times the rate of women for most of the last half of this century, even as the suicide rate for each sex tripled. Suicide now ranks among the three leading causes of death for college-age persons in the general population.

Paralleling this increase in suicide rate for college-age men and women is an increase in the proportion of all suicides committed by firearms. For women this increase has enabled firearms (at 40 percent) to replace substance ingestion (at 30 percent) as the most common method of suicide. Among men, for whom a firearm has long been the most common method (45 percent from 1900 to 1945), it now accounts for about two-thirds of all completed suicides, twice as many as all other methods combined.

The demography of a campus (primarily the ratio of men to women and secondarily the age and ethnic distributions) and the point in time when it is studied are crucial to interpreting data about suicide. Equally important is an appreciation of the large statistical uncertainty (e.g., standard deviation or 95% confidence interval) associated with findings derived from even apparently large studies.[14,19] For example, in 1985 the national suicide rate for women in the 20 to 24 year age group, of whom there were approximately ten million, was 5.0. The 95% confidence interval for the true suicide rate for that group extended from 3.5 to 6.5, a range approximating a factor of two. It is easy to see why it is difficult to show that female college students suicide at a rate that is "significantly" different from their age peers in the general population. Statistical difficulties notwithstanding, it seems clear that students at American colleges and universities suicide at a rate that is about one-half the rate for college-age persons in the general population.[14,16,17] This is in direct contradiction to the belief, still popular among both professionals and the public, that students suicide at a rate as much as half-again the suicide rate for the general population. The substantially lower rate that has been reported for students is both a statistically significant difference (based on 567 suicides) and a relatively robust finding.

Factors associated with suicide may vary from campus to campus. The following summarizes what we know of several of these.

## INSTITUTIONAL PRESTIGE AND SIZE

These two factors had been suspected of contributing to what was erroneously believed to be an elevated student suicide rate.[13,20] Neither has been found to affect student suicide rates. The role of institutional prestige, as measured by the highest degree awarded, was assessed;[9] working with a total of 78 suicides, among a geographically restricted sample of more than 50 schools, institutions awarding doctoral degrees – the most prestigious ones – did have higher absolute (i.e., crude or uncorrected) suicide rates. When campus demography was taken into account, however, the apparent association between higher prestige and elevated student suicide rates disappeared.

Institutional size was also assessed.[13] No association was found between size and student suicide rate, based on an analysis of 120 suicides. The small number of suicides associated with small campuses required pooling all campuses with enrollments below 8,000 students. Still, across the four groups of campuses (full-time enrollments of 0-8,000; 8,000-15,000; 15,000-20,000; over 20,000), no association was evident, and these groupings represent a factor of five in respect to institutional size.

## STATUS AS UNDERGRADUATE, GRADUATE, OR PROFESSIONAL STUDENT

Suicide rates do not appear to be significantly related to undergraduate class (i.e., freshman vs sophomore) or to undergraduate versus graduate student standing.[17] While this finding is based on a very limited number of studies and suicides (61 undergraduates and 32 graduate student suicides based on two reports[1,8]), it does not appear to be an artifact of the limited data available. The numbers of suicides reported compare very closely with those that would be expected given the populations studied.

A study of suicide by medical students at 88 of 116 schools surveyed provides a very tentative indication of differential suicidality among these post-baccalaureate professional students.[21] Suicide by nine female medical students yielded a suicide rate significantly higher than expected for women of this age. However, the 34 suicides reported for male medical students represented a suicide rate that was significantly lower than expected. For the entire sample of 52 suicides (9 had no gender specified), the suicide rate was not significantly different than expected for a cohort with the age and sex distribution reported.[22]

## GENDER

The reduced rate of suicide, or "benefit," for students, relative to the general population, accrues largely and perhaps exclusively to men. Analyses of 116 suicides from three studies[6,7,8] that distinguished male and female student suicides were applied to the total pool of student suicide data. Male students were found to suicide at 46 percent of the expected rate, female students at 91 percent of the expected rate.[16] The difference for males is statistically significant; the difference for females is not. Hence the "benefit" implied by a substantially lower suicide rate for students may derive wholly from a reduction in the suicide rate for male students.

## SEXUAL ORIENTATION

Gay and lesbian youth belong to two groups at high risk for suicide: youth and homosexuals. A majority of suicide attempts by homosexuals occur during their youth, and gay youth are two to three times more likely to attempt suicide than other young people.[23] They may comprise up to 30 percent of completed youth suicides annually. The earlier that youth are aware of their sexual orientation and identify themselves as gay, the greater the conflicts they have. Suicide is the leading cause of death among gay male, lesbian, bisexual, and transsexual youth. Risk factors in gay and lesbian youth suicide are outlined in Appendix A.

## OTHER DEMOGRAPHIC DESCRIPTORS

Considered here are race/ethnicity, religious affiliation, socioeconomic status (SES), citizenship, and marital status. SES has not even been mentioned in epidemiologic studies of suicide among students at American colleges and universities. This is a contrast with studies of students at British institutions.[24,25] There, however, the prominence of "social class" is reflected in the publication of annual national mortality data as a function of social class. In the U.S. annual suicide data are not reported as a function of SES.

Other demographic variables have been mentioned in studies of U.S. institutions. There were no differences when suicide rates for students of different races were compared with their respective race-matched age peers.[5] Additionally, no significant differences existed in suicide rates based on students' religious affiliation.[15] Two reports of suicides based on marital status[1,7] showed that rates for different levels of marital status were not significantly different for these reports, but there are too few suicides for an effective test of this dimension. Similarly, while one study noted the number of suicides based on ethnic background and commented on suicide by foreign nationals, there were either too few suicides to evaluate or no data were actually presented.[7]

In general, then, no effective tests have been done on the role of demographic descriptors, apart from gender, in determining student suicide rates. The potential role of these factors on student suicide is suggested, however, by their effects in the general population.[26] Black males and females of college age tend to have lower suicide rates than their white counterparts. This comparatively lower rate of suicide holds as well for Hispanics. In both groups the generally lower rate of suicide (vis-a-vis whites) occurs in the context as an even more dramatic imbalance in male over female suicide rates.

Native Americans, a much smaller group than either black or Hispanic Americans, have suicide rates, among college-age persons, that are more than double those of their white age peers.

With respect to nationality, suicide rates of nationals from the industrialized nations tend to be higher than or comparable to those for U.S. citizens; nationals from Second and Third World countries generally have comparatively lower suicide rates.[27] This is a pattern that has been stable, or intensifying, over the past 25 years. Additionally, many of the trends seen in the U.S. over the past 30 years (e.g., dramatically increasing suicide rates among youth) have also appeared in other countries. Finally, the fact of attending college in the U.S. can be expected to moderate the pattern of suicidality found in a student's country of origin, decreasing the suicide rate of foreign students if this is higher in their country of origin and raising it if that rate is lower.[28]

Religious affiliation[29] and marital status[30] both influence suicide rates in the general population. Protestants have been found to have the highest rates, roughly twice the rate of Jews and three times the rate of Catholics. Among those of college age, married persons have historically had the lowest suicide rates, about half that of their single same-sex age peers. The divorced have rates that are 50 percent to 250 percent higher than those of single persons. Among college-age males, compared to their single same-sex peers, the death of a spouse implies a tenfold increase in rate of suicide while females show a much more modest increase, double or triple the rate of single persons.

In the absence of empirical findings specifically for students, these trends in the general population must serve as the best available guides for regarding suicidality for persons with these particular demographic features.

## METHOD OF SUICIDE

The comparatively lower suicide rate found for students, and perhaps exclusively for male students, may well be an unintended result of policies that make firearms relatively inaccessible on campus. Method of suicide has been identified for 124 suicides by male students and 31 by females.[1,2,7,8,15] The latter is too few to sustain any meaningful method-specific analysis for women. For the men, however, the method-specific rates of suicide for both firearms and hanging are significantly lower than in the general population.[22] The reduction is dramatic for firearms, a factor of 3.7, while for hanging it is lower by a factor of 1.6. No method showed a significant elevation for male students.

## MONTH, DAY, AND HOUR

It is well known that academic stresses vary considerably over the course of an academic year. While different rates of suicide in certain months might reflect developments over the academic and calendar year, differences on certain days of the week or hours of the day can suggest phenomena with a relatively short cycle. Studies have looked at the relationship between each of these temporal indices and student suicide rates.[1,5,8,16]

The only significant finding is a higher-than-expected proportion of student suicides (versus both chance and general population) occurring on weekdays (Monday-Thursday) versus weekend days. This finding suggests that excessive episodic alcohol use, a significant characteristic of weekend life on campuses, does not result in increased student suicide. It also suggests that the diminished availability of faculty, administrators and campus health professionals is not associated with increased student suicide rates. The life-threatening and sometimes fatal behaviors associated with acute alcoholic intoxication, like automobile accidents and falls, may be misclassified as accidental rather than suicidal events. This possibility, however, would not explain the contrast between students and the general population. No convincing account of the finding has yet been suggested.

Non-significant trends were found in analyses of month of suicide. September and March, and to a lesser extent January, were months with elevated suicide rates. These findings suggest that psychosocial events unrelated to classes, such as those associated with beginning or returning to school in the Fall, or with the Christmas holiday and Spring break, are more prominent as precipitants of suicide than examinations or other specifically academic demands.

## RISK FACTORS

The development of a set of coherent risk factors for college students who suicide is a complex and daunting task. For example, persons completing suicide may be contrasted with those attempting suicide; either of these cohorts may be compared with those exhibiting only suicidal ideation; any of these three may be compared with psychiatric populations or with "normals," and so on. In comparison to other college students, risk factors for suicide by college students[16] include male sex (factor of 2 versus females), symptomatic depression (a factor of 2 versus asymptomatic students), contact with campus medical psychiatric facilities (a factor of 6 versus non-users), and major psychiatric illness including major depression, bipolar disorder, schizophrenia, and other psychoses (a factor of 200 versus students without these illnesses). It is perhaps noteworthy that for late adolescents and young adults in the general population, poor school performance is negatively related to likelihood of suicide.[31] This is consistent with descriptive reports focused on college students.[4,8,10,11,16]

## PREVENTION PROGRAMS
## AND INSTITUTIONAL RISK MANAGEMENT

There is as yet no evidence supporting the effectiveness of suicide hotlines, walk-in suicide crisis units, or related resources in reducing a community's suicide rate.[32] One reason for this may be that the processes of self-identification and self-referral that these resources require are too unlikely for them to be effective. On the campus, as in the broader community, some more active processes, like raising public awareness of the signs of impending suicide (e.g., giving away valued possessions) and community training in suicide assessment and referral skills, may be required to reach potential suicides.[33] Such initiatives may also enhance the climate of mutual caring and concern, of openness and inclusion. These achievements will reduce isolation and anomie, two of the cultural/community factors that have been linked to suicide.[26,29] Within the limits of the resources that are provided, a balance will need to be struck between a reliance on the help-seeking capacities of individuals at risk for suicide and on the help-giving capacities of the campus and the broader community.

It can be tempting for campus mental health professionals to pursue the reduction or elimination of those student stressors that are within the control of campus authorities. The death of a student's parent or spouse is obviously not among these, but academic requirements clearly are. These requirements, moreover, have been identified, at least clinically and anecdotally, as contributing to student suicide.[15,34] It was noted above that a balance must be struck between proactive and respondent approaches to the suicidal individual. Here again a balance must be struck between advocating for the academic accommodations that may benefit those very few students who will attempt suicide and preserving the institutional framework that is more generally growthfully challenging to students. Perhaps the best option is for mental health professionals to provide admissions personnel with knowledge that will enable them to make a better match between incoming students and the challenges they will encounter at the institution.

There is a third, related balance that must be struck. The more initiative the institution self-consciously undertakes in order to prevent student suicide, the greater its responsibilities in this regard. Take as an example the training of residence halls staff to recognize suicidality. Besides lacking any demonstrated effectiveness in preventing suicide, taking this step begins to create an implied contract between the institution, its students, and its parent clientele, a contract to prevent student suicide. Mental health professionals can contribute to discussions aimed at balancing the legal risks that attend such implied contracts against both the benefits associated with such programs and the costs of foregoing them.

## SUMMARY

The cumulative evidence from epidemiologic and descriptive studies of suicide by students at American colleges and universities is that the principal contribution of the academic environment is a protective one. Specifically, the relative absence of firearms on campuses limits students' access to perhaps the most highly lethal method of suicide. The close proximity of others on a 24 hour-a-day basis may also contribute to diminished use of hanging, a significant but less substantial feature. The result is a dramatic reduction in student suicide, particularly by male students.

In terms of clinical management and therapeutic treatment, suicidal college students should be approached as one would any person of comparable sex and age. Suicide will occur in individuals rendered vulnerable by constitutional, familial, and other environmental factors. It will occur when object loss or events resulting in diminished self esteem evoke depressive responses in a context where the individual has access to a highly lethal method of suicide and, influenced by normative social scripts, chooses to use them.[35]

There is as yet no consensus regarding the treatment of suicidality as a symptom of an underlying psychiatric disorder versus as a primary disorder warranting treatment in its own right,[36] though the former position is the majority point of view at this time.[37] An approach that integrates initiatives based on both of these perspectives, and that concurrently seeks to prevent suicide by restricting access to highly lethal methods that students may employ, is perhaps the most conservative one. In view of the fact that suicide is irreversible, a conservative approach is easily advocated.

# REFERENCES

1. Bessai J: College student suicides: A demographic profile. Paper presented at the annual meeting of the American Psychological Association, Washington DC, August 1986

2. Braaten LJ, Darling CD: Suicidal tendencies among college students. Psychiatric Quarterly 36:665-692, 1962

3. Bruyn HB, Seiden RH: Student suicide: Fact or fancy. J Am Coll Health Assoc 14:69-77, 1965

4. Fry CC, Rostow EG: Mental Health in College. New York, Commonwealth Fund, 1942

5. Heinrichs EH: Suicide in the young: Demographic data of college-age students in a rural state. J Am Coll Health Assoc 28(4):236-237, 1980

6. Kagan D: A survey of student suicide 1984-85 through 1986-87. The California State University, Office of the Chancellor, Long Beach, California, March 3, 1988

7. Kraft DP: Student suicides during a twenty-year period at a state university. J Am Coll Health Assoc 28(5):258-262, 1980

8. Parrish NH: Epidemiology of suicide among college students. Yale Journal of Biology and Medicine 29:585-595, 1957

9. Peck ML, Schrut A: Suicidal behavior among college students. HSMHA Reports 86(2):149-155, 1971

10. Peck M, Schrut A: Suicide among college students, Proceedings: Fourth International Conference for Suicide Prevention. Edited by NL Farberow. Delmar Publishing Company, Inc, Los Angeles, 1968

11. Raphael T, Power SH, Berridge WL: The question of suicide as a problem in college mental hygiene. Am J Orthopsychiatry 7(1):1-14, 1937

12. Riggs AF, Terhune WB: The mental health of college women. Mental Hygiene 12:559-568, 1928

13. Schwartz AJ, Reifler CB: Suicide among American college and university students from 1970-71 through 1975-76. J Am Coll Health Assoc 28(4):205-210, 1980

14. Schwartz AJ, Reifler CB: College student suicide in the United States: Incidence data and prospects for demonstrating the efficacy of preventative programs. J Am Coll Health 37(2):53-59, 1988

15. Temby WD: Suicide, Emotional Problems of the Student. Edited by GB Blaine and CC McArthur. New York, Appleton-Century-Crofts, 1961

16. Schwartz AJ, Whitaker LC: Suicide among college students: Assessment, treatment, and intervention. Suicide Over the Life Cycle. Edited by SJ Blumenthal, DJ Kupfer. Washington DC, American Psychiatric Press, 1990, pp 303-340

17. Schwartz AJ: The epidemiology of suicide among students at colleges and universities in the United States. J College Student Psychotherapy Vol 4, 3/4, 1990

18. U.S. Public Health Service: Vital Statistics of the United States. Washington, DC, U.S. Government Printing Office

19. Schwartz AJ: Inaccuracy and uncertainty in estimates of college student suicide rates. J Am Coll Health Assoc 28(4):201-204, 1980

20. Ross N: Suicide among college students. Am J Psychiatry 126:106-111, 1969

21. Pepitone-Arreola-Rockwell F, Rockwell D, Core N: Fifty-two medical student suicides. Am J Psychiatry 138:198-201, 1981

22. Schwartz AJ: Student Suicide. Poster Presentation, American College Health Association Annual Meeting. San Antonio, Texas, May, 1990

23. Gibson P: Gay male and lesbian youth suicide, Report of the Secretary's Task Force on Youth Suicide, vol 3. Edited by MR Feinleib, ADAMHA, DHHS Pub no. (ADM)89-1623. Washington DC, U.S. Govt Printing Office, 1989, pp 110-142

24. Parnell RW: Mortality and prolonged illness among Oxford undergraduates. Lancet: 731-733, 1951

25. Carpenter RG: Statistical analysis of suicide and other mortality rates of students. British J of Preventive and Social Medicine 13:163-174, 1959

26. Earls F, Escobar JI, Manson SM: Suicide in minority groups: Epidemiologic and cultural perspectives, Suicide Over the Life Cycle. Edited by SJ Blumenthal, DJ Kupfer. Washington, DC, American Psychiatric Press, 1990, pp 571-598

27. Diekstra, RF: An international perspective on the epidemiology and prevention of suicide, Suicide Over the Life Cycle. Edited by SJ Blumenthal and DJ Kupfer. Washington, DC, American Psychiatric Press, 1990, pp 533-569

28. Stengel E: Suicide and Attempted Suicide. New York, Jason Aronson, 1974

29. Durkheim E: Suicide. Glencoe IL, Free Press, 1967

30. National Center for Health Statistics: Vital Statistics of the United States: 1987. Rockville, MD, 1989

31. Brent DA, Kolko DJ: The assessment and treatment of children and adolescents at risk for suicide, Suicide Over the Life Cycle. Edited by SJ Blumenthal, DJ Kupfer. Washington, DC, American Psychiatric Press, 1990, pp 253-302

32. Miller HL, Coombs DW, Leeper JD et al: An analysis of the effects of suicide prevention facilities on suicide rates in the United States. Am J Public Health 74:340-343, 1984

33. O'Carroll PW: Community strategies for suicide prevention and intervention, Suicide Over the Life Cycle. Edited by SJ Blumenthal and DJ Kupfer. Washington, DC, American Psychiatric Press, 1990, pp 499-514

34. Raphael T, Power SH, Berridge WL: The question of suicide as a problem in college mental hygiene. Am J Orthopsychiatry 7:1-14, 1937

35. Blumenthal SJ, Kupfer DJ: Clinical assessment and treatment of youth suicide. J Youth and Adolescence 17:1-24, 1988

36. Winchel RM, Stanley B, Stanley M: Biochemical aspects of suicide, Suicide Over the Life Cycle. Edited by SJ Blumenthal, DJ Kupfer. Washington, DC, American Psychiatric Press, 1990, pp 97-126

37. Blumenthal SJ, Kupfer DJ: Epilogue, Suicide Over the Life Cycle. Edited by SJ Blumenthal, DJ Kupfer. Washington, DC, American Psychiatric Press, 1990, pp 735-737

## APPENDIX A
## RISK FACTORS IN GAY AND LESBIAN YOUTH SUICIDE[23]

**General**
Awareness/identification of homosexual orientation at an early age
Self-acceptance of homosexual orientation
Conflicts with others related to homosexual orientation
Problems in homosexual relationships
**Society**
Discrimination/oppression of homosexuals by society
Portrayal of homosexuals as self-destructive by society
**Poor Self-Esteem**
Internalization of image of homosexuals as sick and bad
Internalization of image of homosexuals as helpless and self-destructive
**Identity Conflicts**
Denial of a homosexual orientation
Despair in recognition of a homosexual orientation
**Family**
Rejection of a youth due to homosexual orientation
Abuse/harassment of child due to homosexual orientation
Failure of youth to meet parental/social expectation
Perceived rejection of youth due to homosexual orientation
**Religion**
Youth's homosexual orientation seen as incompatible with family beliefs
Youth feels sinful, condemned to hell due to homosexual orientation
**School**
Abuse/harassment of homosexual youth by peers
Lack of accurate information about homosexuality
**Social Isolation**
Rejection of homosexual youth by friends and peers
Social withdrawal of homosexual youth
Loneliness and inability to meet others like themselves
**Substance Abuse**
Substance use to relieve pain of oppression
Substance use to reduce inhibitions on sexual feeling

**Professional Help**
    Refusal to accept homosexual orientation of youth
    Refusal to support homosexual orientation of youth
    Involuntary treatment to change homosexual orientation of youth
    Inability to discuss issues related to homosexuality
**Residential Programs**
    Refusal to accept/support homosexual orientation of youth
    Isolation of homosexual youth by staff and residents
    Inability to support homosexual youth in conflicts with residents
**Relationship Problems**
    Inability to develop relationship skills like heterosexual youth
    Extreme dependency needs due to prior emotional deprivation
    Absence of social supports in resolving relationship conflicts
**Independent Living**
    Lack of support from family
    Lack of support from adult gay community
    Involvement with street life
**AIDS**
    Unsafe sexual practices
    Secrecy/unplanned nature of early sexual experiences
**Future Outlook**
    Despair of life as hard as the present
    Absence of positive adult gay/lesbian role models

# 20

# Violence and Sexual Assault on College Campuses

TOBY SIMON, MED

Violence on college campuses has gained national attention. Campuses everywhere are experiencing noticeable increases in incidents of bigotry and prejudice, violence in relationships, and intolerance for difference.[1] Universities have reported murders, violent physical assaults, larcenies, suicides, and sexual assaults. Concern over campus safety has resulted in recent federal legislation, Public Law 101-542, which requires that campus crime statistics be made more available to the public. Under the Crime Awareness and Campus Security Act and the Student Right to Know Act, as of July 1992, any university receiving state and federal funds will be required to publish annually, in a variety of official university documents and pamphlets, crime statistics for their campus. This increased attention to issues of public safety has forced universities to address the overall safety and well being of students as well as the safety of employees.

Attention to campus crimes has emphasized the importance of collaboration between Offices of Police and Security and other university offices, e.g., Student Affairs, Health Services, and Public Relations. The American College Health Association (ACHA) has created a task force on campus violence and human dignity "to focus attention on issues of violence and human dignity as they relate to the health and welfare of college students." College health professionals have daily evidence of the clinical manifestations of attacks on human dignity. In addition to physical injury, "these manifestations include chronic stress, anxiety, depression, substance abuse, eating disorders, suicidal ideation, general feelings of malaise, and dis-ease."[2]

Although any crime that is committed on a college campus is a concern to all, by and far the most prevalent crime on campus today is sexual assault. It is estimated that in approximately 85 percent of reported sexual assaults on campus, the victim is acquainted with her/his assailant.[3] This chapter will focus chiefly on sexual assault on the college campus.

# THE COLLEGE SETTING

The sexual experiences of college students range from abstinence to intercourse, with a variety of activities in between. For many students, sex is not "a many splendored thing." Dating can be dangerous and love can be abusive. Sexual activity may be conceptualized along a continuum of consent and coerciveness ranging from voluntary to altruistic, from verbally coercive to physically coercive.[4,5] A continuum of adolescent sexual behavior has been proposed, beginning with mutual sexual exploration (initiating sexual activity, touching, and mutual pleasure giving). This part of normal adolescent psycho-sexual development has in common some of the elements of the next stage of the continuum, persuasion of a reluctant partner. When persuasion is used, both partners may feel good about the encounter if the reluctant person is treated with respect and his or her feelings are taken into account. The next stage is exploitative sexual activity that may involve the same behaviors as persuasion; the difference is that the reluctant partner's feelings and wishes are not taken into account. The spectrum continues with sexual coercion, harassment, and rape.[6]

In some instances, when a woman is sexually assaulted by a male acquaintance, neither party may recognize the encounter as a rape. The difficulty in recognizing a sexual encounter without consent as rape is exacerbated by popular rape myths and societal norms about sexual behavior: beliefs that women say no when they mean yes, advertisements that portray women as sex objects, popular rock and rap groups that exploit and objectify women, and social norms about sexual "duties." The existence of the myths is supported by Brown University survey findings in which 42 percent of men and 26 percent of women agree with the statement, "Even if someone says no to sex, you can't always tell if they want sex or not."[7]

Research has focused primarily on women's experience with unwanted sexual activity, but there is evidence that men also experience unwanted sexual activity. One study that examined sexual assault among university students, faculty, and staff showed that 6 percent of the men reported having been sexually assaulted.[8] A study done at Texas A&M exploring dating situations provides evidence that men experience unwanted sexual activity due to both physical and verbal coercion.[9]

Heterosexual students are not alone in experiencing sexual harassment and other forms of sexual assault. Gay men and lesbian women on college campuses are victims of violence and sexual harassment as well. In 1989, almost 20 percent of the reported incidents of violence and victimization against homosexual men and women involved college students.[10] These data, from the National Gay and Lesbian Task Force, demonstrated that the 1,329 anti-gay incidents on college campuses in 1989 included acts of verbal harassment, acts of vandalism, assaults, bomb threats, and arson. While on the one hand, many gay and lesbian students are feeling more comfortable being out and visible on campuses, their increased visibility may have contributed to the increase of harassment and violence against these students.

## EPIDEMIOLOGY OF RAPE

Rape is by far the most prevalent, serious, and violent crime committed on college campuses. Sexual assault affects one-quarter to one-third of all women in college today. Rape is under-reported and it is believed that federal statistics do not reflect the reality of its prevalence.[11] Approximately half of all reported rapes are acquaintance rapes. The majority of reported victims and offenders are college age, with the rate of rape victimization highest among 16-to-19-year-olds.[12] Under-reporting is much more common among victims/survivors of acquaintance rape than among victims/survivors of stranger rape. In a national survey of college students, only 27 percent of women who described assault by acquaintances and whose assault met legal definitions of this crime, believed their assault qualified as rape.[11]

In a recent survey of college-age students, one out of six female students reported having been a victim of rape or attempted rape during the preceding year. One out of fifteen male students reported committing rape or attempting to commit rape during that same period.[11] These statistics imply that on a hypothetical campus of 12,000 students where the ratio of males to females is equal, one could expect approximately 1000 incidents of rape or attempted rape per year. Approximately 400 men per year on such a campus would have admitted to being associated with these occurrences. One campus found that 11 percent of the male respondents answered that they had had sex with someone who was not completely willing.[7]

The prevalence of rape on college campuses has resulted in the creation of special terminology: sexual assaults that occur in residence halls, fraternity houses, libraries, walkways are referred to as "campus rapes." The majority of these assaults are also called "acquaintance rapes," with "stranger rape" being a less common occurrence on most campuses. There is a typical pattern to acquaintance rape: It may occur at fraternity parties or in student residence halls, both students involved may have been drinking heavily, and some of the victims may have been assaulted by more than one student.

Because of the disproportionate frequency of victimization among 16 to 19 year olds, first-year women on a college campus are a highly vulnerable group. Some experts have speculated that since college students are typically in a new setting, they probably are a group at increased risk compared to adolescents of the same age living at home. A variety of environmental factors influences their health-enhancing and health-compromising behavior. They are away from home, some for the first time, and are not yet sure of their identity. As typical adolescents, they are still under the impression that they are immortal, invincible and that "bad" things won't happen to them. They continue to be risk takers in all aspects of their behavior. And college students live among others who are experimenting with new freedoms, thus creating a population at risk for victimization.[13]

## THE ALCOHOL CONNECTION

Studies on the behavioral aspects of alcohol use have shown that sexual judgments, including judgments as to both partner and practice, are affected by alcohol.[14] Most of the data on alcohol and date rape are anecdotal, gathered by interviews with victims/survivors who present to college health and counseling services. Although recent studies have clearly shown that alcohol use is associated with sexual assault, date rape, sexual harassment, and coerced sexual activity, more data are needed that illuminate the relationship between alcohol use and acquaintance rape. Half of the women in one study reported that, while drinking, they had been the targets of other drinkers' sexual aggression.[15] The Ms. Project on Campus Sexual Assault reported that approximately 75 percent of men and 55 percent of women involved in date or acquaintance rape were drinking or taking drugs just before the attack.[16] Another study, conducted on 16 campuses nationwide, found that alcohol is involved with half of the date rape incidents; men in the study consumed on the average five or more drinks, women consumed one or two.[17]

It is important to remember that alcohol is not the direct cause of rapes on campus. Alcohol has a mood-altering quality that may help set the stage by reducing men's and women's inhibitions. It also helps men excuse or rationalize abusive behavior, although campus policies should view alcohol abuse as an exacerbating rather than mitigating factor in discipline cases. Students use alcohol for the same reasons adults do; it helps them unwind, feel more relaxed, and more comfortable in social settings. Women report that alcohol makes them feel "sexier" and that drinking lessens their sexual inhibitions.[15] It is most likely that college men and women drink in order to become more comfortable with themselves as sexual beings.[18] Alcohol may also weaken a woman's ability to assess dangerous situations, and diminish her capacity to take effective steps to protect herself. Alcohol and other drugs distort reality and cause both men and women to expose themselves to dangers or to disregard social constraints that might otherwise influence them.[16] Alcohol consumption increases aggressive behavior, and decreases inhibitions against behavior usually considered unacceptable.

Recent studies have focused on college athletes who, as a group, may be overrepresented in date rape cases. Athletes were involved in one-third of date rape cases on one campus.[19] Other research has shown that 38 percent of the men involved in gang rapes on several college campuses were athletes.[20]

## PREVENTION STRATEGIES

It is common for a number of offices on campus to be involved with sexual assault prevention. University Police and Security offices can provide rape alert/ rape precaution workshops, self-defense programs, and other safety information. The university women's center may be involved with rape education programs in the dorms that focus on raising awareness about sexual assault and harassment, providing legal definitions, and discussing options available to students who are sexually assaulted or harassed. Often Health Service personnel and health educators are involved with primary prevention programs that must involve men and women and should attempt to engage students in open and honest discussions about sexuality.

Primary prevention of sexual assault and harassment asks college students to talk about sex, to communicate their sexual needs and desires to each other, to recognize the potential for coercion, and to be sure there is consent in sexual encounters. Ideally, the prevention messages should begin at an earlier age. Comprehensive sex and family life education beginning in elementary school should include discussions of sexual assertiveness, sexual boundaries, sexual expectations, dating expectations, sexual orientation, and attitudes about rape. Younger children today have attitudes that imply that sexual abuse is okay. In a study by the Rhode Island Rape Crisis Center, nearly one-fourth of the boys and one-sixth of the girls in grades six through nine said that a man had the right to force a woman to have sexual intercourse if he had spent money on her. Sixty-five percent of the boys and 47 percent of the girls in the same study felt it was acceptable for a man to force a woman to have sex if they had been dating for six months to a year.[21] Young children have to be taught, long before they begin to date, that there are appropriate, non-violent ways to deal with personal conflict and anger, that misuse of alcohol and other drugs can lead to sexual misadventures, and that sex-role stereotyping can be hazardous to one's health.

Other primary prevention strategies must address men's perceptions of acquaintance rape, since 84 percent of the men who committed acquaintance rape said that what they did was definitely not rape.[16] Prevention strategies for men should attempt to validate men's feelings about sexuality and relationships and should avoid alienating men. Male vs female attitudes about sex, what sexual encounters mean to women and men, and "what's love got to do with it" are necessary workshop topics. Together, men and women must examine communication patterns. More and more research is reporting on the differences between male and female communication patterns. A woman may be communicating "no" the best way she can and yet a man may not interpret it as "no." Although it can be politically unpopular with certain students, the use of levity in discussions about sexual conduct can be highly effective.

Given the specific data on aggression and sexual assault, universities need to provide some transitional training for male athletes; for example, players are taught to behave aggressively on the playing field, ice rink, or baseball diamond but need to understand that what is appropriate aggressive behavior in sports should be left on the playing field and not brought back to dormitories and fraternity houses where it can interfere with relationships with women and other men. There is a sense of entitlement among some athletes that is difficult to counter. Athletes have been afforded many opportunities, have a strong sense of self, and experience a great deal of prestige. As a result, they may have a more difficult time hearing "no" from a woman, interpreting the "no" as a statement of her needs, and accepting it at face value.

Some educators argue that programs on sexual assault should be conducted by men in all-male settings, citing that when women participate in these discussions the men tend not to participate. Other campuses have had success using peer educators to engage students in productive dialogue about sexual communication and sexual decision-making. Some campuses have active male groups (e.g., Men Can Stop Rape, Men Helping Men) that are involved with dormitory outreach programs. One potential problem with this approach is that these students are often not "traditional" men and may have some difficulty effectively reaching fraternities, athletes, and other "traditional" male groups.

In developing sexual assault and harassment prevention programs, it is important that **hetero**sexuality is not assumed. Role plays and case scenarios involving gay, lesbian, and bisexual students should be part of workshop programs, written materials, and media development. It is important to remember that women who are lesbians and/or bisexual are victims of rape and that perpetrators of these crimes can be both hetero- and homosexual.

Marketing of date rape education programs is important. Many universities have discovered that programs entitled "How to Be a Better Lover," "What's Love Got to Do With It?," or "Sex at 7:00 - How to Get What You Want But Not More Than You Bargained For" are much more enticing to students than programs called "Date Rape Prevention." Clearly the issues of sexuality – sexual communication, sexual assertiveness, good love-making, sexual decision-making – as well as issues of consent, need to be addressed in these workshops. Numerous college sex surveys have found that students have adequate factual sexual knowledge but are lacking in the skills needed to negotiate and communicate about sex.

There are some concrete prevention strategies often included in rape awareness programs. The advice and guidance given to women is to avoid men who:

- emotionally abuse (through insults, belittling comments, ignoring a woman's opinion)

- tell women who to be friends with, try to control other elements in a woman's life

- talk negatively about women in general

- get jealous when there is no reason

- drink heavily or use drugs

- berate women for not wanting to get drunk , get high, have sex

- attempt to get  women drunk

- are unable to handle sexual and emotional frustrations without becoming angry

- act in intimidating ways (sit too close, touch women when told not to)

It may also be advisable to be aware of men who refuse to let women share any of the expenses of a date and who get angry when women offer to pay, since studies have shown that there are indeed certain sexual expectations among men and women when money is spent.[21]

For men there are also guidelines that ask men to rethink their beliefs about women and sex and to change their behavior. The burden should perhaps be on men to make sure they have a "yes" before they proceed sexually with a partner.

The following are typical of points offered by rape-awareness advocates to men:

- never force or pressure a woman to have sex

- stay sober, know your limit, and stay in control of your drinking

- don't buy into the myth that a drunken woman "deserves" to be raped

- do not confuse "scoring" or "scamming" with having a successful social encounter

- don't assume that you know what a woman wants, and vice versa

- speak up if you feel you're getting a double message from a woman

- communicate with women

- communicate with other men

Since socialization is responsible for many attitudes about sexuality, both men and women must be willing to examine the importance of traditional socialization on their behavior. The next generation of men hopefully will learn to view women as equals, will appreciate the importance of communicating their feelings clearly, and will have the skills to do so. We can also hope that the next generation of women will feel better about themselves as sexual beings, more comfortable and assertive with their sexuality and less dependent on the use of alcohol and other drugs to help them feel okay about being sexual. Careful attention must be paid as well to issues of homosexuality so that the next generation of adults will also be less homophobic and more accepting of diversity.

## HEALTH SERVICES RESPONSE

Rape victims seeking immediate medical attention usually do so at a hospital emergency room. Often college health professionals are not encouraged, and sometimes not permitted, to do rape exams. This reluctance has more to do with state laws pertaining to "expert witnesses" in rape cases than with unwillingness to get involved. Many health services are staffed by pediatricians, adolescent medicine specialists, and internists. In some states the only expert testimony allowed in court is that of a board certified obstetrician/gynecologist, even though the majority of physicians working in college health provide routine gynecologic care. Whatever the protocol of the university health service, it is important to establish good working relationships with nearby emergency rooms. Women who seek medical attention immediately following a rape require both physical and psychological crisis intervention. Women who wait will need emotional help but perhaps less medical attention for physical problems associated with the rape.

If university health service staff is providing medical services immediately following a sexual assault, then it is imperative that they be trained by a local rape crisis center. A proper history must be taken and questions should be asked in a nonmoralistic, nonjudgmental manner. Since the medical record may become part of the court proceeding, all entries should be legible and detailed. A summary of the victim's statements with a professional evaluation of her status provides sufficient information to be fully defensible legally, as the medical record is a professional evaluation.[22] The following is a summary for conducting and documenting the rape exam.[23] Information should include findings from the physical exam with the student's description of the rape. The following elements should be present:

- length of time between rape and exam

- presence of pain, dysuria, or tenesmus

- type of sexual penetration (anal, vaginal, oral)
- cultures of any areas that were penetrated
- evidence of stains on clothing that fluoresce using ultraviolet light
- victims' activities following the assault (such as bathing, douching, urinating, etc.)
- photos and a description of the precise location and description of the injuries
- results of the pelvic exam

Most victims of acquaintance rape do not fight with their assailants and are rarely physically injured. They may also be unlikely to report the incident immediately following the attack. Therefore, health care providers will probably see victims/survivors of acquaintance rape, but the rape victimization will not be obvious. Many do not identify the experience as a rape and only do so weeks, months, or even years after the incident has occurred. It may be past the time when discussion of pregnancy is relevant. However, the routine physical exam and STD evaluation may still be indicated.

Since assailants and victims of acquaintance rape are usually between the ages of 15 and 25, it is certainly appropriate for a discussion of acquaintance rape to be part of the medical history.[24] Some of the questions health care providers can include in the history and physical include:

- Have you ever had sex when you didn't want to?
- Have you ever been forced to have sex?
- Do you have difficulty saying "no" when you don't want to have sex?

Providers are often leery of asking these questions because they may be unsure of what the next step should be. It is extremely important for anyone dealing with affirmative responses to these questions NOT to proceed with questions that can be a form of victim-blaming. Questions such as "Were you drunk at the time?", "Have you had sex with this person before?", or "Did you report this to the police?" can make a woman feel that she was somehow responsible for being raped. The most important next step when dealing with a disclosure is to support the individual and not blame her for what has happened. Questions such as "How can I help you?" or "What do you think you would like to do about this?" are helpful to the woman involved. Equally important during the history taking is to ask questions that pertain to alcohol/drug use and eating disorders. In our experience at Brown University, we have found that many women suffering from either alcohol misuse or eating disorders (or both) have a history of sexual assault (acquaintance or stranger rape or incest). If providers see women students brought to the infirmary for alcohol intoxication, it may be useful to inquire if there have been any recent incidents or problems that may have caused the student to engage in high-risk drinking.

The most important part of healing for rape victims is to regain control over their lives and to place blame and responsibility for the rape where it belongs – with the perpetrator. Health care providers should offer medical services, referrals, and counseling for victims of rape. The following is a partial list of suggested approaches for those working in college health settings that may serve to minimize some of the trauma victims may experience:[24]

- express regret that the woman has been assaulted

- reassure her that she is safe with you

- even if you do not believe her, act as if you do

- do not blame her

- help to give her back control by doing as she asks

- let her have someone she trusts to comfort her during the exam

- ask her questions in a way she will understand

- explain procedures to the woman before and during the exam

- refer her to a trained counselor for emotional help

- help arrange an appointment with the counselor and follow up to make sure she went

- don't use the term "rape" to describe the incident unless she already has done so

- learn more about rape

## INSTITUTIONAL RESPONSE

The responsibility of the university is to provide education, information, and training to students, faculty, and staff on sexual assault and sexual harassment. These programs should be designed to provide accurate information and promote open discussion. They should also encourage reporting of sexual assault and harassment and address the specifics of campus rape.

Sexual harassment is a serious offense and is understood to encompass a wide range of behavior, including coercing a person into a sexual relationship, subjecting a person to inappropriate verbal or physical sexual attention, and retaliating for a refusal to comply with sexual demands. In a larger context, the federal government has stipulated that sexual harassment is illegal and a violation of Title IX of the Higher Education Amendment of 1972. Examples of unwelcome behavior that can constitute sexual harassment include the following:

- repeated, abusive phone calls

- graffiti putting down women, gay men, and lesbians

- verbal insults on the street against women of color, gays, and lesbians

- someone in a dorm bothering certain individuals

- anti-gay or lesbian slurs or threats

- an unwanted arm around a shoulder

- a break-up that won't end

Experiences such as these of unwanted sexual attention often create feelings of frustration, guilt, helplessness, and/or confusion. The university's commitment to deal with these cases has to be as apparent as its commitment to handle cases of sexual assault.

There are many steps the university should take to address the issues adequately. There should be written, clear statements that explain the university's policy on sexual assault and harassment. The student code of conduct should include a statement on sexual assault. Statements describing expectations of student behavior (such as Brown University's Tenets of Community Behavior) should be read and signed by all students prior to enrolling at the university. There should be clear procedures to modify living arrangements if the victim/survivor and the accused live in the same dormitory or residential unit. There should be written protocols for the university's response to sexual assault cases that include immediate medical treatment, campus-based rape crisis teams, referrals to trained therapists, and competent coordination with university police as well as local police.

Sexual harassment cases should be treated with the same seriousness and in the same manner that cases of sexual assault are handled. Universities should regard sexual harassment as part of a continuum of sexual assault behavior. Since there is evidence that gay and lesbian students are often targets of sexual harassment, it is imperative that universities be sensitive and educated on issues of homosexuality. There needs to be a commitment at the highest level of the institution to provide in-service education and training to staff on this topic. Universities with a designated staff liaison to the lesbian, gay, and bisexual student community are demonstrating this type of support. One of the difficulties many universities face is how to actually handle sexual assault cases. Campus rape is both a criminal violation of state sexual assault laws and a violation of college codes of student conduct. However, some university legal counsel have prohibited their university judicial systems from hearing criminal cases, thereby leaving criminal proceedings outside the university as the only option available to students. In criminal proceedings, the same laws and penalties apply to stranger sexual assault as to acquaintance rape; however, the court system does present some problems: the conviction rate for rape offenders is low, cases take a long time to come to trial, and jurors often are unfamiliar with the reality of college life and students' behavior. Given the complications that often accompany date rape, it is difficult to be optimistic about the courts' ability to find a college student guilty of raping his date. On the other hand, a university hearing panel or judicial system is more familiar with campus life, the sexual mores of students, and the use and misuse of alcohol. If such a group is established, it is able to hear cases, determine the guilt or innocence of the student charged and decide on the appropriate measures to take based on the outcome of the hearing.

Some universities offer another option for students who are victims of sexual harassment and sexual assault. This involves a confrontation and encounter in the form of a Dean's Conference. This process is particularly useful if the woman (or man) involved chooses not to press charges with the local police nor to pursue the case through the university disciplinary route. Such an approach is useful when the student feels she wants some action taken and wants the offender to understand the gravity of the offense but does not wish to pursue a judicial action. The charged student is contacted and required to meet with a Dean. At the meeting the student filing the complaint may choose to be present and is accompanied by a female Dean or staff member. This method has been satisfactory to many of the students involved and, if done properly, the charged student leaves with an understanding of the severity of the action. This process should avoid the label "mediation" since this implies "settling a dispute" and is inappropriate in acquaintance rape cases. These sessions allow the two students to discuss the incident, the behaviors, and express their perceptions of what transpired. Often mandatory alcohol counseling, sexuality counseling, and/or a room change are required of the student who has been charged. Students (primarily women) involved with this process often regain a sense of control and feel that future encounters with the other student will be less awkward and uncomfortable.

## SOME POLITICAL CONSIDERATIONS

This chapter would be incomplete if it did not address some of the aspects of campus politics regarding sexual assault. Rape is a topic that is highly charged, emotional, and political. Often students feel that the university sexual assault policies and services are inadequate and unresponsive to student needs. In many cases, the students are right. As a result of student activism and certain militant tactics, universities are forced to confront these issues in an honest and sometimes painful way. The tactics used by certain student groups will not be universally accepted by administrators, or even fellow students. Some tactics can be quite effective in getting the attention of university officials, the President included. Other tactics can be divisive on the issue of sexual assault and can even become newsworthy. These "other" tactics also usually succeed in getting the attention of the proper officials.

Our experience at Brown University in the fall of 1990 is an interesting example. Women students began writing on the bathroom walls of various campus buildings names of men they say sexually assaulted or harassed them. The media was intrigued with this tactic and overnight our campus gained national attention. The most disturbing aspect of this "event" was that the media did, in fact, trivialize an important issue. The tactic itself was so radical that it managed to divide students, faculty, and staff. Discussions centered around such subjects as how to stop the spread of this "graffiti," due process issues, and first amendment rights. Many students and staff felt exploited by the press and looked forward to the "newsworthiness" quieting down in order to continue working on the issue.

The other part of the "politics" has to do with being "PC" – politically correct. College health personnel attempt to address the issue of date rape in a sensitive yet realistic manner. We are concerned with the primary prevention of date and acquaintance rape and talk about "high-risk behavior," "sexual communication," and "sexual assertiveness." We address issues of sexuality and communication in our assault-prevention discussions. We acknowledge that alcohol misuse is a behavior that puts students at risk for dangerous outcomes and view alcohol abuse as a contributing factor to the incidence of date rape on college campuses. The majority of college students are willing to attend these workshops and find these discussions useful. However, this approach may not be "PC" in the eyes of some students – students who are not comfortable with any discussion in which sexuality and rape are both addressed, students who feel that sexual assault is **only** about violence and oppression against women, and that women cannot prevent rape since in 98 percent of the cases, they are not the perpetrators. Some students make accusations of insensitivity and victim-blaming behavior on the part of the health professionals. This is intended as a warning to those involved with programming and training. It is not intended to suggest a departure from a discussion of primary prevention issues but to recognize differing and valid student views on the subject. We must also be prepared to acknowledge that some of what we say may be interpreted by some students in ways we did not intend. To address the complexities of date rape adequately, it is important to talk about the politics of rape, to pay attention to language, and to challenge students' views on male and female relationships.

Finally, universities must come to terms with their ambivalence about date rape. Most college administrators know that rape is a fact of campus life. Resistance to acknowledge this is often based on fears about the public's perception of open discussions of sexual assault. There is an assumption that highly intelligent young men are not as likely to commit such crimes. Some campuses are afraid the messages sent to the potential student cohort will imply that their campuses are not safe. Campus rape is not likely to go away, and the best rape awareness programs are in vain unless the university provides institutional support. Universities that are reluctant to allocate funds to educate all members of the university, that do not schedule discussions of date rape during first-year student orientation programs, and that fail to collect and publish sexual assault statistics are missing important teachable moments for all members of the university community. Support has to be visible at the top. University presidents must be willing to publish strong statements condemning violence and sexual assault on campus and they must be prepared to provide strong leadership in combatting this national problem.

## CONCLUSIONS

As we enter the 1990s, attention to the issues underlying sexual assault on campus is becoming increasingly prominent. It appears that more universities are now confronting this problem, although perhaps more as a means of protecting their reputations and to avoid lawsuits than as a sincere response to a reprehensible problem. There are now growing numbers of universities less ambivalent about rape. Although there is not yet a model system in place, it is important for universities to "not let the perfect get in the way of the possible." The challenge for colleges and universities is to develop innovative educational programs to prevent sexual assault and to create support services and judicial systems to address cases of sexual assault and harassment adequately.

## REFERENCES

1. Boyer E (ed): Campus Life: In Search of Community. Carnegie Foundation for the Advancement of Teaching, Princeton University Press, 1990

2. American College Health Association Task Force on Campus Violence and Human Dignity (comments on proposed statement) 1990

3. Brown University Report to the Community, November 1990

4. Bart PB, O'Brien PH: Stopping Rape: Successful Survival Strategies. New York, Pergamon, 1985

5. Koss MP, Oros CJ: Sexual experiences survey: A research instrument investigating sexual aggression and victimization. J Consulting Clin Psychol 50, 1982

6. Bateman P, Stringer G: Where Do I Start? A Parent's Guide to Talking to Teens About Acquaintance Rape. Teen Acquaintance Rape: A Community Response Project, Seattle, WA, 1984

7. Brown University Office of Health Education Annual Report, 1988

8. Lott B, Reilly ME, Howard DR: Sexual assault and harassment: A campus community case study. J Women in Culture and Society 8: 296-319, 1982

9. Muehlenhard CL, Cook B: Men's self reports of unwanted sexual activity. J Sex Research 24: 58-72, 1988

10. Anti-gay Violence, Victimization & Defamation in 1989, National Gay & Lesbian Task Force, Washington, DC, 1990

11. Koss MP, Gidycz CA, Wisniewski N: The scope of rape: Incidence and prevalence of sexual aggression and victimization in a national sample of higher education students. J Clin Consulting Psychol 55:162-170,1987

12. Adams A, Abarbanel G: Similarities and differences between stranger and acquaintance rape. Paper presentation, APHA Annual meeting, 1981

13. Roark ML: Preventing violence on college campuses. J Counsel Dev: 65-69, 1987

14. Bowen O: Public Health Reports Vol 103 No. 6, 1988

15. Klassen AD, Wilsnack SC: Women, alcohol and sexual aggression. Arch Sexual Behav 15, 1986

16. Warshaw R: I Never Called It Rape: The Ms. Report on Recognizing, Fighting, and Surviving Rape and Acquaintance Rape. New York, Harper & Row, 1988

17. Bruskin RH and associates: Inview: Issues and Insights for the College Woman. New York, Whittles Communications, 1990

18. Brown University Sex Survey, Brown University Office of Health Education, 1987

19. Koss MP: Hidden Rape: Incidence and Prevalence of Sexual Aggression and Victimization in a National Sample of College Students. Sexual Assault, Vol II, Edited by AW Burgess. New York, Garland, 1988

20. O'Sullivan C: Acquaintance gang rape on campus, Acquaintance Rape: Hidden Crime. Edited by A Parrot. New York, John Wiley and Sons, 1991

21. Kikuchi JJ: What Do Adolescents Know and Think About Sexual Abuse? Paper presentation, National Symposium on Child Victimization, Anaheim CA, 1988

22. Beckmann CRB, Groetzinger LL: Treating sexual assault victims: A protocol for health professionals. The Female Patient 14:78-83, 1989

23. Burgess AW, Holstrom LL: Treating the adult rape victim. Medical Aspects of Human Sexuality 22:36-43, 1988

24. Parrot A: Date rape. Medical Aspects of Human Sexuality, pp 28-31, April 1990

## Suggested Additional Reading

Adams A, Abarbanel G: Sexual Assault on Campus: What Colleges Can Do. Rape Treatment Center, Santa Monica Hospital Medical Center, 1988

Bass E, Davis L: The Courage to Heal. New York, Harper and Row, 1988

Cassell C: Swept Away. New York, Simon and Schuster, 1984

Eskenazi G: Athletic Aggression and Sexual Assault. New York Times, June 3, 1990

Ledray L: Recovering From Rape. New York, Holt and Company, 1986

Parrot A, Bechhofer L (eds) Acquaintance Rape: Hidden Crime. New York, John Wiley and Sons, 1991

# 21

# Cholesterol and Other CHD Risk Factors in the College Population

RALPH MANCHESTER, MD

Coronary heart disease (CHD) remains the leading cause of death in most developed countries, and it costs billions of dollars each year for medical care and lost productivity. It is clear that control of this disease requires a preventive approach, focusing on the major modifiable risk factors for CHD: smoking, hypertension, and hypercholesterolemia. Sedentary life-style is also an important modifiable risk factor. Age, male gender, and family history of premature CHD (< 55 years old) are risk factors that are not modifiable, but should not be overlooked because of their interactions with the modifiable risk factors. In theory, college health professionals are in the right place at the right time to have a significant impact on these risk factors while primary prevention of CHD is still possible.

In most college student populations, sedentary life-style1 and high blood cholesterol will be the most prevalent modifiable risk factors, followed by smoking and hypertension.[2] Smoking is covered in more detail in the chapter on tobacco. Hypertension is reviewed briefly in this chapter and in more detail in references 3 and 4. This chapter will focus on cholesterol as a risk factor for CHD; a review of cholesterol metabolism can be found in reference 5.

## DETECTION OF HIGH BLOOD CHOLESTEROL

Since hypercholesterolemia itself causes no symptoms and (apart from some rare genetically determined disorders of cholesterol and triglyceride control) no physical findings, detection prior to onset of clinical CHD requires some type of screening. The National Institutes of Health created the National Cholesterol Education Program (NCEP, which is modeled after the National High Blood Pressure Education Program) in recognition of the need to identify adults with high blood cholesterol. The NCEP's Adult Treatment Panel has recommended that every adult should know his/her cholesterol level.[5] The Panel's recommendations are summarized in Figure 1. A few points merit further discussion.

Applying the NCEP guidelines to the typical young adult college student population would mean selective screening of the 17- to 19-year-old students and then mass screening in the older students. Direct comparison of these two screening strategies has shown that voluntary mass screening of all entering students (during the pre-college health evaluation) is more effective and more efficient than selective screening, on a residential campus.[6] Other screening methods, such as cafeteria programs, special "Healthy Heart" promotions, and clinic-based testing have all been used to advantage. One should be aware, however, that screening programs

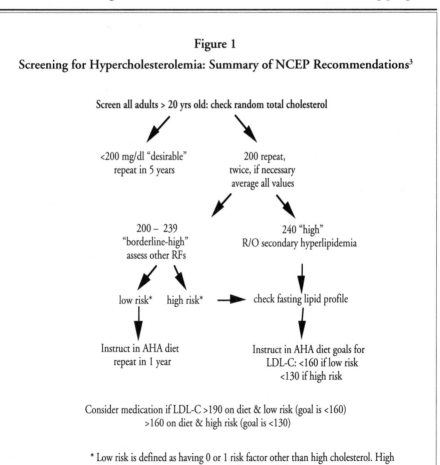

**Figure 1**

**Screening for Hypercholesterolemia: Summary of NCEP Recommendations[3]**

Screen all adults > 20 yrs old: check random total cholesterol

<200 mg/dl "desirable" repeat in 5 years

200 repeat, twice, if necessary average all values

200 – 239 "borderline-high" assess other RFs

240 "high" R/O secondary hyperlipidemia

low risk*    high risk*  →  check fasting lipid profile

Instruct in AHA diet repeat in 1 year

Instruct in AHA diet goals for LDL-C: <160 if low risk <130 if high risk

Consider medication if LDL-C >190 on diet & low risk (goal is <160) >160 on diet & high risk (goal is <130)

* Low risk is defined as having 0 or 1 risk factor other than high cholesterol. High risk is defined as having 2 or more risk factors. Risk factors are listed in the text.

that rely on students "volunteering themselves" for testing may selectively recruit those students who are already aware of the importance of cholesterol; such programs may fail to reach those who are at greatest risk of developing CHD in the future.

The NCEP recommends testing for total cholesterol as the initial screening tool, rather than checking any of the cholesterol fractions (e.g., HDL- or LDL-cholesterol) or triglycerides. This is convenient since total blood cholesterol can be measured accurately in the nonfasting state. Furthermore, reliability is much better for total cholesterol measurement than it is for HDL-cholesterol measurement. However, many young adults with mildly elevated total cholesterol levels simply have a generous amount of HDL-cholesterol and are probably at lower than average risk of developing CHD later in life.

A total cholesterol level below 200 mg/dl has been defined as "desirable" for adults aged 20 and older. While this is at the 75th percentile for people in their forties, it is close to the 90th percentile for young adults around age 20. Because cholesterol levels tend to rise in young adults, many of the younger screenees in the 180s and 190s will soon be over 200. Choosing a lower "cut-off level" (e.g., 180 mg/dl) for those 18 to 25 years of age would classify more individuals as needing further evaluation, many of whom would not be at increased risk (due to high HDL-cholesterol levels). The optimal cut-off level for the college student population remains to be determined.

In summary, every college student should know his or her cholesterol level before graduating. The current recommendation is to check a nonfasting total cholesterol level during routine medical visits on everyone age 20 and older. An efficient variation on this strategy is to include a cholesterol test in the pre-college health evaluation. Further refinements of this approach will be worked out in the future.

## EVALUATION

Just as a single elevated blood pressure reading is not sufficient for a diagnosis of hypertension, a single cholesterol level of 200 or higher is not sufficient evidence to diagnose hypercholesterolemia. Total blood cholesterol in any individual varies from day to day, and several measurements are needed to be sure of the true level. Furthermore, laboratory precision and accuracy have been problematic. All health care professionals who order cholesterol tests should know how well their laboratory performs.

The evaluation of individuals with an initial cholesterol level of ≥200 mg/dl is shown in Figure 1.[5] After confirming the total cholesterol level, the care provider must determine whether the patient needs to have the cholesterol fractions measured. If this is done, further decisions are based on the LDL-cholesterol level. Everyone with a confirmed LDL-cholesterol level of 130 or above should be instructed about how to lower cholesterol; other modifiable risk factors should also be addressed.

A fairly common problem is how to manage the young woman with a high cholesterol level who is or wants to be on an oral contraceptive. There are no absolute rules; clinical judgment will have to be individualized. Obviously, the situation should be discussed with the patient after measurement of the entire lipid profile. Oral contraceptive formulations that contain norgestrel appear to have a worse effect on lipid levels compared with those that do not.[7] A practical approach is to discourage strongly the use of an oral contraceptive for any woman in whom its use would require cholesterol-lowering medication.

## INITIAL INTERVENTION

Since most people with elevated blood cholesterol levels do not have a genetic hyperlipidemia, initial intervention should focus on reversing the most common **underlying** causes: excess intake of saturated fat and cholesterol, excess intake of calories (obesity), and inadequate amounts of aerobic exercise. Even patients with extreme elevations of cholesterol who need to take cholesterol-lowering medication should be on an appropriate diet and exercise regimen in order to minimize the amount of medication necessary to achieve goal-cholesterol levels. Anyone with an LDL-cholesterol level of 130 or higher should take steps to lower his/her cholesterol level.

Instruction in proper initial diet and exercise patterns should be available in the primary care setting. College health service staff should be able to advise students with elevated blood cholesterol levels how to follow a low-fat, low-cholesterol diet using the brochures, videotapes, and software now available. Somewhat different approaches will be necessary for students who eat in a cafeteria compared to students who purchase and cook their own food. However, the general guidelines are the same for both groups: decrease saturated fat intake by cutting down on red meat, whole milk dairy products, and tropical oils; decrease cholesterol intake by limiting use of organ meats, egg yolks, and red meat in general; consume adequate amounts of fiber and avoid excess calories. Referral to a dietitian is appropriate for patients who need to follow a more stringent diet or who have complicated conditions.

Many students with elevated cholesterol levels can benefit from regular aerobic exercise. Exercise can assist in weight control and help raise HDL-cholesterol levels. The specific type of exercise is less important than the frequency, duration, and intensity. Almost any activity that raises the heart rate to 65 to 85 percent of the predicted maximum and is performed for 20 to 30 minutes three or more times per week will have some beneficial effect.

Cholesterol levels should be checked four to six weeks after making a significant diet and/or exercise change in order to give the student an initial indication of how much improvement has occurred. Another level, checked at 3 months, should show the maximum response. However, the diet should be continued for at least 6 months before putting someone on cholesterol-lowering medication.

## DRUG TREATMENT

The vast majority of college students with elevated blood cholesterol levels do not need to be treated with medication. However, on any medium to large campus there will be a number of students with familial hypercholesterolemias (approximately 1 percent of the population) who cannot be managed with diet, weight reduction, and exercise alone.

The NCEP guidelines have set threshold recommendations for initiation of drug therapy: LDL-cholesterol of 160 mg/dl or higher for an individual with CHD or more than one other risk factor; or an LDL-cholesterol of 190 mg/dl or higher for those with no more than one other risk factor. These levels are intentionally higher than the goal LDL-cholesterol levels for these two groups (130 and 160 mg/dl, respectively). Thus, a few patients will not reach their goal LDL-cholesterol level but will not be candidates for drug therapy.

If drug therapy is indicated, it is important to include the patient in the decision of which drug to use. Each of the first-line drugs (bile acid binding resins and niacin) has significant side effects: the binding resins cause constipation and bloating, and niacin causes flushing, headache, and gastrointestinal problems. The long-term safety of lovastatin is unknown. An informed patient will probably be more compliant with the regimen prescribed.

A detailed description of the various drugs is beyond the scope of this chapter. Further readings are listed in the references. Patients should be seen every 3-4 months until they achieve their goal LDL level, and then every 6-12 months.

# HYPERTENSION: DETECTION, EVALUATION, AND INITIAL MANAGEMENT

Hypertension is a very important risk factor for CHD as well as for stroke, congestive heart failure, renal failure, and other problems. Current recommendations for the detection, evaluation, and initial management of individuals with high blood pressure have been published recently.[3] As with cholesterol, these guidelines should be interpreted with some flexibility when dealing with the college student population.

Blood pressure measurement is less expensive than cholesterol measurement, but both require attention to proper technique and equipment. Each student health center should have appropriate programs to assess the frequency and accuracy of blood pressure measurement. Also similar to cholesterol, blood pressure should be checked several times before starting someone on treatment. Students should have their blood pressure measured as part of the pre-college health evaluation and during visits to the health center. The classification of blood pressure levels and follow-up recommendations are shown in Table 1.

The critical components of the medical history, physical examination and laboratory evaluation of individuals with definite hypertension are reviewed in reference 3 and in Table 2 (next page). The major questions to be addressed are:

1. Is there evidence of secondary hypertension?
2. Does the patient have target organ damage? and
3. Are other CHD risk factors present?

The initial approach to lowering elevated blood pressure should be through nonpharmacologic therapy. Weight reduction, restriction of alcohol intake, reduction of sodium intake, and regular aerobic exercise can all help normalize blood pressure. Decreasing saturated fat intake and increasing one's intake of calcium and potassium may lower blood pressure, but the evidence is somewhat scanty.

If these measures do not bring the blood pressure down to goal levels (DBP of 90 or less, SBP of 140 or less) within 3 - 6 months, drug treatment should be considered. While in the past all hypertensive patients were started on a thiazide

---

**Table 1**

**Classification and Initial Follow-up Blood Pressure Guidelines[2]**

| BP Range: mm Hg | Category | Recommended Follow-up |
|---|---|---|
| Diastolic < 85 | Normal BP | Recheck within 2 yrs |
| 85 - 89 | High-normal BP | Recheck within 1 yr |
| 90 - 104 | Mild Hypertension | Confirm within 2 mos |
| 105 - 114 | Moderate Hypertension | Evaluate/refer w/in 2 w |
| ≥ 115 | Severe Hypertension | Evaluate/refer immediately |
| | | |
| Systolic, when diastolic < 90 | | |
| < 140 | Normal | BP Recheck within 2 yrs |
| 140 - 159 | Borderline isolated systolic hypertension | Confirm within 2 mos |
| ≥160 | Isolated systolic hypertension | Confirm within 2 mos evaluate/refer w/in 2 wks if SBP >200 |

diuretic initially, the modern approach allows for more flexibility in choosing the type of medication. In addition to diuretics, beta-blockers, angiotensin-converting enzyme inhibitors, and calcium-channel blockers are all recommended as first-line treatments. Considerations such as the patient's age and race, concomitant diseases, and financial situation can all play a role in selecting an antihypertensive drug.

Treatment of hypertension with combination drug therapy is beyond the scope of this chapter, but is reviewed in reference 3.

## PUBLIC HEALTH APPROACHES

In addition to identifying individuals with high blood cholesterol, high blood pressure, and other risk factors, and helping them modify those risk factors, college

---

Table 2

Essential Items in Initial Evaluation of Hypertensive Patients

History
Duration and severity of known hypertension
Previous treatment and side effects
Current meds: BP meds, estrogens, amphetamines, steroids, thyroxine,
    NSAIDs, decongestants, TCAs, MAOIs
Diet, weight history, exercise patterns, smoking, and ETOH use
HAs, palpitations, sweating, weakness, nocturia
Angina, MI, stroke, renal disease, diabetes

Family history of hypertension and cardiovascular diseases

Physical Exam
VS - temp, HR, supine and upright BP in both arms
Ht and Wt
Fundi
Thyroid exam
Cardiovascular exam
Abdomen - bruits, masses, aorta
Peripheral pulses and edema
Neurologic exam

Laboratory evaluation
U/A, Hct
$K^+$, $Ca^{++}$, creat, chol, uric acid, gluc
EKG, CXR

health services can also help groups of students work toward risk factor modification – the public health model. Since a sizeable minority of young adults have elevated blood cholesterol levels and/or other risk factors, and since a "healthy heart" diet, smoking cessation, and moderate amounts of aerobic exercise are generally safe, the public health approach may be an effective adjunct to the strategies described earlier in this chapter.

## SUMMARY

College health professionals can play a major role in helping young adults lower their risk of CHD later in life. The most prevalent reversible risk factors for CHD are hypercholesterolemia and sedentary life-style. Cholesterol, blood pressure, and other risk factors should be assessed on all college students. Students with elevated blood cholesterol, high blood pressure, and/or other risk factors should receive appropriate intervention based on current guidelines. Only a small minority will require medication.

## REFERENCES

1. Centers for Disease Control: Coronary Heart Disease Attributable to Sedentary Lifestyle - Selected States, 1988. MMWR 39:541, 1990

2. Manchester RA, Greenland P: Prevention of coronary atherosclerosis: The role of a college health service. J Am College Health 35:261, 1987

3. 1988 Joint National Committee: The 1988 Report of the Joint National Committee on Detection, Evaluation, and Treatment of High Blood Pressure. Arch Int Med 148:1023, 1988

4. The U.S. Preventive Services Task Force: Guide to Clinical Preventive Services: An Assessment of the Effectiveness of 169 Interventions. Baltimore, Williams and Wilkins, 1989

5. The Expert Panel: Report of the National Cholesterol Education Program Expert Panel on Detection, Evaluation, and Treatment of High Blood Cholesterol in Adults. Arch Int Med 148:36, 1988

6. Manchester RA, McDuffie C, Diamond E: Screening for hypercholesterolemia in college students. J Am College Health 37:149, 1989

7. Mishell DR: Contraception. N Engl J Med 320:777, 1989

# 22

# Injuries: Problems and Prevention in College Student Populations

KAREN A. GORDON, MPH AND DIANE H. JONES, MSW

This chapter reviews concepts of injury related to college student populations, psychosocial and environmental factors associated with the occurrence of injuries in campus settings, and problems with injury data collection and analysis. Guidelines for establishing campus-based injury prevention programs are outlined.

## INJURY AS A PUBLIC HEALTH PROBLEM

Injury is a major public health problem in the United States and is the major cause of death among children and young adults.[1,2,3] On an average day, more than 170,000 people in the U.S. sustain injuries that warrant use of medical care resources. More than 145,000 injury deaths occur each year in the U.S.[2] Unintentional injuries account for 84 percent of injury-related hospitalizations.[2] Unintentional injuries are the fourth leading cause of death in the U.S. for all age groups, with young males being more likely to be injured and die from these than females.[2]

Of the 56.9 million people injured in the U.S. in 1985 approximately 12.8 million or one-fourth were between the ages of 15 and 24. The three leading causes of death in this age group are unintentional and intentional injuries, homicide, and suicide. Injuries are also the leading cause of morbidity and each year account for over 70 percent of deaths among 15 to 24 year olds. Unintentional and intentional injuries are the primary cause of death among African-Americans age 15 to 24.[2] Motor vehicle accidents account for the greatest proportion of deaths due to unintentional injury. Males are three times more likely to die than females due to auto accidents. The risk of death from firearms is highest among African-Americans than other racial and ethnic groups. Suicide rates among males are twice as high as for females in this age group.[2] Other causes of morbidity and mortality result from drowning, poisoning, fires and burns, falls, use of public transportation, and exposure to other objects.[3]

Among males and females 15 to 24 years, injury rates are similar to other Western industrialized societies. The exception is excessive death due to homicide among young men in the U.S. The rate for U.S. females is one-fourth that of U.S. males, and rates for U.S. females are higher than the male rates in three comparison countries. Injury data from four industrialized countries show that motor vehicle crashes, falls, suicide, and homicide account for the majority of total injury deaths in the U.S., Japan, France, and the United Kingdom. However, in the U.S. homicide rates for male adolescent and young adults were excessively high.[4]

College campuses across the U.S. have no uniform injury surveillance system. Off-campus sources of medical care for injuries and temporary shifts of residence and work among student populations make surveillance difficult. Morbidity and mortality from injuries in the U.S. college student population can only be estimated with limited national data sources. In general, information about injuries not requiring hospitalization is less complete than for injuries requiring medical care or that result in death.[3] When medical attention for injuries is required, the severity, type, time of occurrence, and outcome are not always recorded. The few campus-based studies that have examined the distribution of injuries among students have focused on injuries resulting in visits for specific emergency care on or near campus.[5,6,7] At one large public university a survey was conducted of student visits to the local (off-campus) hospital emergency room. In this study, 46 percent of all visits were found to be due to injury and poisoning, which included contusions, sprains, lacerations, and fractures. Serious injuries were more likely to be seen on weekends.[5,6] A study of the distribution of injuries in a small residential college showed that alcohol-related injuries (sprains, contusions, lacerations) seen at the local hospital emergency room and campus health services were more likely to occur on weekend midafternoons and in the pre-dawn hours. Graduate students had significantly lower injury incidents than undergraduates. Underclass males were more likely to be injured than females. In this study neither the cause nor mechanism of injury was recorded or reported.[7]

The National Health Interview Survey, conducted each year by the National Center for Health Statistics, provides the best estimate of the national distribution of injuries among college students. In these data, college student status is assumed by identifying respondents with 12 years or greater of education whose current main activity is going to school. Estimated injury rates are based on two-week recall.[8] Five years of data (1982-1986) have been aggregated to maximize stability of injury estimates.[9] Approximately 40 percent of college men and 24 percent of women ages 18 to 24 were estimated to have a medically attended injury in a year. Older students (21 to 24 years of age) were more likely to report severe injuries (such as broken bones or head injuries) than younger students (18 to 21 years of age). Injury estimates were found to vary depending on living situations. Those students living with their family of origin were found to have lower estimated injury rates than those living in dorms, and students living alone or with non-relatives in off-campus housing had higher estimated rates than those living at home or in dorms.[9]

Data from the 1985 Health Promotion Disease Prevention Supplement to the Health Interview Survey were examined to explore possible determinants for the observed differences in injury estimates in college students.[9] In this study risk behaviors such as drinking, use of seat belts, and smoking followed a pattern similar to the distribution of estimated annual injury rates by living situation, age, and sex. For example, students who do not use seat belts regularly or who smoke are more likely to be injured. Approximately 40 percent of the 18- to 21-year-old and 48 percent of the 22-to-24-year-old men reported having had five drinks on two or more occasions in the past two weeks. Eleven percent of younger and 18.3 percent of older males reported drinking and driving in the past year, compared to 3.1 percent of younger and 12.8 percent of older college women.[10] The lower rates found among students living in dorms may be due to the limitation of mobility (especially regarding access to automobiles), and the social control over students in dorms as contrasted to students living in off-campus housing. Alcohol and drug use has a greater chance of detection in dorms. However, dormitory living may also increase the occurrence of some kinds of injuries by exposing individuals to a pro-risk-taking value system among peers (especially in regard to alcohol use). These results suggest that injuries vary due to differences by age, sex, of social organization, and exposure to hazards.

The limited data available on the types of injuries in college student populations come from research on sports. Sports and recreational activities may often result in lacerations and contusions, and musculoskeletal injuries such as rupture of tendons, back strains, fractures, and joint dislocations.[11] High rates of sports injuries have been found to be related more to low levels of conditioning.[12] Environmental conditions combined with alcohol may increase significantly the incidence of certain types of injuries such as falls. Alcohol has been linked to injury in a number of studies.[5,6,7] One study examined incidence and severity of injury after falls from bunk beds. Alcohol was implicated as one of several significant co-factors in falls from students' self-designed and constructed bunk and loft beds.[13] The distribution of injuries at football games was studied at a large university to see if a ban on bringing alcoholic beverages into the stadium would alter injury and illness patterns; it did not seem to show a significant association.[14] Other campus-based case studies have been conducted but are not generalizable due to inadequate methods to obtain information on contributing factors or on which to base prevalence rates.

In sum, limited local and national data suggest that injuries vary by such factors as sex, age, and race as well as by the social-ecologic setting of students. The setting shapes both the exposure to dangers and response of the student to his or her environment.

There can be little debate about the high cost of injury to our campus communities. Non-fatal injuries result in substantial economic costs due to restricted activities and substantial use of medical, social service, legal, and financial resources.[15] For example, costs attributed to physical and psychological therapy to overcome trauma of an injury experience such as a violent assault can be especially high. Regardless of outcome – death, disability or discomfort – the impact of a student's injury affects the individual, roommates, family, and the campus community both emotionally and socially. Though the direct costs of medical care and rehabilitation have been shown to be excessively high, the morbidity costs through loss of social activity, productive academic or work life, and uncompensated caregiver time can never be adequately quantified.[16] Yet, despite the prominence of injuries, funding, programming, and policy development for prevention of injury in student populations has not been a high priority on most campuses and in local communities.

## INJURIES AS A NATIONAL PRIORITY

At the national level, prevention of premature morbidity and mortality due to injury has gained new recognition as a national health priority. Increased awareness of injuries as both costly and preventable has led to federal funding for injury prevention research centers and sponsorship of research and surveillance through the National Institutes of Health and the Centers for Disease Control.[17] Such efforts are necessary to build a more comprehensive knowledge and data base for future policies, interventions, and research. Healthy People 2000: National Health Promotion and Disease Prevention Objectives has identified 71 objectives and recommendations as elements of a national priority.[2] Of these 71 objectives related to injury, most address prevention and control of unintentional injuries; other objectives related to injuries are included in sections dealing with occupational health and safety, alcohol and other drugs, mental health, physical activity, and violent and abusive behavior. Some objectives refer to reducing circumstances that lead to injury while others refer to improvement of responses to injuries, surveillance issues, or prevention through education. The objectives relating to reduction of unintentional injuries refer primarily to non-fatal, highly costly head or spinal cord injuries and non-fatal poisoning, while objectives relating to homicide, sexual assault, and suicide are included under violence and abusive behavior. Examples of injury-related national health objectives relevant to college populations are listed in Appendix A.

Several aspects of Healthy People 2000: National Health Promotion and Disease Prevention Objectives address injury prevention for student populations or campus settings. Examples of such objectives are: use of safety belts and cyclist helmets, mouth guards for sports, sprinklers and smoke detectors, and reduced consumption of alcohol. These national objectives, when translated to a campus setting, provide a useful framework for identifying areas of injuries in a specific student population or institution and developing responsive prevention programs. Understanding what constitutes an injury is important in improving the capacity to detect, classify and respond to injuries. The following sections address types and determinants of injuries and data sources, as well as guidelines for campus wide preventive interventions.

# WHAT IS AN INJURY?

"Injury" can be generally categorized into five classes: 1) fatal, 2) injury requiring hospitalization, 3) injury requiring medical attention without hospitalization, 4) injury resulting in one or more days of self-reported restricted activity without medical attention, and 5) injury resulting in temporary discomfort or disability but not requiring medical resources or restricted activity. Injured persons discharged from hospitals are more likely to be classified into one of 24 injury categories, defined by severity and body region affected. Although one or more coding systems, such as ICD-9CM can be used, none is used uniformly in all medical care facilities in the U.S.[3]

Injury is defined as damage to the body resulting from acute exposure to thermal, mechanical, electrical, or chemical energy, or from the absence of such essentials as heat or oxygen.[17] Understanding energy transfer, as well as the absence of energy as the basis for injuries, is important in constructing descriptions of causation. An injury event is the set of circumstances and place where the physical injury occurred, as illustrated in Box 1 (next page).

"Intentional" is used to differentiate interpersonal violence and suicide from other forms of injury. Intentional injuries involve such categories as aggressive assault or suicide, while unintentional injuries involve motor vehicle accidents, drowning, or falling from a ladder. Intentional self-destructive behavior rests on a continuum, ranging from self-denial to suicide.[18] Some experts have argued that a distinction between intentional and unintentional is not useful in terms of prevention and control, since injuries may fall into both categories or neither one.[17] Certain occupational and recreational injuries cannot be described as purely unintentional if employers, co-workers, fellow students, or acquaintances have deliberately exposed a person to risk resulting in injury, such as drinking games.

Violence, broadly defined, is the use of physical force with the intent to inflict injury or death upon oneself (suicide) or others (assault). It sometimes refers to specific activities or behaviors and sometimes to outcomes of violent behaviors, which result in injuries.[19] Assault denotes violent actions resulting in injury. Homicide is defined as death due to injuries purposely inflicted by another person, not including deaths caused by law enforcement officers.[2] These definitions tend to focus on physical outcomes but do not fully explain psychological dimensions of cause or outcome.

At a popular level injuries are often accepted as "accidental," uncontrolled, unpredictable fates of nature or behavior. Denial of the seriousness of injury is often reflected in stereotypical attitudes such as "it's just an accident," "she/he could not help it – she/he was drunk," "it was inevitable, boys will be boys," "it's part of being in college." These mask factors that precipitated the injury, such as use of alcohol leading to interpersonal violence or sponsorship of social events that included alcohol use and lead to interpersonal violence and broken limbs. Popular attitudes toward injuries often reflect pro-risk-taking as favorable, but discount the severity or consequences.

## DETERMINANTS THAT INCREASE
## THE LIKELIHOOD OF INJURY

Campuses offer unique social and ecologic settings that may protect young adults from some kinds of injuries, while increasing risk for other types of injuries. Behavioral and psychosocial factors combine with environmental conditions to shape the risks of injury. For example, adolescents and young adults engage in a constellation of behaviors that place themselves in situations that compromise

---

**Box 1**

**Injury Event**

| Injury Event | Injury | Consequences of Injury |
|---|---|---|
| fall from bicycle | broken leg | use of emergency room, missed classes |

**Factors contributing to injury event:**
**Environmental** - wet, uneven pavement on side walk; dark;
**Legal/policy** - lack of adherence to biking rules to stay on streets;
**Technical** - faulty brakes, no bike light;
**Behavioral** - drinking at party, no helmet used, unsteady steering, lack of proper bike equipment.

safety. Binge drinking that can be associated with exam time and high levels of stress may impair judgment and increase risk of motor vehicle accidents, sports injury or interpersonal violence. Behavioral **indiscretion** is often a precursor of injury when, for example, protective gear is not used in sports, a laboratory, or art class. A head laceration from acquaintance assault while walking to a dorm after a Saturday night party is another example of an injury that results from a combination of environmental circumstance and human behavior.

## INDIVIDUAL AND SOCIAL FACTORS THAT LEAD TO INJURY

The conventional age of undergraduates, 18 to 22 years, coincides with a phase characterized by a continuation of adolescence. Unlike their non-college peers who are largely in the work force, the period of being a student is a time when transition to adult role responsibilities continues to be delayed. The risk-taking behavior of adolescence combines with a marked decrease in adult supervision and control. The "here and now" orientation, along with strong influence of peers, further compounds problems of social control. One study suggests that while students know how to avoid risks they engage in behaviors that increase risks due to concern about negative peer opinion.[20] Lack of orientation toward long-term consequences for behavior and feelings of invulnerability make it difficult for students to see a relationship between "risky" behavior and the likelihood of injury and the long-term effects of injuries.

Contemporary advertising and media also glamorize risk-taking behavior, while downplaying the likelihood or seriousness of injury. Aggression, especially in the context of sports and abusive behavior toward others, is frequently glorified and presented as an acceptable form of conflict resolution. Mind-altering substances are portrayed as part of enjoyment and recreation. Alcohol and other drugs impair judgment and capacity to react to danger. In recent years such campus activities as "hazing" and drinking games have gained greater notoriety among student peers, parents, and administrators as greater numbers of serious injuries and deaths occur. The coupling of such on-campus traditional events as football or basketball with alcohol consumption overshadow critical consideration of individual safety or community responsibility.

## DATA SOURCES AND LIMITATIONS

A major limitation in describing the incidence and prevalence of injuries in student populations is the lack of comprehensive databases. No single national data source provides a complete picture of the distribution and magnitude of injuries by campus or student group. Data on the frequency and types of injuries can be derived from a variety of published and unpublished sources. See Appendix B.

The first two sources are anecdotal evidence based on systematic or unsystematic observation and studies conducted at individual campuses or communities. These sources for data rarely provide reliable estimates of injury incidence and/or prevalence. Even when data are carefully collected on a campus-wide survey, they can give only a snapshot of a community with no general comparability. A third source of data is national mortality and morbidity data, which reports injuries by large age groups and cannot be broken down into college versus non-college populations. Some of these data are reported in different age ranges, as 15 to 24 years, 18 to 25 years, or 15 to 44 years, so that student versus non-student status is not distinguishable.

A fourth source is local, regional, or national trauma registries and crime reports, which also cannot be broken down to college populations.[17]

A final source is national household survey data. This data source provides us with the best estimates of injury incidence and prevalence, but have a number of caveats: First, a self report of "going to school" as the respondents' major activity and a self report of 12 or more years of education might eliminate working students who identify their main activity as "working" or being at home but who nevertheless attend school. Because students are transient and move on and off campus, and thus may seek medical attention for an injury other than on campus-based student health services, this estimation of true prevalence or incidence rates may be vastly underestimated. Secondly, most data sources do not identify the cultural or ethnic background of the injured person or have such small samples that race or ethnic variation in injuries cannot be determined with confidence.[19] Statistics of injuries treated at student health centers or a university hospital may provide only a partial picture of injuries on campus.

Comparisons of different injury rates as reported in campus annual reports or in published studies must be viewed with caution because of: 1) how the numerator is defined (e.g., what constitutes an injury); 2) the denominator (the population at risk for injury); and 3) temporal and other problems involved in determination of the denominator population on which the rate is based.

To gain a complete picture of the magnitude and impact of injuries in the college student population a mandatory surveillance system is needed. In order to assure comparability, injury reporting using International Classification of Diseases (ICD) external cause of injury or poisoning coding scheme (E codes) needs to be applied consistently.[21] Injuries such as alcohol poisoning or acquaintance rape, often not perceived as an injury, need to be recorded appropriately. The number of E codes for certain types of injury events limits some detailed information important for campus settings or a specific population.

# KEY PRINCIPLES IN DESIGN
# OF INJURY-PREVENTION PROGRAMS

Development of injury prevention and control programs requires a practical collaborative rather than a fragmented approach. For example, safety and injury prevention is the collective responsibility of such organizations as campus security, an occupational health office, and student health services. Campus employment offices and work-study programs also play a role in assuring that students are assigned to jobs that provide proper safety precautions and training. A student's injury may require not only medical attention but also legal, financial, and technical resources from other campus departments. Furthermore, understanding differences between and complementary roles of community and individuals (students, administrators, faculty, and staff) is important in delineating areas of responsibility for policy and education.[22] Implementing a dormitory fire-prevention program, for example, requires individual student cooperation in reducing use of equipment that can be a fire hazard in a dorm room. Institutional compliance is also needed by enforcing fire codes and providing smoke detectors in each room. The individual's role is based on decision-making and behavior change, while the community role focuses more on environmental conditions, social norm setting, and policies.

Developing a comprehensive injury prevention and control program begins with a coordinated surveillance or data-gathering system.[17] A first step in developing an injury-prevention program is to establish a multidepartmental campus committee or task force. This committee can assess potential and existing injury patterns by considering injury causation in five general categories:

| Category of prevention: | Examples: |
|---|---|
| Individual (psychological): | campus norms, attitudes, motivations, perceptions, beliefs that being drunk is OK at football games |
| Individual (behavioral): | skill level and competence in avoiding injury, consistent use of protective gear or safety precautions |
| Environmental: | conditions that make injury more likely, such as poorly marked crosswalks, uneven sidewalk pavements |
| Technological: | easy-to-use bike helmets, tamper-proof smoke detectors |
| Legal: | drinking age, disciplinary policies for drug use, parking regulations |

Establishing a surveillance system can serve as an ongoing needs assessment for interventions, a means for estimating incidence and prevalence within the student population, and a data base for describing patterns of injuries or injury complications.

Next, the focus can proceed to formulating a combination of educational and service programs that focus on: 1) reducing risks, 2) modifying injuries, 3) creating policies that address risk factors relevant to specific groups within a student population, and 4) coordinating policies and procedures for responding to injuries and their longer-term consequences.

For a comprehensive intervention approach a broader community profile of injury patterns can be developed. Information from such a profile, gathered over time, can allow for better targeting of educational programming. Examples of profile questions are listed below:

1. What are the characteristics of the population "at risk"?
2. Who is sustaining the injuries?
3. What types of injuries are sustained?
4. When and where did the injuries occur?
5. What is the community perception of the injury(ies)?
6. What are the estimated costs (time lost, financial loss) related to the injury(ies)?: medical care; loss of days from work, studies, or sports competitions; property damage; or caregiver time.

A coordinated surveillance system can be established by developing a simple injury event log to be used by campus security, health services, and other campus offices.[17] An example is given in Box 2 (next page).

Based on data from an injury log, interventions to modify the injury event or injury itself can be designed at three levels:

1. **Primary level** – Interventions to reduce events or circumstances that result in injuries: (pedestrian injuries at a cross walk from cars and bikes, banning alcohol at sports events, change in rules related to sports competitions)
2. **Secondary level** – Interventions to prevent or modify severity of an injury (airbag inflates in car after crash, redesign of a football helmet)
3. **Tertiary level** – Interventions to modify the severity of an injury by providing medical care and rehabilitation after an injury (EMS system, trauma care at Student Health Service or local medical facility).

At the tertiary level many campus settings do not have the financial resources, facilities, or large-enough student body to support an extensive 24-hour response system. In many cases formal relationships are established with local community hospitals, trauma centers, and rescue squads.

Effective interventions for prevention and control of injuries generally combine approaches that can minimize factors contributing to an injury event or modify severity of an injury. **Active interventions** are behavioral, more complicated, and direct. They focus on the decision-making process and behavior change such as consistent use of a bicycle helmet, use of mouth guards in football or ice hockey, or no-alcohol policies for under-aged students or at campus-based parties and sports events. Trauma from sports can be reduced by training in proper application of technique and athletic conditioning. **Passive interventions** are designed to protect individuals or groups by modifying an environment or product design in order to eliminate or reduce risk of potential injury. Examples of passive interventions are:

1. Policies: 15-25 MPH speed zones on campus; changes in judges' scoring criteria to reduce risky moves or overly demanding routines in gymnastic competitions;
2. Environmental changes: Installing speed bumps in dorm areas, better lighting in parking lots, or non-slippery surfaces in bathtub and shower floors;

---

**Box 2**

**Sample Individual Injury Event Log**

Time/Date:
Name/Office completing log:
Place:        on/off campus; type-road, residence hall; sports arena
Person(s):        sex, age, race/ethnic group, status at institution for injured and uninjured (if exposed to same conditions)
Injury type:        Severity, location (fracture, burns, poison)
Intention:        self-inflicted, assault, force of nature, accident
Cause(s):        faulty equipment, lack of skill in operating machine, electrical connection, etc.
Circumstance:        impaired judgment from alcohol use, existing disability, environmental conditions, non-use of protective gear
Medical care:        emergency facilities, hospitalization, rehabilitation, self-treatment, use of campus security, health service staff
Outcome(s):        death, short/long-term disability, leave from school/work, effect on campus climate, environmental/policy changes

3.  Injury Control/Monitoring: Monitoring building codes or checking for presence of functioning smoke detectors in every dorm room; establishing uniform testing standards for football helmets and other protective gear in sports.

Some passive interventions have a significant behavioral component, such as driving habits and adherence to speed limits or consistent fastening of the seat belt. Others may have a strong public awareness component but have limited effect on changing factors leading to certain injury patterns. The increase in legal drinking age has not necessarily reduced alcohol consumption among students and may function to increase consumption of alcohol in rooms and other private settings. Institutional regulations such as banning alcoholic beverages from a stadium during college sports events may not reduce overall injury rates among spectators because of other uncontrollable factors such as hot weather or pre-game drinking at tailgate parties.[14]

Patterns of injuries should be analyzed in order to assess the potential effectiveness, cost, efficiency, and expediency of a proposed intervention. A monthly or periodic summary of injury events as illustrated in Box 3 can provide a rough but quick snapshot of patterns in injury type, population group, or location. It can also provide a basis on which more detailed and sophisticated analysis of factors can be undertaken for a specific group or type of injury. Such information can be used by

---

**Box 3**

**Sample Injury Event Summary Sheet**

| | M=male   F= female | Month/Year: | |
| Category of Injury | Undergrad 1  2  3  4 | Grad. student 1  2  3  4  5+ | Employee staff/faculty |
|---|---|---|---|
| burns | | | |
| poisonings | | | |
| fires | | | |
| drowning | | | |
| falls | | | |
| assaults | | | |
| firearms | | | |
| vehicular | | | |
| pedestrian | | | |
| other | | | |
| | | | |
| Total / month | | | |
| Total / year | | | |

clinicians working in student health services to amplify their own injury-prevention teaching and counseling during patient encounters.

Development of systematic record keeping and an ongoing analysis process are important elements of collaborative prevention strategies. Information about the location and type of injury will help determine what environmental or policy changes can be made or from which department an educational program should be based. For example, it may be more effective for campus security staff to focus on education related to seat belt use, drinking, and driving since they control campus driving regulations and parking permits. An assault-prevention program may combine the efforts of several offices such as campus security and the campus health services creating a peer security escort service in conjunction with the maintenance department's efforts to install campus emergency phones and lighting for walkways.

Haddon's general guidelines for modification of injury-producing circumstances can be used for developing general or injury-specific educational, environmental, and policy interventions:

1.  Prevent the creation of an injury-producing hazard.
2.  Reduce the amount of a hazard.
3.  Prevent the hazard that already exists.
4.  Modify the rate or spatial distribution of a hazard.
5.  Separate, in time or space, the hazard from people at risk for injury.
6.  When possible, separate the hazard from people by a material barrier.
7.  Modify the dangerous aspects of the hazard.
8.  Make what is to be protected more resistant to damage from the hazard.
9.  Quickly work to counter the damage done by the hazard.
10. Stabilize, repair, and rehabilitate the person or people injured.[23]

Intentional and unintentional injuries in the U.S. are a leading cause of morbidity and mortality among young adults and a major contributor to restricted activity and disability.

As such, students as young adults are in a developmental period characterized by adopting and engaging in new behaviors, many of which are risky and result in injuries to themselves and others. Most injuries are not "accidents." The injury event and severity of an injury consist of a constellation of social, environmental, physical, and psychological determinants. A clearer picture of injury patterns and causes can be obtained by establishing a campus surveillance system. Injury events can be a point of coalition building among different offices and services within a community. Most injuries can be prevented through interventions that are appropriate to the age of the target group and setting. Through effective comprehensive programming, patterns of morbidity and mortality related to injury will be significantly reduced by the Year 2000.

## REFERENCES

1. Baker SP, O'Neil B, Karpf RS: The Injury Fact Book. Lexington KY, Lexington Books, 1984

2. U.S. Public Health Service, Dept. of Health and Human Services: Healthy People 2000-National Health Promotion and Disease Prevention Objectives. Washington, DC, U.S. Govt. Printing Office PHS 91-50213, 1991

3. National Research Council and Institute of Medicine: Injury In America - A Continuing Public Health Problem. Washington, DC, National Academy Press, 1985

4. Rockett IR, Smith GS: Homicide, suicide, motor vehicle crash, and fall mortality: United States' experience in comparative perspective. Am J Public Health 79:1396, 1989

5. Kraft DP: Alcohol-related problems seen at the student health services. J Am Coll Health Assoc 27:190, 1979

6. McKillip J, Courtney CL, Locasso R et al: College students' use of medical services. J Am Coll Health 38:289, 1990

7. Meilman PW, Yanofsky NN et al: Visits to the college health service for alcohol-related injuries. J Am Coll Health 37:205, 1989

8. Thornberry OT, Wilson RW, Golden PM: Health Promotion Data for the 1990 Objectives, Estimates from the National Health Interview Survey of Health Promotion and Disease Prevention: United States, 1985. Hyattsville, MD, National Center for Health Statistics, 1985

9. Jones DH, Harel Y, Levinson R: Patterns of Physical Activity Among Noncollege Youth in America: Remembering the "Forgotten Half." Cardiovascular Health Branch, Div. of Chronic Disease Control and Community Intervention, Centers for Disease Control, Atlanta, GA, presentation at Am Public Health Assoc. Annual mtg. Chicago, IL, October, 1989

10. Harel Y, Jones DH: Social determinants of non-fatal injuries among college-aged youth in America: Results from the 1982-1986 national health interview surveys. Presentation at Am Coll. Health Assoc. Annual mtg. Washington, DC, June, 1989

11. Torg JS (ed): Athletic Injuries to the Head, Neck, and Face. Philadelphia, Lea & Febiger, 1982

12. Willmore JH, Costilli DL: Training for Sport and Activity. 3rd ed. Dubuque, IA, Wm C Brown, 1988

13. Dedrick DK, Burney RE et al: Bunk bed injuries in college students. J Amer Coll Health 36:279, 1988

14. Spaite DW, Meislin HW et al: Banning alcohol in a major college stadium: Impact on the incidence and patterns of injury and illness. J Am Coll Health 39:125, 1990

15. Harlan L , Harlan WR, Parsons EP: The economic impact of injuries: A major source of medical costs. Am J Public Health 80:453, 1990

16. Rice DP, MacKenzie EJ et al: Cost of Injury in the United States - A Report to Congress 1989. Atlanta, GA, Centers for Disease Control, Kroger Center, 1989

17. The National Committee for Injury Prevention and Control: Injury Prevention: Meeting the Challenge. New York, Oxford University Press as a supplement to the American Journal of Preventive Medicine 5, 1989

18. Firestone RW, Seiden RH: Suicide and the continuum of self-destructive behavior. J Am Coll Health 38:207, 1990

19. Mercy JA: Assaultive Injury Among Hispanics: A Public Health Problem: Proceedings - Research Conference on Violence and Homicide in Hispanic Communities, UCLA, Kraus J et al (eds). Office of Minority Health, U.S. DHHS, Washington, DC, 1988

20. American School Health Assoc for the Advancement of Health Education, Society for Public Health Education, Inc: The National Adolescent Student Health Survey - A Report on the Health of America's Youth. Oakland, CA, Third Party Publishing, 1989

21. Smith SM, Colwell LS, Sniezek JE: An evaluation of external cause-of-injury codes using hospital records from the Indian health service, 1985. Am J Public Health 80:279, 1990

22. Schelp L: The role of organizations in community participation: Prevention of accidental injuries in a rural Swedish municipality. Soc Sci Med 26:1087, 1988

23. Haddon W: Advances in the epidemiology of injuries as a basis for public policy. Public Health Rep 95: 411, 1980

# Appendix A

## Examples from: Healthy People 2000: National Health Promotion and Disease Prevention Objectives

4.7    Reduce the proportion of high school seniors and college students engaging in recent occasions of heavy drinking of alcohol beverages to no more than 28 percent of high school seniors and 32 percent of college students. (Baseline 33 percent of high school seniors and 41.7 percent of college students in 1989) Note: Recent heavy drinking is defined as having 5 or more drinks on one or more occasion in the previous 2-week period as monitored by self-reports.

6.2    Reduce by 15 percent the incidence of injurious suicide attempts among adolescents aged 14 through 17. (Baseline data available in 1991)

7.6    Reduce assault injuries among people aged 12 and older to no more than 10 per 1,000 people. (Baseline: 11.1 per 1,000 in 1986)

7.17   Extend coordinated, comprehensive violence prevention programs to at least 80 percent of local jurisdictions with populations over 100,000 (Baseline data available in 1993)

9.3    Reduce deaths caused by motor vehicle crashes to no more than 1.9 per 100 million vehicle miles traveled and 16.8 per 100,000 people. (Baseline: 2.4 per 100 million vehicle miles traveled [VMT] and 18.8 per 100,000 people -age adjusted- in 1987) 9.3b Youth aged 15-24; 1987 Baseline 36.9; 2000 Target 33 (Youth aged 15-24, 2000 target 33 per 100,000 crashes)

9.12   Increase use of occupant protection systems, such as safety belts, inflatable safety restraints, and child safety seats, to at least 85 percent of motor vehicle occupants. (Baseline: 42 percent in 1988)

9.13   Increase use of helmets to at least 80 percent of motorcyclists and at least 50 percent of bicyclists. (Baseline: 60 percent of motorcyclists in 1988 and an estimated 8 percent of bicyclists in 1984)

9.19   Extend requirement of the use of effective head, face, eye, and mouth protection to all organizations, agencies, and institutions sponsoring sporting and recreation events that pose risks of injury. (Baseline: Only National Collegiate Athletic Association football, hockey, and lacrosse; high school football; amateur boxing; and amateur ice hockey in 1988)

9.21   Increase to at least 50 percent the proportion of primary care providers who routinely provide age-appropriate counseling on safety precautions to prevent unintentional injury. (Baseline data available in 1992)

# Appendix B

## Databases Relevant To Student Populations*

Many sources of databases are already established. Data may be incomplete, uneven in quality, or not representative of student population or campus setting.

**National Center for Health Statistics**
Scientific and Technical Information Branch, Center Building, 3700 East-West Highway, Hyattsville, Md. 20782, Tel. 301-436-8500
National Health Interview Survey - an annual household survey on illness, injuries,and chronic diseases.
Special supplements include Health Promotion Disease Prevention Supplement (1985,1990) and Child Health Supplement (1988)

**National Injury Information Clearinghouse**
Directorate for Epidemiology, U.S. Consumer Product Safety Commission, 5401 Westbard Avenue, Room 625, Washington, DC, 202207, 301-492-6424
National Electronic Injury Surveillance System - based on sample of injuries seen in emergency rooms involving consumer products.

**Indian Health Service Data Base**
Indian Health Service Office of Planning, Evaluation, and Legislation, Division of Program Statistics, Parklawn Building, 5600 Fishers Lane, Rockville, Md 20857, 301-443-1180

**Centers for Disease Control**
Behavioral Risk Factor Surveillance Survey - telephone random sample survey of adults 18 years and older. Conducted in 33 states. Quarterly reports in Morbidity and Mortality Weekly Reports: Office of Surveillance and Analysis, 1600 Clifton Road, NE, Atlanta, GA 30333, 404-488-5302
Also contact Division of Adolescent and School Health (404-488-5330)

**Drug Abuse Warning Network (DAWN)**
National Institute on Drug Abuse, Div. of Epidemiology and Statistical Analysis, Parklawn Building, Rm 11a-55, 5600 Fishers Lane, Rockville, MD, 20857, 301-443-6637
Drug-abuse-related surveillance data for 27 metropolitan areas. Methods vary by facility.

**Big Ten Injury Surveillance (sport-related injury)**
University of Iowa Hospitals, 1189 Carver Pavilion, Iowa City, IA 52242, 319-338-0581
Tracks selected sports injuries from Big Ten Conference.

**National Head and Neck Injury Registry**
University of PA Sports Medicine Center, Weightman Hall E-7,235 South 33rd St., Philadelphia, PA, 1910,215-662-6943 Information on football-related cervical spine and head injuries.

A variety of federal and private organizations and resources are described in the **Unintentional Injuries, Occupational and Safety and Health, and Violent and Abusive Behavior Resource Lists.** These are obtained through the Office of Disease Prevention and Health Promotion (ODPHP), Public Health Service, National Information Center, P.O. Box 1133, Washington, DC, 20013-1133;

800-336-4797; or 301-565-4167. With regard to National Health Promotion and Disease Prevention Objectives for the Year 2000 and lead agencies, federal contacts can be made through Division of Injury Control, Center for Environmental Health and Injury Control, Centers for Disease Control, Mail Stop F36, 1600 Clifton Road, NE, Atlanta, GA, 30333, Tel. 404-488-4646, or through National Institute for Occupational Safety and Health, Centers for Disease Control, Mail Stop D29, 1600 Clifton Road, NE, Atlanta, GA 30333, Tel. 404-639-3794. Minority health-related materials are available through the Office of Minority Health Resource Center, U.S. DHHS, Office of the Assistant Secretary for Health, P.O. Box 37337, Washington, DC, 20013-7337, Tel. 1-800-444-6472.

* Adapted from Injury Prevention, Meeting the Challenge,  pp 43-44. Table 1. Data Sources and Appendix A, pp.283-286.

# SECTION III

# ISSSUES FOR SPECIAL POPULATIONS

# 23

# Disabled Students on the College Campus

JOEL GRINOLDS, MD, MPH AND ELIZABETH BACON, MS

College and university campuses must be prepared to serve a growing number of students with physical and psychological disabilities. Increasing numbers of these students will enroll in college with documentation of their disability and experience with how that disability affects their academic endeavors. Others may acquire or become diagnosed with a disability during their academic career. The actual number of students with disabilities on college campuses can only be estimated. In the fall of 1986 over 1.3 million, representing 10.5 percent, of the 12.5 million students enrolled in post-secondary institutions reported having at least one disability.[1] Six percent of full-time/first-time college freshmen report having at least one disability, a figure that has more than doubled since data on this subject was first collected a decade ago in 1978.[2] Over 50 percent of all students with disabilities on campuses have so-called "hidden disabilities" that are health related, or they have learning disabilities.[3]

In the past decade, with an increasing awareness and recognition of the prevalence of disabilities and with new types of disabling conditions, it has become important for student health practitioners to gain familiarity with the characteristics and needs of this student group.

## DEFINITIONS AND DESCRIPTION OF THE POPULATION

Section 504 of the Rehabilitation Act of 1973 provides the following definition of handicapped (disabled): "...any person who (i) has a physical or mental impairment which substantially limits one or more major life activities, (ii) has a record of such impairment or (iii) is regarded as having such impairment."[4] A qualified handicapped person with respect to post-secondary education is defined in these regulations as: "A handicapped person who meets the academic and

771

technical standards requisite to admission or participation in the recipient's education or activity."[5] Most institutions have policies based on state and federal legislation that further define a handicapped or disabled student. These policies usually establish categories of disability with specific definitions based primarily on function and used largely for reporting purposes.

Definitions of specific disabilities can be legal, medical, or functional. They are promulgated by sources such as medical associations, national associations, state and federal governmental agencies, and institutions of higher education. Whatever the source, differences in definitions must be anticipated. Blindness, as an example, pertains to anatomic and functional disturbances of the sense of vision to cause total loss of light perception. However, the American Medical Association in 1934 defined legal blindness as: "a person shall be considered blind when central visual acuity does not exceed 20/200 in the better eye with correcting lenses or whose visual acuity, if better than 20/200 has a limit to the central field of vision to such a degree that its widest diameter subtends an angle of no greater than 20 degrees." Visual impairment may be defined in many different ways but is generally thought to mean the loss of visual function that is less than legal blindness.

Another example is deafness, usually defined as a severe to profound hearing loss over 90 dB (decibels). Individuals are considered deaf although they may have some residual hearing. Deafness may be further defined as either prelingual or postlingual. Postlingual deafness occurs after language development and is severe enough to make the understanding of conversational speech, with or without a hearing aid, difficult or impossible. Prelingual deafness occurs before language skills are developed and these individuals usually require oral or sign language interpreters. Persons with less severe decibel loss are considered **hard-of-hearing** although the area of 70 to 90 dB loss is considered borderline between hard-of-hearing and deaf. Functionally, deafness may be defined as the inability to use hearing for purposes of communication. Speech disability is defined generally as a speech impairment that causes speech to be unintelligible in normal conversation.

In the college setting functional definitions are usually more appropriate than strict medical definitions. The important issue is the degree to which the disability interferes with the academic process of the student. If the disability interferes significantly, supportive programs or services will be necessary for the student to be successful.

Of the 1.3 million disabled students in 1986, distribution by specific type of disability among commonly used categories is illustrated in Table 1, next page. The numbers do not add to total, since some students reported two or more disabilities. However, the vast majority of students reported only one disability.

Visual handicap is by far the most prevalent disability, accounting for 39 percent of all disabled students and 4 percent of all post-secondary students. It is of note that only a small percentage are actually blind. Health-related disability was the second most prevalent disability, comprising almost one-quarter of all disabled students. Included in this category are persons who have chronic diseases such as asthma and cystic fibrosis, cardiovascular disease, arthritis, diabetes, systemic lupus, seizure disorders, multiple sclerosis, cancer, AIDS, and psychiatric disorders. Decreased hearing function without deafness is the next most common disability accounting for 20.1 percent of all disabled students. Orthopedic handicaps comprise 17.6 percent of all disabled students with the deafness category and speech disability category accounting for 6.1 and 4.7 percent, respectively.

Although learning disability has been recognized for a long time as a significant disability affecting students in post-secondary education, there still is not a consensus as to its definition. Many experts in the field agree that the definition by

---

### Table 1

**Students enrolled in postsecondary institutions, by type of disability: Fall 1986**

| Type of disability | Number of postsecondary students | Percentage of all students | Percentage of disabled students* |
|---|---|---|---|
| Total, any disability | 1,319,229 | 10.5 | 100.0 |
| Specific learning disability | 160,878 | 1.3 | 12.2 |
| Visual handicap | 514,681 | 4.1 | 39.0 |
| Hard of hearing | 265,484 | 2.1 | 20.1 |
| Deafness | 80,910 | 0.6 | 6.1 |
| Speech disability | 62,525 | 0.5 | 4.7 |
| Orthopedic handicap | 231,491 | 1.8 | 17.6 |
| Health impairment | 320,272 | 2.6 | 24.3 |

*Comprises students who reported that they had one or more of the following conditions: a specific learning disability, a visual handicap, hard of hearing, deafness, a speech disability, an orthopedic handicap, or a health impairment.
NOTE: Details do not add to total, since some students reported two or more disabilities.
SOURCE: Reference 1.

the National Joint Committee on Learning Disabilities is the best comprehensive statement regarding learning disabilities:

> Learning disabilities is a general term that refers to a heterogeneous group of disorders manifested by significant difficulties in the acquisition and use of listening, speaking, reading, writing, reasoning, or mathematical abilities. These disorders are intrinsic to the individual, presumed to be due to central nervous system dysfunction, and may occur across the life span. Problems in self-regulatory behaviors, social perception, and social interaction may exist with learning disabilities but do not by themselves constitute a learning disability. Although learning disabilities may occur concomitantly with other handicapping conditions (for example, sensory impairment, mental retardation, serious emotional disturbance) or with extrinsic influences (such as cultural differences, insufficient or inappropriate instruction), they are not the result of those conditions or influences.[6]

The types of learning disabilities most frequently seen on college campuses are the following:

1.  dyslexia - a measurable difficulty with reading;
2.  dysgraphia - a measurable difficulty with writing language; and
3.  dyscalculia - a measurable difficulty with mathematics.

Students may have more than one of these types at a time. Other types of learning disabilities encountered are auditory perceptual problems; auditory discrimination; auditory directional problems; short-term memory problems; and speed perception problems.

In 1986, students with learning disabilities accounted for 12.2 percent of all disabled students and 1.3 percent of all post-secondary students. The number of learning-disabled students currently enrolled in post-secondary education is not known with precision although an estimate of 6 to 10 percent of all students is frequently used. The increase since 1986 is due to a combination of factors, including increasing public and campus awareness, a reduction in the stigma associated with learning disabilities, and changing definitions. In any event, there has been a substantial increase in demand for services for these students.

Other classifications are used by institutions that stress functional groups different from the classifications in Table 1. As an example, the California State University System Policy[7] uses "communication disability" to classify limitations in the process of speech and/or hearing that impedes the education process. A separate category exists for deafness. "Orthopedic handicaps" is not used; it is included in a broader category of "mobility limitations" that encompass both medically-based problems (such as asthma) and orthopedic disabilities that limit motor function. Health-related impairment is included in the systems' category of "other functional limitation," defined as "any other dysfunction of a body part or process which necessitates the use of supportive services or programs, and which does not fall within the other categories."[7] Finally, disabilities also can be classified by their origin or temporal characteristics. These would include congenitally acquired, late onset, temporary, intermittent, permanent, acute, or chronic. Use of these classifications is primarily for reporting purposes and does not affect the student's eligibility for services.

Some characteristics of the disabled population are of interest because of similarities and differences to the nondisabled student population. According to the report, Profile of Handicapped Students in Post-secondary Education, 1987,[1] similarities were that the majority of disabled students, like other students, attend public institutions – especially two-year colleges. Also, most disabled students attend full time, and most lived off the campus, not with their parents. Differences of note in the two populations are that disabled students were more often male, veterans, older, and more likely to be undergraduates than were nondisabled students.

# HISTORY AND CURRENT STATUS
# OF DISABLED STUDENT SERVICES

The earliest programs to serve students with relatively severe disabilities were established on campuses in the 1960s. Some, such as the Cowell Hall Program at the University of California at Berkeley, utilized the student health services facility as a central component of the program. Pressures on colleges and universities to accommodate disabled students continued to grow with the increasing number of adults surviving catastrophic injury, including war veterans. In addition, an increased number of students received support services in the primary and secondary education systems with the passage of Public Law 94-142, the Right to Education for all Handicapped Children Act.

The requirement to provide support services at the university level became institutionalized with the passage of the Rehabilitation Act of 1973 and its following regulations promulgated in 1977. Service programs developed at public colleges and universities, some with broadly based public funding. At the same time, general institutional policies and guidelines began to emerge. For example, in California, funding and guidelines emerged first for the 107 community (two-year) colleges, followed by policies on the 19-campus California State University System and the eight University of California campuses. These policies established guidelines regarding which students would be served and the nature of services offered.

Today, the typical disabled student services program may provide a wide array of services, ranging from loosely structured services defined by the presenting needs of the disabled students to larger programs with specifically defined and sophisticated services and eligibility criteria. Some programs may be self-contained and segregated from the regularly available campus services. However, the more common model, particularly at four-year colleges and universities, strives to refer and integrate students into existing service programs to the maximum extent possible. Thus, while some programs may include a cluster of special classes and study laboratories, and a small number may cater to specific disability groups (i.e., Gallaudet College for hearing-impaired students, or Landmark College for learning disabled students), most programs provide services that cross all disabilities.

Almost all programs have as their primary mission the integration of disabled students into the regular classroom setting through the provision of services necessary to accommodate the disability. This is accomplished in a number of ways, including direct assistance to the student through the provision of readers, notetakers, sign language interpreters, or tutors; and staff services such as counseling, academic advising, or assistance with financial benefits. Many disabled-student programs will also make available special equipment either on campus or in the student's home. Some programs may provide comprehensive assessment of learning or physical disabilities. Most will coordinate formal or informal activities to educate faculty and staff, to assist with architectural access, or to implement special admissions procedures. Regardless of program size, at a minimum, campuses must consider themselves responsible for providing: architectural access; nondiscriminatory admissions procedures; academic adjustments necessary to accommodate a disability; auxiliary aids; course examinations that measure true academic achievement; and equivalent access to other programs such as financial aid, physical education, social organizations and, of course, student health services.

## SPECIAL ISSUES

### PERSONAL INTERACTION WITH DISABLED STUDENTS

The choice of verbal and written language relative to disability is generally a quick indicator to the disabled student of the general health care atmosphere. While specific medical terms may be a necessary part of communication, it is important to avoid generalizing these terms. It is preferable to refer to the person first using the disability as a defining characteristic rather than using the disability as a noun. Therefore, it is more appropriate to say, "a student who has epilepsy," than to refer to "the epileptic." Avoid emotionally laden terms such as "victim" or "crippled." Language should convey independence. "Confined to a wheelchair" ignores the obvious fact that wheelchairs provide mobility, not confinement. "Disability" is the generally preferred generic term used to describe ones physical condition. The word "handicap" defines the interface between the disability and the environment. Thus a person who has a "disability" such as a spinal cord injury may become "handicapped" by the steps into a building or a bus.

## ARCHITECTURAL ACCESSIBILITY

The physical accessibility of the student health services facility is probably the first and most tangible indication of a nondiscriminatory philosophy to the disabled student. Federal law requires programmatic accessibility. This means that where architectural design does not allow full access, programs must be modified or moved to an accessible location. When facilities are designed or reconstructed they must comply with the American National Standards for Accessibility or to State Building codes, whichever is more stringent. Because of the unique nature of a student health facility, campus policy might be expected to go beyond the minimums. While codes require access to parking, entrances, telephones, drinking fountains, toilet facilities, service counters, work stations and upper levels, student health services should also direct attention to access to examining rooms, dressing rooms, exam tables and equipment, and offices to ensure that design allows for adequate space to move about and close doors for appropriate privacy.

## COMMUNICATION

Sensitivity to the communication needs of disabled students sets the tone for good doctor-patient and professional exchange. Communication issues occur for deaf and hard-of-hearing students. Deaf students must be provided an interpreter if they wish, at no additional cost. Health services professionals should communicate directly to the deaf student rather than to the interpreter, maintaining a clear visual contact as much as possible. Since deaf students may have differing levels of language skills, information should be defined or explained in concrete terms if possible and also should be provided in writing. Similarly, students with diagnosed auditory perceptual learning disabilities benefit from good visual contact and back-up material in writing. It is always appropriate to enquire of the student which communication style is the most beneficial.

Access to telephone communication with deaf patients may be accomplished by installing a telecommunication device for the deaf (TDD). This allows for direct private communication with the deaf patient over telephone lines. In addition, under new federal regulations a national network of Telecommunication "Relay Services must be put into place by 1992 by all common carriers. This will allow for voice-relayed communication when a TDD is not available. It is never appropriate to depend on hearing family members, especially children of deaf adults, to provide interpreting support personally or by phone for medical situations.

Blind students, students with limited vision, and those with visual/perceptual learning disabilities may depend on verbal review of written material. In addition, regularly produced written materials such as pamphlets or handbooks should be made available in large print, Braille, or on cassette if requested.

## EMPLOYMENT

Both public and private colleges and universities are prohibited under federal law from discriminating against qualified individuals with disabilities in employment. This means that an individual who can perform the essential functions of the job with or without reasonable accommodations is protected. As an employer of professional and student staff, the student health center has the opportunity to provide model programs with regard to application, hiring, and advancement of employees with disabilities. In addition, student advisory boards and committees should appropriately include one or more representatives of the concerns of the student with disabilities. Where the campus health services is involved in medical screening of applicants for personnel services, attention should be given to federal requirements that limit the employer's ability to inquire into or test for an applicant's disabilities. Once an employer makes a job offer, the employer may condition the offer on the results of a medical examination if all entering employees are subjected to an examination regardless of disability. Current employees may not be required to take a medical exam unless it is job-related.

## HOUSING

In order to provide adequate support to a student with a disability, attention should not be limited to medical or academic issues only. A student's on- or off-campus living situation may be the single most influential feature in academic success. Appropriate safe access to toilet and kitchen facilities should be provided in all campus housing. Students requiring the assistance of a personal care attendant may require some assistance in formulating appropriate interview questions and communication techniques. Funding for personal care attendants may be provided by the State Vocational Rehabilitation agency, through Title II or Title XVI funds (Medicare, Medicaid) or through special state programs.

## ACADEMIC ISSUES

Student health service staff may become involved when physical or emotional problems impact directly on the academic success of a student. Students may need documentation of the need for curriculum modification, course substitutions, extended time to complete academic or degree requirements, late withdrawals, incomplete semester or leave of absence requests, accommodations or modifications to classroom facilities, or testing procedures. Health personnel may be asked to evaluate the impact of the disability itself, or related medications, on cognitive functioning, perceptual speed, energy level and fatigue, mobility, and/or the specific logistic requirements of a particular academic experience. Great care must be taken to distinguish the true impact of the disability from other life or personal factors and abilities when justifying modifications or accommodations to academic requirements. It is important that the student be provided the accommodations needed to demonstrate his/her true abilities rather than the disability. However, consideration must be given to the impact of waiving or substituting requirements that may affect the student's ability to enroll – or succeed – in later course work. Whenever possible, students should be accommodated to complete course work that is equivalent to that expected of others.

## FINANCIAL BENEFITS

In addition to student insurance available to all students, disabled students may be eligible for other benefit programs to cover medical costs. These may include Medicaid, Medicare, and state or veteran rehabilitation funding. Students may require assistance in determining eligibility for these programs or in seeking appropriate off-campus professionals willing to provide services under these programs. The disabled student services program on campus or community-based Independent Living programs may be resources for these benefits.

An increasing array of special equipment has become available to accommodate a variety of physical conditions, ranging from manual and power wheelchairs to adapted computers. Most campuses will provide some types of adapted equipment to be used by students on the campus to accommodate visual, dexterity, learning, or hearing limitations. Equipment for personal use must be purchased by the student. Student health staff may be asked to assist with this purchase through third-party reimbursement of benefit programs by providing necessary medical verification and documentation of need.

Finally, special programs often exist in university communities that will provide for some of the medical needs of disabled students at reduced or no cost. It should be an acknowledged responsibility of the student health center to assist with accessing and referral to these sources. The financial burdens that disabled students and their families often shoulder are considerable and this is nowhere more evident than with medical costs.

## DEVELOPMENTAL ISSUES

One of the most important roles that a college or university plays is in assisting students toward a more mature self image. Some students with disabilities may have been sheltered excessively by families or in an inappropriate school setting. These students may need assistance to evaluate objectively the effect of their disabilities on their life goals and may need encouragement to take more risks in order to learn from their failures. On the other hand, some have come by their disabilities as a result of risk-taking behaviors. These students often continue to take risks in the form of poor management of their disability-related responsibilities and general abuse of their health. They may need assistance in incorporating their limitations more realistically into their life goals and perhaps in identifying any unresolved anger about these limitations. Some disabled students may be newly diagnosed or experiencing physical changes. In all cases health services personnel may be among the first to note behavior that is indicative of these issues. A balanced approach to reviewing not only symptoms, but energy levels and physical responsibilities in relationship to the campus environment, may be necessary for some students. For example, a student who is accustomed to getting around his small high school on crutches may find it necessary to use a wheelchair on a large campus in order to preserve his energy for the more important pursuits of college life. This decision requires new information about equipment, access and, perhaps most importantly, a re-examination of self image.

## CONSULTATION

Meeting the needs of disabled students on a campus requires a team approach that may include special academic programs, counseling services, special-purpose clinics on the campus, such as speech or reading clinics, and disabled student services. In some cases the health center may be the first point of contact for a student. Initial identification and assessment of the physical disability must include both the nature and extent of the condition. Attention should be given to whether the condition will affect mobility and academic function. Students with temporary disabilities are more likely to be unaware of services available on campus. Referrals to the disabled student services programs and other campus resources should stress the practical value of such services. Some students may express concern with labeling or identification as a disabled student. Confidentiality of records is of particular concern to these students with non-visible disabilities. Assuring reluctant students of the voluntary nature of services and providing them a role in planning their approach to problem-solving may assist them in making initial contacts.

In many cases students may make their initial contact through the disabled student services office. This is more often the case for students with previously diagnosed permanent disabilities. The disabled students services office may thus take primary responsibility for collecting initial documentation and doing general case management. However, the health center may be called upon to provide consultation when records provided are unclear or inadequate, when a second opinion is necessary, or when disabled student services staff needs additional information. When a new disability group or service area is emerging, dialogue and in-service training may be necessary to define new policies and procedures. Special assistance may be needed to define and assess students with specific learning disabilities or those with psychological disabilities.

Mutual efforts may commonly occur when students are requesting special parking, on-campus transportation, the ordering of books on tape, assistance with academic adjustments such as late withdrawals (for medical reasons) or course/curriculum adjustments, and purchase of special equipment. Occasionally health services may be called upon to serve as an advocate for the student with an agency or organization outside the campus such as the Social Security Administration or a state or federal rehabilitation agency.

## CONCLUSION

As a result of changing laws and attitudes and available support programs, the numbers of disabled students on campus can be expected to continue to increase, resulting in increased demand for services from the student health centers. Current epidemiologic data on prevalence and incidence of disabilities is inadequate to assist with precise program planning and development. It is clear, however, that in an era of shrinking public funding it is important for the student health services to work cooperatively with all campus service programs to adequately meet the needs of the growing number of disabled students on the college and university campus.

## REFERENCES

1. U.S. Department of Education Office of Educational Research and Improvement: Profile of Handicapped Students in Postsecondary Education, 1987 (SP-NPSAS-86/87-10). Washington, DC, U.S. Government Printing Office, June 1987

2. American Council on Education: The American Freshman: National Norms for Fall 1988. University of California, Los Angeles, Higher Education Research Institute, 1989

3. Hidden Disabilities, Information from Heath (National Clearinghouse on Postsecondary Education for Individuals with Handicaps) 8:1, p 7, 1989

4. Public Law 93-112: Rehabilitation Act of 1973

5. Federal Register 42:86, May 4, 1977, p 226-84

6. California State University: Policy on the provision of services for students with disabilities, Jan 1989

# Appendix A

**Summary of federal legislation important to people with disabilities***

Americans with Disabilities Act (ADA), 1991, PL 101-336 (See also, Appendix B)

Individuals with Disabilities Education Act Amendments of 1990 (IDEA), PL 101-476

Carl D. Perkins Vocational and Applied Technology Act Amendments, PL 101-392

National Affordable Housing Act, PL 101-625

Supported Living: Omnibus Reconciliation Act of 1990, PL 101-508

Television Decoder Circuitry Act, PL 101-431

*Developmental Disabilities Board, State of California bulletin

# Appendix B

**Americans with Disabilities Act (ADA) - Public Law 101-336***

Public Law 101-336 (signed July 26, 1990) enacts the Americans with Disabilities Act (ADA), a new federal law that provides civil rights protections to individuals with disabilities that are like those provided to individuals on the basis of race, sex, national origin and religion. It guarantees equal opportunity for individuals with disabilities in these five areas: employment, public accommodations, transportation, state and local government services, and telecommunications. (Each Title goes into effect on a different date.)

*Developmental Disabilities Board, State of California bulletin

# 24

# College Health Care for
# International Students

PAMELA A. COOPER BOWEN, MD, MPH AND MURRAY M. DEARMOND, MD

Providing health care for international students is a complex challenge for many institutions of higher education in the United States. Not only are college health professionals challenged to provide health care for people from diverse cultural backgrounds, they and their student health services are drawn into the arena of international education. Few practice settings in the U.S. offer such opportunities. Through global educational exchange, student health care providers can touch the lives of people from all over the world. Such an opportunity should not be taken lightly as it may lay the foundation for better understanding among cultures and the exchange of ideas that are essential for real international cooperation and peace.

This chapter will provide demographic information about international students studying in the U.S., outline the unique challenges and health issues of these students, and describe ways in which to deal with them effectively.

## DESCRIPTION OF THE
## INTERNATIONAL STUDENT POPULATION

Who are these international students who come to study in the U.S.? In the 1989-1990 academic year, there were more than 385,000 international students enrolled in American institutions of higher education, and more than 35,000 students enrolled in U.S. Intensive English Language Programs. Over 50 percent (53.8) of the 385,000 international students came from Asia, 12.4 percent from Latin America, 11.9 percent from Europe, 9.7 percent from the Middle East, 6.4 percent from Africa, 4.8 percent from North America, and 1.0 percent from Oceania. During 1989-90 the ten countries with the most students in the U.S.

were: China (33,390 students), Taiwan (30,960), Japan (29,840), India (26,240), Korea (21,710), Canada (17,870), Malaysia (14,110), Hong Kong (11,230), Indonesia (9,390), and Iran (7,440). More than 30 percent (33.4) of students in Intensive English Language Programs came from Japan, 7.5 percent from Korea, 5.2 percent from Mexico, and 4.5 percent from China.[1]

Significant changes in the international student population have occurred over the past decade. In 1979-80 there were only slightly more than 286,00 international students in the U.S. The ten countries with the most students in the U.S. were: Iran (51,310), Taiwan (17,560), Nigeria (16,360), Canada (15,130), Japan (12,260), Hong Kong (9,900), Venezuela (9,860), Saudi Arabia (9,540), India (8,760), and Thailand (6,500).[2] But by 1989-90 China, Korea, Malaysia, and Indonesia were newcomers to the top ten; whereas Nigeria, Venezuela, Saudi Arabia, and Thailand were no longer to be found among them. In 1982 the Committee on Foreign Students and Institutional Policy appointed by the American Council on Education projected an international student enrollment of 804,000 in 1988-89.[2] This, of course, did not come to pass, due to those political and economic forces that inevitably impact upon international student enrollment.

International students come from all parts of the world. They present unique opportunities and challenges to U.S. institutions of higher education, among which is the delivery of health care. To address these, in 1986 two national organizations, the American College Health Association (ACHA) and the National Association for Foreign Student Affairs' (NAFSA) Association of International Educators, began working together to improve the delivery of culturally appropriate health care to international students and their dependents.

## UNIQUE CHALLENGES
## AND HEALTH ISSUES OF INTERNATIONAL STUDENTS

Caring for international students often requires student health care providers to go above and beyond what is normally required when providing health care for domestic students. For example, there may be language and communication difficulties to overcome and different expectations about ways of healing. There may be unfamiliar tropical diseases to treat and the need to collaborate with colleagues in international services and other offices on campus. As with all patients, health care providers must seek to understand individual lives, not just the symptoms that are presented for treatment, if they are to effectively respond to their patients' physical, emotional, social, and spiritual well-being. These are the elements that must be in harmonious balance for good health. In the case of international patients such understanding may require a greater commitment of energy, time, and resources on the part of health care providers and the institutions in which they practice.

The following represent some of the topics most important to caring for the health of international students and suggested ways to address them effectively.

## INTEGRATING CULTURAL BELIEFS

Integrating cultural beliefs about health into the assessment, diagnosis, and treatment of illness will contribute to successful health care for international students. All patients, whether from the U.S. or a foreign culture, carry a rich fabric of experience and convictions regarding their health and illness. Without acknowledging and understanding these, health care providers will have little success in helping them. Patients themselves are valuable sources of such information, so providers may wish to ask them questions such as:

1.  What is the meaning of their illness?

2.  Is it a good or bad illness to have?

3.  How would healing normally take place?

4.  Who is responsible for an individual's health (the individual or the health care provider)?

5.  What remedies have they brought from home?

Medical anthropologists and literature from other cultures will also help to provide valuable insight into these matters.[3]

## ORIENTATION TO THE U.S. HEALTH CARE SYSTEM AND HEALTH INSURANCE

The U.S. health care system is the most complex and most expensive in the world; hence, it is difficult to understand, especially for international students who often come from countries where medicine is socialized or nationalized and available to everyone regardless of income level. Thus, our private enterprise system with its soaring costs is totally foreign to most students and requires detailed explanation.

It is essential for student health care providers and foreign student advisers to work together to provide the necessary information to students. It is best if such information is sent to students and their sponsors before they leave their home country. This allows them to obtain adequate health insurance for themselves and their dependents at home, or bring adequate funds with them to purchase it immediately upon their arrival in the U.S.

Once they arrive in the U.S., students should be provided with additional information about our health care system and insurance as part of an ongoing orientation program. The program should include an orientation to the student health service if there is one on campus and to medical resources in the community.

It is highly recommended that health insurance be made mandatory for these students and their dependents, and it is necessary to ensure that they continue to pay their insurance premiums. In addition, it is necessary to explain to them that insurance does not cover all medical bills and, therefore, that they should set aside additional funds to cover deductibles, prescriptions, dental and eye care, and other services outside the benefit package.[4]

## CULTURAL ADJUSTMENT

Health care providers should be aware of the phenomenon known as "culture shock" and how it may affect the health and educational experiences of international students. Students may experience some of the following symptoms as they pass through various phases of adjustment to a new culture:

- helplessness and dependence on compatriots

- greater irritation than usual when things go wrong

- a fear of being cheated, robbed, or injured

- excessive concern about cleanliness, pains, skin eruptions, or minor health problems

- a strong desire to be home with those who understand them

- delaying or refusing to learn the language of the country

- insomnia and fatigue

- loss of appetite and stomach problems

- headaches

- loneliness, homesickness, and depression

- poor concentration

Since students experiencing such symptoms often come to the student health service for care, it is important for health care providers to have some knowledge of the phases of cultural adjustment people experience.

**Stage I.** This may be called the "tourist stage" or the stage of euphoria. Students are fascinated by all that is new and tend to see similarities with their home country.

**Stage II.** Students slowly tend to feel uncomfortable. Differences with home stand out and cause misunderstandings and feelings of alienation. At this stage students may be very critical of the new culture and they may become depressed.

**Stage III.** Students slowly recover. Interest in and sensitivity to the new culture and other people emerge. A sense of humor and an ability to joke about new experiences and difficulties return.

**Stage IV.** A meaningful understanding of the new environment occurs. Students stop assessing the new culture by using their own cultures as models. They accept the new culture and people for who and what they are – not better or worse, just different.[3]

It is also important for international students themselves to have some knowledge about "culture shock" and the stages of adjustment to the new culture, so that they are better prepared to deal with them. Student health services may enlist the help of the counseling service and international office on campus to share such information with them at orientation programs. Armed with an understanding of adjustment, students are better able to avoid adverse outcomes of the experience. Viewing the videotape "Cold Water" (copyright 1986, Noriko Ogami; Intercultural Press), followed by discussion, may also be helpful to sensitize international students to these issues several weeks after their arrival.

One caution about "culture shock" – do not confuse the symptoms of a clinical depression with the symptoms of "culture shock." The results of such a mistake could lead, on the one hand, to an unnecessary hospitalization and, on the other an undetected depression or, in the extreme case, a suicide attempt.

## TROPICAL DISEASES

Not only do international students have the same maladies as domestic patients, they also may suffer from various tropical diseases often unfamiliar to health care providers in the U.S. Tropical diseases such as malaria, cholera, typhoid, yellow fever, and parasitic illnesses and certain cancers and infectious diseases in diverse parts of the world may present new challenges for student health services. Information about such illnesses should be available to health care staff so that they can deliver the best care possible to international students. Student health center continuing education programs should address these on a periodic basis. Other good sources of this information include:

- texts on tropical medicine, medical parasitology, and epidemiology;

- the U.S. Public Health Service Centers for Disease Control;

- infectious disease specialists and gastroenterologists; and

- physicians from foreign countries practicing in the area.

## HEALTH CARE FOR DEPENDENTS

As stated earlier, it is highly recommended that colleges and universities require health insurance for international students and their dependents. However, insurance sometimes does not meet the health care needs of dependents since they are often ineligible to use student health services. Illness in a family member can have a profound effect on a student's ability to cope with day-to-day activities. In addition, a lack of support systems for spouses and children makes them vulnerable to loneliness and stress-related problems, and they can become the targets for abuse when tensions overwhelm the international student.

Thus, student health services should seek resources in the community that will be responsive to the health care needs of students' dependents. Cooperative arrangements may be established with on- and off-campus resources such as: schools of public health, dentistry, nursing, optometry, education, psychology, and social work; public health programs (such as immunization clinics, well-baby clinics, family planning and maternity-care programs); and physicians, dentists, psychologists, and optometrists who are immigrants, have foreign language skills, or are sensitive to different cultural norms.

## THE SPECIAL HEALTH CARE NEEDS
## OF INTERNATIONAL WOMEN

At the present time one-third of the international students in the U.S. are women, not including the wives of students. These women bring a variety of health practices and beliefs with them that may vary from U.S. custom and require sensitivity by health care providers. Such practices include: taboos against gyneco-logic examination of virginal women, female circumcision, the requirement that they be examined only by female health care practitioners, the insistence on remaining clothed while being examined, or on having a friend or husband accompany them for examinations. Student health services should be aware of such cultural differences and be prepared to accommodate them. In particular, it is important that there be female practitioners available to provide care for these international women.

It is common to find that international women have had incomplete gynecologic care. Thus, it is important to provide regular screening for cervical and breast cancer and sexually transmitted diseases (STDs), to teach the technique of breast self-examination, and to provide information about contraception and protection against STDs in culturally sensitive ways. The health service staff should consider employing group, individual, and peer counseling, and translated written materials to accomplish these goals.[3]

While in the U.S., international women may question or alter their identity as women, and their changing roles may affect their psychosocial and physical health. It is important for health care providers to recognize that this may occur and to be ready to offer support and counseling services if necessary. Peer support groups are useful for addressing these problems.

## IMMUNIZATIONS AND TB
## POLICIES AND PROTOCOLS

The prevention of communicable diseases is important to institutions of higher education and local public health authorities. Student health services and local and state health departments should work together to ensure proper immunization and testing of international students and their families. Although international children of school age are required by state laws to receive adequate immunization, spouses and infants may be overlooked. State or local health department personnel can be very helpful in providing access to information and immunization consent forms in many languages through the Centers for Disease Control.

The prematriculation immunization requirements (PIRs) of the American College Health Association stipulate that all students, including international students, should be immune to measles, mumps, rubella, diphtheria, tetanus, and polio. In addition, international students should be required to have a skin test for tuberculosis (PPD) before being allowed to matriculate. If the PPD is positive, a chest x-ray should also be required, regardless of whether the student has had BCG vaccination, since those who have had BCG can still become infected with pulmonary tuberculosis. Individuals under the age of 35 with a positive PPD (10 mm or more of induration) and a negative chest x-ray, regardless of whether they have had BCG vaccination, should receive INH prophylaxis for six months provided there are no contraindications to its use. Local and state health departments often provide and monitor INH prophylaxis at no cost.[3] In addition, staff who work closely with international students should receive skin testing for TB at regular intervals.

# HEPATITIS B

Hepatitis B infection is prevalent in many parts of the world, including China, southeast Asia, sub-Saharan Africa, and the Amazon basin. In these regions, 15 to 20 percent of individuals with acute hepatitis B may become carriers of the virus. Carriers are at risk of developing liver failure and hepatoma, and are capable of infecting their children at birth and others through intimate contact.

International students from countries with high prevalence of hepatitis B infection should therefore be offered the opportunity to be screened for the presence of hepatitis B core antibody. If uninfected students are identified, they should be offered hepatitis B vaccine. If students are identified with a positive hepatitis B core antibody, they may be screened further for the presence of hepatitis B surface antigen. If the antigen is present, they should be counseled about the transmission of the virus to others, they should be followed to detect the development of liver failure or hepatoma, their sexual partners should be offered hepatitis B vaccine, and children born to female carriers should be treated at the time of birth in an effort to prevent their becoming carriers.

The relatively high cost of the vaccine should not deter student health services from establishing a program to address hepatitis B. By immunizing uninfected individuals and by treating children born to women who are carriers of hepatitis B, the health of many people may be preserved.[3]

# DENTAL AND EYE CARE

Even though dental and eye care traditionally are not covered by insurance policies, international students are often in great need of such care and sometimes even delay seeking it until they reach the United States. Student health services not offering such care should be prepared to refer students for reasonably priced care in the community. Sources might include the university dental or medical school, public health clinics, or practitioners in the community who are immigrants or who have foreign language skills.

# NUTRITION

It is essential that students have adequate nutrition in order to participate fully in their program of study. As part of "culture shock," international students may experience aversion to American foods, anorexia, and weight loss. To compound the problem, they may be unfamiliar with purchasing, storing, and cooking foods, especially if they are living on their own for the first time.

Student health services, in cooperation with international student offices, should assist students in obtaining adequate nutrition. This may involve providing them with lists of local ethnic grocery stores, taking them on expeditions to large grocery stores where familiar foods are often packaged in unfamiliar ways, providing information on safe storage of foods, and conducting cooking classes. Students in nutrition programs, community volunteers, public health departments, and other international students and their spouses may be willing to assist with such programs.

Information may also be provided using foods specific to a culture. Since women are often the ones preparing the meals, meetings with wives are frequently necessary to address specific dietary restrictions, especially when treating patients for chronic problems such as diabetes, hypertension, and obesity. Otherwise little in the way of nutritional management can be achieved.[3]

# SEXUALLY TRANSMITTED DISEASES INCLUDING HIV INFECTION AND AIDS

International students may fear studying in the U.S., because the U.S. is perceived as having a high prevalence of sexually transmitted diseases and AIDS. At the same time, U.S. institutions and individuals may discriminate against students from foreign countries with a high prevalence of AIDS. Thus, it is essential that universities develop institutional policies and provide appropriate educational programs about HIV infection/AIDS and STDs to allay fears and prevent discriminatory actions.[5] In the case of international students, close cooperation among the student health service, the international office, and the students will be helpful in providing flexible, culturally sensitive STD and HIV/AIDS programs.

Student health services should provide treatment or referral for treatment of STDs and HIV-related illnesses. They should also provide information about treatment of sexual partners and about health care resources for partners, if they are not eligible to use the student health service.[3]

## HEALTH PROMOTION AND DISEASE PREVENTION

Preventing health problems before they arise is of paramount importance for students experiencing the stress of living in a foreign culture. Without good health little else can be accomplished. In most respects, the health promotion and disease prevention challenges facing international students are similar to those of all students. These include the use of tobacco, alcohol, and other drugs; obesity; poor physical fitness; using effective contraceptives and STD protection; and coping with stress. The health education staff, in collaboration with the international office and the international students should develop appropriate prevention programs to address these problems.

Prevention may be an entirely new concept to international students, but once they have adopted the idea they may become some of the strongest proponents on campus. It is important to include families in these prevention programs since spouses are often in charge of health care for the family, and since they may be health care providers at home and have a great deal of expertise to contribute.[3]

## PREPARING STUDENTS FOR THE RETURN HOME

Just as international students experience "culture shock" upon arrival in a new culture, so too do they experience problems resulting from re-entry into their home culture. Often just the anticipation of returning home and leaving behind a newly adopted life-style can result in stress, causing the student to come to the student health service with stress-related symptoms. Thus, it is important to record the date international students plan to return home on their medical charts, since this may help to explain some of the problems they may experience at that time.

The international office, counseling center, and students who have been home and returned to the U.S. can work together to develop re-entry workshops and exit interviews that will provide international students with opportunities to explore their feelings, discuss their role changes, share experiences, reduce stress, and prepare for the return home.[3]

## CONCLUSION

The number of international students studying in the U.S. is expected to remain high in the years ahead. In turn, the increasingly interdependent nature of our times calls for institutions of higher education across the country to seek ways to enrich the international perspective for all students. Failure to do so will risk the very relevance of the higher education experience. Currently, only 2 percent of U.S. undergraduates study abroad, lowest among the developed nations of the world. Many universities have set ambitious goals to increase this to 10 percent by the end of the century. In all respects, health care for international students will continue to present exciting opportunities and challenges to college health practitioners. By meeting these challenges with skill and caring, those who work in the field will have the opportunity to influence the health and well-being of people all over the world.

Acknowledgments

The authors are indebted to both ACHA and NAFSA, and to all past and present members of the NAFSA/ACHA Joint Committee on Foreign Student Health Care for their work in this area and for their contributions to this chapter. We would like also to acknowledge the U.S. Information Agency for partially funding the work of the Joint Committee.

## REFERENCES

1. Zikopoulos M (ed): Open Doors: 1989/90, Report on International Educational Exchange. New York, NY, Institute of International Education, 1990

2. A Report of the Committee on Foreign Students and Institutional Policy: Foreign Students and Institutional Policy, Toward an Agenda for Action. Washington, DC, American Council on Education, 1982

3. NAFSA/ACHA Joint Committee on Foreign Student Health Care: Optimizing Health Care for Foreign Students in the U.S. and American Students Abroad. United States of America, National Association for Foreign Student Affairs/American College Health Association, 1989

4. NAFSA Insurance Advisory Committee: The Risks and Realities of Health Insurance: A Guide for Advisers to Foreign Students and Scholars. United States of America, National Association for Foreign Student Affairs, 1988

5. Keeling RP (ed): AIDS on the College Campus, A Special Report of the American College Health Association, Second Edition. Rockville, MD, American College Health Association, 1989

## SUGGESTED READINGS

David M. Kennedy Center for International Studies, Brigham Young University: Culturgrams: The Nations Around Us. Vol. I & II. Provo, UT, Garrett Park Press, 1988

Gunn ADG, Zwingmann CAA: Uprooting and Health: Psycho-social Problems of Students from Abroad. Geneva, Switzerland, World Health Organization, 1983

Helman CG: Culture, Health and Illness: An Introduction for Health Professionals. Second Edition. London/Boston, MA, Wright, 1990

Jong EC: The Travel and Tropical Medicine Manual. Philadelphia, PA, W. B. Saunders Co., 1987

Pedersen P: Handbook of Cross-Cultural Counseling and Therapy. New York, NY, Praeger, 1987

Wood CS: Human Sickness and Health: A Biocultural View. Palo Alto, CA, Mayfield Publishing Co., 1979

# 25

## Non-traditional Students in Colleges and Universities

MYRA LAPPIN, MD, MPH

The popular image of a college campus is based less on fact than on recall. Many of us think back on our experience in college a decade or more ago. Colleges of the 1950s and 1960s served a homogeneous population, primarily white males age 18 to 23 from the middle and upper class. These were students who lived away from home for the first time in a dormitory setting, were supported by well-to-do parents, and usually finished college in four years. Their challenges were academic, their problems were dating, and few had financial concerns. Then, only 20 percent of high-school graduates went on to college. Most women never completed their degrees.

Several important changes are occurring that challenge this conventional wisdom about the demographic, social, cultural, and economic characteristics of college student populations. For example, according to the U.S. Census Bureau Statistics, nearly 40 percent of college students in 1985 were 25 years of age or older. The trend toward older students is especially noticeable for females. Over 40 percent of female college students were 25 years of age or older in 1985, compared to about 25 percent in 1970.[1] In the 1980s and 1990s, in many urban settings, the commuter campus is the norm. Younger students live at home or in apartments, while older students often live with friends, family, or spouse. Up to 80 percent have part-time or full-time jobs, most of which are necessary to provide funds for college.

The design and implementation of student health services in the past reflected the characteristics of the campus. College students were individually unique, but the "cohort approach" to their medical problems was common. Students of the same age and similar background were presumed to have the same medical needs. Ordinarily student health services provided ambulatory care for simple health complaints – upper respiratory problems, dermatologic problems, sprains and injuries sustained while in athletic competition – while only the most forward-thinking campuses addressed "problem pregnancies, VD, and drugs."

The diversification of college students now requires that college health services address not only the health issues of "traditional" groups of young adults but also those issues associated with a much more heterogeneous student body. This influences both clinical service delivery and planning for health promotion services.

Students under age 25 require clinical services for birth control, pregnancy testing and referral, sports physicals, bulimia and anorexia, treatment of sexually transmitted diseases, and psychological services aimed at the developmental issues of young adults. Older students, on the other hand, are more likely to need medical consultation for manifestations of chronic disease such as hypertension, cardiovascular disease, cancer, adult-onset diabetes, arthritis, and gynecologic problems not associated with contraception.

With respect to health education and health promotion services, traditional activities in the areas of sexually transmitted diseases and AIDS education, nutrition counseling, smoking cessation, and drug and alcohol counseling, may need to be supplemented with programs that address mid-life stress and transitional issues such as divorce counseling and cancer awareness. As the composition of student groups changes and as advances in medical care translate into improvement in functional capacities for certain individuals, universities must accommodate their facilities for the disabled, for students who are visually and hearing impaired, and for those who are wheel-chair bound. Plans must be made to address the needs of students who bring their pediatric diseases into young adulthood, such as students with severe asthma, cystic fibrosis, renal transplantation, muscular dystrophy, or osteogenesis imperfecta.

## DEFINITIONS

"The Non-traditional Student" was initially coined as a phrase describing the "adult female learner" returning to academia after an absence of several years to pursue higher education or complete her degree.[2] This name was debated in the 1960s and 1970s in the educational field concurrent with the work of the 1971 Commission on Non-traditional Study, which was established under the joint auspices of the College Entrance Examination Board and the Educational Testing Service. Commission members agreed that non-traditional study "puts the students first and institution second, concentrates more on the former's need than the latter's convenience, encourages diversity of individual opportunity ... (and) has concern for the learner of any age and circumstance."[3] Later, the term "non-traditional" was broadened to include "adult learners" of any gender or age.[4]

As the "traditional student" is described as the 18 to 24 year old, living in residential housing, supported by parents, readers must acknowledge the diversity of the group currently labeled "non-traditional." Non-traditional students are now a varied group comprised of the displaced homemaker, the empty-nest mother, the blue-collar wife, the single parent, the career woman or man with or without children who requires additional training for career advancement or career change, students in the 55-75 age bracket participating in Elderhostel or Extended Education, the international student whose only college contact is enrollment in English language programs, the first generation college student of an immigrant or minority family, and the commuter student.

## IMPORTANT ISSUES AND PROBLEMS

What then are the unique challenges to providers of student health services for such a diverse population on college campuses? The following must receive attention from health workers in college and university settings and may be considered the "problem list and chief complaints" of the students of the 1990s.

### ACADEMIC STRESS AND THE COMMUTER STUDENT

The goal of late adolescence is separation from family and redefinition of self.[5] Landmark publications conclude that attendance at the university is a "self-engendered remaking of the personality,"[6] "which is attributable to the college experience."[7] Chickering's study found significant relationships between the psychological achievements of dorm residents versus commuters living at home during the freshman year.[8] Those living at home had negative self-perceptions in four major areas: public speaking ability, leadership ability, social self-confidence, and popularity.

Commuter students tend to fall into many more sets of subgroups than do resident students (e.g., ethnic backgrounds, various types of socioeconomic status). Commuters tend to be the first generation of college attenders in their families. Their parents are more frequently blue-collar workers with less education than the parents of dormitory resident students.[9] Commuters tend to be less well prepared for the academic demands of college.[10]

Smith has noted that significant relationships with peers, faculty, campus organizations, and parents stimulate the college student with new ideas, values, and beliefs while providing the student with "support during periods of emotional stress."[9] Resident students' relationships with their parents often improve as a result of separation. Commuter students living at home are not as free to work out their own approach to life. Parents and preexisting social groups apply pressure on students to remain the same as they were before college.[11] Gains in upward mobility also bring the loss of a familiar past, including a past self. First-generation students report an anguish and conflict that may be complicated by living at home.[12] Dorm living and proximity to campus increase the frequency with which interactions with faculty occur. This social integration with faculty is more difficult to attain by commuters, which they recognize with consequent anxiety.

In sum, commuter students may miss out on some powerful advantages of the college experience. Status as a commuter student can have an impact on retention and completion of academic goals. The concomitant stress can have deleterious effects upon health and well being.

## WOMEN'S HEALTH ISSUES

Women now constitute over one-half of all students in higher education.[1] Medical services rendered must provide for a range of needs from the late adolescent to the post-menopausal woman. Routine gynecologic care and birth control, education for the prevention and treatment of sexually transmitted diseases, including AIDS and the diagnosis and treatment of pelvic inflammatory disease, certainly must be available. Services that overlap age groups but meet the more specific needs of older patients should be available. These include: cervical cancer screening, colposcopy and biopsy, breast care and mammography, infertility counseling, and the care of postmenopausal problems. Most campuses do not offer obstetrical care or pre-natal care despite the large percentage of women who are of child-bearing age. The provision of such services places demands on student health services that could not have been anticipated one or two decades ago.

Because required services are more extensive than in prior years, and all health facilities are not equally prepared or funded to offer comprehensive women's services, substantial variations are seen from campus to campus. Some centers offer education and referral only. Others offer services utilizing nurse practitioners, with physician/specialist consultation and referral, while still others offer the above with a team of nurse practitioners and gynecologists on staff. Regardless of available services, coordination with prior medical services and established referral relationships with local medical resources are a must. The cooperative management of these patients is essential for a high quality of medical care.

Circumstances have been changing with respect to the availability of family planning services in many communities in which college students reside. This is due to a combination of political and economic factors. Traditionally, students have been eligible for community services based simply upon their ability to pay. But funds are becoming more limited and since the late 1980s Planned Parenthood and similar family planning facilities have been required to charge full-fee to all clients having "health coverage" elsewhere. The assumption is often made that college students can obtain a full range of family planning care through their student health center. Thus, fewer low-cost women's services are available in the community and an increasing proportion of their needed gynecologic services must come from the campus health center.

## ACADEMIC STRESS, STUDENT FAMILIES, AND HEALTH STATUS

Juggling school, family, and job responsibilities is common among non-traditional students. It is the rare older student who comes to the college or university without financial demands to maintain his/her family, continue a job, and attend school part-time. The major demands placed on students with families are lack of reasonably priced child care and inflexibility of class schedules resulting in inability to complete required courses due to work schedules.[4] Most studies find that students contending with the challenges associated with juggling school re-entry, work, and family considerations do exceedingly well.

Marital status, single-parent families, and parenthood (motherhood and fatherhood) have profound effects on the quantity of time available for studies. A comparison of the levels of stress among re-entry women students (ages 26 to 66 years; mean 36.2 years) with traditional college women (ages 18 to 29 years; mean 20.9 years) showed that although re-entry women experienced significantly more time constraints, they had less stress in the academic arena and fewer stress-related symptoms than did the traditional younger women.[13] There were no significant differences between the two groups on self-reports of overall health, energy, and spirits.

Marital status,[14] economic forces,[15,16] and parenthood[4] can be driving forces for self-improvement[17] and higher self-esteem.[14] These forces may affect career aspirations and advancement positively; contribute to increased marital happiness;[14,18,19] and lead to closer relationships with children.[19] Self-improvement, hope of improved job satisfaction, and anticipated completion of a challenge (the academic degree) all contribute to the positive attitude that a parent-as-student experiences.[4]

A comparison of 106 middle-aged student (outwardly oriented) and nonstudent (home-oriented) women on attitudes toward age, perceived happiness and satisfaction, perceived physical health, number and severity of depressive symptoms, self-esteem and autonomy revealed that the student group reported better health, fewer and less severe depressive symptoms, and higher autonomy than did those in the nonstudent group.[20] This study is supported with additional findings, which conclude that those older women aged 50 to 73 who have found a channel for the development of self, in this case through university studies, feel healthier both mentally and physically.[21]

One of the most comprehensive studies on re-entry women and their problems is entitled "Student Support Services: Re-entry Women Need Them Too" prepared in 1980 for the Association of American Colleges – Project on the Status of Women.[22] This national look at the barriers re-entry women often encounter as they attempt to use college support services points out that student health services often exclude use by part-time or evening students, a problem that persists to this day. Other excellent suggestions about "what the institution can do" to address these problems are included in this document.

## PSYCHOLOGICAL STRESS, ISOLATION, OVERCROWDING, AND THE DISTURBED STUDENT

The isolation and adjustment problems of spouses and families of international students are acknowledged[23] but there is little reported in the literature of the impact that this has on health. These students are often poor by U.S. standards, and, based on federal rulings, visa-holding students and their families are not eligible for the "safety net" programs such as Medicaid, or other governmental support for perinatal or pediatric care. Health insurance plans exist but are costly by the foreign students' standards. Many come from countries where there is national health insurance. Others come from countries where fee-for-service visits are set in proportion to the wages of the student-family rather than on prevailing community standards.

Campus student affairs and counseling personnel generally agree that the number of students with serious mental health problems is on the rise.[24] In California, it is not uncommon to encounter students who are being advised by vocational rehabilitation workers to "return to school" as a part of their rehabilitation process. Sometimes this plan is implemented because the individual is too unstable to maintain a job. Once they are on campus, these students often require intensive help from many student service offices. This group is disproportionately represented among those who cannot repay their financial aid loans. After their attempt at a college career they may apply for permanent disability and as a result apply to have their financial responsibilities waived. This often draws student health personnel into the process of making decisions about health and functional status. Careful coordination must occur between the health center and financial aid personnel to assure that each student's loan responsibility is considered individually, and that appropriate consideration is given to the student's needs, current vs permanent difficulties, and the institution's financial obligations to the lender for loan repayment.

As a result of the "baby boomlette" that caused enrollments to peak in the early 1980s, many public universities are finding that the demands on classrooms, faculty, student services, and funds exceed the availability of resources. Students sit on the floor in large classes. Lines for registration, meals, and library use are long. Student services offices are understaffed in comparison to the numbers requiring services. Although some of the best teaching can occur in informal settings[25,7] the availability of faculty for such informal time is limited. This is stressful for all persons involved – students, staff, and faculty.

## GEOGRAPHIC MOBILITY AND STRESS

Geographic mobility is a given in the U.S. One-fourth of college students will move during their college career.[26] Students who have completed some of their higher education in one location inevitably face difficulties in the admission process when they move to another locale. It is complicated to obtain credit for previously taken subjects, some of which have changed tremendously over the years, especially in the sciences. Older students may request "life-experience credit"[14] but universities have been slow to respond. A proposal has been made to create, at the national level, a computer-based counseling and guidance system (based in local libraries) that would provide counselor and learner with current and accurate information at their fingertips about all post-secondary educational opportunities for which the learner might qualify.[26]

It is believed that the consequences of mobility and its effect on transferability costs students on average an extra year to attain a degree. This is a year without wages, a year's more tuition, unavoidable postponement of career plans, a 20 percent increase in overall costs, and additional debt. The stress that surrounds degree attainment includes anger aimed at the institution because students may feel that they cannot get accurate academic advisement. This is a reason students often present to a variety of student services offices, including the student health center.

# IMPLICATIONS AND AGENDA FOR THE FUTURE

The foregoing illustrates that student health service staff must be sensitive to a complex set of current administrative, economic, and social issues. This is in addition to the expectation that a broader range of clinical services must be offered different from a decade ago. The challenge to serve equitably the non-traditional population in the year 2000 and beyond will be more complex, as 50 percent of the overall enrollment in higher education will be over the age of 25.

What are the implications for the day-to-day duties of student health professionals? Health center staff who acknowledge the stresses facing university students can advocate for their needs within the university, to faculty and administrators, planners and legislators. They can be brokers of care for students between outside facilities and other sources of medical care. They can influence the type and cost of the health insurance plan that the university selects. They can acknowledge the time constraints of students and attend to their medical needs while being mindful of these constraints. They can diminish the "red tape" regarding health requirements such as how to comply with matriculation requirements for adult students. They can attempt to include spousal and dependent coverage or services where possible to help conserve students' financial and emotional resources.

Because of changing demographics, medical personnel should consider whether it is appropriate to re-evaluate the need for and types of pre-enrollment medical documents. These might include pre-identification of a primary source of medical care for older students, a list of medical problems and medications in case of emergency, and an update of adult immunizations.

Health service personnel will certainly find themselves referring a larger percentage of students to community resources as the population becomes more varied. Thus, systematic methods of referral, follow-up, and plans about how to cooperate in the care of referred students will help the student maintain a sense of attachment and continuity with the student health center.

That a majority of students in higher education by the year 2000 will be older than 25 has significant implications for the issue of health insurance. Traditionally, college students have been covered by a family health insurance plan until age 23. For those with coverage, financial resources to solve major medical problems did not present a serious problem. At San Francisco State University in 1989 a student mail survey[27] was conducted to define more precisely the health insurance needs and current coverage of students. Among a student body of approximately 30,000 (50 percent minorities; 23 the average age of undergraduates) it was shown that 26 percent of all students did not have any type of health coverage. In the 23 to 25 age group, the percentage was 38. It is worth noting that 59 percent of all students felt they could pay $200 or less for an annual premium and 7 percent felt they could not pay anything for health insurance.

A national survey conducted by the Employee Benefit Research Institute demonstrated that between 18 and 24 percent of college students do not have health insurance. When extrapolated, this suggests that approximately 3 million of the 34 million uninsured in this country in 1989 are students.[28] The challenge to the student health service is to ensure that the plan sponsored on campus is responsive and appropriate to the student population and its needs. Referral of students with major acute and chronic care needs are more costly if health insurance coverage is not universal and/or mandatory for all enrolled students.

Student schedules, with the demands of work, school and family, should influence the design, operation, and staffing of health centers. Plans for accommodating evening students and commuters, utilization of personnel who have experience treating adults and not just youth, revisions in the formulary to include medications needed by an older age group, mandating CPR training, and acquiring appropriate equipment may all be necessitated by the attendance of "non-traditional students" on the university campus.

Finally, changing enrollment patterns have implications for the development of new therapeutic strategies and the creation of appropriate group supports and services. Programming aimed at student-parents; "significant others" dealing with fatal diseases of loved ones or themselves; mid-life crises due to separation, divorce, or death; racism; homophobia; career change; re-entry; changing roles of women and men; addictions of all kinds; and "fear of success" issues may all be necessary. And may consequently serve students better than ever before.

## REFERENCES

1. National Education Association: The 1989 Almanac of Higher Education, 1989, pp 6, 43

2. Cross KP: Telephone Communication, October 1990

3. Commission on Non-Traditional Study: Diversity by Design. San Francisco, CA, Jossey-Bass, 1973

4. St. Pierre S: Understanding the non-traditional female student. NASPA Journal, 26-227, Spring 1989

5. Erikson E: Identity, Youth and Crisis. New York, Norton, 1968

6. Bloom B: Psychological Stress in the Campus Community—Theory, Research and Action. New York, Behavioral Publications, 1975

7. Astin A: Four Critical Years: Effects of College on Beliefs, Attitudes, and Knowledge. San Francisco, CA, Jossey-Bass, 1977

8. Chickering AW: Commuter versus Resident Students. San Francisco, CA, Jossey-Bass, 1974

9. Smith BM: The personal development of the commuter student: What is known from the comparisons with resident students? An ERIC Review. Community College Review, 17(1)-47, Summer 1989

10. Pascarella ET: Reassessing the effects of living on campus versus commuting to college: A casual modeling approach. Review of Higher Education, 7- 247, 1984

11. Barclay AM, Crano WD, Thornton C et al: To a Certain Degree: A Guide to Contemporary College Life. New York, Behavioral Publications, 1972

12. London H: Breaking away: A study of first-generation college students and their families. Am J Educ 97:144-170, February 1989

13. Jacobi M: Stress among Re-entry Women Students: A Contextual Approach. Association for the Study of Higher Education (Conference Paper) February 1987

14. Brandenburg JB: The needs of women returning to school. Personnel and Guidance J 53-11, 1974

15. Adelstein D, Sedlacek WE, Martinez A: Dimensions underlying the characteristics and needs of returning women students. J National Association for Women Deans, Administrators, and Counselors 47-32, 1983

16. Clayton DE, Smith MM: Motivational typology of reentry women. Adult Educ Q 37(2)-90, 1987

17. Lamb-Porterfield P, Jones CH, McDaniel ML: A needs assessment of reentry women at Arkansas State University. College Student J 21(3)-222, 1987

18. Roehl JE, Okun, MA: Depression symptoms among women reentering college: The role of negative life events and family social support. J College Student Personnel 25 (3), 251, 1984

19. Spreadbury C: Family adjustment when adult women return to school. J National Association for Women Deans, Administrators, and Counselors 47-26, 1983

20. Hooper JO, Traupmann JA: Older women, the student role and mental health. Educational Gerontology 9-233, 1983

21. Traupmann J: Mid-life Women in Continuing Education: A Comparative Study. American Education Research Association (Conference Paper), March 1982

22. Creange R: Student Support Services: Re-entry Women Need Them Too. (Field Evaluation Draft.) Association of American Colleges, Project on the Status and Education of Women, October 1980

23. Vogel SH: Toward understanding the adjustment problems of foreign families in the college community: The case of Japanese wives at the Harvard University health services. J Am Coll Health 34-274, 1986

24. Hoffman F, Mastrianni X: The mentally ill student on campus: Theory and practice. J Am Coll Health 38(1)-15, July 1989

25. Wilson R, Gaff J, Dienst E et al: College Professors and Their Impact on Students. New York, John Wiley & Sons, 1975

26. Wilson R: Toward a national counseling system in lifelong learners, A New Clientele for Higher Education. Edited by D Vermilye. San Francisco, CA, Jossey-Bass Publishers, 1974, pp 108-112

27. Public Research Institute: Student Health Care Survey. San Francisco State University, August 1989

28. Collison MN-K: Officials warn of a crisis in student health insurance as medical costs soar and companies revise policies. The Chronicle of Higher Educ, June 7, 1989, p A31

# 26

# Unique Health Care Needs of Health Sciences Students

## Wylie C. Hembree, MD

Health Science students are a unique group requiring routine primary care services, a high level of specialty care, and special preventive services occasioned by their identity as health care workers. To insure safe and effective pursuit of learning in a health care setting, a very high rate of utilization is required, while proximity to and within the health care system engenders expectations of "high tech" and high cost utilization. These students are older than most student populations, although colleges and universities with large graduate programs share in part the age profile of this population. Funding and access to health care outside the educational environment is limited since most can neither maintain coverage on parents' plans nor can they afford independent coverage. The true uniqueness of these students is defined by three factors:

1. Health care risks occasioned by contact with patients within an active health care system;

2. Perception of needs for health care that is often magnified in a complex manner by: a) exposure to a curriculum comprised of medical knowledge, and b) the process of transition from layman to health care professional; and,

3. Increased frequency of personal or family health problems that may have occasioned the career choice of a health care profession.

This third factor has yet to be verified because of lack of access to an age-matched and socioeconomically matched database for comparison. The only data that may support the importance of this factor are derived from health certificates completed by more than 75 percent of students prior to registration; 30 percent have histories of significant hospitalizations and/or chronic medical problems. The first two factors have been well established over the past decade by a careful analysis provided by our own Computer-assisted Utilization Study (CAUS).[1,2] This system has made it possible to develop a continuing database of health care needs and problems, real and perceived, of the students on the Health Sciences Campus of Columbia University and of the patterns of clinical behavior exhibited by students and providers utilizing the program of services available.

## GENERAL ISSUES

### DEMOGRAPHY OF HEALTH SCIENCE STUDENTS

Health sciences students are those whose education either: 1) requires direct patient contact; or 2) occurs primarily within a health care setting and/or may be associated with exposure to personnel, blood, and tissues derived from a health care setting. Nationally, there are more than 400,000 graduate and undergraduate students who fall into this category. This population includes not only medical, nursing, and dental students but also research and allied health professionals (Table 1, next page). Data are incomplete regarding the demographics of these students but include roughly equal numbers of men and women, primarily 20 to 40 years of age, with wide variation in the gender, racial, and ethnic distribution in each school.

The health sciences student body at most university medical centers consists of medical, dental and nursing students; students from the schools of public health, occupational and physical therapy, dental hygiene, graduate nursing and dentistry; graduate students in arts and sciences on the health sciences campus (e.g., biochemistry, genetics, microbiology); and often post-doctoral fellows. Most other health sciences students attend schools that are not physically associated with hospitals or medical centers.[3]

### HEALTH SERVICE PROGRAM ISSUES

The Association of American Medical Colleges' (AAMC) Committee on Student Affairs recently completed a summary of Health Policy and Health Care Services for Medical Students, to which 62 percent of schools responded.[4] Review of the responses makes it clear that there is no uniform approach to the structure or content of a program of health care services for these students or to the funding of the services provided. Only 50 percent have a health service available at the medical school and only one-third of the schools provide services for other health sciences students (e.g., dental and nursing students). Those health sciences schools in which the majority of health sciences students are enrolled are not affiliated with hospitals or universities with student health services. Only 12 percent of allied health professional students are affiliated with an academic health center or medical school and only 20 percent with a 4-year college or university. In New York City, less than 25 percent of nursing students have access to a student health service. Thus, as few as 20 percent of students who have regular patient contact during their professional education have access to health care services that are designed to meet the unique health care needs of health providers. An examination of health care services and health insurance programs for undergraduates found similar inconsistencies among four-year colleges and universities.[5]

Table 1

Health Science Students

| Category | # Students Enrolled | Percent Men | Percent Women |
|---|---|---|---|
| Medicine[1] | 65,000 | 64 | 36 |
| Graduate Students[1] | 18,000 | | |
| Postdoctoral[1] | 5,622 | | |
| Dental[2] | 16,412 | 68 | 32 |
| Public Health[3] | 3,200 | | |
| Nursing (RN)[4] | 182,947 | 12 | 88 |
| Nursing (LPN)[4] | 30,313 | 4 | 96 |
| Occupational Therapy[5] | 8,013 | 8 | 92 |
| Physical Therapy[6] | 6,000 | | |
| Osteopathy[7] | 8,661 | 70 | 30 |
| Social Worker[8] | 9,500 | 17 | 83 |
| Dental Hygiene[9] | 8,073 | | |
| Music Therapy[10] | 3,209 | | |
| Allied Health Professionals[11] | 79,576 | 25 | 75 |

1. Jonas HS, Etzel SI, Barzansky B: Undergraduate Medical Education. JAMA 264:801, 1990
2. American Association of Dental Schools Enrollment Survey, 1990
3. Association of Schools of Public Health, Letter #512, December 9, 1988
4. American Nurses Association: Nursing, Data Review, 1988; Nursing Student Census, 1989
5. 1990 Education Data Survey, The American Occupational Therapy Association
6. American Physical Therapy Association
7. American Osteopathic Association
8. National Association of Social Workers
9. Dental Hygiene Education Programs, American Dental Hygienists Association.
10. National Association Music Therapy Students Enrolled Academic Year 1989-1990
11. Gupta GC, Hedrick HL: Allied Health Education and Accreditation. JAMA 262:843, 1990

Financing of health services for medical students exhibited a non-uniform pattern, despite recommendations to the contrary.[4,6] Two-thirds of medical schools require health insurance, but outpatient mental health services are covered in only 50 percent; a similar number require hospitalization insurance and only one-third provide complete coverage for physician and hospital charges and/or for medication. The annual cost for each student varies with the number of services covered, but usually ranges between $200 and $600 annually.

## GENERAL HEALTH CARE ISSUES

There are no comprehensive studies that analyze health care needs or health care services utilization for health sciences students. Health care problems fall into three categories: 1) those determined alone by the age, sex, and socioeconomic characteristics of health sciences students; 2) those uniquely occasioned by their educational program; and 3) those that occur because a high level of exposure to information about diagnosis, treatment, and prevention of illness.

Health care needs that are uniquely occasioned by being a health science student include those designed to prevent nosocomial illnesses, to prevent illnesses acquired during patient care,[7,8] to diagnose and treat psychiatric disorders associated with professionalization,[9,10] to recognize and prevent dependency disorders[11,12] and to learn behaviors that enhance personal health and improve the efficiency and effectiveness of the health care system.

Certification of immunization status and freedom from communicable diseases is required in no more than 75 percent of 90 medical schools responding to the AAMC survey.[4] Tests for tuberculosis and immunity to rubella are required in 75 percent, but hepatitis B serology is required in only 20 percent and hepatitis B immunization in 32 percent. Polio, rubeola, and mumps immunity requirements range from 51 to 59 percent and HIV antibody tests are required in only one school. These tests and immunization are paid for by students in 56 percent of the schools, while only 26 percent of the schools reported paying for these services. New York state law requires that all health care workers, including students, exhibit no abnormal physical findings the reasons for which could impair their ability to perform their required duties and interact safely with patients; demonstrate immunity to rubella, rubeola, and mumps; and have no contagious illness, especially tuberculosis. Federal law prevents discrimination based on health during the admissions process, making it impossible to require pre-matriculation proof of immunity or absence of illness. However, recent changes in New York state regulations include rubeola testing for all students, in 1991 requiring proof of immunity for admission to colleges or universities.

There is little information available to health services or in the literature about the extent, range, and type of psychiatric services required by health sciences students. Students rarely present to a psychiatric service with complaints of drug and/or alcohol dependency. For this reason, many medical schools have initiated independent programs for the recognition and treatment of impairment due to substance abuse.[12,13,14] More than 20 medical schools currently have "impaired medical student" programs, each of which has identified between 10 and 20 students. The goal of these programs is the early detection and treatment of substance abuse and dependency among students before the problem jeopardizes their education and careers. If chemical dependency affects 10 to 12 percent of the general population and is, in fact, higher among health sciences professionals, additional services and studies are needed.

## EXPOSURE TO INFECTIONS

For the health science student population perhaps the health care problems that present the greatest challenge and opportunity are those related to real or potential occupational exposure to infectious disease, especially to patients with HIV, hepatitis B and tuberculosis infections. The greatest risk to the student exposed to blood or body fluids of an infected patient is that from viral hepatitis, especially hepatitis B.[15] The risk of this exposure can be virtually eliminated by requiring demonstration of immunity of all health care workers, especially those performing invasive procedures, oral procedures, phlebotomy, or handling body fluids in the clinic or in the laboratory.

Students who experience parenteral or non-parenteral HIV exposure must have available immediate access to someone knowledgeable about the risks, who can guide the student in the analysis of his/her own risk, provide data regarding the potential efficacy of prophylactic AZT and, when appropriate, be able to initiate AZT treatment promptly. The most widely published rate of seroconversion after parenteral exposure from an HIV-positive patient's blood is 0.4 percent[16,17] and, recently, the risk from non-parenteral exposure is 0.02-0.04 percent.[18] Data suggesting the efficacy of AZT in preventing this seroconversion (infection) rate are derived from a limited number of animal studies, while published anecdotes concerning large parenteral exposures in humans have failed to demonstrate efficacy.[19] Nevertheless, following clear parenteral exposure to blood from a patient known to have HIV infection, it remains difficult to reject the potential benefit of prophylactic AZT in healthy individuals when the acute side effects are minimal. When barriers to taking AZT use (cost, counseling, reporting procedures, loss of confidentiality) are minimized, medical students opt for treatment in high frequency, while house officers and staff health care workers choose to take AZT at a lesser frequency.

Health services should urge students reporting occupational exposure to document their current state of health on exam, routine laboratory tests, and serologic testing for viruses frequently found in seriously ill patients. If the source-patient exhibits evidence of hepatitis, immune globulin may be administered. A mechanism must be provided by which the source patient's history can be assessed for possible contagious illness and by which the patient can be testing for HIV antibodies. This is often difficult but crucial in the outpatient setting, especially in dental clinics. Counseling and appropriate follow-up must be provided, even if the student elects no AZT treatment. Clinicians familiar with acute manifestations of HIV infection must be available to students within the first 3-6 months following an exposure and advice should be given regarding appropriate measures to prevent HIV transmission until lack of seroconversion can be demonstrated. Recent discussions regarding the risk of HIV transmission from health care provider to patient emphasize the need for informed and enlightened counseling, as well as for measures to assure confidentially.[20,21] Under-reporting of clinical exposures is as high as 50 percent and many health care workers who seroconvert cannot recall specific incidents probably responsible for their infection.[22] Highly visible information about the highly invisible (confidential) but easily accessible procedure all students should follow in the event of occupational exposure will increase reporting and reduce physical and psychological morbidity. Universal precautions and vigorous education efforts will reduce non-parenteral exposures and, in students, perhaps parenteral exposures.[23,24] The potential adverse effects of a needle stick upon learning, professionalization, and career choices seem obvious,[25,26] but the actual impact is undocumented.

Finally, exposure to tuberculosis is developing as a renewed problem for health care workers. This phenomenon is associated with the recent increase in HIV infections, and exacerbated by socieconomic and demographic changes in the population and the emergence of strains of this organism resistant to traditional therapy. The Centers for Disease Control guidelines[27] should be monitored closely for current recommendations as to management of and therapy for tuberculosis-exposed students.

## COLUMBIA UNIVERSITY PROGRAM

It is instructive to describe here how we have developed our program at Columbia. Demographic characteristics of health sciences students at Columbia have remained relatively constant over the past ten years. For the year 1989-90, the age distribution of enrolled students had a median of 23 to 25 years for both men and women, with approximately 30 percent falling within this age bracket. Only 10 percent were younger than 22 years old, whereas 30 percent were over 29 years old and 60 students (3 percent) were over 40 years of age. Fifty percent of the total enrolled students are women, although there is large variation among individual schools. This sex distribution is true only for students in the Graduate School of Arts and Sciences; 60 to 64 percent of medical, dental, and postdoctoral students are men and 75 to 88 percent of the nursing, occupational and physical therapy, and graduate nursing students are women. Sixty-three percent of public health students are women. These figures reflect the national picture for health sciences students, to the extent that data are available.[3]

The experience at Columbia, as well as that reported in the literature,[28,29] strongly suggests that health care services that are necessary for health sciences students cannot be addressed adequately only by providing insurance coverage, or access to a health service, or assignment to a managed care program; rather, efforts must be made to target the structure and content of the program specifically for health science students. The program of services for health sciences students at Columbia University has been designed to meet those health care needs that arise during or because of their educational program. The goal is to deliver efficient, accessible, high-quality medical care, without undue financial burden, preventing and treating health problems that might interfere with a student's educational and professional goals while attending Columbia University/Health Sciences Campus. Only those services approved by and coordinated through the student health service are covered. Exclusion criteria are based on the impact of the medical condition upon the patient's studenthood. The program does not include a dental plan, although an optional one is available. A fee of $500 covers complete medical and psychiatric outpatient costs and inpatient professional costs, while a $450 University-based Blue Cross hospitalization policy covers emergency room care and inpatient hospital charges.

Since 1973, Columbia Health Science campus has provided confidential psychiatric care within its program of services. Fifteen visits are covered and the average number of visits/student has ranged between eight and ten for the past decade. The utilization rate has remained constant at 10 percent with the utilization by women being three-fold higher than that of men. One-third of students seen by staff psychiatrists are referred for extended treatment after 15 visits. School-related problems occasion 40 percent of the service use, with Mixed Personality Disorders accounting for 70 percent of the diagnoses assigned. As has been reported by others, the majority of students report that the reasons for psychiatric visits are occasioned by interpersonal problems.[30] There are four to six psychiatric hospital admissions annually and there have been no deaths by suicide.

At Columbia, the AIMS Program (Assistance for the Impaired Medical Student) is now in its fourth year, staffed entirely outside the Health Service and Office of Student Affairs. The other health sciences schools at Columbia have similar programs.

The full program of services for health sciences students is self-funded, supported entirely by a student health fee set annually by the Board of Governors. This Board also has the responsibility for setting the policies from which the Program of Services is designed. The fee has risen from $210/student in 1980-81 to $500/student in 1990-91. This increase in cost of care can be attributed almost entirely to increases in cost of ancillary services, not an increase in number or type of medical problems, nor in the number of encounters, nor in physician payments. As is true for most health care systems, the cost of services among students has been driven up by increases in cost of new medical technologies (e.g., CT scans, MRIs) and medications. The health care system's response to AIDS and related illnesses has heightened expectations and increased the University's awareness of its liability to protect the health of students educated within a health care setting. Thus, preventive and educational services have been added to the Program.

Since 1981, we have been engaged in a Computer-assisted Utilization Study (CAUS) designed to define an appropriate program of services and to analyze its clinical adequacy and costs. Data sources are registration cards, health certificates completed by students and their physicians prior to matriculation, encounter forms for each visit to the central facility, referral forms and consultation forms for panel physicians outside the facility and coded registration cards for psychiatric visits. For each patient care visit, the data are captured in fields for date and time, provider(s), the reason for the visit, diagnoses, procedures, laboratory tests, x-rays, medications, consultations, and dispositions recorded on the encounters forms. To define whether the program adequately meets the needs of health sciences students and to define their health care needs more precisely, we have relied upon analyses of the CAUS database. The software integrates five distinct databases: 1) enrollment - including demographic data; 2) encounters for each patient care visit; 3) laboratory results; 4) referrals to specialists; and 5) psychiatric visits.

Utilization varies by school and by sex, but does not correlate with age of the student. The average number of visits/student is six to seven annually, with 15 percent having more than 15 encounters/year. More than 80 percent of the students utilize the service at least once during the academic year, with the proportional utilization varying among schools. Virtually 100 percent of the medical and dental students utilize the service, while 75 to 80 percent of graduate students and only 60 percent of dependents are seen. The temporal pattern of utilization annually is the same for all schools. Among the total numbers of students seen during the academic year (September 1 through August 31), 75 percent visit the facility for the first time within the first four months.

Outpatient services for Columbia's Health Sciences Campus Student Health Program have been delivered through a facility located in the principal dormitory complex. Students have access to primary care services at the facility on both walk-in and appointment bases. Providers in the facility are internists, nurses, nurse practitioners, nurse midwives, gynecologists, and orthopedists. Annually, there are 10,000 to 12,000 patient visits to the facility with 1500 to 2000 referral visits outside the facility.

An active psychiatry service exists in a separate facility in the same building. Approximately 10 percent of the students occasion 2000 to 2500 psychiatry visits annually. Utilization of psychiatry services varies widely among the schools and from year to year, with women utilizing the services more than men, medical students and public health students having the highest and dental students the lowest rates of psychiatric utilization. These patterns of utilization differ from those at the medical facility. There is no significant difference between the utilization rate of men and women for medical services.

Ancillary services, medications, specialist referrals, and primary care visits are provided at no cost to the student. Physician fees for hospitalization and hospital-based services are also paid in full from the student health program budget. Students are referred only to those physicians who agree to be on the student health panel and to take as payment in full a reduced fee. Each year, more than 300 physicians agree to participate in this panel. The student health allowance is approximately 30 percent of the fees usually charged. Ancillary services are financed by annual contracts with vendors and providers wherever possible.

Utilization of ancillary services varies from year to year and has been found to be more dependent upon the clinical behavior of the providers than upon variations in the diagnostic impressions attributed to patient encounters. The total number of laboratory tests and x-rays varies from year to year, as does the frequency of each diagnostic category. Yet, the number of laboratory tests $(0.55 \pm 0.08)$ or x-rays $(0.04 \pm 0.01)$ ordered **per encounter** is independent of year, utilization, or types of illnesses seen.

High levels of student expectations within a university setting have made cost constraints very difficult. During the 1987-88 academic year, we estimated that $2.5 million in health care services were delivered to 2000 students at a cost of $750,000. Overall, the average patient care visit cost $50, including ancillary services, medications, professional fees, and administrative cost. This encounter cost varied with the type of visit: Psychiatric visits were $67 each, referral visits averaged $40 each, and a medical visit to the student health facility cost $28. Fifty percent of the cost of facility visits was allocated to staff (professional) costs, while laboratory tests (15 percent) medications (15 percent) and x-rays (20 percent) accounted for the remainder.

Unlike most HMOs and managed care programs, the design of services for health sciences students must minimize barriers and provide educational materials that will lower students' threshold for seeking medical care and/or advice. Thus, a high rate of utilization is sought. In a recent random analysis, 119 students generated 331 problems with 800 encounters, or 2.5 encounters/ problem. The number of encounters/problem ranged between 1 and 12. The average number of problems/student treated was 3, while the number of encounters/student was 7. More than 85 percent of the student visits to the facility are "medical encounters," defined as a patient visit at which a diagnosis is made; and/or laboratory tests, x-rays, or consultations are ordered for diagnostic purposes; and/or medications are given to treat a defined problem. Each medical encounter contains a diagnostic code. A modified medical diagnostic coding system, derived from the pathophysiologic groups of the ICD-9 codes, was used. Sixteen diagnostic groups are defined, each of which contains codes for 20 to 30 more or less specific diagnoses. Over 75 percent of the medical encounters occur for conditions in eight pathophysiologic groups: reproductive, infectious disease, dermatology, ENT, orthopedic, urology, health maintenance, and gastroenterology.

A four-year analysis (1983-1987) of the top 15 diagnostic codes demonstrated a high degree of consistency from year to year. The top 15 diagnostic categories each year made up 45 to 59 percent of the total medical encounters. They reflected diagnosis and treatment of primary care problems, including vaginitis, upper respiratory tract infections, dermatitis or rash, acne, sore throat, possible pregnancy, and urinary tract infection. In addition, health maintenance concerns ranked among the top 15, as did routine physical exams and routine gynecology exams. Since 1984, with the advent of hepatitis B vaccine, immunizations have accounted for 8 to 9 percent of the total medical encounters. Musculoskeletal problems ranked in the top 15 due to 200 to 300 encounters annually for orthopedic injuries. More than 300 encounters each year were occasioned by allergy injections.

It is clear that patient education about preventive programs increases the utilization for non-preventive problems. For example, we examined the effect of immunization screening and the availability of the vaccine upon our utilization. Not surprisingly, those who received hepatitis B vaccine had, on average, 3 more encounters than those who did not. The additional encounters, however, were not for hepatitis B vaccine injections alone. When the encounters related to immunization were subtracted, those who elected to have hepatitis B vaccine generated more encounters ($6.2 \pm 0.2$ vs $3.6 \pm 1.0$). Women also had more encounters than men, although the significance was borderline. We also attempted to examine the behavior of women and men with regard to hepatitis B vaccine. Between 30 and 40 percent of the students enrolled in the medical school are women. During the 1984-85 academic year, 95 percent of the women were treated, but only 72 percent of the men. Only 50 percent of the men elected to be tested for hepatitis B antibodies and of those tested, only 38 percent chose to receive the hepatitis B vaccine; by contrast,

82 percent of the women were tested and 62 percent immunized. Based on this analysis, we targeted men of the medical and dental classes, increasing the immunization rate to 84 percent in one year. More recently, over 90 percent of both men and women who see patients during their health science education receive hepatitis B immunization.

The University-based group Blue Cross policy is experience-rated and covers hospitalizations and emergency room visits. The number of non-maternity hospitalizations ranged from 20 to 40, including four to six for psychiatric reasons. There are 20 to 30 childbirths each year with approximately 40 voluntary abortions. Of the annual hospital claims, 60 percent are maternity (20 to 30 newborns), 20 percent minor surgical, 10 percent medical, 5 percent psychiatric, and 5 percent accidents. Recently, ambulatory surgery has accounted for 20 percent of the claims. Orthopedic surgery, usually for repair of injuries, is approved 20 to 25 times annually. Surgery (ENT, gynecologic, and urologic) makes up the remainder of the hospital utilization. There are 75 to 100 emergency room visits each year for sudden and serious illness (40 percent) and accidents (60 percent). These data reflect those of the general population in the same age brackets and there appear to be no unique hospitalization coverage requirements for health sciences students.

## AGENDA FOR THE FUTURE

Health Sciences schools invest far more than tuition income into the education of health professionals. If the obligations, responsibilities, and liabilities implied in this investment are to be met successfully, the students must have easy access to comprehensive health care services. These services must include health education, preventive services, strict confidentiality both for psychiatric problems and for medical problems that may alter their capacity to participate in their educational programs or their career choices, as well as procedures to comply with state and local regulations concerning immunizations and freedom from contagious disease for health care workers. Within university medical centers, it may be possible to provide these services at discounted costs. However, the cost of insurance coverage for these services would be prohibitive. Having defined more precisely the health care needs of health sciences students, it will be necessary to provide, through a national network of health sciences schools, insurance coverage at reduced cost by virtue of a larger pool of shared risks. Health services must also work to provide mechanisms for liability insurance for incidents that may occur during their education in the health care setting, for compensation for occupational (educational) exposure and for disability that may occur as a result of health risks incurred.

The impact of personal illness and personal health risks upon professionalization and career choice must be studied in order to design appropriate health services and curriculum within each school. Greater emphasis must be placed upon the risks to health professionals of substance abuse and drug dependency. Each school must have clear, well-publicized policies regarding not only services available for impaired students, but also, to eliminate barriers to access, the consequences of using these services upon their status within the school. Each school should have an independent policy study group, composed of students and faculty, which recommends to the Administration policies and procedures for students infected with human immunodeficiency virus (HIV), acquired through occupational exposure or by virtue of life-style or medical treatment. Such groups should have available resources that reflect the breadth of the ethical, legal, and economic issues involved.

No national or regional organization exists that collects data, provides information or acts as advocate for the health care of health sciences students. Most parent organizations of the schools for health sciences professionals do not have the resources or mandate to provide these services and those who do, such as the AAMC, represent only a small fraction of students at risk. Failure to address the health issues of health sciences professionals has an obvious negative impact on the public. Health care organizations whose scope extends broadly, such as the American College Health Association, should seek private and public funds to sponsor national networking of health services for health sciences students, to provide computer software that will allow schools to capture data concerning health care needs and their costs for health sciences students and to sponsor research concerning the impact of health care services for students upon professional behavior.

## SUMMARY

Design of a program of services for health sciences students should be determined not only by the real health care needs of this population, but also by policies regarding the appropriate role of the student health service in the transition from layman to health professional. Actual needs can be defined if the program has access to 100 percent of the students and possesses the ability for facile analysis of a database that documents the needs. All patients are made vulnerable to some degree by their reaction to real or perceived illness; health science students are doubly vulnerable as patients because of the professionalization process they are undergoing. When double vulnerability is perceived to be an opportunity for student health providers, as role models and educators, not only are students well treated, but the encounter with the health service may also serve to reinforce and enhance their educational outcome. All too often, when this opportunity is not recognized and incorporated into the policies and goals of a health service program, the impact of personal health care encounters upon students is negative. Such a policy is unique among health care systems and has broad program implications.

Yet, nowhere else in health care is this approach as critical as it is for health science students. If, as student health professionals, we do our job properly in this regard, we could alter the quality and character of the practice of medicine.

# REFERENCES

1. Clark KH, Clark AS, Hembree WC: Analysis of health care assisted by a microcomputer. AAMSI 2:129 1983

2. Hembree WC, Clark AS, Clark KH: Microcomputer-assisted utilization analysis: Changing patterns of health care in a health sciences student health program. SCAMC 6:343 1985

3. Gupta GC, Hedrick HL: Allied health education and accreditation. JAMA 264:843, 1990

4. GSA Committee on Student Affairs, Association of American Medical Colleges: Survey of Health Policies and Health Care Services for Medical Students, 1990

5. Patrick K: Student health: Medical care within institutions of higher education. JAMA 260:3301, 1988

6. McManus M, Brauer M, Weader R et al: The adequacy of college health insurance coverage. J Am Coll Health 39:177, 1991

7. Mast EE, Berg JL, Hanrahan LP et al: Risk factors for measles in a previously vaccinated population and cost-effectiveness of revaccination strategies. JAMA 264:2529, 1990

8. Guidelines for Preventing the Transmission of Tuberculosis in Health-Care Settings, with Special Focus on HIV-related Issues. MMWR 39:1, 1990

9. Sherry S, Notman MT, Nadelson CC et al: Anxiety, depression and menstrual symptoms among freshman medical students. J Clin Psychiatry 49:490, 1988

10. Dickstein JJ, Stephenson JJ, Hinz LD: Psychiatric impairment in medical students. Acad Med 65:588, 1990

11. Forney MA, Ripley WK, Forney PD: A profile and prediction study of problem drinking among first year medical students. Int J Addict 23:767, 1988

12. Baldwin DC, Hughes PH, Conrad SE et al: Substance use among senior medical students: A survey of 23 medical schools. JAMA 265:2074, 1991

13. Coombs RH, Perell K, Ruckh JM: Primary prevention of emotional impairment among medical trainees. Acad Med 65: 576, 1990

14. Schwartz RH, Lewis DC, Hoffmann NG et al: Cocaine and marijuana use by medical students before and during medical school. Arch Int Med 150:883, 1990

15. Update: Universal precautions for prevention of transmission of human immunodeficiency virus, hepatitis B virus, and other blood-borne pathogens in health-care settings. JAMA 260:462-464, 1988

16. Henderson DK, Fahey BJ, Willy M et al: Risk for occupational transmission of human immunodeficiency virus type 1 (HIV-1) associated with clinical exposures. Ann Int Med 113:740, 1990

17. White AC, Miller SM: HIV infection after needlesticks. Ann Int Med 114:253-254, 1991

18. Fahey BJ, Koziol DE, Banks SM et al: Frequency of non-parenteral occupational exposures to blood and body fluids before and after universal precautions training. Am J Med 90:145, 1991

19. Public Health Service Statement on Management of Occupational Exposure to Human Immunodeficiency Virus, Including Considerations Regarding Zidovudine Postexposure Use. U.S. Dept of Health and Human Services Public Health Service: CDC MMWR 39: 1990

20. Mishu B, Schaffner W, Horan JM et al: A surgeon with AIDS. JAMA 264:467, 1990

21. Gilbert B, Bleecker T, Miyasaki C et al: Possible health care professional-to-patient HIV transmission. JAMA 265:1845, 1990

22. Tandberg D, Stewart KK, Doezema D: Under-reporting of contaminated needlestick injuries in emergency health care workers. Ann Emer Medicine 20:66-70, 1991

23. Klein RS: Universal precautions for preventing occupational exposures to human immunodeficiency virus type 1. Am J Med 90:41, 1991

24. Wong ES, Stotka JL et al: Are universal precautions effective in reducing the number of occupational exposures among health care workers? JAMA 265:1123-1128, 1991

25. Simmonds AC, Robbins J, Brinker MR et al: Factors important to students in selecting a residency program. Academic Medicine 65:640, 1990

26. Ness R, Killian CD, Ness Ed et al: Likelihood of contact with AIDS patients as a factor in medical students' residency selections. Acad Med 64:588, 1989

27. The Use of Preventive Therapy for Tuberculosis Infection in the United States. MMWR 39:9-12, 1990

28. DeArmond M, Bridwell MW et al: College health toward the year 2000. J Am Coll Health, 39:249, 1991

29. Parkerson GR, Broadhead WE, Tse CKJ: The health status and life satisfaction of first-year medical students. Academic Medicine, 586-587, 1990

30. Golinger RC et al: Reasons that medical students seek psychiatric assistance. Acad Med 66:121-122, 1991

# 27

# Intercollegiate Athletes

RICHARD STRAUSS, MD

## POPULATION

Intercollegiate athletes represent a small but visible segment of the student population of most colleges and universities. The number of intercollegiate, or varsity, teams supported by a university can vary from two or three at a small college to 30 at a large university. In addition, some universities lend modest support, such as the use of facilities, to "club" sports that compete against clubs at other universities. Also, intramural sports participation is encouraged at most universities to allow students within the university to participate in sports with their peers.

Both men and women at all levels are involved, with the exception of a small number of single-sex colleges. Federal legislation (Title IX) promotes the access of women to athletic facilities and funding. However, at most universities the number of men involved in collegiate athletics is greater than the number of women.

## ROLE OF THE STUDENT HEALTH SERVICE

The student-athlete has the same access to the student health service that general students have. At some small universities, no additional services may be available to competing athletes. However, one or more physicians may have a particular interest in sports medicine, and athletes tend to gravitate toward such individuals for their care.

At large universities, the athletic department usually assumes the responsibility for making certain additional medical services available to intercollegiate athletes because of their risk of injury during athletic participation. The athletic department often contracts with a group of physicians or with individual physicians to provide care for the athletes. This process may be politicized because teams such as football and basketball are not only highly visible in the community but also may be prominent nationally and may generate large sums of money that support the athletic department and the other intercollegiate sports.

The care of athletic injuries may be contracted to a group of orthopedists or primary physicians in private practice or associated with the university's medical school. In this case, the student health service sees little of the injured athlete but often cares for the medical (nontraumatic) problems such as infectious diseases. Alternatively, the athletic department may reimburse the student health service for extra surgical and medical services required by intercollegiate athletes.

## ROLE OF THE TEAM PHYSICIAN

Since the doctor is paid directly or indirectly by the athletic department but treats the athlete, where do priorities lie? The answer is clear, both legally and ethically: the doctor's first concern must be for the patient. In other words, the coach does not practice medicine and the doctor is not an assistant coach.

However, the practice of sports medicine sometimes requires compromises as compared to a more standard practice of medicine. That is, after an injury or illness, the athlete is highly motivated to return to practice and competition as soon as possible. An average patient with a sprained ankle is often happy to avoid strenuous activity involving the ankle for many weeks or even months. In contrast, the athlete wants to be back in action within days. The sports physician implicitly agrees to use all reasonable methods to help the athlete return as soon as possible. This generally means getting the athlete back into participation as soon as his or her performance permits, with the minimization – but not elimination – of possible further injury to the sprained ankle. For example, an athlete with a sprained ankle can return to running or jumping while wearing an "air cast" so that the normal motion of the ankle is allowed but lateral bending in an abnormal fashion is prevented.

Most athletes choose to attend classes even if prevented by injury or illness from participating in practice.[1] On rare occasions, an athlete will attend practice but want a note excusing him or her from a particular class activity; that policy is inconsistent with university goals.

Athletic trainers are paramedical personnel who have been trained to work with athletes. They attend many practices and games at which physicians may or may not be available. Thus, athletic trainers become the initial medical contact for athletes in systems large enough to support their services. The athletic trainer usually screens and cares for minor injuries and refers more significant injuries and medical problems to physicians either on site or at another medical facility. Athletic trainers began years ago as individuals who performed ankle taping. Now, however, the certified athletic trainer is college-educated and has passed an examination covering the skills required in athletic training.

## STRESSES ON THE STUDENT-ATHLETE

Many of the stresses associated with studying and athletic participation revolve around the limited time available to complete a multitude of activities. A major question is, what are the student's long-term goals? If these are not clear, which is frequently the case, the athlete may stress the immediate demands of athletic participation and let academics slide. Many athletic departments employ academic counselors to help monitor the student's academic progress and advise on specific academic problems.

In addition to academic requirements, the athlete is faced with large blocks of time being used for one or more practices each day, for competition, and for travel. Physical demands are such that even if the athlete is uninjured, practices may be physically exhausting and may diminish motivation for studying in the evening. Psychologically, the student-athlete is encouraged to do well both academically and in his or her sport. The conflict may be considerable.

Finances can also be a problem. Some athletes get scholarships, either partial or full. Scholarship athletes are frequently prohibited from additional employment in order to discourage overcommitment of time. However, athletes not on scholarships may need to work for pay in order to remain in school, depending on family finances.

The above-mentioned time constraints may leave little additional time available for social activities, and friends may be drawn primarily from among teammates. Still, most athletes find free time to socialize, sometimes to the detriment of studies. The traditional song that suggests, "You've got to be a football hero, to get along with the beautiful girls..." emphasizes social opportunities available to athletes.

Lowest in priority appears to be time for sleep. This occasionally results in students who are too exhausted to perform decently either academically or in their sport.

## DISTRIBUTION OF RESOURCES

Some athletic departments pay part or all of the medical care required for injuries that result directly from athletic participation. Beyond that, the student's own resources or health insurance are necessary to finance health care. Athletic department training rooms and sports medicine clinics are generally accessible to all intercollegiate athletes. Athletic trainers are often in attendance or readily available at practices and competitions.

Physicians sometimes drop in for certain practices and attend some competitions. Which games a physician attends often depends on the amount of injury anticipated in that sport, the public visibility of the sport, and the personal interest of the physician. Thus, football games, with a high injury rate and high public visibility, are almost always attended by one or more physicians at the college level. Basketball games have a relatively low incidence of injury, but because of high visibility and interest, are frequently attended by a physician. In contrast, lacrosse and field hockey games are less often attended by physicians.

## DELIVERY OF MEDICAL CARE

Sites of medical care often include training rooms, the student health service, and the office of a private physician or surgeon, all of which have their own sets of medical records. This may present a challenge in terms of coordinating the medical care of a given athlete. Needless to say, communication among the various physicians is important.

Injuries are often first brought to the attention of an athletic trainer. If the injury is significant, the patient is seen by a physician for diagnosis and a treatment plan. Rehabilitation is often supervised by athletic trainers, some of whom are registered physical therapists.

Athletes are highly motivated to return to activity as quickly as possible. In general, this rapid return is facilitated by daily rehabilitation and re-evaluation. Frequently, the athlete must be restrained from returning to activity too soon for his or her own good. That is, the athlete may feel well enough to jump into full activity after a few days of recuperation. However, the physician is wise to advise repeated strength or other testing to assure that the athlete has recovered sufficiently in order to avoid further damage to a weakened structure. The majority of sports injuries can be handled by a primary physician who is experienced in sports medicine. Orthopedic consultation is required when injuries are serious or may require surgical intervention.

Illnesses are largely the same as those affecting the general student population. However, they may interfere with physical performance and the athlete may be better off excused from practice to facilitate recovery. In addition, certain sport-specific problems exist. For example, the individual with infectious mononucleosis should remain out of contact sports until the spleen shows no sign of enlargement. Swimmer's ear (otitis externa) usually can be treated or prevented without having the competitive swimmer lose any practice time. Skin problems from abrasion, sweating, or infection are common in football and wrestling. Menstrual irregularities are frequent among women participating in track.

Keeping weight under control is frequently a concern for female gymnasts and male wrestlers, as well as in other sports. These concerns may lead to eating disorders, more frequently among women than men. Their resolution may require consultation with the coach, a dietitian, and a psychologist.

Overtraining can occur from the extended physical and emotional demands of practice. The overtrained individual's performance diminishes and the question of an underlying illness sometimes brings the athlete to the physician. The identification of the overtraining syndrome is rarely clear-cut. However, several days of diminished or no practice are frequently curative.

Psychological consultation can be helpful in cases of emotional stress stemming from academic, social, or athletic performance problems or crises. In addition, a sports psychologist may assist in improving performance by optimizing attention levels, using imaging techniques, or enhancing relaxation.

Both physical demands and personality traits may differ considerably from sport to sport. For example, a mild wrist sprain will cause no problem to a football lineman but may well incapacitate a gymnast.

## COMMUNICATION

The physician's ability to communicate with the patient is of utmost importance. This is generally easy to accomplish because the patients are anxious to get better and tend to pay attention to instructions that help them achieve this goal. In addition, physicians who work in sports medicine are usually interested in sports and physical activity and tend to develop rapport with their patients.

As mentioned above, communication with other physicians who are acting as consultants or primary physicians is important in order to keep care optimal and consistent, as well as to avoid confusing the patient with differing instructions.

The diagnosis and plan of treatment must be communicated clearly to the athletic trainer working with the patient because the trainer frequently has the responsibility of assuring that the athlete-patient carries out medical instructions and returns to practice in a manner that is consistent with good medical care. The athletic trainer frequently communicates the medical plan to the coach so that he or she can make appropriate coaching decisions. The physician may also communicate directly with the coach.

The question of patient privacy versus team planning requirements sometimes arises. The diagnosis and treatment plan for an athletic injury is usually common knowledge within the team and coaching staff. In contrast, sexually transmitted diseases are kept confidential in the medical tradition.

In high-visibility sports such as football, the mass media seek information about the diagnosis and return to participation of the athlete when an injury occurs. Communication with the media is best done through one member of the medical team who is accustomed to dealing with the media. The information to be given out is generally agreed to ahead of time by the patient and the treating physician. In emergency situations, the appropriate physician or representative makes a statement to the press.

## PREVENTIVE MEDICINE

Identifying medical trends within a team on a day-to-day basis is helpful. For example, if shin splints start to occur at about the same time in several athletes on the same team, the coach may be advised of this finding so that he or she can alter running practice. Similarly, eating disorders may cluster within a team, as may certain communicable diseases.

Immunizations against tetanus, measles, mumps, and rubella should be consistent with current national guidelines. Travel by intercollegiate teams is usually restricted to their home country. However, regional epidemics may occur and should be taken into consideration, and any international travel requires planning.

## ALCOHOL AND DRUGS

As with many college students, alcohol is the drug of choice and causes the most problems for the student-athlete. One problem associated with alcohol is that fights may ensue. The relationship between aggressive behavior during games and violence in social situations is unclear. However, it is my impression that athletes in contact or collision sports tend to get into fights in bars more frequently than do noncontact athletes. Athletes appear to use street drugs such as marijuana and cocaine at a level that is no greater than their college peers.

Anabolic-androgenic steroid hormones are male hormones that are used by athletes in an attempt to increase strength and muscle mass. They are used by some male athletes and a smaller number of female athletes. Anabolic steroids are effective in helping to increase strength and muscle mass when used in conjunction with hard physical training and good nutrition.[2] However, they are banned by almost all sports organizations and their presence in urine is tested for by the National Collegiate Athletic Association (NCAA) and by many universities under various sets of rules. Deleterious effects on health include masculinization in women, and diminished testicular production of sperm and testosterone, increased acne, and increased male baldness pattern in men. Gynecomastia occurs in some men. Long-term risks appear to include an increased chance of heart disease and increased risk of liver tumors. Irritability and aggressiveness associated with anabolic steroid use ('roid rage) can lead to disruptive behavior.

## PREPARTICIPATION MEDICAL EXAMINATION

A preparticipation medical examination is performed annually at many universities. Some universities prefer to do a full preparticipation examination when the athlete first enters the system and then to perform an annual medical update. In any case, it is important for the athlete to be in communication with the medical system of the university at least annually at the beginning of the practice season. How to perform a preseason examination and what elements to include are the subject of many review papers and chapters (see Suggested Readings).

One of the purposes of performing a preparticipation examination is to detect the presence of any abnormalities that may be limiting or disqualifying for a given sport. For example, the existence of only one functioning testis is generally considered compatible with noncontact sports but is reason for concern in sports such as football and hockey. Even in these sports, the participant may choose to acknowledge the increased risk of participation and to wear additional protection. Similar problems arise with the absence of one of a paired organ such as the eye. Certain cardiac conditions or abnormalities may be associated with a sufficiently high risk of sudden death that the individual who is affected must be excluded from athletic participation.[3]

## LEGAL ISSUES

The presence of medical risks may lead to considerable conflict between the highly motivated athlete vs the medical consultants and the university. In several cases, the decision has been made by the courts. The tendency in U.S. courts has been to let the athlete make the final decision. However, the question of informed consent becomes a thorny legal issue. The fact that the athlete and parents sign a waiver does not seem to be the final answer.

Given the litigious nature of the United States, sports physicians are concerned about medical liability. As described earlier, the doctor, not the coach or administrators, has the responsibility for assuring the health of the athlete. When several physicians are involved, it should be clear when the primary physician makes the decision and when the consulting specialist is responsible for the decision. Frequently, a consultant will recommend that an athlete be allowed to play or not play. The team physician must then review this recommendation to make sure that it is consistent with the information of which the team physician is aware. The team physician should assure that he is covered by liability insurance when practicing on the field as well as in his usual medical setting.

## REFERENCES

1. Strauss RH, Lanese RR, Leizman DJ: Illness and absence among wrestlers, swimmers, and gymnasts at a large university. Am J Sports Med 16:653-655, 1988

2. Yesalis C, Wright J, Lombardo J: Anabolic-androgenic steroids: A synthesis of existing data and recommendations for future research. Clin Sports Med 1:109-134, 1989

3. Thomas RJ, Cantwell JD: Sudden death during basketball games. Phys Sportsmed 18(5)75-78, 1990

## SUGGESTED READINGS

Collins HR (ed): Office practice of sports medicine. Clinics in Sports Medicine, Vol. 1, Number 3, July 1989. Philadelphia, WB Saunders

Garrick JB, Webb DR: Sports Injuries: Diagnosis and Management. Philadelphia, WB Saunders, 1990

Mellion MB (ed): Office management of Sports Injuries and Athletic Problems. St. Louis, CV Mosby, 1988

Scott WN, Nisonson B, Nicholas JA (eds): Principles of Sports Medicine. Baltimore, Williams & Wilkins, 1984

Ryan AJ, Allman FJ (eds): Sports Medicine (2nd ed). San Diego, Academic Press, 1989

Strauss RH (ed): Sports Medicine (2nd ed). Philadelphia, WB Saunders, 1991

# 28

# Students of the Performing Arts

RALPH MANCHESTER, MD

The performing arts are a significant part of campus life, and students at colleges and universities across the country devote countless hours developing their skills in music, dance, and theater. These students, like professional performers,[1] are at risk for developing a number of performance-related medical problems. For purposes of this chapter, students of the performing arts are considered to be those who are preparing for a career as performing musicians, dancers, or actors. It must be remembered, however, that students studying to become performing arts teachers or who are performing in various extracurricular arts programs may also develop similar problems. According to U.S. Census Bureau data, 200,000 people in this country are professional performers and about 46,000 degrees in the performing and visual arts are awarded each year. Music students can be found in both two- and four-year programs, at smaller institutions that offer only music degrees, and at large universities with music departments or schools.

Students of the performing arts share several common characteristics. In many cases they are required to take a full course load in addition to spending several hours per day in practice and performance. Virtually all of them face an uncertain vocational future with very little chance of job and financial security as performers. Finally, many of them have devoted much of their earlier adolescence to performance-related activities and therefore are likely to be at different stages of psychosocial development compared with their contemporaries. Sexual identity may still be uncertain for some of these students. In short, students of the performing arts are generally under more stress than most other students.

This chapter will review the major performance-related health problems of students who are instrumental musicians, singers, and dancers. Actors have some of the same voice problems as singers.

# INSTRUMENTAL MUSIC STUDENTS

Students who are studying piano, violin, and other instruments are at risk for developing several musculoskeletal and neurologic syndromes as well as a variety of other performance-related medical problems.[2,3] The more common ailments are discussed in this section. Less common problems are covered by the references.[1,2]

The most frequently occurring performance-related medical problems in instrumentalists are the musculoskeletal disorders of the upper extremities. Most of these are repetition strain injuries (also called cumulative trauma disorders), similar to the problems encountered in other occupations, such as keypunch operators, meat packers, and typists. They result from repeated motion of the arm and hand, which overtaxes the capability of the muscle-tendon-ligament structures. Data reported from one school showed 8.5 new cases per 100 students per year.[4] A survey done at an Australian school showed that about 9 percent of the students were affected at any one time.[5] Several studies have shown that women are more frequently affected than are men, and wind instrument players are at lower risk than are string and keyboard players.[4,5] Students present with pain or other symptoms in various parts of the upper extremities. Physical findings are often subtle, but it may be helpful to watch the student play. X-rays and laboratory tests are usually not necessary.

The diagnoses most commonly made are muscle and muscle-tendon overuse, with true tendonitis being less common. Treatment consists of resting the affected structures for a few days, ice followed by heat and occasional use of anti-inflammatory medication. Aspercreme™ was shown to be effective in one study.[6] The outcome is generally quite good, with only one in six showing impairment at one year.[7] Rehabilitation requires the gradual return to playing, with avoidance of any factors that precipitated the problem. Of equal importance is the prevention of these overuse problems; taking breaks frequently during practice, knowing one's own limits, and working closely with one's teacher to develop good technique are all important. Some experts believe that regular exercise may help music students avoid some performance-related problems.

A few other performance-related upper extremity problems of instrumentalists deserve brief mention.[2] Several peripheral neuropathies, including carpal tunnel syndrome, are fairly common for various instruments. In some cases these are also a type of repetition-strain injury. They can take somewhat longer to heal than the muscle-tendon problems. Thoracic outlet syndrome is a controversial entity that may be a fairly common cause of arm and hand symptoms in musicians. Focal dystonia is the general term for writers' cramp, a rare but nearly untreatable problem. Most often seen in keyboard players, this neuromuscular disorder results in one or more fingers flexing into the palm involuntarily as one starts to play. Botulinum toxin injection into the affected muscle has shown some promise in experimental use.

Instrumentalists are also prone to several skin problems resulting from contact with wood, metal, and other substances in their instruments. These have been reviewed recently in the dermatologic literature.[8] Hearing loss due to prolonged exposure to high sound pressure levels has been reported in orchestral as well as rock and jazz musicians.[9] Young musicians should be aware of this phenomenon and avoid noise exposure that could cause significant hearing loss later in life.

In summary, musculoskeletal arm and hand problems are fairly common among instrumental musicians. In addition to those that are brought on by practice, some are due to acute or cumulative trauma in other activities. Most can be managed conservatively in the primary care setting in cooperation with the student's music teacher.

## VOICE STUDENTS

Singers are subject to a variety of problems affecting the sound-producing apparatus. In the broadest sense, this includes the entire body. In this section we will review the most important causes of vocal dysfunction and suggest a clinical approach.[1,10]

Almost any systemic condition can affect the voice. Some of the diseases more frequently seen in young adults include rapid weight gain or loss, diabetes, hormonal changes related to the menstrual cycle and/or oral contraceptive use, and thyroid disease. Many commonly used medications can affect the vocal cords: antihistamines, decongestants, high-dose vitamin C, and diuretics can cause excessive drying of the larynx. Oral contraceptives can cause problems due to their effect on fluid balance.

Laryngitis that lasts more than a few days is most commonly due to post-nasal drainage, allergies, or esophageal reflux. After taking an appropriate history and examining the head and neck, the vocal cords should be examined with the indirect laryngoscope or other equipment if available. Singers are always concerned about having nodules on the cords so visualization of the cords can be very reassuring.

Singers with voice problems usually respond to conservative treatment involving a few days of voice rest and treatment of the precipitating factors. Of course, medications should be avoided that can cause more harm than benefit (e.g., antihistamines and decongestants). Nonetheless, referral to an interested ENT specialist is often helpful and reassuring.

## PERFORMANCE ANXIETY

Most people who have performed in public have experienced the nervousness, dry mouth, palpitations, and tremor that result from being in a stressful situation. While these symptoms usually do not interfere with dance performance, they can be disabling for some musicians and actors. The pathophysiology of the somatic symptoms involves release of epinephrine and stimulation of beta-receptors on muscle, heart, and salivary glands. Even experienced professional performers have significant performance anxiety, most typically in solo performance circumstances. Twenty-five percent of symphony orchestra musicians reported having serious performance anxiety.[11]

Performing arts students who seek treatment for performance anxiety require evaluation of both the psychological and somatic components of the disorder. Students who have generalized anxiety or signs of depression should have a more detailed mental health workup. History and physical exam should focus on diseases that could cause secondary anxiety (e.g., hyperthyroidism) or could contraindicate use of beta-blockers (asthma and certain heart diseases).

Appropriate treatment of performance anxiety may include both psychological and pharmacologic approaches. While a variety of psychobehavioral therapies have been studied, only systematic desensitization seems to be effective.[12] Use of a beta-blocker (e.g., propranolol 20 mg one hour before the performance) has been shown to be effective in controlling the somatic symptoms of performance anxiety,[13] although the use of beta-blockers for performance anxiety is somewhat controversial. Some performers are able to wean themselves off medication after getting through a few successful performances. Singers may not benefit from beta-blockers.[14]

## DANCE MEDICINE

Injury is probably more common among dancers than among musicians, and many dance careers are cut short by one or several injuries.[15] While this brief discussion of dancers' problems will cover all types of dance, it is important to recognize that ballet dancers, modern dancers, and theater dancers each have specific patterns of injuries. The musculoskeletal problems of dancers will be reviewed first, and then other medical problems of dancers will be discussed.

In general, the foot and ankle are the most common sites of injury, accounting for 25 to 70 percent of dancers' injuries. Next most frequent are injuries of the knee, and then the leg, hip, thigh, and lumbar spine. Male dancers may injure their shoulders while lifting their partners. This pattern applies to dancers at the university student level as well as to professional dancers. Most studies have shown that a majority of dancers experience at least one injury per year. Seventeen percent of the dancers in one professional company were disabled at any one time during the performing season.[15]

Several factors contribute to the occurrence of injuries among dancers. Each type of dance style requires a certain body habitus with various anatomic requirements. Individuals without the proper anatomy will eventually be unable to progress further or will suffer an injury while trying to do so. Those who have the proper anatomic characteristics must pay continuous attention to training and technique. Pre-season training is designed to have the dancer ready for the performance season. Training must focus on the dance style that the dancer will use, and warm-up before lessons, rehearsals, and performances is essential. The schedule of dance activities during the week can play an important role in preventing injuries by allowing adequate rest periods. Temperature and relative humidity of the practice room and performance hall are important, and the floor characteristics can be a critical factor in preventing problems. Finally, the dancer's diet and stress level can predispose to or protect from injury.

The treatment and rehabilitation of specific musculoskeletal injuries in dancers is beyond the scope of this chapter. College health services on campuses with dance programs should develop a good working relationship with an interested orthopedic specialist. Common dance injuries are discussed in reference 15.

Dancers are likely to suffer from various non-musculoskeletal problems. Due to the extremely thin body habitus that is the ideal for classical ballet dancers, eating disorders are fairly common.[16] Amenorrhea, which is related to the low body weight and active life-style of ballerinas, is fairly common as well. Dancers should be educated to understand their basic nutritional needs, and those with a definite eating disorder should receive appropriate multidisciplinary intervention.

## SUMMARY

Students of the performing arts are at risk for developing a variety of performance-related problems. College health professionals can help these students prevent such problems, recognize them early when they occur, and return quickly to their artistic endeavors.

Acknowledgment

Harris Faigel, MD, of Brandeis University contributed to the section on performance anxiety.

# REFERENCES

1. Sataloff RT, Brandfonbrener AG, Lederman RJ (eds): Textbook of Performing Arts Medicine. New York, Raven Press, 1990

2. Lockwood AH: Medical problems of musicians. N Engl J Med 320:221, 1989

3. Brandfonbrener AG: An overview of the medical problems of musicians. J Am Coll Health 34:165, 1986

4. Manchester RA: The incidence of hand problems in music students. Med Probl Perform Art 3:15, 1988

5. Fry HJH: Prevalence of overuse (injury) syndrome in Australian music schools. Br J Indust Med 44:35, 1987

6. Hochberg FH, Lavin P, Portney R et al: Topical therapy of localized inflammation in musicians: A clinical evaluation of Aspercreme versus placebo. Med Probl Perform Art 3:9, 1988

7. Manchester RA, Lustik S: The short-term outcome of hand problems in music students. Med Probl Perform Art 4:95, 1989

8. Rimmer S, Spielvogel RL: Dermatologic problems of musicians. J Amer Acad Derm 22:657, 1990

9. Westmore GA, Eversden ID: Noise-induced hearing loss and orchestral musicians. Arch Otolaryngol 107:761, 1981

10. Sataloff RT: The professional voice: Parts I, II, & III. J Voice 1:92, 191, 283, 1987

11. Fishbein M, Middlestadt S: Medical problems among ICSOM musicians: Overview of a national survey. Med Probl Perform Art 3:1, 1988

12. Clark DB: Performance-related medical and psychological disorders in instrumental musicians. Ann Behav Med 11:28, 1989

13. Brantigan CO, Brantigan TA, Joseph N: Effect of beta blockade and beta stimulation on stage fright. Amer J Med 72:88, 1982

14. Gates GA et al: Effect of beta blockade on singing performance. Ann Otol Rhinol Laryngol 94:570, 1985

15. Ryan AJ, Stephens RE (eds): Dance Medicine - A Comprehensive Guide. Chicago, Pluribus Press, 1987

16. Braisted JR, Mellin L, Gong EJ et al: The adolescent ballet dancer - nutritional practices and characteristics associated with anorexia nervosa. J Adolesc Health Care 6:365, 1985

# 29

# Chronic Illness
# and the College Student

DONALD F.B. CHAR, MD

The terms "illness" and "disease" are frequently used interchangeably by all of us, as if they were synonymous. Unfortunately, they imply very different meanings. Illness is a state associated with the phenomenon of not feeling well or being sick, an expression of the person afflicted. Disease, on the other hand, implies an organic deviation involving structural or chemical changes and results from a diagnosis or label, generally based on a decision involving a health professional. When chronic, these conditions commonly involve a state of disability as well.

With the emphasis of college medicine involving primary health care principles, the term "illness" will be utilized for this chapter. We intend to focus our attention on the ailing student and on what brings such a person to the Student Health Service, rather than be subjected to the arbitrary concept of how we health professionals view the student. It is important to keep these distinctions in mind when surveying and evaluating the literature on this subject.

From 1949 to 1956, a national voluntary group called the Commission on Chronic Illness met to discuss this broad health care topic for the United States. This group, made up of 46 different health and social welfare professionals, health care organizations, insurance companies, and lay people, assisted by 59 technical and staff advisers, grappled with this compelling health care challenge and issued multiple reports on the subject. Focusing largely on the concept of prevention at the end of this protracted study, the Commission adopted the following definition for chronic disease:

> "Chronic disease comprises all impairments or deviations from normal which have one or more of the following characteristics: are permanent; leave residual disability; are caused by nonreversible pathologic alteration; require special training of the patient for rehabilitation; may be expected to require a long period of supervision, observation, or care."[1]

The Commission ultimately decided to focus their efforts on the following disorders: arthritis and rheumatism, blindness, cancer, cardiovascular diseases, cerebral palsy, diabetes mellitus, epilepsy, impaired hearing, mental illness, multiple sclerosis, poliomyelitis, late manifestations of syphilis, and tuberculosis. They considered the following factors as strong influences on these diseases: industry, heredity, malnutrition, obesity, dental factors, and emotional factors. If discussed today, I am certain that education would be considered another significant factor in chronic illness.

Since the report was issued, much has transpired in this area of caring for chronic illness. It is most fascinating to reflect on a presentation given by Dr. David Seegal to the Commission in 1951 in which he stated that "with this fine record over the past 40 years and the present pace of research, is it not possible that the medical student of 1975 or 2000 may add hypertension or arteriosclerosis or cancer or all three to the list of preventable or controllable chronic diseases?"[1] Indeed, the Journal of Chronic Diseases, initiated in 1955, decided to change its name to the Journal of Clinical Epidemiology in 1988 because "chronic diseases became part of the mainstream of pathophysiologic research; and with increased specialization in medicine, many other journals became available as locations for studies...."[2]

In focusing on the concepts of chronic illness, rather than disease, the role of college medicine in providing basic primary medical care must be emphasized. The ideal student health center provides first contact, as well as continuing care, and coordinates, integrates, and facilitates comprehensive and personalized care for the individual student-patient.

It should also be stressed that one cannot demarcate and clearly define chronic illness, no matter what factors are applied. One must accept the fact that for everyone, the terms of illness, disease, handicapped, and disability will remain by necessity vague and unclear, and one must remain sensitive to the context of how it is being utilized and who is involved in the discussion.

## AN OVERVIEW OF CHRONIC ILLNESS IN COLLEGE STUDENTS

As American society begins to implement the mainstreaming of special-needs students into our communities, it can be expected that their numbers will continue to grow on all college campuses. The tasks and responsibilities for college health services will no doubt be expanded correspondingly, bringing greater numbers and more complex and difficult health care problems to student health centers.

It is crucial that the management of chronic illness and disease be accomplished in a way that is sensitive to the psychosocial and developmental needs of young adult students. The patient's need to work on the establishment of a stable identity, to develop independence from parents, to search for meaningful relationships with the opposite sex, and, ultimately, to find a career and vocation, must be acknowledged. At times, these students may have been overprotected and sheltered, and thus might be unable to cope with the multiple needs of growing up with an illness. Uncoupled from their home environment and needing to establish themselves in the academic community might cause asthma attacks or seizures to increase, or arthritis to worsen. In fact, the first signs of any problem or distress by these students with chronic illness may be a visit to the campus clinic to consult the nurse or physician. Some of these individuals are accustomed to the use of highly specialized, sometimes technologically demanding, services from several different health professionals and specialists. It is crucial that their problems be approached holistically, focusing on the total and comprehensive needs of the person, rather than targeted exclusively on the disease or illness itself.

## SCOPE OF CHRONIC ILLNESSES
## ON COLLEGE CAMPUSES

In 1986, the Chronic Disease Planning Group of the Centers for Disease Control of the U.S. Public Health Service discussed the many problems connected with defining the problem of chronic illness. Employing a public health, largely preventive approach to this problem and using mortality, morbidity, and cost expenditures, they defined chronic diseases as: ischemic heart disease, cancer, stroke, chronic obstructive pulmonary disease, diabetes, cirrhosis of the liver, rheumatoid arthritis, inflammatory bowel disease, osteoporosis, and degenerative neurologic disease (specifically, multiple sclerosis, Parkinsonism, and Alzheimer's disease) with mental retardation, and congenital anomalies during childhood.[3]

Continuously since 1970, the Hawaii State Department of Health has conducted the Health Surveillance Program, modeled after the National Health Interview Survey of the National Center for Health Statistics. Surveying noninstitutional residential households, it collects continuous information relating to the incidence and prevalence of chronic and acute morbidity, accidents, injuries, and disabilities/impairments in the general population through direct questioning of the individuals. This study found that in 1987, for those between 17 and 44 years of age, the leading chronic conditions in rank order included: 1) impairment of back or spine, 2) hay fever without asthma, 3) chronic and allergic skin condition, 4) chronic sinusitis, 5) asthma with or without hay fever, 6) hypertension, 7) hearing impairment, 8) hemorrhoids, 9) arthritis/rheumatism, 10) bronchitis/emphysema, 11) mental and nervous condition, and 12) stomach ulcer.[4]

In 1990, the American Medical Association pointed out that serious, chronic medical and psychiatric disorders affect approximately two million adolescents or 6 percent of the adolescent population. The AMA Report points out that 32 percent of these were mental disorders involving psychoses, anxiety and personality disorders, substance dependence syndromes, and retardation; 21 percent involved respiratory conditions, primarily asthma and bronchitis; 15 percent were musculo-skeletal disorders including arthritis; 6 percent were nervous system disorders such as multiple sclerosis, cerebral palsy, epilepsy; 4 percent were ear problems consisting of deafness and other impairments; and 22 percent involved disease of other parts of the body. Other chronic conditions affecting adolescents include hypertension, scoliosis, dysmenorrhea, myopia (25 percent of adolescents), obesity, dental decay, malocclusion, and gum disease.

Studies on the incidence and prevalence of chronic illness involving college students have not been reported. One approach that has been used to study the prevalence of chronic illness among college students is to evaluate the information provided on the health form completed by the personal physician submitted for admission of the student into the university. In the Fall semesters of 1987 and 1990, a total of 2046 and 2176, respectively, of such health forms was submitted to the Student Health Service of the University of Hawaii to initiate student medical records. A study of the information on these forms revealed that a consistent 17 percent of them contained medical information documenting some chronic illness of the student, based on personal comments of the student as well as diagnosis of the physician.

As seen in Table 1, next page, respiratory conditions comprise the leading cause of chronic morbidity at 28 percent, with skin, cardiovascular, and musculoskeletal illness ranking significantly below it at one-half of this rate. Neuropsychiatric illness and metabolic endocrinologic conditions were noted at approximately 10 percent with gastrointestinal, genitourinary, and blood disorders trailing far behind. Of greater interest may be the specific illnesses noted on these health forms as seen in Table 1.

Asthma was found to be the leading cause of chronic illness among these college students, with back problems, including scoliosis, and acne trailing significantly behind it. The surprising number of cardiovascular disorders noted, with the diagnosis of mitral valve prolapse exceeding that of hypertension and rheumatic fever, was interesting. Indeed, the presence of an undifferentiated heart murmur without further specific clarification, such as "innocent," was rather striking. Back problems, including the diagnosis of scoliosis, were also frequently noted. Thyroid disorders, involving goiter and hyperthyroid states, and obesity were also frequently mentioned, as were depression, headaches, eczema, diabetes, and stomach ulcers or stomach "problems."

Diagnoses of systemic lupus erythematosus, hepatitis, ulcerative colitis, arthritis, especially involving the temporomandibular joint, regional enteritis or Crohn's disease were mentioned less frequently. Of interest, anorexia, bulimia, and chronic Epstein-Barr virus (EBV) syndrome (chronic fatigue syndrome) were each noted

Table 1

Chronic Illnesses According to Systems and Numbers Involved*

| Systems Involved | Percent of chronic illness |
|---|---|
| 1.  Respiratory conditions | 28% |
|     Commonly noted: Asthma (138) | |
|     Sinusitis/Bronchitis (28) | |
| 2.  Skin conditions | 14% |
|     Commonly noted: Acne (55) | |
|     Eczema (17) | |
| 3.  Cardiovascular Conditions | 14% |
|     Commonly noted: Mitral valve prolapse (25) | |
|     Hypertension (22) | |
|     Undifferentiated heart murmur (16) | |
|     Rheumatic Fever (8) | |
| 4.  Musculoskeletal Conditions | 14% |
|     Commonly noted: Back problem, scoliosis (41) | |
|     Temporomandibular joint problem (6) | |
| 5.  Neuropsychiatric Conditions | 11% |
|     Commonly noted: Headaches/migraine (20) | |
|     Depression (18) | |
|     Seizures (8) | |
|     Worry/anxiety (7) | |
| 6.  Metabolic-Endocrine Conditions | 10% |
|     Commonly noted: Obesity (24) | |
|     Thyroid/Goiter (18) | |
|     Diabetes mellitus (10) | |
| 7.  Gastrointestinal Conditions | 5% |
|     Commonly noted: Stomach problems/ulcers (14) | |
| 8.  Genitourinary | 3% |
| 9.  Blood | 1% |

*Taken from University of Hawaii health forms submitted by newly admitted students for Fall semesters 1987 and 1990

only one time on these forms. Anemia was not noted, with the exception of one diagnosis of Thalassemia. Sickle cell anemia was never noted – no doubt a reflection of the relative lack of African-Americans in this student body. Cystic fibrosis was also never noted, again probably reflecting the fact that two-thirds of the student body is not of Caucasian origin.

## THE MANAGEMENT OF CHRONIC ILLNESSES IN COLLEGE

The specifics of the management of individual chronic illness are beyond the scope of this book; however, some general principles apply. How these chronic illnesses are evaluated, diagnosed, and treated will depend greatly on the nature, size, and complexity of the Student Health Service and its staffing, reflective of the depth of the financing of the program as well as the extended health insurance coverage. Obviously, the larger programs with greater resources and staffing will be capable of providing more services for these patients on campus. Organizations in smaller college towns may not have the access and availability of specialized services and consultations. Smaller health services directed by a single physician or a nurse may be even more restricted.

Indeed, the biggest disruption in caring for the health of these chronically ill students may well be taking place when he or she leaves home for the first time to set up an independent lifestyle, free of parental influence, on the college campus. The dependable and familiar network of medical services and support in the home environment will need to be planned and developed for the new college setting. The transfer of appropriate medical records and suggestions for follow-through care and management is vitally needed to ensure successful transition to this new life. Colleges that continue to require a complete medical examination by the personal physician of the student and the submission of a health form describing the findings upon enrollment are obviously at a great advantage for getting useful information on these problems.

Students should be strongly encouraged to contact the student health service regarding a chronic illness and the special needs that may be required. Too often, these chronic illnesses are precipitated by special requirements and administrative problems that a student encounters once on campus. It is recommended that this problem of chronic illness and special requirements should be addressed in the general catalogue of the institution, thereby encouraging the parents and students to address these problems before the student arrives on campus. This will ensure a smoother transition from the home to the new institutional environment, and all of the specialized health care needs could be anticipated and developed.

How each different model of student health service carries out management plans for students with chronic illnesses depends largely on its capacity to act as a primary service provider, overseeing, monitoring, and providing a basic level of medical services, but also aware of the need to consult and coordinate other specialists in health care whenever necessary. Above all, one must not lose sight of the fact that the student must be permitted to pursue fully and actively his or her academic and educational tasks and programs, and learn to cope with and hopefully overcome the deleterious and possible disabling effects of the chronic illness. Special note should be made of those with chronic mental illness. These are common problems, seen daily at college health centers. Most primary health care professionals in the college setting are skilled and capable of managing mental health problems directly. Each organization ultimately learns how to provide the necessary services through its own staff, or how to refer these problems for consultation and/or management by other mental health professionals.

In a small institution, the nurse or the physician may be the only clinician available and must provide much of the counseling and treatment, referring only the more severely depressed or anxious student to a psychologist or psychiatrist off-campus. Many larger student health services are capable of providing directly for an array of mental health services, with some able even to provide hospitalization for more intensive care.

Most primary care physicians are comfortable and skilled in prescribing psychotropic medications useful in treating many mental health disorders. Nevertheless, the use of these medications is attended with some risks, particularly when applied to illnesses such as those that crop up chronically and recurrently. It is of utmost importance to recognize that the average undergraduate student is in transition and growing into adulthood. These drugs must never be used over protracted periods of time, unless they are specifically required and are closely monitored and adequately supervised. It is imperative that those individuals requiring long-term treatment with medications also receive appropriate counseling and psychotherapy. As a general rule, patients requiring long-term psychopharmacologic treatment are best sent to a university or community psychiatrist for management.

## CONCLUSION

Contrary to the popular notion that college students get sick merely from minor injuries or acute respiratory, gastrointestinal, and skin disorders, many of them have more serious health problems, including those associated with chronic illnesses. Along with chronic conditions of adolescence and young adulthood, the increasing numbers of older students on campus bring with them an increase in the number and complexity of chronic illness presenting to student health centers. College health care providers must be capable of managing all types of medical problems, not just those of young people and not just those that are temporary in nature. Continuing education programs for college health personnel should reflect this fact as should medical quality assurance activities.

## REFERENCES

1. Commission on Chronic Illness: Prevention of Chronic Illness. Cambridge, Harvard University Press, 1957

2. Feinstein AR, Spitzer WO: Happy anniversary and an impending name change. Journal of Chronic Disease (changed name to Journal of Clinical Epidemiology), 1988

3. Chronic Disease Planning Group, Centers for Disease Control: Positioning for Prevention: An Analytical Framework and Background Document for Chronic Disease Activities. U.S. Department of Health, Research and Statistics Office, 1990

4. Hawaii Health Surveillance Program, RES Report: Survey Data, Hawaii State Department of Health, Research and Statistics Office, 1990

# 30

## Issues for Ethnically and Culturally Diverse Campuses: The View from Los Angeles

CONNIE A. DIGGS, RN, NP, MPA AND STEVEN L. HARRIS, MD, MS

The information presented in this chapter focuses on California State University, Los Angeles, and other campuses within the California State University system, and to a lesser extent the University of Southern California and the University of California at Los Angeles (UCLA). These universities have experienced significant changes in their student populations and are confronted with health care issues prevalent in ethnically and culturally under-represented populations. Inasmuch as these population trends represent changes in the general population of urban communities in the West and indeed, across the entire United States, they reflect socioeconomic and ethnic diversity that may be viewed as a glimpse into the future.

## THE POPULATION

The California State University, Los Angeles (Cal State L.A.) Student Health Center provides primary health care to one of the most ethnically and culturally diverse student bodies in the nation. The most recent enrollment data (Fall, 1990) from the University's Analytical Research Department reflect a total student enrollment of 21,596, of which 44.1 percent are from traditionally under-represented populations.

Over the last decade, Cal State L.A. has experienced significant change in the ethnic diversity of its student population (Table 1, next page). The once-majority white, non-Hispanic student enrollment has decreased by 33.8 percent, whereas the Hispanic student enrollment has increased by 37.8 percent. There has been a 26.3 percent decrease in the African-American student enrollment and a 39.2 percent decrease in Native-American enrollment. In addition to that noted for Hispanics, the only other increase in ethnic minority enrollment has been the Asian/Pacific Islanders with a 10.1 percent increase.

Though the enrollment levels of Hispanic and white, non-Hispanics at Cal State L.A. may be in stark contrast to the enrollment levels of their counterparts at other colleges and universities across the nation, these levels are in sync with the ethnic make-up of the general population of the University's service area. The University is surrounded by small communities with large populations of Asian/ Pacific Islanders and Hispanics. Though these communities continue to have a significant number of white, non-Hispanic citizens, they have experienced tremendous ethnic and cultural change.

Cal State L.A. serves a student population that is typically low-income minority, or first-generation college attenders. Two-thirds of the student body is non-white and 57.4 percent are women.[1] The average age of the population is 28 years. The majority are working adults with families. A large number are without health care insurance and have limited financial resources to cover health care costs. The Student Health Center serves as the primary health care provider for a sizable number of students.

## UNIQUE HEALTH ISSUES

In general, the emotional and physical health-related issues for college students from differing cultural and ethnic backgrounds are similar to those of other students. Issues of identity formation, separation from home and family, career choice, academic success and failure, the development of relationships with peers and significant others, accidents, injuries, sexuality and family planning considerations, and illnesses of many types occur with approximately equal frequency

Table 1

Enrollment by Ethnic Groups* – 1980–1990

|  | Fall, 1980 | % | Fall, 1990 | % |
|---|---|---|---|---|
| Total | 18,871 | % | 18,208 | % |
| Asian/Pacific Islander | 4,704 | 24.9 | 5,177 | 28.4 |
| African-American, Non-Hispanic | 2,811 | 14.9 | 2,073 | 11.4 |
| Hispanic | 3,640 | 19.3 | 5,856 | 32.2 |
| Native American | 153 | 0.8 | 93 | 0.5 |
| White, Non-Hispanic | 7,563 | 40.1 | 5,009 | 27.5 |

*Ethnic data are voluntarily reported; only U.S. citizens and resident aliens identifying an ethnic group are included.

among and between culturally disparate groups. On the other hand there are some problems that are either unique to, or occur with a much greater frequency in, given ethnic groups; health problems that either manifest themselves uniquely or have unique needs for diagnosis, management, and/or prevention in ethnic groups; and problems that are simply more characteristic of the underlying socioeconomic status of contemporary immigrant or disadvantaged populations.

In our experience, it is not uncommon to find, in any given day, that we are dealing with medical problems in students living in households where six different primary languages are spoken, such as English, Spanish, Cambodian, Korean, Filipino, and Laotian. As well, the level of financial support for medications, necessary medical supplies, and even basic transportation can vary tremendously. It is important to acknowledge these issues as we assess the background of our patients' problems and develop therapeutic strategies.

## PROBLEMS UNIQUE TO THE ETHNIC POPULATIONS

### Sickle Cell Disease

Sickle cell disease is an autosomal recessive red blood cell disorder that affects the African-American population predominantly. It has also been identified in people from other ethnic groups who come from countries around the Mediterranean and Caribbean seas. Sickle cell anemia was first identified by Dr. James Herrick in 1920, but it was not until 1954 that Dr. Linus Pauling recognized it as a hemoglobin disorder. This disease affects over 50,000 African-Americans and is characterized by a chronic hemolytic anemia.

While over two million African-American people carry the sickle cell trait (Hemoglobin As), it is important to establish that having the trait does not constitute having sickle cell disease. Persons with sickle cell trait are usually asymptomatic. The primary concern for this population should be prospective parenthood. Should two persons with Hemoglobin As conceive, there is a 25 percent chance that the child will have sickle cell anemia. Other common sickle cell disorders are sickle cell C and the sickle beta-thalassemias.[2]

### Tuberculosis

Over the past decade the prevalence of tuberculosis (TB) has doubled. As colleges and universities continue to diversify their student bodies, it is highly likely that they will experience an increase in the number of students who will require evaluation and treatment for active TB. Ethnic populations in which one would expect TB to manifest include Asian/Pacific Islanders, Hispanics, and African-Americans. To aid in the detection of TB infections, our university policy requires that all first-time and readmitted students present a negative tuberculin skin test or chest x-ray within 12 months preceding classroom participation. Transmission of TB is via aerosolized droplets containing tuberculous bacilli, which escape from infected individuals during coughing, sneezing, or speaking. The disease is acquired by inhalation of these bacilli and not by skin contact or from fomites.[3]

One of the challenges to the Student Health Center is the provision of information to newly arrived foreign students in a language they can understand. In explaining the difference between a positive TB skin test and active TB disease, many foreign students indicate an initial understanding of the explanation only to find that the next day they are totally confused by the explanation given so carefully just the day earlier. The need is crucial for staff who can adequately and accurately translate this important medical information.

## Protozoal and Helminthic Infections

Protozoal and helminthic infections affect primarily the lower gastrointestinal tract. Clinical manifestations range from flatulence, mild diarrhea and dysentery to malabsorption. These infections will usually manifest in students from countries where sanitation is poor, including migrant labor camps and Indian reservations in the U.S.[4] It is interesting to note that experience at our university does not support an increased incidence in minority populations. These infections have actually been seen most frequently in white students who have engaged in travel to endemic areas.

## Hepatitis B

The incidence of hepatitis B virus (HBV) infection is increasing in the U.S. with approximately 300,000 new cases each year. The prevalence of hepatitis B (HBsAg) carriers in the U.S. is 0.1 to 0.2 percent of the total population, with substantial variation among ethnic groups. African-Americans and immigrants from certain Asian and Pacific Islands have a higher prevalence.[5] Prevention of hepatitis B, the most important consideration for student health care practitioners, is addressed elsewhere in this book.

## PROBLEMS WITH UNIQUE CHARACTERISTICS IN ETHNIC POPULATIONS

### Hypertension

The racial differences in hypertension do not become apparent until adolescence or early adulthood; however, once established, morbidity and mortality are greater in African-Americans than whites. Although mortality from hypertension has been decreasing in African-Americans since at least 1950, it still remains significantly higher than in whites.[6] Epidemiologic characteristics associated with greater hypertension-associated mortality in African-Americans include low socioeconomic status, less education, stress, and reduced access to health care. Obesity and family history of hypertension are equally important risk factors for both African-Americans and whites.

Behavioral risk factors such as diet, smoking, and levels of physical activity are often part of particular cultural patterns that are grounded in socioeconomic circumstances associated with increased risk. Mortality rates demonstrate linkages with social instability, and an inverse relationship between income and social class. Thus, hypertension control among African-American communities can be improved by interventions that increase levels of social support.

For Hispanics, there is a strong inverse relationship between socioeconomic status and hypertension, much as in African-Americans. Among Hispanic women, this effect remains, even when adjustments are made for the higher rate of obesity among those with lower socioeconomic status. Finally, hypertension represents a significant problem among Filipinos, as a poorer response to antihypertensive medication has been observed. Fewer Filipino women had adequate control of their disease than Filipino men – the reverse of the gender trends for all other ethnic groups studied.[7]

## Gallstone Disease (Cholelithiasis)

Gallstone disease is more prevalent among Mexican-American women than others in the population, although the evidence is somewhat sparse. One study provided evidence that gallstone disease is more prevalent among Mexican-Americans than among Cuban-Americans or Puerto Ricans living in the U.S. and that Mexican-American women were at higher risk than men. This same study demonstrated that only Pima Indians in the southwest U.S. had a higher incidence of gallstone disease than did Mexican-American women.[8]

## Diabetes Mellitus

Diabetes mellitus is a major problem in Hispanics, especially among Mexican-Americans and Puerto Ricans living in the U. S. As well, the prevalence is high among certain Native American groups. With the increasing average age of student populations it is very likely that diabetes will become a more important issue to student health providers in the future.

## PROBLEMS UNIQUE TO THE SOCIOECONOMIC CHARACTERISTICS OF ETHNIC POPULATIONS

### Alcohol and Drug Abuse

Caucasian college students have higher rates of alcohol use than either African-American or Hispanic students even though there are some indications that no difference exists between any of the male groups on the alcohol-related problem scale.[9]

According to the Centers for Disease Control (CDC),[10] cirrhosis-related deaths are disproportionate among African-Americans. While studies of the Hispanic's drinking practices and consequences are less available and not as informative as those for African-Americans, there is some indication that Hispanics, particularly young males, suffer disproportionate health consequences as a result of their use of alcohol. What is not indicated in most studies of this phenomenon, however, is whether or not those studied are students.

Native-Americans are also known to experience disproportionate health consequences as a result of alcohol consumption. On an average, Asian/Pacific Islanders do not consume as much alcohol as the general population. Because of the wide variation in drinking among the different Asian nationalities, it is difficult to arrive at generalizations about cultural factors that contribute to the differences among Asian sub-populations with regard to the use of alcohol.[10]

African-Americans are more likely than whites to have higher rates of drug use for marijuana, cocaine, heroin, and illicit methadone. Hispanics were more likely than whites to report primary problems with heroin, cocaine, or PCP according to data from hospital emergency rooms and drug treatment programs.[10]

## Sexually Transmitted Diseases (STDs)

STDs represent the second most frequent cause for visits to our Student Health Center. Among the most frequently seen STDs are chlamydia, human papillomavirus (HPV), gonorrhea, and syphilis. Though recent statistics from the Department of Health Services, County of Los Angeles (April 1 - June 30, 1990) reveal epidemic proportions of both gonorrhea and syphilis, campus statistics suggest greater prevalence of both chlamydia and HPV infections.

According to L.A. County Public Health statistics, the rate of gonorrhea among African-American males is six times greater than that of white males, and for African-American females, rates are five times greater than for white females. Rates for Hispanic males are nearly twice those of white males while rates for Hispanic females are approximately the same as those for white females. Similar statistics hold for primary and secondary syphilis. Asian/Pacific Islanders were not represented in this group.

Chlamydia has been shown to be a most significant health hazard for young, sexually active women. As on most college campuses, we have noted a much higher rate of chlamydia infections than of gonorrhea. We have not, however, developed any data to suggest ethnic or socioeconomic differences between those infected and those not. The same is true for HPV infections, where we have found that approximately 11 percent of all routine Pap smears performed over the period 1989-90 were Class II or above.

## Mental Health Problems

Suicide rates among adolescents aged 15 to 24 tripled over the last 30 years, despite the fact that suicide rates in the general population have remained remarkably stable.[11] Among all age groups, men outnumber women by as much as 5:1 in completed suicides. Suicide rates for whites have been approximately twice that for non-whites. Attempted suicide has been consistently higher among women, with female-to-male ratios ranging from 2:1 to as high as 9:1.[12]

No one particular type of adolescent or young adult commits suicide. Certain characteristics tend to increase the risk, however, and are relevant to all campus populations. These include age, with risk increasing in the 15 to 24 year age group; gender, with women attempting suicide more often than men but with men succeeding more often than women; and, of particular relevance to this chapter, race, with African-Americans attempting suicide more often (albeit with a lower success rate) than whites. Of all racial groups, Native Americans have the highest rate of completed suicides.[11]

# PROGRAM ISSUES

The physical and mental health issues of under-represented students represent a significant challenge to student health care providers. In most respects, systems of medical and mental health care for ethnically diverse populations should be similar to those that serve more homogeneous populations. The overriding consideration, however, is the need for such systems to accommodate the wide range of cultural and ethnic sensibilities found in our students. At Cal State L.A. the experience has been that in providing health services to students from under-represented populations, the race of the provider is a significant factor. Students tend to gravitate to health care providers from their own ethnic backgrounds, or to providers from backgrounds similar to their own. Staff frequently encounter African-American and Hispanic students, who are first-generation college students and are struggling to overcome racial barriers and family traditions, sometimes in conflict with pursuit of a college education.

It is important to understand that students from the under-represented populations often find it difficult to ask for help. Thus, college health care professionals must recognize the importance of developing and implementing programs that appeal to their needs. However, despite the increasing frequency with which these challenges are being encountered, reports of successful programs aimed at addressing these problems are relatively few.

Programs of peer education have been in existence for as long as 25 years, but it is only recently that they have been aimed at the special needs of under-represented students. Community agencies such as churches and community centers recently have been recognized as sources for reaching ethnic students and much is currently underway in this sector. Health education and promotion in the classroom has long been one way to reach out to all students, and new programs aimed at health education through entertainment and the media are finding their way onto the campus.

The "Health Advocates" program at the University of Southern California has existed since 1975. Originally conceived as a course to teach cardiopulmonary resuscitation, it has been taught by health educators and broadened in scope and purpose over the past five years. Currently, this innovative program is a two-semester general education course designed primarily for freshmen and sopho-mores. The first semester focuses on teaching basic principles of health education, including first aid, cardiopulmonary resuscitation, HIV education, and sexually transmitted disease information. The second semester involves students in design-ing and participating in an outreach program on the campus. This includes educational programs and posters for the campus walkways, as well as presentations to student groups such as fraternities, sororities, and dormitory groups. This course has attracted 20-25 students per semester, and offers two units of credit per semester.

An innovative program has been designed by the First African Methodist Episcopal Church of Los Angeles, aimed at working within the African-American community to reduce gang violence and drug abuse among high-risk youth. Funded in part by a grant from the Governor's Office of Criminal Justice, this early intervention program has as its goals to improve self-esteem and provide direction for youth at risk for anti-social behavior. The "Value Affirmation Model," while designed to reach out to the African-American community, is appropriate for use in any culture and for other areas of concern.

Such a program, coordinated by members of the community, includes small group discussions, expert presentations, presentations on careers or education by role models, video presentations, and mentor-mentee relationships. This model is designed to reach nearly 4,500 youth per year at some 30 churches and community centers in six urban centers in California. Its potential applicability to college communities is great. Health education on the campus of California State Univer-sity, Los Angeles reaches into under-represented groups through such programs as the Coordinated Dietetics program. Through the auspices of the Student Health Center this project addresses special diet therapies for patients consuming a traditionally Hispanic, African-American, or Asian diet. This program utilizes senior students in dietetics to counsel their peers through computer-assisted diet and life-style modification.

Another example of health education programming that is likely to be culturally sensitive is a UCLA program called Kaleidoscope Theatre, sponsored by the Student Health Center. The specially trained UCLA student-actors perform an entertaining play based on an examination of relationships and sexuality issues in the 1990s. Students working in this program undertake an intensive 10-week training course in which they receive guidance in basic acting technique in addition to educational classes on STDs, HIV infection, condom-use skills, safer sex, assertiveness training and communication, gay and lesbian issues, and the effects of alcohol on sexual decision-making. Material for Kaleidoscope scripts is derived from concerns expressed by participants at campus workshops and focused discussion groups on sexuality, AIDS, and safer sex.

Finally, the Multicultural Training Resource Center at San Francisco State University is a state-supported agency that provides training for trainers in the African-American, Latino, and Asian communities. The Center teaches fundamental precepts for meeting the health education needs of students including clearly defining the population, incorporating representatives from each community in program planning and implementation, and education about cultural taboos and language difficulties.

## CONCLUSION

In sum, there are really very few surprises when considering either the health problems of, or health systems designed to serve, highly ethnically diverse populations. While some problems might be different, it is very likely that these differences will diminish as greater levels of cultural assimilation occur. As noted in this chapter, successful programs aimed at under-represented students and their attendant health care needs will utilize health care providers who understand the community. For health education, peers and role models in the community, as well as innovative programming are needed. Only with the above in place will student health providers be able to address the needs of the students of the next century.

Acknowledgment

The authors wish to acknowledge the assistance of Arleen Lageman in researching the background material for this chapter.

# REFERENCES

1. California State University, Los Angeles, Education Equity Report, 1989

2. Rooks Y, Pack B: A Profile of Sickle Cell Disease. Nursing Clinics of North America 18:1, March 1983

3. Dall L, Gritz D: The Changing Patterns of TB: Risk, Treatment, and Prevention. Infections in Medicine, July-August 1978, 4: 6

4. Markell E, Voge M, John D: Medical Parasitology. Philadelphia, WB Saunders Co, 1986

5. Alter M, Hodler S et al: The changing epidemiology of hepatitis B in the United States. JAMA 263:1218-22, 1990

6. Hall M et al: Hypertension in Blacks: Epidemiology, Pathophysiology and Treatment. Chicago, Yearbook Medical Publishers, 1985

7. Heckler M: Report of the Secretary's Task Force on Black & Minority Health, U.S. Department of Health & Human Services, Vol. 1: Executive Summary, 1985

8. Maurer K et al: Prevalence of gallstone disease in Hispanic populations in the United States. Gastroenterology 96:487-92, 1989

9. Gonzalez G: A comparison of alcohol use and alcohol-related problems among Caucasian, black, and Hispanic college students. NASPA Journal, Vol 27:4, Summer 1990

10. CDC: MMWR Vol 33, Nos 43 and 46, Nov 1984

11. Mathiasen R: Evaluating suicidal risk in the college student. NASPA Journal, 25:4, Spring 1988

12. Low B, Andrews S: Adolescent Suicide. The Medical Clinics of North America, Vol 74:5, September 1990

## Suggested Readings

Hafen B, Frandsen K: Youth Suicide: Depression & Loneliness. 2nd ed. Evergreen Co, Cordillera Press, 1986

Hepworth D et al: Research Capsule, Social Research Institute Newsletter, Graduate School of Social Work, University of Utah, February 1986

Neiger B, Hopkins R: Adolescent Suicide: Character Traits of High-Risk Teenagers. Adolescence XXIII:90, Summer 1988, 469-471

# INDEX OF AUTHORS:
## ALL THREE VOLUMES

# INDEX OF SUBJECTS:
## ALL THREE VOLUMES

# APPENDIX A

## BIOGRAPHICAL SKETCHES OF
## CONTRIBUTING AUTHORS FOR VOLUME THREE

**Elizabeth Bacon** is currently the director of Disabled Student Services, San Diego State University. Ms. Bacon has been an active member of San Diego's disabled community for over 15 years; her involvement started 23 years ago when she sustained a spinal cord injury as the result of a parachuting accident. She subsequently completed both bachelors and masters degrees, during which time she became interested in the development of the support services program for disabled students just starting at San Jose State University. Ms. Bacon has served on a variety of local boards and advisory committees to the city, county, the statewide CSU chancellors office, and the White House Conference on Disability. Additionally, she is the founder of Community Service Center for the Disabled, one of the largest independent living centers in the country.

**Pamela Bowen** is currently Director of the Princeton University Health Services. Dr. Bowen received her MD from the University of Toronto and an MPH in Occupational Medicine from the University of Pittsburgh. She is a Fellow of the American College of Preventive Medicine and is board certified in Public Health and General Preventive Medicine. Dr. Bowen is currently a member of the board of directors of the American College Health Association, and she has served as chair, co-chair, or member of several committees and task forces. Her areas of interest in presentations and publications include the health care of international students and healthy life-styles.

**David Burns** is Director, Student Health Service, and Assistant Vice President for Student Life Policy and Services at Rutgers University. He has served as Vice President of the American College Health Association, as the Chair of their Task Force on Alcohol and Other Drugs, and as a consultant for the American Council on Education. At Rutgers University, he worked with Barbara McCrady, Director of the Center for Alcohol Studies, to establish the first on-campus in-patient treatment facility in the country, the New Jersey Collegiate Substance Abuse Program. Rutgers University is nationally known for the development of comprehensive education, treatment, and rehabilitation pro-grams for alcohol and other drug abuse. In addition, David is the Principal

Investigator on two grants from the U.S. Department of Education for alcohol and other drug abuse prevention.

**Donald Char** is currently the director of Student Health Services and Professor of Pediatrics at the University of Hawaii in Honolulu. Dr. Char received his MD from Temple University School of Medicine and completed both a residency in pediatrics and a pediatric cardiology fellowship at St Christopher Hospital for Children in Philadelphia. He has extensive publications in various areas of pediatric medicine, and participates on a wide variety of community, state health, and medical committees, including active participation in the American College Health Association, the American Academy of Pediatrics, and the Hawaii Academy of Science.

**Bill Christmas** received his MD from Boston University and completed a medical residency and infectious diseases fellowship at the University of Vermont. Dr. Christmas pursued private practice for five years in rural Vermont before entering the field of college health at the University of Rochester in 1977. In 1982, he became director of the student health services at the University of Vermont. Dr. Christmas is board certified in internal medicine, is a clinical associate professor of medicine, and is a fellow of the American College of Physicians and of the American College Health Association, which he served as President in 1987-88.

**Dom Cittadino** is currently Dental Director and Staff Dentist, Student Emergency Dental Services, Student Health Program; and Adjunct Assistant Professor in the Dental Hygiene Program at Southern Illinois University at Carbondale. Dr. Cittadino received his DDS from Loyola University School of Dentistry and took advanced training in a General Practice Residency Program. He is active in the American College Health Association, and has served as Chair of the Dental Section. Dr. Cittadino's lecturing and publishing interests include the structure of student emergency dental services, research into pain reduction, and TMJ pain patients.

**MarJeanne (Mimi) Collins** is currently the director of the student health services of the University of Pennsylvania; and Associate Professor of Medicine and Associate Professor of Pediatrics of the Medical School of the University of Pennsylvania. Dr. Collins received an AB from Bryn Mawr and an MD from the University of Pennsylvania Medical School. She has written and lectured extensively in the areas of pediatrics, adolescence, and immunization practices for vaccine-preventable diseases. Dr. Collins is active in the American College Health Association (ACHA), and has served as Chair, Section of Clinical Medicine; and Chair, Committee on Immunizations. Additionally, she has been recognized by the ACHA with a Special Award for Distinguished Service.

**Murray DeArmond** is currently Director, Student Health and Student Life facilities, University of Arizona. Dr. DeArmond received an undergraduate degree from DePauw University and an MD from Indiana University, after which he completed a psychiatric residency. His areas of interest in presentations and publications include mental health care, both generally and involving international students; and the future trends in college health. Dr. DeArmond was the first chair of the NAFSA-ACHA joint committee on foreign student health care, and is a past president of ACHA. He is currently the chair of the ACHA College Health 2000 Task Force, which has produced two documents: a college health model and opportunities in college health for the year 2000.

**Connie Diggs** is the director of the student health services at California State University, Los Angeles. Ms. Diggs is a graduate of the Grady Memorial Hospital School of Nursing in Atlanta, and was one of four RNs employed by the Watts Health Foundation selected to participate in the first pediatric nurse practitioner program established in California. She has received both her undergraduate and masters degree from California State University, Dominguez Hills.

**John Dorman** is currently Director of Public Relations/Outreach, Cowell Student Health Center, as well as Clinical Associate Professor of Pediatrics, at Stanford University. Dr. Dorman received his BA from Williams College and his MD from Harvard Medical School. He is a past chair of the Clinical Medicine Section, American College Health Association; and is currently Executive Editor of the Journal of American College Health.

**James Evans** is currently Assistant Professor of Behavioral Sciences and Director of the Chemical Dependency Counselor Training Program at San Diego City College. Previously Mr. Evans was Substance Abuse Education and Prevention Coordinator at Student Health Services and Counseling and Psychological Services at San Diego State University. He has a Masters Degree in Counseling Psychology from San Diego State University and has been a Certified Chemical Dependency Practitioner in the state of Minnesota. Mr. Evans is co-author of Counseling The Black Client: Alcohol Use and Abuse in Black America. He is a past president of the Minnesota Chemical Dependency Association and a past consultant to the National Football League on Drug Abuse Prevention.

**Karen Gordon** has worked in the field of college health promotion for over ten years as Director of Health Education at Princeton University, where she created the health education department based at the university health center. Ms. Gordon was awarded a BA from Connecticut College, an MPH from Yale University School of Public Health, and is currently working toward an EdD from Columbia University, Teachers College. She has served as chair of the

Health Education Section of the American College Health Association and is currently the chair of the Task Force on National Health Objectives in Higher Education.

**Ted Grace** has just accepted the position of Director, University Health Services, The Ohio State University. Previously, he was the director of clinical services at San Diego State University's Student Health Services and held an adjunct faculty position in the Graduate School of Public Health at the same university. Dr. Grace was awarded an MD from Ohio State University and an MPH from San Diego State University, where he completed a Preventive Medicine residency. In addition, he has completed both Family and Internal Medicine residencies, as well as a Fellowship in Student Health Administration. Dr. Grace expresses an interest in medical history; his research interests include infectious disease epidemiology.

**Joel Grinolds** is currently a staff physician at the student health services at San Diego State University, and co-ordinator for student services at California State University - San Marcos. Dr. Grinolds received his MD at the Medical College of Wisconsin; is board certified as a pediatrician; and received his MPH at the University of California at Berkeley, with an emphasis on adolescent health care in the Maternal-Child Health program. First as a district health officer and later as director of MCH for the state of New Mexico, Dr. Grinolds was in charge of the Crippled Childrens' Services (CCS). His current activities include teaching adolescent health care issues in the Graduate School of Public Health at SDSU, and representing health services as liaison to Disabled Student Services on campus.

**Steven Harris** is currently Clinical Assistant Professor of Family and Emergency Medicine at the USC School of Medicine, and Associate Professor of Health Science at California State University, Los Angeles (Cal State, LA), where he serves as Medical Chief of Staff. Dr. Harris received his MD from the University of Texas Medical School at San Antonio, and a Master of Science degree in Health Care Management from Cal State, LA. He has also completed post-doctoral training in emergency medicine at Martin L. King General Hospital in Los Angeles.

**Nils Hasselmo** is currently President, University of Minnesota, a position he has held since 1989. Dr. Hasselmo received undergraduate degrees from Uppsala University in Sweden as well as from Augustana College in Illinois; a graduate degree from Uppsala, and his PhD in linguistics from Harvard University. He taught language and literature for many years, and has published extensively in those areas. Dr. Hasselmo has been the recipient of numerous fellowships, awards, and research projects; and has served since 1987 on the Executive

Committee of the National Association of State Universities and Land-Grant Colleges, Council for Academic Affairs.

**Wylie Hembree** received his BA from Vanderbilt University in 1960 and his MD from Washington University School of Medicine in 1964. Dr. Hembree's certifications include Certification in Internal Medicine and Subspecialty Certification (Endocrinology Fellow) American College of Physicians. Academic appointments include Associate Professor of Clinical Medicine and of Obstetrics & Gynecology, Columbia University College of Physicians & Surgeons. Hospital appointments include Associate Attending Physician at Presbyterian Hospital, New York City; Dr. Hembree is also the director of the Andrology Laboratory and director of the Steroid/Gonadotropin Laboratory.

**Diane Jones** is a medical sociologist with a research interest in psychosocial determinants of health behavior. She is currently with the Center for Chronic Disease Prevention and Health Promotion at the Centers for Disease Control. She has taught sociology at Emory University and is currently in the final stage of completing a dissertation on job stress, social support, and their impact on health. Since joining CDC, Ms. Jones has been involved in research in the area of psychosocial risk behaviors for chronic disease and injury, with particular focus on adolescents and young adults. In addition, she is principal investigator of an international WHO study of physical activity and its role as a risk factor for, and important health promotion behavior linked to, chronic diseases and premature death.

**Richard Keeling** is currently Director, Department of Student Health, University of Virginia; Associate Professor of Internal Medicine at the School of Medicine; and Consultant, Health Advocates. Dr. Keeling received an MD from Tufts University School of Medicine in Boston. He is a past president of the American College Health Association, of which he is currently the chairman of the Task Force of HIV Infection and AIDS; and is currently the president of the Foundation for Health in Higher Education. Dr. Keeling serves on a number of boards and committees, and as a consultant to many others, with particular expertise in HIV/AIDS. He has written extensively and is currently the Consulting Editor of the Journal of American College Health. Additionally, Dr. Keeling has been awarded several major grants from the CDC to study AIDS seroprevalence, and AIDS education in colleges and universities.

**David Kraft** is Executive Director of the University Health Services, University of Massachusetts at Amherst. Dr. Kraft completed his MD at Northwestern University School of Medicine and residency in general psychiatry at the University of Rochester School of Medicine and Dentistry. In 1984 he assumed his current position, which serves 28,000 students, faculty, staff, and their families with prepaid care. Since 1984, Dr. Kraft has served as an accreditation surveyor for the Accreditation Association for Ambulatory Health Care (AAAHC). In 1988, he was appointed Chair of the Committee on Standards for the American College Health Association (ACHA), and has recently completed efforts to revise the ACHA Recommended Standards and Practices for a College Health Program (5th Edition).

**Felice Kurtzman** is currently a Visiting Assistant Professor in the Department of Biological Chemistry at the UCLA School of Medicine. Ms. Kurtzman is also the team nutritionist for the UCLA Athletic Department and does nutrition consulting in private practice. She received an undergraduate degree in biology from UCLA and an MPH in Public Health Nutrition from Berkeley. Most recently as an assistant director of the UCLA student health services, Ms. Kurtzman directed the health education programs. Her professional areas of interest include eating disorders and sports nutrition.

**Myra Lappin** is currently Director, Student Health Services, San Francisco State University. Dr. Lappin has been working in the field of student health since 1983; her major interest is multi-cultural medicine. She received her BA from Washington University (St. Louis), her MPH from Yale University, and her MD from the University of Texas at San Antonio; additionally, she has completed a residency in pediatrics and a fellowship in adolescent medicine. Dr. Lappin spent several years abroad, doing health promotion and research in Ethiopia and Colombia. She is an advocate for high-quality health care for college students and conducts cross-cultural health research on topics relevant to non-traditional college students.

**Chris Lovato** is currently Assistant Professor, Graduate School of Public Health, San Diego State University. Dr. Lovato received a BA from the University of New Mexico, and an MA in program evaluation and PhD in educational psychology from the University of Texas at Austin. She has been investigator or co-investigator on a number of funded research projects (including NLHBI, NCI, and U.S. DoT), and is currently the principal investigator on the CDC California College Health 2000 project. Dr. Lovato has published and presented on a variety of subjects in health promotion and disease prevention, including health promotion activities in the worksite, seat belt use education, smoking policies, and smoking behavior.

**Ralph Manchester** is currently Medical Chief, University Health Services, University of Rochester; and Assistant Professor of Medicine at the same university. Dr. Manchester was awarded a BS from Tufts University and an MD from the University of Vermont. His current professional interests in publications, research, and presentations include prevention of heart disease in college students and the medical problems of music students. Dr. Manchester was elected a Fellow of the American College of Physicians in 1990.

**Anne Marie Novinger** currently holds the position of Specialist, Health Services, at Glendale Community College, Glendale, CA; in this role, Ms. Novinger directs the activities of the health center. She received her nursing degree from Pasadena City College, a BA in biology from California State University at Los Angeles, and an MA in Health and Safety from the same university. She has written extensively about college health, including a manual on common student health conditions, a resource book for community college health services, and a First Aid guide for college health services. In addition, Ms. Novinger has been the editor of the Stethoscope, a newsletter for California Community College Health Services, for the past 15 years. Her areas of clinical interest include mental health and crisis intervention.

**Kevin Patrick** received a BA from Baylor University, an MD from Baylor College of Medicine, and an MS in Community Medicine from the University of Utah, where he did his residency training in both General Preventive Medicine and Family Practice. After three years' experience on faculty at Utah, he moved to San Diego to direct the Student Health Center at San Diego State University and to develop and direct the University of California, San Diego – San Diego State University General Preventive Medicine residency program. He has served as President of the Association of Teachers of Preventive Medicine and as a member of the Secretary's Council on Health Promotion and Disease Prevention. His primary interests are in the areas of preventive medicine training, college health services research and development, and academic administration.

**George Robb** is currently Associate Vice President for External Relations of the University of Minnesota in Minneapolis, a position he has held since 1983. Mr. Robb received his BS in speech and English from the University of Minnesota, and has spent his professional career in various roles – from Instructor in the College of Education to Associate Vice President – at the University.

**Allan Schwartz** is Associate Professor of Psychiatry and of Psychology at the University of Rochester, and Psychologist at Strong Memorial Hospital. Dr. Schwartz is currently chief of the mental health services of the University Health Service. He received BA and MA degrees from Columbia University, an MS from Rensselaer Polytechnic Institute, and his PhD in clinical psychology from the University of Rochester. Dr. Schwartz is a Fellow of the American College Health Association, and is past president of the ACHA's Section on Mental Health. He has published articles on the personality styles of student activists, the comparative effectiveness of different group interventions and varied models of individual psychotherapy, the treatment of sexual dysfunction, mental health consultation, and psychotherapy with older and returning students.

**Toby Simon** is currently Associate Dean of Student Life at Brown University, where her responsibilities include overseeing and co-managing the university's disciplinary system, including cases of sexual assault; developing sexual assault and alcohol policies and procedures; and team-teaching the human sexuality course. Ms. Simon received a BA from Syracuse University, a masters in education from Tufts University, and spent a summer session at The Johns Hopkins University School of Hygiene and Public Health. Her professional areas of interest in presentations and publications include issues of sexuality, fear of AIDS, and alcohol and sex in the college population.

**Beverlie Conant Sloane** is Director of Health Education at Dartmouth College and Assistant Professor in the Department of Community and Family Medicine at Dartmouth Medical School. Dr. Conant Sloane received her PhD from the Syracuse University Maxwell Graduate School of Citizenship and Public Affairs; and an MPH from the University of Texas School of Public Health in Houston. Since 1979, as the creator of Dartmouth's health education program, she has planned and implemented health education programs and conducted research on college health and peer education. She was the recipient of the Middlebury College Alumni Achievement Award in 1990. Dr. Conant Sloane has served as consultant and advisor on health-related topics to a range of universities and secondary schools. She has been active as a member and officer in the Health Education Section of the ACHA, while serving as an Executive Editor to the Association's Journal. Dr. Conant Sloane is a member of the ACHA's task force on Health Objectives for the Nation in Higher Education and she is also on the Board of Directors of the Sex Information and Education Council of the U.S. (SIECUS).

**Richard Strauss** is currently Associate Professor of Preventive Medicine and Medicine; Associate Director, Sports Medicine Program, Department of Preventive Medicine; Team Physician, Athletic Department, The Ohio State University; and a physician at OSU Hospitals. Dr. Strauss received his BA from Michigan State and his MD from University of Chicago, and completed a fellowship in sports medicine at Harvard Medical School and Children's Hospital, Boston. He is also Editor-in-Chief, The Physician and Sportsmedicine. Dr. Strauss is widely published in the areas of diving and athletics, and has been involved as a team physician for national and international sports (including the Pan American games and the Olympics).

Paula Swinford is currently the director of health education at the University of Southern California; serves as executive editor for health promotion for the Journal of American College Health; and is a member of the board of directors of ACHA. Ms. Swinford received both undergraduate and graduate (Community Health Education) degrees from the University of Illinois, Urbana Champaign, where as a resident advisor in the 1970s, her interest in college sex education began. Currently, she also serves as faculty to National Peer Education Workshops, has received grants to study HIV pre- and post-test counseling, and is a consultant on sex-positive approaches to HIV prevention.

Lee Whitaker is the director of Psychological Services for Swarthmore College, Swarthmore PA. Dr. Whitaker is Adjunct Clinical Professor for the Graduate Institute of Clinical Psychology of Widener University, and is in private practice. He is a Diplomate in Clinical Psychology of the American Board of Professional Psychology, Editor of the Journal of College Student Psychotherapy, current President of the Mental Health Section of the American College Health Association and Consulting Editor for the Association's Journal of American College Health. He is author of about 50 publications on college student mental health, social issues, and schizophrenic disorders, including Assessment of Schizophrenic Disorders: Sense and Nonsense.

Robert Wirag is currently the director of the Student Health Center of the University of Texas at Austin. Dr. Wirag received an undergraduate degree from West Chester University and masters and doctoral degrees from Indiana University (Bloomington). His professional interests include health education and promotion, and the special place of that field in the college health service setting. Dr. Wirag has written and lectured extensively, and currently serves as a consultant to numerous universities (to evaluate their student health service programs). Additionally, he has had a long professional relationship with the American College Health Association and is the immediate past president of that organization.

Joel Yager is a professor of Psychiatry and Biobehavioral Sciences at the UCLA School of Medicine, and Director of Postgraduate Education at the UCLA Neuropsychiatric Institute and West Los Angeles Veterans Administration Medical Center (Brentwood Division). Dr. Yager is also senior consultant in the Adult Eating Disorders program at UCLA and has been an active researcher in the field for more than a decade.

Christine Zimmer is Administrator, University Wellness Programs, Sindecuse Health Center, Western Michigan University; she oversees the planning, implementation, and evaluation of health promotion interventions for students, faculty, and staff within the Health Center and the university community. She currently holds the position of Chairperson, Health Education Section, American College Health Association; and is a member of ACHA's Task Force for Achieving the National Health Objectives in Higher Education. Her expertise includes a wide variety of health promotion issues including the National Health Objectives, peer education, community planning, and program development. Ms. Zimmer holds a BSN from the University of Michigan and a Masters Degree in Community Health Education from Central Michigan University. She is also a Certified Health Education Specialist.

# Appendix B
## Contents, Volume One

Volume One: **FOUNDATIONS**

# Appendix C
## Contents, Volume Two

Volume Two: **SCHOOL HEALTH**

**Section I. Nature and Organization of School Health**